KATE CHOPIN'S
PRIVATE PAPERS

KATE CHOPIN'S
PRIVATE PAPERS

Edited by

Emily Toth and Per Seyersted

Associate Editor, Cheyenne Bonnell

Indiana
University
Press

BLOOMINGTON AND INDIANAPOLIS

This book is a publication of

Indiana University Press
601 North Morton Street
Bloomington, Indiana 47404-3797 USA

www.indiana.edu/~iupress

Telephone orders 800-842-6796
Fax orders 812-855-7931
Orders by email iuporder@indiana.edu

Library of Congress Cataloging-in-Publication Data

Chopin, Kate, 1850–1904
   [Archives]
   Kate Chopin's private papers / edited by Emily Toth, Per Seyersted;
   associate editor, Cheyenne Bonnell.
     p.   cm.
   Includes bibliographical references (p.) and index.
   ISBN 0-253-33112-9 (cloth : alk. paper). — ISBN 0-253-21017-8
 (pbk. : alk. paper)
    1. Chopin, Kate 1850–1904—Notebooks, sketchbooks, etc. 2. Women
authors, American—19th century—Correspondence. 3. Women authors,
American—19th century—Diaries. 4. Chopin, Kate, 1850–1904—
Criticism, Textual. 5. Chopin, Kate, 1850–1904—Correspondence.
6. Chopin, Kate, 1850–1904—Diaries. 7. Women—Louisiana—
Correspondence. 8. Women—Louisiana—Diaries. I. Toth, Emily.
II. Seyersted, Per, date. III. Bonnell, Cheyenne. IV. Title.
PS1294.C63A6 1998
812'.5099287—dc20
[813'.4]
[Bncor95-50476]   95-50398

1 2 3 4 5 03 02 01 00 99 98

To B. T. and S. K.

Contents

Preface

Most present-day admirers of Kate Chopin may find it hard to believe that when I began my work with her in 1959 and tried—with the backing of Edmund Wilson—to get her writings back into print, the reaction of the publishers who went beyond saying only "Kate who?" was that there was "no market for this local colorist."

That was also the aspect of Chopin that Daniel S. Rankin had emphasized in his 1932 book on her. Two decades later, Cyrille Arnavon, in a long introduction to his French translation of *The Awakening*, was the first to discuss her seriously as a writer of realist fiction, and it was he who told me, after I had written on Chopin in a graduate seminar he gave at Harvard, that I ought to write a book on her.

It was a strange feeling to come to the Chopin Collection, untouched for nearly thirty years, at the Missouri Historical Society. Kate Chopin's grandchildren were a little surprised that a Norwegian should come all the way to do research on their ancestor, but they were very cooperative; Robert C. Hattersley, at my urging, even went through old trunks to look for material and came up with her valuable 1894 diary.

Then, in 1969, I was able to publish *Kate Chopin's Complete Works* and my *Critical Biography* of her (both with Louisiana State University Press). Both books have since been republished, and are still in print.

Then things really began to happen. At the 1972 MLA meeting some seventy-five of us took part in the first discussion of Chopin's work. Anthologies of her writings began to appear (including the one I edited in 1974 for the Feminist Press). *The Awakening* was translated into Norwegian, German, Italian, and other languages; and in 1975 Emily Toth started her *Kate Chopin Newsletter*. She and I had already worked together since the MLA meeting, and it was very natural for me to ask her to be assistant editor for the *Kate*

Chopin Miscellany that I published in 1979, bringing together uncollected Chopin stories and poems, her diaries and letters, and other relevant material.

Since then, Emily Toth has diligently continued her Chopin research, and she has come up with a wealth of new information and new material. It is a great pleasure for me that she has thus continued what I started and that this new material makes the present *Kate Chopin's Private Papers* into a much more comprehensive collection than the one we edited in 1979.

We have come a long way since the mention of Kate Chopin elicited only the response "Kate who?" Chopin has finally received the recognition she deserves, from readers and scholars, in America as well as in other parts of the world. In *Kate Chopin's Private Papers* they should find much valuable material for their further study of this fascinating and important writer.

Per Seyersted
Department of British and American Studies
University of Oslo

Acknowledgments

Many individuals and institutions have contributed to this project. It began, essentially, with Per Seyersted's 1959 discovery of Kate Chopin. This volume, published nearly forty years later, supplements his *Complete Works* (1969) and contains everything else by Kate Chopin except the Guy de Maupassant translations available in Thomas Bonner's *The Kate Chopin Companion*. It is unlikely that anything else will be found.

Joan Catapano, sponsoring editor at Indiana University Press, deserves particular accolades for her patience with this book, which is being completed many years after the expected due date. We appreciate her faith, and the excellent support provided by her and her assistants Jennifer Hyde, Grace Profatilov, and Devonia Stein. LuAnne Holladay deserves special thanks for copy editing this volume.

Besides the initial funding Per Seyersted received for his pioneering work (Fellowships from the American Council of Learned Societies and the Norwegian Research Council), Emily Toth is also indebted to the following universities for faculty research grants: Louisiana State University (Manship Research Fellowship, and Manship Summer Research Grant); University of North Dakota; and Pennsylvania State University (College of Liberal Arts, English Department, and Institute for the Arts and Humanistic Studies). This work was also aided by a Travel to Collections Grant from the National Endowment for the Humanities, and by two Research and Publication Grants from the Louisiana Endowment for the Humanities.

Many libraries and librarians have been useful in this project. Particular thanks are due to the Missouri Historical Society in St. Louis, and its past and present staff members and librarians: Beverly Bishop, Martha Clevenger, Janice Fox, Stephanie Klein, Peter Michel, Emily Miller, Wendi Perry, Frances Hurd Stadler, Barbara Stole, Carol Verble, and Dina Young. At the Cammie G. Henry Research Center of the Eugene P. Watson Library (Northwestern State

University of Louisiana), Carol Wells and Mary Linn Wernet have been extraordinarily helpful, as have Sisters Marie Louise Martinez and Mary Cecelia Wheeler from the National Archives of the Society of the Sacred Heart, Villa Duchesne, St. Louis. Sister Martinez also generously shared numerous other materials from her own research.

This book has also been aided by the libraries and librarians at the Historic New Orleans Collection; Louisiana State University; University of Oslo; Pennsylvania State University, especially Charles Mann and Sandra Stelts; the University of Pennsylvania, especially Daniel Traister; the St. Louis Mercantile Library; the St. Louis Public Library; the Newcomb College Center for Research on Women and the Howard-Tilton Memorial Library, Tulane University; the U.S. Library of Congress; and the Olin Library, Washington University, St. Louis.

Marilyn Bonnell, now Cheyenne Bonnell, served as first research assistant on this project.

At Louisiana State University, Judith Stafford and Janet Wondra were able research assistants, researching and preparing notes, and Janet Wondra also transcribed what we are calling the Wondra Manuscript Account Book. Catherine Williamson assisted with final research. Katharine Jensen aided with French translations, and Irene Di Maio (Louisiana State University) and Evelyne B. Hand (Pennsylvania State University) contributed German transcriptions and translations.

The Rankin-Marhefka Fragments were transcribed by an excellent, dedicated, and meticulous group of Louisiana State University graduate students: Brian Arundel, Phyllis Catsikis, Kevin Dwyer, Chris La Jaunie, Cynthia Maxwell, Anna Priddy, Leonard Vraniak, and Steve Weddle.

This book also incorporates notes prepared by Beverly Bishop, Jo Anne Thibault Eresh, Penny Flatin, Per Seyersted, and Emily Toth for *A Kate Chopin Miscellany*. Portions of the manuscript were typed by Kathy Leitzell, Nancy Royer, and Kim Witherite at Pennsylvania State University. Steve Bell assisted with reproductions of newspaper materials. For technical support, Bruce Toth's computer expertise was invaluable.

Among individuals, Kate Chopin's descendants, especially David Chopin, the late George Chopin, and their families, have been both helpful and amusing: they have been a delight to know. Martha Baker has been a valuable contact in St. Louis, as has Frederick Medler.

In Natchitoches, Louisiana, we have been encouraged and edified by the biennial Kate Chopin conferences arranged by Karen Cole, Ada Jarred, and Katherine Kearns. Thomas Fick, Eva Gold, and David Hanson have edited those proceedings and promoted Kate Chopin's contributions to Louisiana literature.

In Cloutierville, Louisiana, many friends have also been sources, especially Lucille Tinker Carnahan, Emma Richter Masson, and Leona Sampite. Lucille Carnahan has been a treasure of knowledge, lore, legend, and delightful stories about the Cane River country, and she has enriched my life.

Linda W. Marhefka, manager of Secured Self-Storage, Inc., in Worcester, Massachusetts, deserves great thanks for rescuing the Rankin-Marhefka Fragments (reproduced in this volume) from oblivion.

Among academic Chopinists, Barbara Ewell in particular has been a perceptive and energetic colleague and sounding board, as well as a lively friend, constant co-panelist and generous research companion. Bernard Koloski's insights into Kate Chopin's bilingualism have been genuine breakthroughs, and his ideas about teaching Kate Chopin enrich us all. Thomas Bonner's generosity and expertise with Guy de Maupassant translations and his *Kate Chopin Companion* have provided continuous help and information: they untie many a knot. Helen Taylor's good humor and skepticism have enlarged my thinking about Kate Chopin. Heather Kirk Thomas's documentary collection of Kate Chopin materials is an invaluable treasure.

Susan Koppelman has been an inspiration and a nudge in my pursuit of the truths about women's lives. She always asks the right questions and has shown me the value of seeking out gossip, humor, and new information.

Many other scholars, authors, and activists have aided my research as co-workers, colleagues, and/or sources for gossip (oral history). Among them I especially acknowledge Patricia Brady, Barbara Davidson, Cathy N. Davidson, Carmen del Rio, Janice Delaney, Linda Gardiner, Carol Gelderman, Sarah Sue Goldsmith, Suzanne Green, Rosan Jordan, Annette Kolodny, Susan Larson, Mary Jane Lupton, Veronica Makowsky, Carol Mattingly, Janet Palmer Mullaney, Robin Roberts, Catharine Stimpson, Linda Wagner-Martin, and Martha Ward.

My family network of supporters also includes Sara Ruffner, Theresa Toth, Dennis Fitzgibbons, Ellen Boyle, Beauregard, Bunkie, and Foxy. While I was working on this book, both my parents, Dorothy Ginsberg Fitzgibbons and John Joseph Fitzgibbons, passed away, but this book, and all my other books, come from what they taught me about curiosity and compassion, wisdom and wit, and wonder, life, and literature.

Finally, Bruce Toth has lived patiently with me and Kate Chopin, providing treats and solace, laughter and silence, for nearly three decades. She and I still appreciate his presence.

Emily Toth
Baton Rouge, Louisiana
For the Editors

PERMISSIONS

Grateful acknowledgment is here given for permission to quote from the following materials:

David Chopin, for Kate Chopin's published and unpublished works.
Missouri Historical Society Archives, St. Louis, for the Kate Chopin Papers ("Leaves of Affection"; Commonplace Book; 1894 diary; Bonnell and

Wondra manuscript account books; the poems "To Blanche," "For Mrs. Ferriss," "Lines Suggested by Omar," "An Hour," and "Alone"; letter to *Youth's Companion*; and Rankin-Marhefka fragments). Also for the Robert E. Lee Gibson Papers (Letter to R. E. Lee Gibson), the Ludlow-Field-Maury Family Papers (Letter to Cornelia Maury), and the Sheet Music Collection ("Lilia Polka").

Cammie G. Henry Research Center, Northwestern State University, for materials first published in *A Kate Chopin Miscellany*, including letter to Marie Breazeale, selected poems, and "Lilia Polka."

American Antiquarian Society for Kate Chopin's letter to Marion A. Baker.

Kate Chopin Collection (no. 9442), Clifton Waller Barrett Library, Special Collections Department, University of Virginia Library, for Kate Chopin's letter to Stone & Kimball.

Herbert S. Stone Papers and Stone & Kimball Papers, the Newberry Library, Chicago, Illinois, for Kate Chopin's Correspondence with Stone & Kimball and Herbert S. Stone (1894–1899).

Manuscripts and Archives, the New York Public Library, Astor, Lenox and Tilden Foundations, for Kate Chopin's correspondence with the *Century* (Century Company records), and Richard Watson Gilder (Richard Watson Gilder Papers).

Waitman Barbe Papers, West Virginia and Regional History Collection, West Virginia University Libraries, for Kate Chopin's letter to Waitman Barbe.

Barbara Sims, for Kate Chopin's "live oaks" version of the poem called "White Oaks."

Ruth McEnery Stuart Papers, Manuscripts Department, Howard-Tilton Memorial Library, Tulane University, for Kate Chopin's autograph to Ruth McEnery Stuart.

Lydia Ward Collection (no. 5672-a), Special Collections Department, University of Virginia Library, for Kate Chopin's letter to Lydia Ward.

Tinker collection, Harry Ransom Humanities Research Center, the University of Texas at Austin, for Kate Chopin's letter to Richard B. Shepard, November 8, 1899.

Special Collections, Olin Library, Washington University, St. Louis, for Kate Chopin's letter to Otto Heller.

Chronology of Kate Chopin's Life

1850 TO MID-1870: ST. LOUIS

February 8, 1850 - Birth of Catherine O'Flaherty. First home: Eighth Street between Chouteau and Gratiot.

Fall 1855 - Kate O'Flaherty enrolls in Academy of the Sacred Heart (which she attends sporadically for the next 13 years); soon becomes friends with Kitty Garesché

November 1, 1855 - Death of Thomas O'Flaherty (father) in railroad accident.

January 16, 1863 - Death of Victoire Verdon Charleville (great-grandmother and teacher).

February 17, 1863 - Death of George O'Flaherty (half-brother), a Confederate soldier.

1863 - Banishment of Kitty Garesché and her family.

1863 - Keeps "Leaves of Affection" autograph book.

1865–1866 - Family moves to 1118 St. Ange Avenue.

Fall 1865 - Kate attends the Academy of the Visitation, then returns to Sacred Heart Academy.

1867–1870 - Keeps Commonplace Book: diary, extracts from authors, original poem ("The Congé"), reactions to flirting and other social obligations.

1868 - Graduation from Sacred Heart Academy.

1869 - Writes "Emancipation: a Life Fable," unpublished.

March-May 1869 - Visits New Orleans.

April 1870 - Julia Benoist Chopin, Oscar Chopin's mother, dies.

June 9, 1870 - Marriage to Oscar Chopin of Louisiana, Holy Angels Church, St. Louis.

June-September 1870 - European honeymoon; keeps honeymoon diary in Commonplace Book.

MID-1870 TO MID-1879: NEW ORLEANS

New Orleans homes: 443 Magazine Street; northeast corner Pitt and Constantinople; 209 (now 1413) Louisiana Avenue.

November 14, 1870 - Victor Jean Baptiste Chopin, Oscar's father, dies.

May 22, 1871 - Son Jean Baptiste born in New Orleans, baptized in St. Louis in August.

September 24, 1873 - Son Oscar Charles born in St. Louis, baptized in St. Louis.

December 27, 1873 - Thomas O'Flaherty (brother) killed in buggy accident, St. Louis.

September 14, 1874 - Oscar in Battle of Liberty Place, with White League and associated companies, New Orleans.

October 28, 1874 - Son George Francis born in St. Louis, baptized in St. Louis.

January 26, 1876 - Son Frederick born in New Orleans (no baptismal record).

January 8, 1878 - Son Felix Andrew born in New Orleans (no baptismal record).

LATE 1879 TO MID-1884: CLOUTIERVILLE ("CLOOCHY-VILLE") IN NATCHITOCHES ("*NACK*-I-TOSH") PARISH, LOUISIANA

December 31, 1879 - Daughter Lélia born in Cloutierville, baptized Marie Laïza in Cloutierville on February 29, 1880.

December 10, 1882 - Death of Oscar Chopin.

1883–1884 - Romance with Albert Sampite.

Mid-1884 - Kate Chopin's return to St. Louis.

MID-1884 TO 1904: ST. LOUIS

1884–1885 - Lives at 1125 St. Ange Avenue, then 1122 St. Ange.

June 28, 1885 - Chopin's mother, Eliza O'Flaherty, dies of "sarcoma."

1886 - Moves to 3317 Morgan Street (now Delmar).

June 1887 - First Cloutierville visit since Oscar's death.

1888 - "Lilia. Polka for Piano" published.

1888 - Writes first draft of what becomes "A No-Account Creole."

September 24, 1888 - Loca Sampite sues for legal separation from her husband, Albert.

1888–1889 - Chopin works on "Unfinished Story—Grand Isle."

January 10, 1889 - First literary publication: "If It Might Be" (poem).

April 24, 1889 - Kate brings Oscar's body back to St. Louis from Cloutierville.

April 30, 1889 - Loca Sampite's suit for separation dismissed.

June 1889 - Chopin writes "Wiser Than a God."

July 5, 1889 - Begins writing *At Fault*.

August 1889 - Writes "A Point at Issue!"

October 27, 1889 - First short story published: "A Point at Issue!" in *St. Louis Post-Dispatch*.

December 1889 - "Wiser Than a God" published in *Philadelphia Musical Journal*.

September 1890 - *At Fault* published at Chopin's expense.

December 1890 - Becomes charter member of Wednesday Club.

June 1891 - John A. Dillon moves to New York.

June 20, 1891 - Loca Sampite's legal separation from Albert Sampite takes effect.

August 20, 1891 - "For Marse Chouchoute" (first Louisiana story) published in *Youth's Companion*.

April 4, 1892 - Resigns from Wednesday Club.

April 9–10, 1892 - Writes "Loka."

July 15–17, 1892 - Writes "At the 'Cadian Ball."

October 22, 1892 - "At the 'Cadian Ball" published in *Two Tales*.

November 24, 1892 - Writes "Désirée's Baby."

January 14, 1893 - *Vogue* publishes "Désirée's Baby."

May 1893 - Trip to New York and Boston.

August 11, 1893 - Houghton, Mifflin accepts *Bayou Folk*.

October 1, 1893 - Devastating hurricane at Chênière Caminada.

October 21–23, 1893 - Writes "At Chênière Caminada."

March 24, 1894 - Houghton, Mifflin publishes *Bayou Folk*.

April 19, 1894 - Chopin writes "The Dream of an Hour" ("Story of an Hour").

May 4, 1894 to October 26, 1896 - Writes "Impressions" (diary).

Late June, 1894 - Attends Indiana conference of Western Association of Writers.

June 30, 1894 - Writes "The Western Association of Writers."

July 7, 1894 - "Western Association of Writers" published in *Critic*.

July 21–28 - Hostile responses to Chopin's "Western Association of Writers" in *Minneapolis Journal*, *Cincinnati Commercial Gazette*.

August 1894 - First national profile: William Schuyler's article in *The Writer*.

December 6, 1894 - "The Dream of an Hour" published in *Vogue* with note about "Those Who Have Worked With Us."

March 1895 - Sends Guy de Maupassant translation collection to Houghton, Mifflin (rejected).

April 10–28, 1895 - Writes "Athénaïse."

January 27, 1897 - Grandmother Athénaïse Charleville Faris dies.

February 3, 1897 - Meets Ruth McEnery Stuart.

June 1897 (?) - Begins writing *The Awakening*.

June 1897 - John A. Dillon makes short trip to St. Louis.

June 24 to July 1, 1897 - Kate Chopin visits Natchitoches Parish.

November 1897 - Way & Williams (Chicago) publishes *A Night in Acadie*.

January 16, 1898 - "Is Love Divine?" (*St. Louis Post-Dispatch*) quotes from novel-in-progress.

January 21, 1898 - Finishes *The Awakening*.

January 1898 - Way & Williams accepts *The Awakening*.

February 6, 1898 - "Has High Society Struck the Pace That Kills?" (*St. Louis Post-Dispatch*).

March 1898 - Goes to Chicago, seeking literary agent.

Spring-Summer 1898 - Son Frederick in Spanish-American War.

July 19, 1898 - Writes "The Storm."

November 1898 - Book contracts transferred from Way & Williams to Herbert S. Stone & Company.

December 1898 - Visits Natchitoches Parish, sells Cloutierville house, visits New Orleans.

March 1899 - Lucy Monroe's favorable review of *The Awakening* in *Book News*.

April 22, 1899 - *The Awakening* published (no documentary evidence that it was ever banned).

July 1899 - Chopin's statement on *The Awakening* published in *Book News*.

November 29, 1899 - Gives reading at Wednesday Club.

February 1900 - Herbert S. Stone returns (declines to publish) *A Vocation and a Voice*.

December 9, 1900 - Publishes "Development of the Literary West: a Review" in St. Louis *Republic*'s Special Book Number.

1900 - Appears in first edition of *Who's Who in America*.

1901 - Is subject of sonnet "To the Author of 'Bayou Folk,'" by R. E. Lee Gibson.

June 4, 1902 - Son Jean marries Emelie Hughes.

July 3, 1902 - "Polly" published in *Youth's Companion* (last publication).

October 15, 1902 - John A. Dillon dies.

December 1902 - Chopin makes her will.

1903 - Moves to 4232 McPherson Avenue.

July 7, 1903 - Death of Emelie Chopin, Jean's wife.

August 20, 1904 - Chopin has cerebral hemorrhage after day at the St. Louis World's Fair.

August 22, 1904 - Chopin dies.

August 24, 1904 - Burial of Kate Chopin.

General Introduction

EMILY TOTH

By the time she died in 1904, Kate Chopin was on her way to becoming, at most, an interesting literary footnote.

Just ten years earlier, she had been nationally acclaimed as the author of *Bayou Folk* (1894), a collection of charming local-color stories set in Louisiana. (Her first novel, *At Fault* [1890] had attracted much less attention.) With her second story collection, *A Night in Acadie* (1897), Chopin pleased some readers but puzzled others with tales that seemed more intimate, untidy, and strange. And then she published *The Awakening* (1899), a sensual novel about a passionate and unhappy wife and mother. Although women readers admired and praised the novel, many reviewers found it morally objectionable. Decades later it was even rumored, falsely, that *The Awakening* had been banned.

By mid-1899 it was clear that Kate Chopin, who drew on such French writers as Guy de Maupassant as her models, would not be able to publish what she chose in the United States. She never sent out her most amoral story, "The Storm," and her last short-story collection, *A Vocation and a Voice*, was cancelled by its publisher. It did not appear in print until 1991, ninety years after originally scheduled.

After 1900 Kate Chopin was also having bouts of ill health, while relatives and friends were ailing and dying. She moved from her own large, Federal-style home to a much less grand rented house. In her last years, she was particularly attending to her son Jean, who suffered a nervous breakdown after the death of his wife in childbirth. The 1904 St. Louis World's Fair proved both exciting and deadly for Kate Chopin. After an intensely hot day at the fair, she suffered a cerebral hemorrhage and died two days later, on August 22.

Although she was no longer a practicing Catholic, Chopin was buried in

St. Louis's Calvary Cemetery, where her grave remains, along the Way of the Second Dolor (Section 17, Lot 47). Buried next to her is one of her five sons; her husband, who died before her literary career began, is buried some distance away. His grave is unmarked.

Kate Chopin was an intensely private person who confided few secrets to her surviving diaries. Most likely, she was also discreet in the letters and diaries which have long been lost or destroyed. In person she always seemed to know more than she was willing to say, and one friend called her "a rogue in porcelain." Even those arresting bits of gossip which can be recovered—notably her romance with Albert Sampite, another woman's husband—come to us through oral histories, not written ones. We have no incriminating photos, spicy notes, or lurid epistolary revelations.

Yet Kate Chopin's surviving private papers reveal a woman of richness and complexity. From beginning to end, her friends were intensely loyal, as shown in her adolescent "Leaves of Affection" autograph book (transcribed here), and in fan letters she received three decades later, after the appearance of *The Awakening*. (These letters are quoted in Emily Toth's *Kate Chopin* and *A Kate Chopin Miscellany*.)

In school at the Sacred Heart Academy in St. Louis, Kate O'Flaherty had inspired admiration as a storyteller, pianist, and honor student, and her Commonplace Book shows a young woman of uncommon discernment and humor. In her honeymoon diary, kept when she was just twenty years old, the newlywed Kate O'Flaherty Chopin had already learned to pick out the colorful details that define a scene. Her notes on her wedding trip to Europe are not a vague, inexpert travelogue, but a brisk set of comments on music, monuments, mummies, military maneuvers, maids and mistresses, and much more—including wine and eels and cigarettes.

But from the period between September 1870 and January 1889, when Kate Chopin began her literary career, we have only a few signed business papers and one 1887 letter from her own hand. As wife, mother, widow, and scandalous woman in Louisiana, Chopin wrote letters and kept diaries, one of which existed as late as 1932—but none were for publication. It was only after her return to St. Louis in 1884, and then her mother's death the following year, that Kate Chopin began writing professionally. She also succeeded with astonishing speed.

Chopin's ambitions and achievements were wide-ranging. In less than a decade, she published two novels and two short-story collections, while also producing some three dozen uncollected stories, as well as poems, newspaper essays and reviews, another novel (unpublished and destroyed) and translations of French stories. She even wrote one play, a romantic comedy called *An Embarrassing Position*.

Yet, like most professional writers, Chopin produced some material that did not sell and was not published—and that forms the core of the last part of this collection. *Kate Chopin's Private Papers* from 1885–1904 include her manuscript account books, showing where she sent stories, her acceptances and rejections. The account books are transcribed for the first time here.

Also appearing in print for the first time are fragments of Chopin stories from a newly discovered cache in Worcester, Massachusetts. Chopin's first biographer, Daniel Rankin, evidently deposited the materials in 1932, and they were left undisturbed until 1992, when they were discovered by Linda W. Marhefka. Most are drafts of stories already known, but there are also some fragments of hitherto-unknown works—showing that Chopin was not the spontaneous author she claimed to be. She did revise; she did reject.

And she was a social critic. Her 1894 diary, reproduced here, includes comments on literary people she knew or read with respect. She also recorded pungent opinions about those she considered hypocritical or misguided. While her diary, entitled "Impressions," was not locked, it was private enough that we can get a sense of the mature Kate Chopin: wry, judicious, clever, and curious.

Among the other items in *Kate Chopin's Private Papers* are the unpublished, very romantic poems she valued highly (although editors did not); her translations of an odd variety of newspaper articles; her cheery children's stories about lucky urchins; and her thoughts about the literary scene, society, and romantic love.

Kate Chopin's Private Papers round out our portrait of the artist as a young and middle-aged woman who was, indeed, a woman for all seasons. She was a pioneer in her own time, in her portrayal of women's desires for independence and control of their own sexuality. But she also resisted continuing to write the same charming tales of Southern life, and instead moved toward a bleaker, stranger vision, and stories that did not have well-made, tightly knit plots.

That literary growth cost her much of her audience. As her account books show, she was finding it much harder to place her more innovative stories. Several years before her death, suffering from her own and others' illnesses and depressions, she was scarcely writing at all.

She might have been forgotten forever—except for a fortunate set of circumstances.

In 1959 Per Seyersted, a thirty-eight-year-old Norwegian graduate student working toward his M.A. at Harvard, was directed to Kate Chopin by Cyrille Arnavon, a French professor especially interested in literary realism. Seyersted read *The Awakening* and, in his own way, asked the question that thousands of later readers have also asked: "How did she know all that in 1899?"

Seyersted, whose mother had been head of the Norwegian Feminist Association, found himself dedicating ten years to pursuing the private, elusive Kate Chopin. Daniel Rankin had published the only book-length study, *Kate Chopin and Her Creole Stories*, in 1932, and Seyersted pursued Rankin to Paris

and interviewed him there. Rankin had little to contribute beyond his original book, which included many of Chopin's stories but was often wrong about
her life. He also said his original notes had been lost.

With fellowships (1964–1968), but without computers or photocopying—
neither of which were yet available—Per Seyersted spent years crisscrossing
the Atlantic, singlehandedly gathering materials. He copied Chopin's stories
in pencil, by hand, from fading manuscripts and newspaper clippings, mostly
at the Missouri Historical Society in St. Louis. He also managed to locate
Kate Chopin's grandson, Robert Hattersley, who generously donated Chopin's
1894 diary (reproduced here). That diary remains our best picture of the writer
in her prime.

Seyersted could not, however, get the *Missouri Historical Society Bulletin*
to publish Kate Chopin's story "The Storm" in 1962: the tale was considered
too sexually explicit. The editor directed Seyersted to provide a discreet syn-
opsis instead.

Seyersted visited the sites of Kate Chopin's homes, interviewed everyone
he could find, and along the way became the first to introduce Women's Studies
courses at the University of Oslo. In 1969 he launched the Kate Chopin revival with his *Kate Chopin: a Critical Biography* and *The Complete Works of Kate
Chopin* (which turned out to be incomplete, as the current volume shows).

Seyersted's rediscovery and promotion of Kate Chopin coincided with
the rebirth of the women's movement in the United States. Chopin, unknown
in 1969, became the first woman writer to be celebrated in the newly revised
American literary canon. Today she is among the top ten most-taught American authors, and *The Awakening* alone appears in more than a dozen U.S.
editions. It has also been translated into, among other languages, French
(twice), Norwegian, Italian, Polish, and Japanese. There are two full-length
movie versions of *The Awakening*, and two films of her "Story of an Hour."
There are Chopin readers and admirers all over the world.

In 1975, after finishing my dissertation on Kate Chopin at Johns Hopkins
University, I founded *The Kate Chopin Newsletter* at the University of New
Orleans, continued it at the University of North Dakota, and then at Pennsylvania State University. Under a new title (*Regionalism and the Female Imagination*), the journal lasted until 1979, the year that Seyersted and I edited *A
Kate Chopin Miscellany* (largely superseded by this volume). Since then I have
published a Chopin biography, *Kate Chopin: A Life of the Author of "The Awakening"*; an edition of Chopin's last short-story collection, *A Vocation and a
Voice*; and soon, *Unveiling Kate Chopin*, for the centennial of *The Awakening*.

Kate Chopin continues to fascinate readers. Her audience continues to
grow, and so do her sales—for *The Awakening* is a staple in classes in fiction,
women's studies, and American literature. More copies of *The Awakening* are
now sold every September than were sold in all of Chopin's lifetime.

The Contributions to This Volume

This volume is a particular tribute to Per Seyersted, long Professor of American Literature and Director of the American Institute (now the Department of British and American Studies) at the University of Oslo. Without him, we would not have Kate Chopin. Seyersted is responsible for gathering most of the letters reproduced here, as well as the 1894 diary and many of the unpublished manuscripts. He drafted the original transcriptions of Kate O'Flaherty Chopin's comments in her diaries; he also transcribed most of the short stories and poems appearing here, and researched or arranged for researching the earliest notes.

Cheyenne Bonnell, a Pennsylvania State University Ph.D. who has also taught at Susquehanna and Shippensburg Universities and is now on the faculty of Northwest College in Powell, Wyoming, is responsible for the transcriptions of what we are calling the Bonnell Manuscript Account Book, as well as the non-Chopin texts in the Commonplace Book. She also researched many of the notes for the Commonplace Book, 1894 diary, and manuscript account books, and is an expert on Sarah Grand, whose novel *The Heavenly Twins* is mentioned in Chopin's diary.

Emily Toth, professor of English and Women's Studies at Louisiana State University, wrote all introductions in this volume; edited translations and transcriptions of diaries and letters; transcribed "Leaves of Affection" and the newspaper pieces; and supervised the Rankin-Marhefka fragment transcriptions. She also put together the chronology, list of Chopin's works, and notes at the end of this volume. She is responsible for the collating and overall editing of this volume, including any errors (which she hopes sharp-eyed readers will call to her attention).

1850–1870

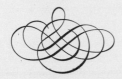

Kate O'Flaherty

Kate O'Flaherty was lucky enough to have female mentors throughout her girlhood. Born into a household of lively, independent-minded widows and then taught by the vigorous, intellectual nuns at the Sacred Heart Academy in St. Louis, young Kate came of age among women who were fervently committed to the life of the mind as well as the life of the home. By the time she was graduated in 1868, Kate O'Flaherty was known as a marvelous storyteller, an accomplished pianist, an honors student, and a youthful cynic.

Born in St. Louis on February 8, 1850, Catherine O'Flaherty was just five and a half when her parents first sent her to the Sacred Heart school on Fifth and Convent. She had to be a boarding pupil: day students were not admitted. The O'Flahertys lived a few blocks away, on Eighth Street between Chouteau and Gratiot, and there was a younger sister, Jane, at home, along with two older brothers, George and Tom. Another sister, Marie, had died in 1853. Jane, also known as Jenny, died in 1860; both brothers died in their twenties. By the time she was 24, Kate O'Flaherty Chopin was an only child.

Young Kate, who looks quite pugnacious in her first childhood picture, lasted just two months into her first term at the Sacred Heart Academy. On All Saints Day, November 1, 1855, her father was among the dignitaries riding on the first train over the new Gasconade Bridge—which collapsed, killing and maiming many passengers. Thomas O'Flaherty was among the dead. Kate came home, to be tutored by her great-grandmother. She could have had no better education.

Kate's mother, Eliza Faris O'Flaherty, was just twenty-seven when her fifty-year-old husband was killed. She may have felt liberated as well as saddened—or so Kate Chopin's "Story of an Hour" (1894), suggests: a wife, hearing of her husband's reported death in a train accident, delights in thoughts of freedom. Eliza had married Thomas when she was barely sixteen, half a year after his first wife died and left him with a son, George. The eldest of seven children in an impoverished but well-established family, Eliza brought social status to the marriage; Thomas, a Galway immigrant and self-made man, brought money. On his death, Eliza became a very wealthy widow. She never remarried.

Kate's grandmother and great-grandmother had also been widowed young and never remarried. There were young aunts and uncles, cousins, and four slaves in the O'Flaherty household, but the strongest individuals were the widows. Kate was in her teens before she ever lived with a married couple (her aunt Zuma and husband John).

But it was the eldest member of the household, her great-grandmother Victoria (or Victoire) Verdon Charleville, who first recognized Kate's special gifts. Madame Charleville, already in her seventies, was the daughter of an extremely unconventional woman: bedeviled by an unpleasant, much older husband, the elder Victoire Verdon had obtained the first legal separation ever granted in frontier St. Louis. Then she learned to read and write, gave birth to another child whose father was unnamed, became a keelboat entrepreneur, and ultimately an eighteenth-century tycoon. Her daughter Victoire, who married the merchant Joseph Charleville, had given birth to fifteen children and retained an indefatigable curiosity about human quirks and follies. Besides coaching Katie in music and speaking French with her, Madame Charleville taught her history and gossip, and stressed the need to look on life clearly and fearlessly.

Then, two years after her father's death, young Kate returned to the Sacred Heart school, where her best friend was also a neighbor, Kitty Garesché. The two girls were voracious readers and writers, as Kate remembered in a much-later reminiscence (reprinted in this volume).

But just nine days after Kate and Kitty made their first communions in May of 1861, the Civil War broke out in St. Louis. Kate, fifteen when it finally ended, suffered devastating losses. Kitty and her family were banished from St. Louis for their Confederate sympathies; Kate's half-brother George, a Confederate soldier, died of typhoid fever; and Madame Charleville passed away in her eighty-third year. Amid the chaos, the Sacred Heart nuns hid their records, and the "Leaves of Affection" autograph book is the only proof that Kate attended school during the conflict. Despite the street fighting and an invasion of the O'Flaherty house by Union soldiers during that July, "Leaves of Affection" is a typical schoolgirl record of friendship—even including the shy admirer who signs on the last page.

Kate O'Flaherty was ten years old when she received a blank, unlined notebook with different-colored pages (tan, green, lavender) from her great-aunt Pélagie Charleville Boyer. "Aunt Boyer," Kate's grandmother's sister, was sixty-one that Christmas and the mother of four children. The gift was a tan copybook, about 6" x 7½", published by Leavitt & Allen in New York—with LEAVES OF AFFECTION stamped in gold on the brown cover, and inscribed "To Katie, from her affectionate aunt Boyer, December the 25th, 1860."

The book, now at the Missouri Historical Society, includes a loose, lace-bordered picture of a young girl in a garland, gazing up at the Virgin Mary: printed under the picture is

Dieu a mis en Marie le plénitude de tout don.
St. Bernard

Kate O'Flaherty wrote under the picture: "May 1st, 1861, My First Communion Picture."

Other bound inserts in the notebook include a drawing of a gloomy thatched castle, labeled "Oakland," and a title page with a picture of a windmill and several figures in a boat. A drawing of a fruit basket and an etching entitled "The ORPHANS Guard" may have come with the book. Seven more cutouts, possibly pasted in by Kate O'Flaherty, include mothers and children; gowned and extravagantly dressed ladies; a chubby child leaning on a half-asleep dog while playing with a toy; and sweethearts leaning toward each other with no space in between (much like the two Grand Isle lovers described nearly forty years later in *The Awakening*). Interspersed with blank pages, there are further drawings and etchings: a cardinal and a flower; a woman in a mantilla looking out over a balcony, labeled "The Proud Lady"; a society matron in a bonnet, carrying a basket to the poor, labeled "VISIT OF CHAR-ITY"; and a pencil drawing of a butterfly with a head resembling a carrot with flowers growing out of it.

Sometime between August 1985 and June 1993, the "Leaves of Affection" notebook sustained serious water damage at the Missouri Historical Society, and some of the texts are no longer easily readable. (The word after "Deep on the convent" has always been unreadable.)

For the texts reproduced in this edition, it is impossible to tell which ones—if any—were actually composed by Kate O'Flaherty. "We Have Been Friends Together" is a popular poem by the English writer Caroline Elizabeth Sarah Norton, and it was evidently a favorite of Kate and Kitty Garesché ("my sweet friend Kitty"), who later became a Sacred Heart nun.

Late in life, Mother Garesché wrote to Chopin's first biographer, Daniel Rankin, that she did not remember who had actually composed the poem: "As the little poem bears my signature, I must have written it in dear Kate's album; but I completely forget having done so. It may have been a poem we both liked and I copied it for her, sure she would know it was *not* original. In those days diminutives were very much used for names. Thus Katherine was always called Katy."

But in her schoolgirl copying, Kitty did change the text somewhat, whether out of carelessness or mischief cannot be known. Kitty's changes do spoil the rhymes: Norton's "And sullen glooms thy brow" became Kitty's "And sullen glooms thy eye," while Norton's "The hopes of early years" became Kitty's "The hopes of early days."

The texts definitely in Kate O'Flaherty's handwriting are the "Dedication"; the poem beginning "I love to linger on my track"; the note "My sweet friend Kitty" above the poem "To Katy"; and the critical comments "very pretty but where's the point?" and "foolishness." The last two, written in pencil and printed here in italics, seem to be later additions from a more cynical Kate.

Dedication.

Let this album be dedicated to friendship. Make it an altere
where every pure offering of affection may be laid. Let the
thought herein inscribed be as untainted as the snowflake; each
wish so pure and bright as the sun beams of Heaven.

Be sure that none but true friends here trace their lines,
and write that alone which is dictated by the purest feelings of
friendship. May thy way of life be fringed with joys; thy hours
pass by in the pleasantest enjoyments, all thy wishes be
gratified, and every aspiration be as spotless as this snowy
sheet.

And
"Should thy heart ever pain with a feeling of sorrow
May it turn to a glittering joy on the morrow."

I love to linger on my track
Wherever I have dwelt,
In after years to loiter back,
And feel as once I felt;
My foot-falls lightly on the sward,
Yet leaves a deathless dint—
With tenderness I still regard
Its unforgotten print.

Old places have a charm for me
The new can ne'er attain
Old faces—how I long to see
Their kindly looks again!
Yes, these are gone:—while all around
Is changeable as air,
I'll anchor in the solid ground
And root my memories there!

very pretty but where's the point?

My sweet friend Kitty.

To Katy

We have been friends together,
In sunshine and in shade,
Since first beneath the chestnut trees
In infancy we played.
But coldness dwells within thy heart
A cloud is on thy brow;
We have been friends together
Shall a light word part us now!

We have been gay together;
We have laughed at little jests;

For the fount of hope was gushing,
Warm and joyous in our breasts.
But laughter now hath fled thy lip,
And sullen glooms thy eye;
We have been friends together
Shall a light word part us now!

We have been sad together
We have wept with bitter tears,
O'er the grass-grown graves, where slumbered
The hopes of early days.
The voices which are silent there
Would bid thee clear thy brow;
We have been sad together
O! What shall part us now!
                                        Kitty Garesché.
                                              1860

The Little Flower Forget-me-not.

There is a modest little flower
To friendship ever dear;
'Tis nourished in her humble bower,
And watered by her tear.

If hearts, by fond affection tied,
Should chance to slip away,
This little flower will gently chide
The heart that thus could stray.

All other flowers, when once they fade,
Are left alone to die;
But this, e'en when it is decayed,
Will live in memory's sigh.

Let cypress trees and willows wave
To mark the lonely spot;
But all I ask to deck my grave
Shall be, "Forget-me-not."
                                        Mary Elder
                                        July 1863

A una Flor

Hojas del arbol caides
fuguete del viento son,
Las ilusiones perdidas,
Ay!! Im hojas despiendidas
Del aubol del corazon.

H. P.

To Katie.
This little emblem of respect.
My youthful friend I give to the
Treat not this motto with neglect.
It is, dear Katie remember me.
And if on native shores I dwell.
And yet am absent still from thee.
Let hallowed friendship deign to tell.
If Katie will remember me.

Annie Shore

July 31st,/63

Il est dans le ciel une puissance divine,
compagne assidue de la religion et de la vertu,
Elle nous aide à supporter la vie / souvent bien
amère) s'embarque avec nous pour nous montrer
le port dans les tempêtes, également douce
et secourable aux voyageurs célèbres et aux
passages inconnus. Quoitque ses yeux
soient couverts d'un bandeau, ses regards
pénetrent l'avenir quelquefois elle tient de
fleurs naissantes dans sa main, quelques
fais une couple pleine d'une liqueur
enchanteresse. Rien s'approache du chacune
de sa voir, de la douceur de son
sourire; plus en avance dans le tombeau,
plus elle se montre pure et brillante aux
mortels consolés. La fin et la chauté
lui disent ma soeur et elle s'appelle
l'Espérance

Chateaubriand

Lead me - oh! lead me to those sparkling groves
Whose every sight is beauty—every sound
Is love—where sunbeams tip the trees around
With gold or starlight—through their foliage roves
And I will muse on pleasure—as a dream
Of lands where marble palaces do shine,
And radiant forms on verdant banks recline,
Till all the senses of my frame shall seem
To pass into a rich Elysium bright!
As though a spirit from some mountain height
Had plucked undying roses for a wreath
To bind fair brows with all who sleep beneath;
Then lead! oh, lead me to those sparking groves
Whose sunlight wanders, and where starlight roves.

Yes   Loving is a painful thrill,
And not to love more painful still,
But oh! it is the worst of pain,
To love, & not be loved again!

       foolishness—

Deep on the convent onof!tce

    O wad the powers the giftie gie us
    To see oursel's as others see us—
    It wad from among a blunder free us,
    And foolish notion.

    My name shall be last in your album.
        Jennie.
    and ought to be forever in your heart miss Katrine
guess who I am for I cannot place my name after the above sweet
injunction.

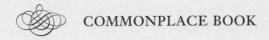 COMMONPLACE BOOK

Her early losses had given young Kate O'Flaherty a certain sad nature. But after the war, a lively, intelligent Sacred Heart nun, the beloved Madam O'Meara, recognized the loneliness of a creative child. Young, Irish-born Mary O'Meara evidently assigned sixteen-year-old Kate to keep a Commonplace Book, the first sustained collection of her writings that has survived.

Kate began by duly copying passages from other writers, but could not resist recording her own thoughts. After graduation, the same notebook became a belle's diary, and then finally a honeymoon journal. It is a rare record of a young woman's passage from student to debutante to bride.

In her Commonplace Book, Kate O'Flaherty develops her own voice as a writer. The first passages she copies are bombastic and impersonal, in the thundering, self-important style that her editor friend William Marion Reedy would satirize some thirty years later. The mature Kate Chopin also loathed the creaking machinery of fustian, old-fashioned writing.

But even the schoolgirl Kate O'Flaherty seems to be less than enthralled. She makes silly spelling and copying mistakes that show inattention; later, she rewrites and simplifies the lines of famous authors. Even at sixteen, the young author made self-confident judgments: Madame Swetchine's volume, often assigned as penance in Sacred Heart schools, is "a queer little book." The contemporary Queen Isabella of Spain, one of few women mentioned, is "beloved by her subjects, but her character is not stainless."

Sacred Heart students all over the world were pressed to be discerning, to see through disguises. For Kate O'Flaherty, Sacred Heart education was the perfect continuation of Madame Charleville's unconventional tutoring, for the young Miss O'Flaherty knew she was different. She satirizes her own clumsiness in the original poem "The Congé," which concludes the schoolgirl portion of the diary. During a play day, "the Brights" are assigned to clean out the chemistry lab, and so—

> . . . Katie O'F. poor unfortunate lass,
> Broke Implements stoutest as though they were glass.

She was indeed one of the brightest and most popular young women. Her classmates and teachers elected her to the Children of Mary, the Sacred Heart honor society, and on graduation day (June 29, 1868), she played in an instrumental duet and read her own prizewinning essay, on "National Peculiarities." But graduation by no means ended her interest in self-improvement, for her Commonplace Book became a diary of her intellectual and social life. She notes her membership in the German Reading Club, as well as her unhappiness with endless social "spreeing." She despises dancing till dawn with men "whose only talent lies in their feet," and she gives worldly wise advice on "the art of making oneself agreeable in conversation": let men talk about themselves.

Although she seems to have had male friendships—"A friend who knows me as well as anyone is capable of knowing me—a gentleman, of course," she writes once—Kate O'Flaherty does not write about Oscar Chopin until their engagement.

Born in 1844 in Little River (Natchitoches Parish) in northwest Louisiana, Aurelian Roselius Oscar Chopin had spent the Civil War years in France, probably at the instigation of his French-born father, Dr. Victor Jean Baptiste Chopin. (Dr. Chopin, a cruel man and brutish husband who also treated his slaves mercilessly, hated everything American.) Oscar was more playboy than scholar at the Collège de la Madeleine in Château-Thierry, where he spent much of his time pursuing young women in dens of iniquity, and failed his baccalaureate. After the war, he moved to St. Louis to learn banking at the firm of his mother's relatives, the Benoists, a prominent and very wealthy family in St. Louis as well as in Louisiana. Oscar Chopin and Kate O'Flaherty probably met at one of the lavish parties at Oakland, the Benoists' Italian-style villa outside St. Louis.

Nothing is known about their courtship. In spring of 1869, when Kate and her mother visited New Orleans with several friends and relatives, they may have met Oscar's parents, then living in the French Quarter—but she does not mention them in her diary. Oscar's mother died two months before Kate and Oscar's wedding, which took place in Holy Angels Church in St. Louis on June 9, 1870.

The last part of Kate O'Flaherty Chopin's Commonplace Book is the diary of her three-month European honeymoon with Oscar. As was typical for women of her era, she does not mention sexual matters, although she seems to be recording the consummation of the marriage on June 12 in Philadelphia. The headaches she records also fall into a monthly pattern, evidently a menstrual notation. Throughout, she enjoys poking fun at her own and Oscar's linguistic and mountaineering failings, as well as their reluctance to go to mass.

Yet she never loses her intellectual approach. The young Mrs. Chopin comments thoughtfully on what she and Oscar saw in Germany, Switzerland, and France—where the Prussians, at the start of what we now call the Franco-Prussian War, were poised to invade Paris. Oscar presumably negotiated their trip to Paris despite the war, and the American ambassador in Paris, Elihu Washburne, may also have helped. His wife was Adèle Gratiot, from the old St. Louis family Kate knew well. The Chopins escaped Paris barely in time. A week later, the Parisians closed the city gates to keep the Germans out, and settled down to months of slow starvation. But by then the Chopins had returned to the United States, and the Commonplace Book ends. They settled in New Orleans and awaited the birth of their first child, evidently conceived in France.

Cut off from the women of her family, who remained at home in St. Louis, Kate O'Flaherty Chopin stopped writing in her Commonplace Book. She began her life as an adult woman, wife, and mother, in Louisiana.

The Commonplace Book, housed at the Missouri Historical Society, is a plain notebook, 8" x 9¾", with black spine and black corners, and a green and black mottled cover on which is printed "Katie O'Flaherty, St. Louis." Kate O'Flaherty wrote on both sides of the lined pages, in black ink, and numbered the pages. The pages, probably originally cream or white, are now brownish. Because it has been read by so many researchers in the last twenty years, the notebook is now in poor condition: the back is broken and pages are loose.

Kate used several very different handwritings in the Commonplace Book. Her schoolgirl writing is flowery, curly; the beginning of her honeymoon diary has tiny script, as if she worried about having enough paper. But toward the end, she writes with large flourishes and a more angular hand.

The Commonplace Book has occasional misspellings and errors, and "Shakespeare" is often misspelled, but we should not conclude that Kate O'Flaherty Chopin was a chronically poor speller. With a dipping ink pen (one repeatedly dipped into an ink well), corrections could be made only by crossing out mistakes—a messy and troublesome process. The dipping pen may also account for odd word breaks, such as young Kate's writing "Longfellow" as "Long fellow." Her spelling is best in the schoolgirl section, which would have been read by Madam O'Meara, and worst in the honeymoon diary, presumably for her eyes only. Possibly the young Mrs. Chopin was also rebelling against Sacred Heart training when she repeatedly and flagrantly left out French accent marks.

We have left intact Kate O'Flaherty Chopin's misspellings, except for one kind. In her honeymoon diary, she frequently writes that she and Oscar stayed in a "holet," when she obviously meant to cross the T and write "hotel." In those cases, we have transcribed the word as "hotel." Overstrikes represent words crossed out; [   ] indicates unreadable words (in other instances, we have provided our best guesses). The page numbers in parentheses are hers through p. 175 of the Commonplace Book. After that, someone else seems to have numbered the pages. Through page 100 of this volume, Kate O'Flaherty's own comments are designated by italics. After that, Kate Chopin's diary is all in her own words.

**Katie O'Flaherty,
St. Louis
1867.**

Index.

Pages
 1—Extracts from "My Novel." Bulwer.
 3—Macaulays "Ranke's History of the Popes"
 5—Frome "Life Mme Swetchine."
 9—Composition—"The early Dead"
12—Reigning Sovereigns of Europe—Victoria.
13—France—Napoleon.
15—Italy—Victor Emanuel.
17—Netherlands—Wm III—Wertemberg Wm I.
18—Portugal—Pedro V—Spain Isabella II.
19—Prussia Wm I.—Austria—Francis Joseph I.
20—Russia Alexander II.—Composition "Memories."
23—Last words of Celebrated Personages.
27—The Rothschilds.
28—Character of a Scotchman = Chas Lamb.
31—Composition—"Christian Art."
40—Composition—"The Congé"
43—Extracts from Longfellow's "Hyperion"
58—Le Montagnard Emigré—Chateaubriand.
60—Character of Louis XIV=From Macaulay's Essay
63—Sicilian Vespers.
64—Espousals of the Adriatic.
65—Duke of Malbourough.
68—Prince Eugene of Savoy.
69—Extracts from Mrs Jamisons' Sketches of Art &c.—
78—" from Goethes' Wilhelm Meister.
83—" " Lady Blessington's Con. with Byron.
95—Bilderbuch ohne Bilder. (Erste Abend.)
97—Gefunden—Goethe.
" —Schlaf ein mein Herz.—(Rüchert.)
98—Knights of the Garter.
100—Blue Stockings.==Abbotsford.
102—Le Lac—Lamartine.

(1)

EXTRACTS FROM BULWER'S "MY NOVEL".

"To many minds at the commencement of our grave and earnest
pilgrimage, I am vandal enough to think that the indulgence of
poetic taste and reverie does great and lasting injury; that it
serves to enervate the character; give false ideas of life,
impart the semblance of drudgery to the noble tools and duties of
the active man. All poetry would not do this—not for instance
the Classical in its diviner masters,—not the poetry of Homer,
of Virgil, of Sophocles, not, perhaps even that of the indolent
Horace. But the poetry which youth usually loves and appreciates
the best—the poetry of mere sentiment—does so in minds already
over-prediposed to the sentimental, and which require bracing to
grow into the healthful manhood.—On the other hand even this
latter kind of poetry, which is peculiarly modern, does suit many
minds of another mould—minds which our modern life with its hard
posative forms tends to produce. And as in certain climates
plants and herbs, peculiarly adapted as antidotes to those
diseases most prevalent in the atmosphere, are profusely sown, as
it were by the benignant providence of Nature—so it may be that
the softer and more romantic

(2)

species of poetry, which comes forth in the harsh, money-making,
unromantic times, is intended as curatives and counter-poisons.
The world is so much with us now-adays, that we need have
something that prates to us, albeit in too fine an enthusiasm of
the moon and stars."

"When we look back upon human records, how the eye settles upon <u>Writers</u> as the main land marks of the past! We talk of the age of Augustus, Elizabeth, Louis XIV, of Anne, as the notable eras of the world. Why? Because it is their writers who have made them so. Intervals between one age of authors and another lie unnoticed, as the flats and common lands of uncultured history. And yet, strange to say, when these authors are living amongst us, they occupy a very small portion of our thoughts and fill up but desultory interstices of the bitumen and tripe wherefrom we build up the Babylon of our lives!"

"Oh! it is such a joy in youth to be alone with ones day dreams. And youth feels so glorious a vigor in the sense of its strength, though the world be before and against it! Removed from the chilling counting house—from the imperious will of a patron and master—all friendless but all independant—the young adventurer felt a new being—felt his grand nature as man. And

(3)

in the man rushed the genius long interdicted and laid aside—rushing back with the first breath of adversity to console—No! The man needed no consolation—to kindle to animate to rejoice! If there is a being in the world worthy of our envy, after we have grown wise philosophers of the fireside, it is not the palled voluptuary, nor the care worn statesman, nor even the great prince of arts and letters, already crowned with the laurel, whose leaves are as fit for poison as for garlands; it is the young child of adventure and hope. Ay and the emptier his purse, ten to one, but the richer his heart, and the wider the domains which his fancy enjoys, as he goes on with kingly step to the future."

FROM T. B. MACAULAY'S "RANKE'S HISTORY OF THE POPES."

"There is not and there never was in this earth, a work of human policy (?) so well deserving of examination as the Roman Catholic Church. The history of that church joins together the two great ages of human civilization. No other institution is left standing which carries the mind back to the time when the

smoke of sacrifice rose from the Pantheon, and when camelopards
and Tigers in Florian ampitheatre. The proudest royal houses are
but of yesterday when compared with the line of the Supreme
Pontiffs. That

(4)

line we trace back in an unbroken series from the Pope who
crowned Napoleon in the nineteenth century, to the Pope who
crowned Pepin in the eighth; and far beyond the time of Pepin,
the august dynasty extends, till it is lost in the twilight of
fable. The Republic of Venice came next in antiquity. But the
Republic of Venice was modern when compared with the Papacy; and
the republic of Venice, ~~remains~~ is gone, & the Papacy remains.
The papacy remains, not in decay, not a mere antique, but full of
life and useful vigor. The Catholic Church is still sending forth
to the fartherst ends of the world, missionaries as zealous as
those who landed in Kent with Augustus, and still confronting
hostile kings with the same spirit with which she confronted
Atilla. The number of her children is greater than in any former
age. Her acquisitions in the New World have more than compensated
for what she has lost in the Old. Her spiritual, as~~quisitions~~
cendency extends over the vast countries which lie between the
plains of Missouri and Cape Horn, countries which, a century
hence, may not improbably contain a population as large as that
which now inhabits Europe."

(5)

*It is to me a subject of wonder that a mind such as
Macaulay's, so enlightened and free from bigotry, should have
considered the Catholic Church a mere work of "human policy." He
yields however to this politic work a superiority and primacy, in
which we (Catholics) see every evidence of a divine Institution.*

FROM "LIFE OF MADAME SWETCHINE"

"Monsieur de Fontenelle took cognizance of nothing but mind.
He had no vices and consequently no battle to fight. He never
laughed. One day I said to him 'M. de Fontenelle did you ever
laugh?' 'No—I never executed an ah! ah! ah!' That was his idea
of laughter. He only smiled at fine things, and never knew what
it was to feel. He received no impressions from others. He never
interrupted any body, but listened attentively till his
interlocuter had finished, and was in hurry about his reply. If
you had brought an accusation against him, he would have heard
you all day, without saying a word. From his birth up nothing had

ever moved him. He resembled some very delicate little machine which will last forever, if placed in a corner where it cannot be rubbed or jostled. It is to his

(6)

absolute apathy that his long life must be attributed. His mother was like him. He speaks of both his parents with the same indifference. He used to say: 'My father was a brute, but my mother had mind; she was a quietish; a sweet little woman, who used often to say to me,—my son, you will be damned: but it did not trouble her.' Fontenelle never raised his voice upon any occasion whatever, and did not speak in a carriage for fear he would be obliged to do so. He disliked music, and did not care for painting or sculpture, expect in their relation to the imagination. He loved no one. People pleased him, but the word 'love' he never pronounced. 'Do you esteem me?' Madame Geoffrin once asked him. 'I think you are very agreeable.'—'But what if some one should come and tell you I had cut one of my children's throats, should you believe him?' 'I should reserve my judgment.'"— Portrait of Fontenelle.

"It was often said of Diderot that he liked to converse with the most commonplace people, because they would listen to him. He was like a man playing ball against a wall, who exclaimed at each rebound 'That

(7)

wall plays remarkably well'!"
"A correspondent of Ferney once said, 'I have just received a delightful letter from Voltaire. Let me read you my reply'."
    "Voltaire cared very little for the country; and it was wittily said of his 'Henriade' that there was just grass enough in it for the horses."
    "M. Dubucq, who has left a brilliant record of his administration in our colonies, once said, 'The gibbet is a species of flattery to the human race. Three or four persons are hanged from time to time, for the sake of making the rest believe that they are very virtuous.'"
    "Mr Thomas said that an expressionless face is born deaf and dumb."

"'They blame you,' 'They accuse you;' they say of
you'—last but not least—'they will say'—Who then is this king
They whose authority is thus proclaimed. It is a king without
state splendor or visible throne, yet all obey his voice and
tremble before him. A remarkably king in this respect that he is
sovereign in great things as well as in small.

---

*The "Life of Madame Swetchine is a queer book—which did
not interest me much. In fact translations from the French*

(8)

*or German rarely interest me; because French and German notions
and ideas are so different from the English—that they loose all
their naive zest by being translated into that practical of
tongues. That "portrait of Fontenelle" is given in a piquant
manner;—I should have preferred reading it in French, but was
unable to procure the book. I like it because I can glance over
it as an occasional reminder that a monster once lived upon
earth; and besides I know persons who resemble M. de Fontenelle
in more respects than one. His only redeeming trait is the
patience with which he could listen. His dislike for music
reminds me of a joke told at my expense. Mama one afternoon sent
me in the parlor to entertain a gentleman, who, though deemed
bashful has never yet succeeded in making that ingredient in his
composition known to myself. I immediately took to the piano as
the most pleasing way both to himself and me of fulling my
mission of entertainer. Wishing to suit his taste what ever it
might be—I played pieces of every variety: Operas—Sonatas—
Meditations—Galops—Nocturnes—Waltzes & Jigs—after
accomplishing which—I turned to him*

(9)

*expecting approbation if not praise and admiration; when to my
utmost dismay, he cooly informed me that there was nothing on
earth he disliked more than music — at any time — in any place
— and of any kind from a brass band to a jews harp.*

COMPOSITION.
THE EARLY DEAD. (TO THE MEM. OF MINNIE ERVINGER 1866)

Death comes not among us, without bringing sorrow to the heart. Even though it be upon the soul of the aged that he lays his icy hold, we still, in sadness, heave a sigh over the bier of the departed one, and breathe a silent prayer for her eternal happiness. How then express the grief with which we follow the young, the gifted, the beautiful to the silent tomb. Alas why should this spring flower, so favored with graces, so dowered with loveliness, in preferance to the faded and drooping be snatched from our midst? Where is now the rich fresh intellect, the visions of future womanly happiness to which she is eagerly looked forward, and which were to form the accomplishment of those many and varied hopes? Ask it of Death!

(10)

But draw away the ghastly pall so illsuited to that childish loveliness, and gaze for a while upon the motionless form. The essence of purity breathes around us; it rests upon the frank open brow, and nestles in the curve of the still lip. Lift one of those marble hands, which clasps so confidingly the jeweled cross; how cold it is—its chill sends a shiver through the frame; drop it,—hear how heavily it falls against the alabaster bosom. The silken tresses wave as naturally around her forehead as when she herself smothed them away. The closed lids hide the merry sparkle of her eye, but you have seen them so before as she rested in happy unconscious slumber, this then surely cannot be a part of death. Ah be not deceived; it is indeed a slumber from which there is no awakening. And that heart, so lately the well spring of joyous life, has ceased responding to earthly cares. Peering into the dim future we see nothing, but much do we fear; and from these very objects of our terror, the dead are, by the hand of a kind and loving Providence, happily rescued. Sin might have dimmed that halo of purity which now floats around the death-

(11)

robed form; sorrow might have threaded the sunny hair with silver, and left its furrows on the brow; the light of the beaming eye might have been quenched in grief, and disease have

*deposed that glorious intellect from its throne. Our future lies
before us,—bright perhaps with many a splendid promise—but
enshrining unnumbered woes, which Providence in mercy veils from
our sight. Would we if we could, in selfishness call back the
silent sleeper to those dread possibilities? She has already
touched the confines of that land "from whose bourne no traveller
returns." She will not, as we may yet do, weep in anguish over
the graves of the loved and mourned, or over the sealed tomb of
blasted hopes. Nestled in the arms of her heavenly Father,
temptation and sin dare not approach her now.*

*Mourn not therefore, when Death comes into our gardens
culling the flowers of Spring, for in their early beauty, how far
more pleasant an offering are they to God than when sere and
drooping. Then in their fragrant purity, their happy innosence,
they tell the Saviour in language of eloquence, that He has not
visited us in vain, that all on earth is not corruption, and that*

(12)

*there are still flowers awaiting to be plucked; beautiful flowers
untainted by the rankling weed.*

*Blessed indeed are the holy living struggling with hope and
love in the combat of life, but doubly blessed are the youthful
dead!*

REIGNING SOVEREIGNS OF EUROPE.
1867.
ENGLAND————VICTORIA.

Was born at Kensington Palace, May 24th 1819. She is the
daughter of Edw Duke of Kent fourth son of Geo. III. As Geo. IV
and his next brothers the dukes of York and Clarence were
childless, she was soon looked upon as heiress presumptive of the
british throne. On the death of her uncle Wm IV in l837, the
crowns of England and Hanover which had been worn by the same
persons since the accession of Geo III, were separated, the
former devolving upon Victoria, the latter by virtue of the salic
law, falling to the duke of Cumberland. Victoria was crowned in
Westminster Abbey, June 28th 1838. In 1840—she was married to

(13)

Albert of Saxe Coburg-Gotha.

The rebellion in India having been crushed, the
possessions of the East India Company were transferred to the
crown, and Queen Victoria was proclaimed Queen of Hindoostan.
She travells frequently—both in her dominions at home and
abroad. She visited Louis Philippe in the Chateau D'Eu, the King
of Belgium in 1843; and the Emperor Louis Napoleon in 1845. Her
mother and Prince Albert died in 1861. She has nine
children—Victoria married to the Prince of Prussia; Albert
Edward to Alexandria of Denmark; Alice married to Louis of Messe;
Alfred, Helena, Louisa, Auther, Leopold and Beatrice.

FRANCE———NAPOLEON III

Was the son of Louis Napoleon and Hortense Beauharnais,
the daughter of the Empress Josephine, and was born in the palace
of the Tuilleries, April 30th 1808. After the fall of the Empire
he went to Rome and in 1830, during the disturbances there, he
received an order to leave the Papal States. A sentence of exile
was pronounced against him. Accompanied by his mother, he threw
himself

(14)

upon the generosity of France, and begged the favor of being
admitted into the army, even as a common Soldier; but this was
refused, and shortly afterwards sentance of exile was pronounced
upon him here also. They fled to England, but afterwards returned
to Switzerland. In 1838 the Strasburg insurrection, of which he
was the soul, broke out, but he was arrested and sent to the
United States. After a brief residence here, he set out for
Europe, to attend at the death-bed of his mother. Shortly after,
the Swiss Government was requested to deliver the person of Louis
to the French, and this was refused. War would have been the
consequence had not Louis voluntarily gone to England. Returning
to France in 1840, he tried to excite a revolution at Bologne. He
was arrested, examined, and doomed to perpetual imprisonment in
the castle of Ham. After five years his father addressed a letter
to Louis Philippe asking him to permit his son to attend him in

his last hours. This was refused and Louis Napoleon thought
himself justified in attempting an escape. In this he succeeded,
and retired to England. When the revolution of 1848

(15)

broke out, he returned to France, where after many vicissitudes
he was elected president of the Republican party. When his term
had expired and France was on the point of another election, by a
coup d'état unparalled in history, he seized the reigns of
government in his own hands, and one year later, by the unanimous
consent of the whole nation, assumed the title of Emperor of the
Republic.

June 25th 1843—he married Eugenie de Montigo, countess of
Tibe, and 1854 was marked by the birth of the Prince of Algiers.

ITALY——VICTOR EMANUEL II.

Son of Charles Albert, King of Sardinia, and Theresa a
daughter of the duke of Tuscany, born 1820. He was carefully
educated, and in 1842 married to Adelaide of Austria. He was
wounded in the battle of Gigo, which followed the first out break
of revolution in 1848; and after the defeat of this day, Chas
Albert abdicated in favor of his son, who came to the throne with
any thing but happy prospects. He now restored order, signed a
peace with Austria,

(16)

and then attacked the clergy,—secularized the property of the
Church, and took from religious associations the monoply of
education hitherto enjoyed. For these acts he was excommunicated
by the Pope, and when shortly after he lost his mother, his wife,
his brother and his youngest child, and fell dangerously ill
himself, many regarded it as a proof of the anger of heaven. The
marriage of his daughter Clotilde, to prince Napoleon Jerome, was
followed almost immediately by the war of Italian Independence in
which France and Sardinia fought against Austria. The Austrians
every way were defeated, and after the battle of Solferina, the
peace of Villa Franca seemed to crush his hopes for the union of
Italy. But by revolutions in Tuscany, Parma, Modena, Sicily,

Naples and the Papal States, he became master of all Italy, save Venice and a small territority immediately surrounding Rome, which is still in possession of the Pope. The revolution of Naples was instigated and led by Garabaldi.

---

(17)

THE NETHERLANDS——WM III.

Son of William II and brother of Alexander I of Russia, born at the Hague in 1817, educated in England, and mounted the throne in 1849. In 1859 he married the princess Sophia of Wertemberg.

WERTEMBERG——WM I.

Born in 1781. For some years he shared the wanderings of his father, during which time he lost his mother. His education was conducted by his father whose severity caused a lasting misunderstanding between the two. In 1803 when the father assumed the title of Elector, he went to France and Germany chiefly for the purpose of keeping away from court, but returned in 1806 and lived in great seclusion in Stutgart. In 1808 he married the princess Caroline Augusta of Bavaria, whom six years later he divorced, and who became the fourth wife of Francis I of Austria. In 1861 he married Catherina, grand dutchess of Russia, who died after three years leaving him two daughters, one of whom is present Queen of the Netherlands.

---

(18)

PORTUGAL—PEDRO V.

Son of Donna Maria II, and Ferdinand of Saxe Coburg, was born in 1837. His mother dying in 1853, he succeeded under the regency of his father. He ascended the throne in 1855, and in 18589 married the princess Stephany of Hohenzollern who died one year after.

SPAIN—ISABELLA II

Daughter of Ferdinand VII and his fourth wife Maria
Christina. Her father having no son repelled the salic law,
introduced by Philip V, and named her his successor, thus
excluding his brother Don Carlos, who would otherwise have been
heir presumptive. At her father's death, Isabella at the age of
three ascended the throne and Don Carlos took up arms to oppose
her; but after a year her claim was confirmed by the Cortez. The
period of her minority was an uninterrupted series of agitations,
during which time the person and education of the young queen
were entrusted to the care of popular generals. These latter were
finally compelled to resign, and the Cortez, by advancing the ma-

(19)

jority of the young queen eleven months, placed her on the
throne in 1843. In 1846 she married her cousin Don Francisco duke
of Cadiz; while at the same time her sister, Maria Ferdinando was
married to the duke de Mont Pontessier, son of Louis Philippe.
She is beloved by her subjects, but her character is not
stainless.

PRUSSIA—WM I

Second son of Frederic Wm III was born in 1797. He succeeded
his brother Frederick Wm IV, and was crowned at Kingsburg in
1861. In 1839 he married Marie Louise of Saxe-Weimer, by whom he
had two children,—the crown prince Frederic Wm who married
Victoria the princess royal of Great Britain, and Louise Marie
who married the grand duke of Baden.

AUSTRIA—FRANCIS JOSEPH I.

Son of the Arch duke Charles, and Sophia of Bavaria, and
grandson of Francis II, was born in 1830. His education was
intrusted to count Bourbilles, who made him a good linguist, and
a skillful rider,

(20)

fond of militery display, but evincing no particular talent. In 1854 he married Elizabeth, daughter of a Bavarian duke, who was the mother of two children, Gisela and Rudolph.

RUSSIA—ALEXANDER II

The son of Nicholas I born in 1808, was most carefully educated under the eye of his father, with whom he lived on very affectionate terms. Ascended the throne in 1855.

COMPOSITION.
"MEMORIES." (18667)

The old man sat in his easy chair,
With nerveless hand and vision dim;
But the soul was bright, like halls that glow
With festal light, though the walls be grim.

For Memory her spell had laid,
And awakened by the talisman bold
The past gave up its silent dead—
The cherished forms and scenes of old

Over life's battled way once more

(21)

He strayed where 'ere its bright path led,
And breathing memories of yore
Sprang up at each elastic tread.

Proud manhoods course was sadly traced
By many a gleaming shaft of stone,—
Fair monumental piles, which graced
The sights where boyhood's hopes had flown.

He strayed where childhood's roseate light
Spread witchery over hill and dell.

He climbed the rocky mountain's height,
Whose every echo he knew so well.

He heard the rush of Avons stream,
A low, sweet, music to his ear,
Which had haunted his soul like a holy dream,
Through the gloom of many a buried year.

His cottage home in his jasmine frame,
Still smiled beneath the linden shade,
When the south-wind an early pilgrim came,
And the wild flowers a rich mosaic made.

He knelt again at his mother's knee,
The flushed brow cooled by the gentle hand,—

(22)

Oh! Why had she gone, why left him there
The last crushed link of that broken band.

At the altar he stood, where his bride was won—
The sharer of childhood's joys and care;
While the myrtle blossom starlike shone,
Through the glossy folds of her braided heir.

Then he saw mid his tears a mossy grave,
Where hope and joy with his bride were laid,
There he heard the wail of oceans wave,
Not half so wild as his own heart made.

Ah! vains' the thought and vain's the man
Who from his wiser self would screen
The visions fair in childhood's span
The images of youths bright dream.

The present drives us to the past,
To muse o'er joys it kindly brought.
The light the future o'er us casts
Is with too many shadows frought.

For in the futures vista dim
What ills are shrouded from our sight—

Cold sorrows known to none, save Him
Who governs destiny with might.

(23)

But memories gladden while they last;
And every power of art combined
Can dim not visions of the past
Nor draw a veil o'er manhood's mind.

LAST WORDS OF CELEBRATED PERSONAGES.

Socrates.	When about to take his last drink. "Krito, we owe a cock to Æsculapius; discharge the debt and by no means omit it."
Sir Hugh Percy.	"I have saved the bird in my bosom."— Fighting for Henry VI when mortally wounded, in reference to the faith he had pledged to his Sovereign.
Tasso	"Into thy hands O Lord!"
Ferrar—Bishop of St. Davids	On being chained to the stake at Carmarthen Cross. "If I stir through the pains of my burning, believe not the doctrine I have taught."
Chas V	"Ay, Jesus!"
Raleigh	To the executioner who was pausing "Why dost thou not strike—strike man."
Cromwell	"It is not my design to eat or sleep, but my design is to make what haste I can to be gone."
Pope	There is nothing meritorious but vir-

(24)

tue and friendship—and indeed friendship
is but a part of virtue."

Haller	"The artery ceases to beat."
Dr Franklin	When desired to change his position in bed—"A dying man can do nothing easy."
Dr Wm Hunter	"If I had strength to hold a pen I would write what an easy and pleasant thing it is to die."
Fontenelle	"Je ne souffre pas mes amis, mais je sens un certain difficulté d'Etre."
Thurlow	"I'm shot—if I don't believe I'm dying."
Mirabeau	"Let me die to the sounds of delicious Music."
Washington	"It is well."—
Nelson	"I thank God I have done my duty."
Wm Pitt	"Oh my country—how I leave my country!
Napoleon	"Mon Dieu—La France—tête d'Armée."
John Adams	"Thomas Jefferson still survives."
Thomas Jefferson	"I resign my soul to God—my daughter to my country."
Byron	"I must sleep now."
Walter Scott	"God bless you—all
Goethe	"Mehr Licht"—More light.
Lord Chesterfield	"Hand the gentleman a chair"
Josephine	"Isle of Elba—Napoleon."

Catherine   "O, if I knew death could be so
Macaulay.   sweet I had never feared it so much."

(25)

Aristotle   "I entered this world in sin, I have
                     lived in anxiety. I depart in
                     perturbation. Cause of Causes pity me."

(26)

THE ROTHSCHILDS.

A jewish family of European bankers, whose founder was Meyer Anschene Rothschild. He was educated for a ~~banker~~ Rabbi, but commenced business on a small scale as a trader; and eventually procured a situation in a Hanovarian banking house. He subsequently opened an establishment of his own at Frankfort, his native city. In 1806 when Napoleon decreed the forfeiture of Hesse Castle and Brunswick and sent an army to enforce his decree, the elector was unable to offer resistance, but he had five million dollars in silver which he was unwilling to give up, and unable to carry with him.—Sending for Anslem Rothschild, he offered him the use of the money without interest, if he would remove it to a place of safety. The banker and his three sons enjoyed the use of this large sum for eight years, and this laid the foundation of their future greatness. His five sons were Anslem, who succeeded his father in Frankfort, Solomon who established himself in Vienna, Nathan Mayer the ablest financier of the family at London, Charles at Naples, and

(27)

James at Paris. The five brothers constituted but one firm, in which all had an equal share, but conducted their business under differant branches, each under the charge of one of his brothers. Nathan is said to have known the results of the battle of Waterloo, eight hours before the British Government, and is said to have realized $1,000,000 by that knowledge. The house has often made peace between the European states by refusing to furnish loans. The Austrian Emperor for the courtesy with which they responded to his appeal in 1813, bestowed on each of the brothers a patent of nobility, with the title of Baron of the Empire. Nathan Lionel Rothschild of London is now the leading

partner; he succeeded to his father's titles in 1836. He was
elected a member of the house in 1847, but declining to take the
oath in the "true faith of a christian" did not take his seat
till 1858, when the objections were removed. He is the first
adhearent of the Jewish religion, that ever held seat in
Parliament.

---

(28)

CHARACTER OF A SCOTCHMAN.
FROM CHARLES LAMB'S "ESSAYS OF ELIA"

"I have been trying all my life to like Scotchmen, and am
obliged to desist from the experiment in despair. They cannot
like me—and in truth, I never knew one of that nation who
attempted to do it. There is something more plain and ingenuous
in their mode of proceeding. We know one another at first sight.
There is an order of imperfect intellects (under which mine must
be content to rank) which in its constitution is essentially
anti-Caledonian. The owners of the sort of faculties I allude to,
have minds rather suggestive than comprehensive. They have no
pretences to much clearness or precision in their ideas, or in
their manner of expressing them. Their intellectual wardrobe (to
confess fairly) has few whole pieces in it. They are content with
fragments and scattered pieces of Truth. She presents no full
front to them—a feature or a side face at the most. Hints and
glimpses, germs and crude essays at a system, is the utmost they
pretend to. They

(29)

beat up a little game peradventure—and leave it to knottier
heads, more robust constitutions, to run it down. The light that
lights them is not steady and polar, but mutable and shifting:
waxing and again waning. Their conversation is accordingly. They
will throw out a random word in or out of season, and be content
to let it pass for what it is worth. They cannot speak always as
if they were up on their oath—but must be understood, speaking
or writing, with some abatement. They seldom wait to mature a
proposition, but e'en bring it to market in the green ear. They
delight to impart their defective discoveries as they arise,

without waiting for their full development. They are no
systematizers and would but err more by attempting it. Their
minds, as I said before, are suggestive merely.

The brain of a true Caledonian (if I am not mistaken) is
constituted upon quite a different plan. His Minerva is born in
panoply. You are never admitted to see his ideas in their
growth—if, indeed, they do grow, and are not rather put together
upon principals of clock work. You never catch his mind in an
undress. He never hints

(30)

or suggests anything, but unlades his stock of ideas in perfect
order and completeness. He brings his total wealth into company,
and gravely unpacks it. His riches are always about him. He never
stoops to catch a glittering something in your presence to share
with you, before he knows whether it be true touch or not. You
cannot cry halves to any thing that he finds. He does not find,
but brings. You never witness his first apprehension of a thing.
His understanding is always at its meridian—you never see the
first dawn, the early streaks. He has no flatterings of self
suspicion. Surmises, guesses, misgivings, half-intuitions,
semi-consciousnesses, partial illuminations, dim instincts,
embryo conceptions, have no place in his brain or vocabulary. The
twilight of dubiety never falls upon him. Is he orthodox—he has
no doubts. Is he an infidel—he has none either. Between the
affirmative and negative there is no broader band with him. You
cannot hover with him upon the confines of truth, or wander in
the maze of a probable argument. He always keeps

(31)

the path. You cannot make excursions with him—for he sets you
right. His taste never fluctuates. His morality never abates. He
cannot compromise, or understand middle actions. There can be but
a right and a wrong. His conversation is as a book. His
affirmations have the sanctity of an oath. You must speak upon
the square with him. He stops a metaphor like a suspected person
in an enemy's country. "A healthy book!" said one of his
countrymen to me, who had ventured to give that appelation to
John Buncle,—'Did I catch rightly what you said? I have heard of
a man in health, and of a healthy state of body, but I do not see
how that epithet can be properly applied to a book."' &c. &c.

COMPOSITION.
CHRISTIAN ART. 1867.

Great indeed were the mighty empires of long ago, that could lay their hold upon nations and call them theirs. But this greatness and glory are fading away. Palmyra and Persepolis would be forgotten, did not

(32)

their storied columns tell a tale of ancient splendor and magnificence, and, as time pushes onward, the echoes from the widespread plain of Philippi, the fields of Pharsalia, and the bleeding ground of Cannae, grow fainter and fainter in the distance, and would die away, in the distance did not History's page catch up the lingering strain and re-echo it back to the silent past. But Rome needs no other eulogist to sound her praise than

"Sully's voice, and Virgils lay, and Livy's pictured page,"

which, with her many glorious works of art, have drawn aside the curtain which would shut the past into oblivion; while the breathing canvass and chiseled forms of sculpture that still speak of ancient Greece render undying the glory of her name. However, without depreciating the rich legacies bequethed us by the past, we yet cannot attribute to them a perfection which Christian genius finds unattainable; but on the contrary, in the works of modern art, we find a superiority, while far from tracing this improvement to the

(33)

advanced state of civilization, its origin may be traced referred to that great source whence springs all good—Christianity.

A brief summary will prove that not even in the golden age of Pericles did the arts flourish with such luxurniance as they have since Christ came upon earth. Where is there a more prolific theme for the rovings of fancy than Religion, with all its beauties celestial and terrestrial. The pagan knew it and drew his grandest inspirations from great Olympus height where dwelt his many gods; the Christian also knows it, but instead of transporting his muse to an earthly mount, he soars to a realm whose glories human eye has never witnessed, where he mingles

*with myriads of spiritual beings, wrapt in a vesture of mystery
and beauty, while faith and genius lead him admiringly within the
penetralia of Omnipotence itself, where pen, and brush, and
chisel fall powerless to execute, and the soul can only worship.*

*Among the most magnificent remains of ancient art are its
architectural mon-*

(34)

*uments, which, several of them, still undefaced by time, embody
some of the grandest conceptions of man's genius; the sunny
shores of the Aegean and the Isles of Greece are still whitened
by their glorious ruins—their tall shafts proudly pointing back
through the gloom of ages to the era when art was born and
nurtured beneath the olive-shades of Attica, and from the
Acropolis gave laws to the world. Some of their many temples are
still extant—in their beautiful and harmonious varieties—the
grand and sublime Doric, the fantastic and graceful Corinthian
and the not less beautiful though less striking Ionic, all alike
evidencing the rich and versatile genius of the masters who
called them forth. But forcibly can Christianity oppose "Diana's
Marvel," the Coliseum or even the Temple of Theseus, for has she
not St Peters, the master conception of Angelo and Raphael, St
Sophia's, St Paul's and Versailles? Her superiority lies in the
pre-eminence given to spirit over matter. Her temples may not
rival those of antiquity in costliness of*

(35)

*material, or in their elaborate finish, but they are unparalleled
in general effect and in the graceful symbolism of detail. The
Gothic has own peculiar kind of architecture, is unequalled by
any of the Grecian orders in awakening the grandest ideas of
majestic sublimity, and that religious awe which is so allied to
worship. It is modelled upon the gloomy pine woods of the North,
and we may distinguish in its lofty pillars the tall shafts of
the forest monarchs while the quaintly traced arches and domes
define the overhanging and pyramidal foliage.*

*In Sculpture alone must Christianity cede to Antiquity the
palm of equality; for the rigidity of marble is unfavorable to
the delicate shadings of sentiment and feeling, whose expression
is the crowning glory of Christian art. While the ancients
studied to fashion every outline of their works to the blending
and perfect undulations of grace and symmetry, Christian genius*

strove to develope in form and feature the evidences of an
indwelling soul; it has aimed, not alone at reproducing the
symmetrical shapes of earth-

(36)

ly beauty, but at eliciting from each breathing lineament, of the
figure chiseled by God's own hand, the "Image and likeness" He
stamped upon it. There breathes a spiritual soul through the
"Adam & Eve" of Fra Bartolomeo, and a sturn dignity in Michael
Angelo's statue of "Moses," that Praxitiles could never have
imparted to a Venus a Hebe or an Achilles.

    In painting however the influence of Christianity is more
discernable. By her fundamental doctrine of the omnipresence of
God, she has added a new charm to nature; a charm which makes the
artist feel the presence of a Supreme Being brooding over valley
and river, woodland and mountain, which inspired the pencil of a
Claude Lorraine and a Salvator Rosa, and which has ushered the
artist into the realm of landscape painting, of which pagan art
seemed forgetful. Again—the associations which have hallowed
western Asia, have opened to art a theatre upon which genius has
revelled at will. The patriarchal simplicity of oriental manners,
the pic-

(37)

turesque costumes and flowing draperies of the East, and the
soul-lit features of its ardent children, but above all the
absorbing interest in its marvellous history, have furnished
subjects for the most magnificent productions of Raphaël, Angelo,
Murillo and others, till the whole inspired record has been
illustrated, from the scene where Satan saw among

> *"Groves whose rich trees wept odorous gums & balm"—*
> *"Two of far nobler shape, erect and tall,*
> *God-like erect with native honor clad."*

to the consummation of the awful tragedy enacted on Calvery.

    Poetry whose existance may be accounted coeval with that of
man, has received from Christianity its loftiest inspirations.
While the ancient bard leads the fancy to the earthly abodes of
Pagan deities, the Christian Milton carries it into Paradise, for

*it is in the unseen world that the master spirits of our race
breathe freely and are at home, where in language the noblest
that ever sprang from man's heart or intellect, he depicts the*

(38)

*characters and occupations, not of men but of Angels. It was
Christianity which impulse to the genius of Dante, & Tasso, while
Virgil, Horace and Homer looked for inspiration but from the
world around.*

*There remains yet to be considered the influence of
Christianity upon music, that art so powerful as an agent in
awakening the slumbering passions in the heart of man. From the
time that David tuned his harp on Salem, and Jeremias, with
prophetic voice sang forth his "Lamentations," music has
continued to gain in perfection of expression and harmony without
entirely abandoning the imitation of the voices of nature. It
arose to the dignity of an art, only when Christianity ennobled
the muses, by accepting their services to add to the splendor of
her ceremonial; then was heard for the first time beneath the
gothic arch of the Cathedral of Milan the exultant strains of the
"Te Deum" which have lost none of their original power after
sixteen centuries—Then was heard amid the pillard isles of the
Sistine Chapel the*

(39)

*harmony of that wondrous "Miserera," now, now stealing forth from
the darkness like the first wail of a broken heart, growing
fainter and fainter till it dies away in silence as if the grief
were too great for the strain; then leaping forth, not like the
voice of song, but of agony—floating and swelling with
irresistable power till it sinks again into the low broken tones
of intense anguish. Mozart, Hayden and Handel laid upon Melody
the spell of their Christian genius, and have made their names as
imperishable as their sacred harmonies.*

*Hence though we cease not to regret that "the works of the
age of Pericles lie at the foot of the Acropolis in
indiscriminate ruin, that the plough share turns up the marble
which the hand of Phidias chiselled into beauty, and that the
Mussulman folds his flock beneath the falling columns of the
temple of Minerva," we still feel convinced that Christianity has
entrusted to art a nobler destiny than she ever fulfilled in the*

*palmiest days of pagan greatness, and a like destiny awaits her
in future, if she seeks at the same source, the well spring of
her inspiration.*

(40)

COMPOSITION.
THE "CONGÉ"—1867.

— *The "Congé" the last at which the day scholars were
permitted to mingle with the boarders—was given in honor of
Mother Galwey's feast. The "Madam" alluded to was our much loved
teacher Madam O'Meara. The day following, for a class-exercise,
were were given ~~were~~ the subject of the past day's amusement.*

The Congé is past and the frolic and fun
Was over, before it seemed scarcely begun;
For with playing and romping and teasing away,
The quick fleeting hours soon filled up the day.
But the morning was not to amusement devoted
For <u>Madam</u> to all of her "Brights" had alloted
The task (this displayed a heart eer trusting)
Of arranging and breaking and mending & dusting,
Her chemical tools, which of delicate make
We could easily handle and—easily break.
There was Lizzie who thought with importance of air
That we could do nothing if she were not there,
And Frank—thinking much, and speaking but little
Who handled with safety tools e'en the most brittle;

(41)

While Katie O'F. poor unfortunate lass,
Broke Implements stoutest as though they were glass.
But this war of destruction, thanks, soon was to cease
And the room and its contents left happily in peace.
For kind Madam Hamilton, with due form and state,
Announced the dinner no longer could wait,
And arranging the girls with artistical taste,
Led the way to the hall without trouble or haste.
But ye Fates! on arriving I found 'twas my doom,
For want I presume of more benches or room,
To sit between Lizzie and Nina my cousin

Who seemed to have appetites due to a dozen,
And gave me scarce time to breathe or to think
With asking for butter—the bread—or a drink.
But between these demands which indeed were not few—
I found time to admire an arrangement or two
Of the garlands of flowers and pigs à la fry
Which in every direction were greeting the eye.
But all these howere beautiful sink into nought,
In considering the fun which the afternoon brought,
For through cellar and basement and garret so high,
We tumbled and tossed in the game of "I Spy."
Now into the barn yard—the loft or the stable,
Hiding in every place—any place that we were able;
And thrown into ecstacies of foolish delight
At not being found or at seeking aright.

(42)

But at length Madam M. with mysterious air,
Comes whispering that the girls must prepare
To enter a room, shut out from all light,
To see a strange thing—a most wonderful sight:
~~Got up by "our Madam~~
Which sight we soon found was a new source of pleasure
Got up by "our Madam" whose mind is a treasure,
Ever teeming with jewels of science and fun,
And in whom we all think sets and rises the sun.
'Twas a strange magic lantern whis displayed a queer sight
Of devils in every conceivable plight.
Of hills and volcanoes; St. Peter's at Rome;
Of Pantheons at Paris—or a neat cottage home.
Of monkies and tigers and elephants rare—
All displayed with precision and mentioned with care.
But my keen disappointment one cannot conceive,
When, at the best part we are told we must leave;
For fear that the already fast fading light
Would leave us in fear at the coming of night.
And as I reluctantly arose to obey,
Though my reason said "homeward" my heart bade me stay.
So greatly put out—nearly ready to cry,
I kissed my companions—bade Madam good bye—
And secretly knowing I'd no time to waste
Turned my steps towards home with all possible haste.

(43)

EXTRACTS FROM LONGFELLOW'S "HYPERION."

"'The Rhine! the Rhine! a blessing on the Rhine!'"

"O the pride of the German heart is this noble river! And right it is; for of all the rivers of this beautiful earth, there is none so beautiful as this. There is hardly a league of its whole course, from its cradle in the snowy Alps to its grave in the sands of Holland, which boasts not its peculiar charms. By Heavens! If I were a German I would be proud of it too; and of the clustering grapes that hang about its temples, as it reels onward through vineyards in a triumphal march, like Bacchus crowned and drunken.

But I will not attempt to describe the Rhine; it would make this chapter much too long. And to do it well, one should write like a god; and his language flow onward royally with breaks and dashes, like the waters of that royal river, and antique, quaint and Gothic times be reflected in it. Flow then into this smoke-colored goblet, thou blood of the Rhine! out of thy prison house,—out of thy long necked tapering flask, in shape not unlike a church spire among thy native hills; and

(44)

from the crystal belfry loud ring the merry tinkling bells, while I drink a health to my my hero in whose heart is sadness, and in whose ears the bells of Andernach are ringing noon."

What a subtle charm exists in each line of Long fellow's. He is a poet and a true one—and prose and poetry bear alike the stamp of his soft poetic genius. His Hyperion from beginning to end might be compared to a "river of flowing gold" so rich is it in real and imaginative beauties. I read and reread with the keenest enjoyment his exquisite descriptions of German scenes and scenery; for my passion has always been to travel in that land that cradle and repository of genius. And even while longing, I still fear to visit it lest my long cherished dreams fail of accomplishment and prove but the "baseless fabric of a vision." "Hyperion" would implant in any heart an aching after Germania's beauties—as it has long, long since implanted in mine heigh ho!—Il faut espérer.

(Heidelberg) "High and hoar on the forehead of the Jetten bühl stands the castle of Heidleberg. Behind it rise the oak-crested hills of the Grissberg and the Kaiserstuhl; and in front, from the wide terrace of ma-

(45)

sonry you can almost throw a stone upon the roofs of the town, so close do they lie beneath. Above this terrace rises the broad front of the chapel of St Udalrich. On the left stands the octagon tower of the horloge; and on the right, a huge round tower, battered and shattered by the mace of war, shores up with its broad shoulders the beautiful palace and garden-terrace of Elizabeth, wife of the count Palatine Frederick. In the rear of the older palaces and towers, forming a vast irregular triangle, Rodolph's ancient castle, with its gothic gloriette and fantastic gables; the Giant's Tower, guarding the drawbridge over the moat, the Rent Tower, with the linden trees growing on its summits; and the magnificent Rittersaal of Otho-Henry, count Palatine of the Rhine and Grand Seneschal of the holy Roman Empire. From the garden behind the castle, you pass under the archway of the Giants Tower into the great court yard. The diverse architecture of differant ages strikes the eye; and curious Sculptures. In niches on the wall of St Ulrich's chapel stand rows of Knights in Armor, broken and dismembered; and on the

(46)

front of Otho Rittersaal, the heroes of Jewish history and classic fable. You enter the ~~crossed~~opened and desolate chambers of the ruin; and on every side are medallions and family arms; the Globe of the Empire and the Golden Fleece, or the eagle of the Caesars, resting on the escutcheons of Bavaria and the Palatinate. Over the windows and doorways and chimney pieces are sculptures and mouldings of exquisite workmanship; and the eye is bewildered by the profusion of caryatides and arabesques, and rosettes, and fan-like flutings, and gardens of fruits and flowers and acorns, and bullocks heads with draperies of foliage, and muzzles of lions, holding rings in their teeth. The cunning hand of Art was busy for six centuries in raising and adorning these walls; the mailed hands of Time and War have defaced and over thrown them in less than two. Next to the Alhambra of Grenada, the Castle of Heidelberg is the most magnificent ruin of the Middle Ages.

In the valley below flows the rushing stream of the Neckar. Close from its margin, on the opposite side, rises the mountains of All-Saints, crowned with the ruins of a Convent; and up the valley stretches the

(47)

mountain-curtain of the Odenwald. So close and many are the hills that shut the valley in, that the river seems a lake. But westward it opens upon the broad plain of the Rhine, like the mouth of a trumpet; and like the blast of a trumpet is at times the wintry wind through this narrow mountain-pass. The blue Alsatian Hills rise beyond; and on a platform, or strip of level land, between the Neckar and the mountains, right under the castle stands the town of Heidelberg; as the old song says, 'a pleasant place town, when it has done raining.'"

(Literature) "'What a strange picture a university presents to the imagination! The lives of scholars in their cloistered stillness;—literary men of retired habits, and professors who study sixteen hours a day and never see the world but on a Sunday. Nature has, no doubt, for some wise purpose, placed in their hearts this love for literary labor, and seclusion. Otherwise who would feed the undying lamp of thought? But for such men as these, a blast of wind through the chinks and crannies of this old world, or the flapping of a conquerors banner, would blow it out for ever.

(48)

The light of the soul is easily extinguished. And whenever I reflect upon these things, I become aware of the great importance in a nations history, of the individual fame of scholars and literary men. I fear that it is far greater than the world is willing to acknowledge; or, perhaps I would say than the world has thought of acknowledging. Blot out from England's history the names of Chaucer, Shakespeare, Spencer and Milton only, and how much of her glory you would blot out with them! Take from Italy such names as Dante, Petrarch, Boccaccio, Michael Angelo and Raphael, and how much would be wanting to the completeness of her glory! How would the history of Spain look, if the leaves were torn out on which are written the names of Cervantes, Lope de

Vega, and Calderon? What would be the fame of Portugal without
her Camoens; of France, without her Racine and Rabelais and
Voltaire; or Germany without her Martin Luther (?), her Goethe,
and her Shiller? Nay, what were the nations of old, without their
philosophers, poets and historians? Tell me, do not these men, in
all ages and in all places, emblazon with bright colors the
armorial bearings of their country? Yes and far more

(49)

than this for in all ages and in all places they give humanity an
assurance of its greatness, and say,—'Call not this time or
people wholly barbarous; for this much, even then and there,—
could the human mind achieve!' But the boisterous world has
hardly thought of acknowledging all this. Therein it has shown
itself somewhat ungrateful. Else whence this great reproach, the
general scorn, the loud derision with which, to take a familiar
example, the Monks of the middle ages are regarded? That they
slept their lives away is most untrue. For in an age when books
were few, so few, so precious, that they were often chained to
their oaken shelves with iron chains, like galley slaves to their
benches,—these men, with their laborious hands, copied upon
parchment all the love and wisdom of the past, and transmitted it
to us. Perhaps it is not too much to say, but for these monks,
not one line of the classics would have reached our day.'"

"Glorious indeed is the world of God around us, but still
more glorious is the world of God within us. There lies the land
of song; there lies the poet's native land. The river of life
that flows through streets tu-

(50)

multuous, bearing along so many gallant hearts, so many wrecks of
humanity;—the many homes and households, each a little world in
itself, revolving around its fireside as a central sun; all forms
of human joy and suffering; brought into that narrow compass; and
to be in this, and be a part of this; acting, thinking,
rejoicing, sorrowing, with his fellow men;—such, such would be
this poets life."

(Spring) "It was a sweet carol, which the Rhodian children sang
of old in spring, bearing in their hands, from door to door, a

swallow as herald of the season.xxxxxxx But what child has a
heart to sing in this capricious clime of ours, where Spring
comes hailing in from the sea, with wet and heavy cloud sails,
and the misty pennon of the East-wind pnailed to the mast? Yet
even here, and in the stormy month of march even, there are
bright, warm, mornings, when we open our windows to inhale the
balmy air. The pigeons fly to and fro, and we hear the whirring
sound of wings. Old flies crawl out of the cracks, and sun
themselves; and think it is summer. They die in their conceit;
and so

(51)

do our hearts within us, when the cold sea breath comes from the
eastern sea, and again

'The driving hail
Upon the window beats with icy flail!'

The red flowering maple is first in blossom, its beautiful purple
flowers unfolding a fortnight before the leaves. The moose-wood
follows, with rose-colored buds and leaves; and the dog-wood,
robed in the white of its own pure blossoms. Then comes the
sudden rain storm, and the birds fly to fro and shriek. Where do
they hide themselves in such storms? at what fire side dry their
feathery cloaks? At the fireside of the great hospitable sun;
tomorrow, not before;—they must sit in wet garments until
then.—In all climates Spring is beautiful. In the South it is
intoxicating and sets a poet beside himself. They birds begin to
sing;—they utter a few rapturous notes, and then wait for an
answer in the silent woods. Those green-coated musicians, the
frogs, make holiday in the neighboring marches. They, too, belong
to the orchestra of nature; whose vast theatre is again opened,
though the doors have been so long bolted with icicles, and the
scenery hung with snow and frost like cobwebs. This is the
prelude which announces the opening of the scene. Already the

(52)

grass shoots forth. The waters leap with thrilling pulse through
the veins of the earth; the sap through the veins of plants and
trees; and the blood through the veins of man. What a thrill of
delight in Spring time! What a joy in being and moving! Men are
at work in gardens; and in the air there is an odor of the fresh

earth. The leaf buds begin to swell and blush. The white blossoms of the cherry hang upon the bough like snowflakes; and ere long, our next door neighbor will be completely hidden from us by the dense green foliage. The may flowers open their soft blue eyes. Children are let loose in the fields and gardens. They hold butter-cups under each others chins, to see if they love butter. And the little girls adorn themselves with chains and curls of dandelions; pull out the yellow leaves to see if the school boy loves them, and blow the down off the leafless stalk to find out if their mothers want them at home.—And at night so cloudless and so still! Not a voice of living thing,—not a whisper of leaf or waving of bough,—not a breath of wind,—not a sound upon the earth or in the air! And overhead bends the blue sky, dewy, and soft, and radiant with many stars like the inverted bell

(53)

of some blue flower, sprinkled with golden dust and breathing fragrance. x x x It was thus the Spring began in Heidelberg."

(Life) "'Life is one and universal; its forms many and individual. Throughout this wonderful and beautiful creation there is never ceasing motion, without rest by day or night, ever weaving to and fro. Swifter than a weaver's shuttle it flies from Birth to Death, from Death to Birth; from the beginning seeks the end, & finds it not, for the seeming end is only a dim beginning of a new out-going and endeavor after the end. As the ice upon the mountain, when the warm breath of the summer sun breathes upon it, melts, and divides into drops, each of which reflects an image of the sun; so life in the smile of God's love, divides itself into separate forms, each bearing in it and reflecting an image of God's love. Of all these forms the highest and most perfect in its Godlikeness is the human soul. The vast Cathedral of Nature is full of holy scriptures, and shapes of deep, mysterious meaning; but all is solitary and silent there; no bending knee, no up-lifted eye, no lip adoring, praying. Into this vast cathedral comes the human soul, seeking its Creator; and the universal silence is

(54)

changed to sound, and the sound is harmonious, and has a meaning

and is comprehended and felt. It was an ancient saying of the
Persians, that the waters rush from the mountains and hurry forth
into all the lands to find the Lord of the Earth; and the flame
of the fire, when it awakes, gazes no more upon the ground, but
mounts heavenward to seek the Lord of Heaven; and here and there
Earth has built the great watch towers of the mountains, and they
lift their heads far up into the sky, and gaze ever upward, and
around, to see if the Judge of the World comes not! Thus in
Nature herself, without man, there lies a waiting and hoping, a
looking and yearning, after an unknown somewhat. Yes; When, above
there, where the mountain lifts its head above all others, that
it may be alone with the clouds and storms of heaven, the lonely
eagle looks forth into the grey dawn to see if the day comes not;
when, by the mountain torrent, the brooding raven listens to hear
if the chamois is returning from his nightly pasture in the
valley; and when the soon up-rising sun calls out the spicy odors
of the thousand flowers, the Alpine flowers, with heaven's deep
blue and the blush of sunset on their leaves;—then there awake
in

(55)

Nature, and the soul of man can see and comprehend them, an
expectation and a longing for a future revelation of God's
majesty. They awake, also, when, in the fullness of life, field
and forest rest at noon, and through the stillness are heard only
the song of the grasshopper and the hum of the bee; and when at
evening the singing lark, up from the sweet-smelling vineyards
rises, or in the later hours of night Orion puts on his shining
armor to walk forth into the fields of heaven. But in the soul of
man alone is this longing changed into certainty, and fulfilled.
For lo! The light of the sun and the stars shines through the
air, and is no where visible and seen; the planets hasten with
more than the speed of the storm through infinite space, and
their footsteps are not heard; but where the sunlight strikes the
firm surface of the planets, where the storm wind smites the wall
of the mountain cliff, there is the one seen, and the other
heard. There is the glory of God made visible, and may be seen
where in the soul of man it meets its likeness changeless and
firm standing. Thus, then stands Man;—a mountain on the boundary
between two worlds; its foot in one, its summit far rising into
the other. From this summit

(56)

the manifold landscape of life is visible, the way of the Past
and Perishable, which we have left behind us; and as we evermore
ascend, bright glimpses of the day break of Eternity beyond us!'"

"What most interested our travellers in the ancient city of
Frankfort was neither the Opera not the Ariadne of Dannecker, but
the house in which Goethe was born, and the scenes he frequented
in his childhood, and remembered in his old age. Such, for
example, are the walks around the city, outside the moat; the
bridge over the Maine, with the golden cock on the cross, which
the poet beheld and marvelled at when a boy, the cloister of the
bare-footed Friars, through which he stole with mysterious awe to
sit by the oilcloth-covered table of old Rector Albrecht; and the
garden in which his grandfather walked up and down among fruit
trees and rose bushes, in long morning-gown, black velvet cap,
and the antique leather gloves, which he annually received as
Mayor on Piper's-Doomsday, representing a kind of middle
personage between Alcinous and Laertes. Thus O Genius! are thy
footprints hallowed, and the star shines forever over the

(57)

place of thy nativity."

"Tell me, my soul, why art thou restless? Why dost thou look
forward into the future with such strong desire? The present is
thine, and the past,—and the future shall be! O, that thou didst
look forward to the great hereafter with half the longing
where with thou longest for an earthly future,—which a few days
at most, will bring thee! to the meeting of the dead as to the
meeting of the absent. Thou glorious spirit land! O that I could
behold thee as thou art,—the region of light, and life, and
love, and the dwelling-place of those belovèd ones whose being
has flowed onward, like a silver clear stream into the solemn
sounding main, into the ocean of Eternity!"

"Ere long he reached the magnificent glacier of the Rhone; a
frozen cataract more than two thousand feet in height, and many

miles broad at its base. It fills the whole valley between two
mountains, running back to their summits. At the base it is
arched, like a dome; and above, jagged and rough, and resembles a
mass of gigantic crystals, of a pale emerald tint, mingled with
white. A snowy crust cov-

(58)

ers its surface; but at every rent and crevice the pale green ice
shine clear in the sun. Its shape is that of a glove, lying with
the palm downwards, and the fingers crooked and close together.
It is a gauntlet of ice, which centuries ago, Winter, the king of
these mountains, threw down in defiance to the Sun; and year by
year the Sun strives in vain to lift it from the ground on the
point of his glittering spear."

LE MONTAGNARD EMIGRÉ.
(CHATEAUBRIAND)

"Combien j'ai douce sovenance
Du joli bien de ma naissance!
Ma soeur qu'ils etaient beaux ces jour,!
    De France!
A mon pays soit mes amours!
    Toujours.

Te souvient-il que notre mère,
Au foyer de notre chaumière,
Nous pressait sur son sein joyeaux,
    Ma chère!
Et nous baisons ses blonds cheveux
    Tous deux.

(59)

Ma soeur, te souvient-il encore,
Du Chateau qui baignait la Dore;
Et de cette tant vielle tour
    Du more,
Où l'airain sonnait le retour
    Du jour?

Te souvient-il du lac tranquille

Qu'effleurait l'hirondelle agile,
Du vent qui courbait le roseau
                Mobile
Et du soleil couchant, sur l'eau,
                Si beau?

Te souvient-il de cette amie,
Douce compagne de ma vie?
Dans les bois en cenillant la fleure
                Joli,
Hélène appuyait sur mon coeur
                Son coeur.

Oh! qui me rendra mon Hélène,
Et la montagne et la grande chêne?
Leur souvenir fait tous les jours
                Ma peine.
Mon pays sera mes amours
                Toujours."

(60)

CHARACTER OF LOUIS XIV.
FROM MACAULAY'S ESSAY "MIRABEAU"

"Concerning Louis XIV himself, the world seems at last to have formed a correct judgement. He was not a great general; he was not a great statesman; but he was, in one sense of the word a great king. Never was there so consummate a master of what James I would have called king-craft, of all those arts which most advantageously display the merits of a prince, and most completely hide his defects. Though his internal administration was bad,—though the military triumphs which gave splendor to the early part of his reign, were not achieved by himself,—though his later years were crowned with defeats and humiliations,—though he was so ignorant that he scarcely understood the Latin of his mass book,—though he fell under the control of a cunning Jesuit, and a more cunning old woman,—he succeeded in passing himself off on his people as a being above humanity. And this is the most extraordinary, because he did not exclude himself from public gaze like those Oriental despots, whose faces are never seen, and whose very names it is a crime to pronounce lightly.—It has

(61)

been said that no man is a hero to his valet; and all the world
saw as much of Louis XIV as his valet could see. Five hundred
persons assembled to see him shave and put on his breeches in the
morning. He then kneeled down at the side of his bed, and said
his prayer, while the whole assembly awaited the end in solemn
silence, the eclesiastics on their knees and the lay men with
their hats before their faces. He walked about his garndens with
a train of two hundred courtiers at his heels. All Versailles
came to see him dine and sup. He was put to bed at night in the
midst of a crowd as great as that which had met to see him rise
in the morning. He took his very emetics in state, and vomitted
majestically in the presence of all the grandes and petites
entrées. Yet, though he constantly exposed himself to the public
gaze in situations in which it is scarcely possible for any man
to preserve much personal dignity, he to the last impressed those
who surrounded him with the deepest awe and reverence. The
illusion which he produced on his worshippers can be compared
only to those illusions to which lovers are proverbially subject
during the season of courtship. It was an illusion which affected
only the senses. The contemporaries of Louis

(62)

thought him tall. Voltaire who might have seen him, and who had
lived with some of the most distinguished members of his court,
speaks repeatedly of his majestic stature. Yet it is as certain
as any fact can be, that he was rather below than above the
middle size. He had it seems, a way of holding himself, a way of
walking, a way of swelling his chest and rearing his head, which
deceived the eye of the multitude. Eighty years after his death,
the royal cemetery was violated by the revolutionists; his coffin
was opened; his body was dragged out; and it appeared that the
prince, whose majestic figure had been so long and loudly
extolled, was in truth a little man. That fine expression of
Juvenal is singularly applicaple, both in its literal and in its
metaphorical sense, to Louis the Fourteenth:

> 'Mors sola fatetur
> Quantula sint hominum corpuscula'.

His person and his government have had the same fate. He had the
art of making both appear grand and august, in spite of the

clearest evidence that both were below the ordinary standard. Death and time have exposed both the deceptions. The body of the great king has been measured more justly than it was measured by the courtiers who were afraid to look above his shoe-

(63)

tie. His public character has been scrutinized by men free from the hopes and fears of Boileau and Molière. In the grave, the most majestic of princes is only five feet eight. In history, the hero and the politician dwindle into a vain and feeble tyrant,—the slave of priests and women,—little in war,—little in government,—little in every thing but the art of simulating greatness.

SICILIAN VESPERS.

A famous masacre which took place in Palermo, at the evening vesper hour, March 20th 1232.

Charles of Anjou had established himself in possession of Naples and Sicily; Conradin had perished on the scaffold, but the haughty Charles ruled with an iron sceptre, and the oppressed people applied to Procida a nobleman of Selerno, to deliver Sicily from her sufferings. He had stood high in favor with the King Manfred, and had been stripped of his estates by Charles on account of his attachment to the house of Swabia. Meditating revenge he went to Arragon and invited King Peter, whose wife Constantia was a daughter of Manfred, to undertake the conquest of Sicily. Prosida promised to make all necessary provisions; he accord-

(64)

ingly went to Sicily in disguise, and found the republic favorable to his designs; he then hastened to Constantinople, an prevailed upon the Emperor to promise pecuniary aid to Peter. He next had a private audience with the Pope, and found him inclined to assist in deposing Charles. He then returned to Arragon with a large supply of money, and Peter began to make extensive preparations in pretence of an attack on Africa. When his preparations were completed, he sailed, while Prosida was to stir up the people of Sicily to rebellion. In this he succeeded and the "Vespers of Palermo" was the result. None were spared,— men women and children sharing the same fate. Immediately after Peter

landed, and entered Palermo, while Charles of Anjou fled
precipitately across the straits. In the year following,
Constantia appeared in Sicily with her children, and was received
as the rightful possessor of the island. The succession was
settled on her eldest son James.

ESPOUSALS OF THE ADRIATIC.

A ceremony instituted by Pope Alexsander III. in 1173,
symbolic of the Venetian supremacy.
Annually, on Ascension day, the Doge

(65)

of Venice, leaving the city by the richly gilded gate called the
Bucentaur, accompanied by a splendid retinue in Gondolas, from
the state barge dropped a ring into the Adriatic. The ceremony
was abolished in 1797.

DUKE OF MALBOUROUGH.

John Churchill born June 24th 1650. Died June 16th 1720.
He was page of Duke of York, afterwards James II. He became
a great favorite, and at the age of sixteen, was made ensign in
the gards. In 1678 he married Sara Jennings of good family but
poor: the marriage was unquestionably of affection on his part.
On the occasion of the marriage of the princess Anne to George of
Denmark, Lady Churchill was made chief lady of the bed chamber;
from which resulted a most intimate friendship. At the suggestion
of the princess they laid aside all ceremony and corresponded
under the assumed names of Morley & Fremon. This intimacy
continued for twenty-three years, during which time Lady
Churchill swayed at pleasure the mind of her royal

(66)

mistress. Notwithstanding his intrigues he retained the royal
favor to the last. He offered his services to Wm of Orange, while
his wife used her influence with Anne, to cause her to join the
party of the Insurgents. During the reign of William and Mary he
even wrote to Wm of Orange placing himself at his disposal, and
won many of the nobility from their allegiance. Later he

encouraged Anne to assert her superiority claims to the throne, but was arrested and confined in the tower for some time. After Queen Mary's death he was released, and after the death of William and accession of Anne, he arose to the highest eminence, assuming the title of Duke of Malbourough, and Knight of the Garter. Having concluded all prelimenaries of a war with France, he now entered upon a brilliant career of unexamplled success. He was appointed generalisimo of the allied forces, and by his first victory of Blenheim in 1704, completely humbled the power of Louis XIV. In the ten successive campaigns which he led in person, victory ever attended the allied arms, and the trophies of Ramillies, Oudanarde, and Malplaquet, bear testimony to

(67)

his emininent military talent. On his return to England, he found the country distracted by the contentions of the Whigs and Tories: his politics soon lost for him the royal favor, and he was removed from all his offices, in consequence of which, the power of France again became predominant on the continent. Disgusted with so much ingratitude, he left for the continent and resided principally at Aix. While there, he favored the Hannovarian succession—wrote to George promising his assistance, and advanced him a considerable loan. He landed in England the very day George I took possession of the throne, and by him was reinstated in all his former dignities. He took seven measures against the Pretender and his partisans in 1715, though it was through his representations that the hopes of Charles were first raised. He retained his mental faculties unimpaired to the last, and died in the seventy-second year of his age. His remains were interred in Westminster Abbey, but were afterwards removed to a stately mausoleum in Blenheim palace.

(68)

PRINCE EUGENE OF SAVOY.

Was born in Paris, October 1663. His parents were Eugene Morris, grandson of the duke of Savoy, and Olympia Mancini, a niece of the celebrated Mazarin. He was destined for Holy Orders, but abandoned this course and devoted himself to military reading. Louis XIV refused him a regiment, and he incurred the enmity of Louvois, in consequence of which he tendered his services to Austria, by which they were gratefully accepted. In his first engagement against the Turks, he merited for himself

the command of a dragoon regiment. New successes were followed by
new promotions, and Louis acknowledging his error, made him great
offers if he would but return to the French Army. He refused, and
soon afterwards joined the allies at the head of the imperial
forces, and shared with Malbourough the dangers and glories which
marked the victories of this glorious period. He was afterwards
engaged against the Turks & Italians. His last military service
was in the wars which followed the Polish partition; when he led
a force against the French on the Rhine. Eugene died suddenly at
Vienna in 1736, and his obsequies was

(69)

one of the most magnificent pageants on record; his coffin being
carried by sixteen Marchals of the Empire. He was never married;
was a liberal patron of literature and the arts, and engaged the
favor of several of the most literary men of Europe. While as a
general he was surpassed by none and equalled only by his great
contemporary the Duke of Malbourough.

EXTRACTS FROM MRS JAMISON'S SKETCHES OF ART &C.

(Medusa at Cologne) "This wondrous mask measured about two feet
and a half in height; the colossal features and, I may add, the
colossal expression,—grand without exaggeration—so awfully
vast, and yet so gloriously beautiful; the full rich lips curled
with disdain—the mighty wings overshadowing the knit and
tortured brow—the madness in the large dilated eyes—the
wreathing and recoiling snakes,—came upon me like something
supernatural, and impressed me at once with astonishment, horror
and admiration. I was quite unprepared for what I beheld. As I
stood before it my mind seemed to elevate and enlarge itself to

(70)

admit this new vision of grandeur. Nothing but the two Fates in
the Elgin Marbles, and the Torso of the Vatican, ever affected me
with the same inexpressible sense of the sublime; and this is not
a fragment of some grand mystery, of which the remainder has been
'to night and chaos hurled'; it is entire, in admirable
presentation, and the workmanship as perfect as the conception is
magnificent. I know not if it would have affected another in the

same manner. For me, the ghostly allegory of the Medusa has a peculiar fascination. I confess that I have never wholly understood it, nor have any of the usual explanations satisfied me; it appears to me that the Greeks, in this blending the extreme of loveliness and terror had a meaning, a purpose more than is dreamt of by our philosophy."

(Dannecker's Ariadne)—"The Ariadne occupied the centre of a cabinet, hung with a dark grey color, and illuminated by a high lateral window, so that the light and shade, and the relief of the figure were perfectly well managed and effective. Dannecker has not represented Ariadne in her more poetical and picturesque character, as, when betrayed and forsaken by Theseus

(71)

she stood alone on the wild shore of Naxos, 'her hair blown by the winds all all about her expressing desolation.' It is the Ariadne, immortal and triumphant, as the bride of Bacchus. The figure is larger than life. She is seated, or rather reclined on the back of a Pan ther. The right arm is carelessly extended: the left arm rests on the head of the animal, and the hand supports the drapery which appears to have just dropped from her limbs. The head is turned a little upwards as if she already anticipated her starry home; and her tresses are braided with the vine leaves. The grace and ease of the attitude, so firm and yet so light; the flowing beauty of the form, and the position of the head, enchanted me. Perhaps the features are not sufficiently Greek: for, though I am not one of those who "think all beauty comprised in the antique models, and that nothing can be orthodox but the strait nose and short upper lip, still to Ariadne the pure classical ideal of beauty,—both in form and face, are properly in character. A cast from the divine head she, the Greek Ariadne, is placed in the same cabinet, and I confess to you that the contrast being immediately brought before the eye, Dannecker's

(72)

Ariadne seemed to want refinement in the comparison. It is true that the moment chosen by the German Sculptor required an expression altogether different. In the Greek bust, though already circled by the viny crown, and though all heaven seems to

repose on the noble arch of the expanded brow, yet the head is
declined, and a tender melancholy lingers around the all perfect
mouth, as if the remembrance of an mortal love—a mortal
sorrow—yet shaded her celestial bridal hours, and made pale her
immortality. But Dannecker's Ariadne is the flushed queen of the
Bacchante, and in the clash of the cymbals and mantling cup, she
has already forgotten Theseus. There is a look of life, and
individual truth in the beauty of the form, which distinguishes
it from the long-lived vapid pieces of elegance called Nymphs and
Venuses, which 'Stretch their white arms and bend their marble
necks,' in the galleries of our modern Sculptors. One objection
struck me, but not till after a second or third view of the
statue. The panther seemed to be rather too bulky and ferocious.
It is true, it is not a natural

(73)

but a mythological panther, such as we see in the antique
basso-relievos and the arabesques of Herculaneum; yet, methinks,
if he appeared a little more conscious of his lovely burden, more
tamed by the influence of beauty, it would have been better.
However, the Sculptor may have had a design, a feeling, in this
very point, which has escaped me; I regret now that I did not ask
him. One thing is certain; that the extreme massiveness of the
panther's limbs serves to give a firmness to the support of the
figure, and sets off to advantage its lightness and delicacy. It
is equally certain that if the head of the animal had been ever
so slightly turned, the pose of the right arm, and with it the
whole attitude must have been altered."

(German Women) "In the highest circles a stranger finds society
much alike everywhere. A court-ball—the soirée of an
embassadress—a minister's dinner present nearly the same
physiognomy. It is the second class of society, which is also
every where and in every sense the best, that we behold the stamp
of national character. I was not condemned to see my German
friends always en grande

(74)

toilette; I had better opportunities of judging and appreciating
their domestic habits and manners than most travellers enjoy. I
thought the German women, of a certain rank, more <u>natural</u> than we

are. The moral education of an English girl is for the most part
negative; the whole system of duty is thus presented to the mind.
It is not 'this you must do;' but always, 'you must not do
this—you must not say that—you must not think so;' and if by
some hardy expanding nature, the question be ventured, 'Why?' the
mamma or the governess are ready with the answer 'It is not the
custom—it is not lady-like—it is ridiculous!' But is it
wrong?—Why is it wrong?—and then comes answer, pat—My dear,
you must not argue—young ladies never argue" But mamma—I was
thinking—"My dear you must not think—go write your Italian
exercise,' and so on! The idea that certain passions, powers,
tempers feelings, interwoven with our being by our Almighty and
all-wise Creator, are to be put down by the fiat of a governess,
or the edict of fashion, is monstrous. Those who educate us
imagine that they have done every thing if they have silenced

(75)

controversy, if they have suppressed all external demonstrations
of an excess of temper or of feeling; not knowing or not
reflecting that unless our nature be self-governed and
self-directed by an appeal to those higher faculties which link
us immediately with what is divine, their labor is lost.—Now, in
Germany the women are less educated to suit some particular
fashion; the cultivation of the intellect, and the forming of the
manners, do not so generally supersede the training of the moral
sentiments, the affections the impulses; the latter are not so
habitually crushed or disguised; consequently the women appear to
be more natural, and to have more individual character. x x More
of the individual character is brought into the daily intercourse
of society—more of the poetry of existence is brought to bear on
the common realities of life. I saw a freshness of feeling—a
genuine (not a taught) simplicity, which charmed me. Sometimes I
have seen affectation, but it amused me; it consisted in the
exaggeration of what is in itself good, not in the mean
renunciation of our individuality—the immolation of our soul's
truth to a mere fashion of behavior.

  As Rochfoucauld called hypocrisy, (that last extreme of
wickedness) 'the homage

(76)

which vice pays to virtue'; so the nature de convention,
that last and worst excess of affectation is the homage which the

artificial pays to the natural. The German women are much more engrossed by the cares of housekeeping than women of a similar rank in England. They carry this too far in many instances as we do the opposite extreme. In England with our fasle conventional refinement, we attach an idea of vulgarity to certain cares and duties in which there is nothing vulgar. To see the young and beautiful daughter of the lady of rank running about, busied with household matters, with the keys of the wine-cellar and store room suspended to her sash, would certainly surprise a young English woman, who, mean time, is netting a purse, painting a rose, or warbling some 'Dolce mio Bene' or 'Soavi Palpiti' with the air of a nun at penance. The description of Werther's Charlotte cutting bread and butter, has been an eternal subject of laughter among the English, among whom fine sentiment must be garnished out in something finer than itself; and no princess can be suffered to go mad, or even be in

(77)

love except in white satin. To any one who has lived in Germany, the union of sentiment and bread and butter, or of poetry with household cares, excites no laughter. The wife of a state minister once excused herself from going with me to a picture gallery, because on that day she was obliged to recon up the household linen. She was one of the most charming, truly elegant, and accomplished women I ever met with. At another time I remember that a very accomplished woman, who had herself figured in a court, could not do something or other—I forget what—because it was the "grösse Wäsche," (the great wash), an event, by the way, which I often found very mal-a-propos, and which never failed to turn a German house up side down. You must remember I am not speaking of tradesmen and mechanics, but of people of my own, or even a superior rank of life. It is true that I met with cases in which the women had, without necessity, sunk into mere domestic drudges—women whose souls were in their kitchen and their house hold stuff—whose talk was of dishes and of condiments; but then the same species of women in England, would have been frivolous and silly, without an Idea at all."

(78)

FROM GOETHE'S WILHELM MEISTER.
"Knowst thou the land where citron apples bloom,
And oranges like gold in leafy gloom,

A gentle wind from deep blue heaven blows,
The myrtle thick, and high the laurel grows?
Knowst thou it then?
   'Tis there! Tis there,
O my true loved one, thou with me must go!

Know'st thou the house, its porch with pillars tall?
The rooms do glitter, glitters bright the hall,
And marble statues stand, and look each one.
What's this, poor child, to thee they've done?
     Know'st thou it then?
        'Tis there! Tis there,
O my protector, thou with me must go!

Knowst thou the hill the bridge that hangs on cloud?
The mules in mist grope o'er the torrent loud,
In caves lie coiled the dragons ancient brood,
The crag leaps down and over it the flood.
Knowst thou it then?
     Tis there! Tis there!
Our way runs: O my father, wilt thou go?"
      Mignon's Song

(79)

"'I can easily conceive, how people of high breeding and
exalted rank must value a poet, (Racine) who has painted so
excellently and so truly the circumstances of their lofty
station. Corneille, if I may say so, has delineated great men;
Racine men of eminent rank. In reading his plays, I can always
figure to myself the poet as living at a splendid court, with a
great King befor his eyes, in constant intercourse with the most
distinguished persons, and penetrating into the secrets of human
nature, as it works concealed behind the gorgeous tapestry of
palaces. When I study his Britannicus, his Berenice, it seems as
if I were transported in person to the court, were initiated into
the great and the little, in the habitations of these earthly
gods; through the fine and delicate organs of my author, I see
Kings whom a nation adores, courtiers whom thousands envy, in
their natural forms, with their failings and their pains. The
anecdote of Racine's dying of a broken heart, because Louis XIV
would no longer attend to him, and had shown him his
dissatisfaction, is to me the key to all his works."

(80)

Hamlet=   "Soft, and from a noble stem, this royal flower had
sprung up under the immediate influences of majesty: the idea of
moral rectitude with that of princely elevation, the feeling of
the good and dignified with the consciousness of high birth, had
in him been unfolded simultaneously. He was a prince, by birth a
prince; and he wished to reign, only that good men might be good
without obstruction. Pleasing in form, polished by nature, courteous
from the heart, he was ment to be the pattern of youth and
the joy of the world. Without any prominent passion, his love for
Ophelia was a still presentiment of sweet wants. His zeal in
knightly accomplishments was not entirely his own; it needed to
be quickened and inflamed by praise bestowed on others for
excelling in theirs. Pure in sentiment, he knew the honorable-
minded, and could prize the rest which an upright spirit tastes
on the bosom of a friend. To a certain degree he had learned to
discern and value the good and the beautiful in arts and
sciences; the mean, the vulgar was offensive to him; and if
hatered could take root in his tender soul, it was only so

(81)

far as to make him despise the false and changeful insects of a
court, and play with them in easy scorn. He was calm in his
temper, artless in his conduct, neither pleased with idleness,
nor too violently eager for employment. The routine of a
university he seemed to continue when at court. He possessed more
mirth of humor than of heart; he was a good companion, pliant,
courteous, discreet, and able to forget and forgive an injury;
yet never able to unite with those who overstep the limits of the
right, the good and the becoming.
     Figure to yourself this youth, this son of princes, conceive
him vividly, bring his slate before your eyes, and then observe
him when he learns his father's spirit walks; stand by him in the
terrors of the night, when the venerable ghost itself appears
before him. A horrid shudder passes over him; he speaks to the
mysterious form; he sees it becon him; he follows it and hears.
The fearful accusation of his uncle rings in his ears; the
summons to revenge, and the piercing, oft-repeated prayer,
Remember me! And when the ghost has vanished, who is it that
stands before us?

(82)

A young hero panting for vengeance? A prince by birth; rejoicing
to be called to punish the usurper of his crown? No! trouble and
astonishment take hold of the solitary young man: he grows bitter
against smiling villains, swears that he will not forget the
spirit, and concludes with the significant ejaculation:

> The time is out of joint, O cursed spite,
> That ever I was born to set it aright!

In these words, I imagine, will be found the key Hamlets'
whole procedure. To me it is clear that Shakespeare meant, in the
present case, to represent the effects of a great action laid
upon a soul unfit for the performance of it. In this view the
whole piece seems to me to be composed. There is an oak tree
planted in a costly jar, which should have borne only pleasant
flowers in its bosom; the roots expanded, the jar is shivered.
A lovely, pure, noble, and most moral nature, without the
strength of nerve which forms a hero, sinks beneath a burden
which it cannot bear and must not cast away. All duties are holy
for him; the present is too hard. Impossibilities have been
required

(83)

of him; not in themselves impossibilities; but such for him. He
winds and turns, and torments himself; he advances and recoils;
is ever put in mind, ever puts himself in mind; at last does all
but lose his purpose from his thoughts; yet still without
recovering his peace of mind.

EXTRACTS FROM "LADY BLESSINGTON'S CONVERSATIONS WITH BYRON"

"'The portrait of Lady Blessington in the "book of Beauty" is
not unlike her, but it is still an unfavorable likeness. A
picture by Sir Thomas Lawrence hung opposite me, taken, perhaps,
at the age eighteen, which is more like her, and as captivating a
representation of a just matured woman, full of loveliness and
love, the kind of creature with whose divine sweetness the
gazer's heart aches, as ever was drawn in the painters most in
spired hours. The original is no longer dans sa première
jeunesse. Still she looks somewhat on the sunny side of thirty.—

Her person is full, but preserves all the fineness of an
admirable shape; her foot is not pressed in a satin slipper,

(84)

for which a Cinderella might long be sought in vain; and her
complexion (an unusually fair skin with dark hair and eyebrows)
is of even a girlish delicacy and freshness. Her dress, of blue
satin, was cut low, and folded across her bosom, in a way to show
to advantage the round and sculpture-like curve and whiteness of
a pair of exquisite shoulders: Her features are regular, and her
mouth—, the most expressive of them, has a ripe fullness and
freedom of play peculiar to the Irish physiognomy, and expressive
of the most unsuspicious good-humor. Add to this a voice merry
and sad by turns, but always musical; and manners of the most
unpretending elegance, yet even more remarkable for their winning
kindness, and you have the prominent traits of one of the most
lovely and fascinating women I have ever seen."
Bulwer. "'Towards twelve o'clock Mr Lytton Bulwer announced, and
entered the author of Pelham. I had made up my mind how he should
look; and between prints and descriptions thought I could
scarcely be mistaken in my idea of

(85)

his person. xx I liked his manners extremely. He ran up to Lady
Blessington with joyous heartiness of a boy let out of school;
and the 'how d'y Bulwer?' went round, as he shook hands with
every body in the style of welcome usually given to the best
fellow in the world. Bulwer's head is phrenologically a fine one.
His forehead retreats very much, but it is very broad and well
marked, and the whole air is that of decided mental superiority.
His nose is aquiline. His complexion is fair, his hair profuse,
curly and of a light auburn. A more good natured, habitually
smiling expression could hardly be imagined. I can imagine no
style of conversation calculated to be more agreeable than
Bulwers. Gay, quick, serious, half satirical and always fresh and
differant from every body else, he seemed to talk because he
could not help it, and infected every body with his spirits.
Bulwer's voice is exceedingly lovelike and sweet. His playful
tones are quite delicious, and his clear laugh is the soul of
sincere and careless merriment.

(86)

Byron. "Saw Lord Byron for the first time. The impression for the first few minutes disappointed me; as I had, both from the portraits and descriptions given, conceived a different idea of him. I had fancied him taller, with a more dignified and commanding air; and I looked in vain for the best-looking person with whom I had so long identified him in imagination. His appearance is, however highly prepossessing; his head is finely shaped, and the forehead high, and noble; his eyes are gray and full of expression, but one is visibly larger than the other; the nose is large and well shaped, but, from being a little too thick, it looks better in profile than in front face; his mouth is the most remarkable feature in his face, the upper lip of Grecian shortness, and the corners descending; the lips full and finely cut. In speaking he shows his teeth very much and they are white and even; but I observed that smi in his smile—and he smiles frequently—there is something of a scornful expression in his mouth that is evidently natural and not, as many suppose affected. This particularly struck me. His

(87)

chin is large and well shaped, and finishes well the oval of his face. He is extremely thin, indeed so much so that his figure has almost a boyish air; his face is peculiarly pale, but not the paleness of ill health, as its character is that of fairness—the fairness of a dark haired person; and his hair (which is getting rapidly gray) is of a very dark brown and curls naturally. His countenance is full of expression, and changes with the subject of conversation; it gains on the beholder the more it is seen and leaves an agreeable impression. I should say that melancholy was its prevailing character; as I deemed that, when any observation elicited a smile—and they were many, as the conversation was gay and playful—it appeared to linger but for a moment on his lip, which instantly resumed its former expression of seriousness."

"Byron observed, that he once told Madam de Staël that he considered her 'Delphine' and 'Corinne' as very dangerous productions to be put into the hands of young women. I asked him how she received this piece of candor, and he

(88)

answered: "Oh! just as all such candid avowels are received—she never forgave me for it. She endeavored to prove to me that au contraire, the tendencies of both her novels were supereminently moral. I begged that we might not enter on Delphine as that was hors du ~~combat~~question, (she was furious at this) but that all the moral world thought that her representing all the virtuous characters in Corinne as being dull, common place, and tedious, was a most insiduous blow aimed at virtue, and calculated to throw it into the shade. She was so excited and impatient to attempt a refutation, that it was only by my volubility I could keep her silent. She interrupted me every moment by gesticulating, exclaiming—"Quel idée' "Mon Dieu!" "Ecoutez donc!" "Vous m'impatientez!"—but I continued saying how dangerous it was to inculcate the belief that genius, talent, acquirements, and accomplishments,—such as Corinne was represented to possess could not preserve a women from becoming a victim to an unrequited passion, and that reason, absence, and female pride were unavailing.—I told her that Corinne

(89)

would be considered, if not cited, as an excuse for violent passions, by all young ladies with imaginations exalté, and that she had much to answer for. Had you seen her! I now wonder I had courage to go on; but I was in one of my humors, and had heard of her commenting on me one day, so I determined to pay her off. She told me that I, above all people, was the last person that ought to talk of morals, as nobody had done more to detiorate them. I looked innocent, and added, I was willing to plead guilty of having sometimes represented vice under alluring forms, but so it was generally in the world, therefore it was necessary to paint it it so; but that I never represented virtue under the sombre and disgusting shapes of dulness, severity, and ennui, and that I always took care to represent the votaries of vice as unhappy themselves, and entailing unhappiness on those that loved them, so that my moral was unexceptionable. She was perfectly outrageous, and the more so as I appeared calm and in earnest, though I assure you it required an effort, as I was ready to laugh outright at the idea

(90)

that I, who was at that period considered the most mauvais sujet of the day, should give Madame de Staël a lecture on morals; and I knew that this added to her rage. I knew she never dared avow that I had taken such a liberty. She was, notwithstanding her little defects, a fine creature with great talents, and many noble qualities, and had a simplicity quite extraordinary, which led her to believe every thing that people told her, and consequently to be continually hoaxed, of which I saw such proofs in London. Madame de Staël it was who first lent me 'Adolphe' which you like so much; it is very clever and very affecting. A friend of hers told me, that she was supposed to be the heroine, and I, with my aimable franchise, insinuated as much to her which rendered her furious. She proved to me how impossible it was that it could be so, which I already knew, and complained of the malice of the world in supposing it possible.'"

"Lord Byron dined with us to day. During dinner he was as usual gay, spoke in terms of the warmest commendation of Sir Walter Scott, not only as an author,

(91)

but as a man, and dwelt with apparent delight on his novels, declaring that he had read and reread them over and over again, and always with increased pleasure. He said he was quite equal, nay, in his own opinion surpassed Cervantes. In talking of Sir Walter's private character, goodness of heart &c. Lord Byron became more animated than I had ever seen him; his color changed from its general pallid hue tint to a more lively tint hue, and his eyes became humid; never had he appeared to such advantage, and it might easily be seen that every expression he uttered proceeded from his heart."

"Talking of Alfieri, he told me to day, that when that poet was travelling in Italy, a very romantic, and, as he called her tête montée Italian Principessa, or Duchessa, who had long been an admirer of his works, having heard that he was to pass within fifty miles of her residence, set off to encounter him; and having arrived at the inn where he sojourned, was shown into a room where she was told Alfieri was waiting. She enters agitated and fatigued—sees a very good-looking man seated at a table whom she concludes must be Alfieri, throws herself into his arms—and, in broken words, declares her admiration, and the distance she has come to declare it. In the midst of the lady's impassioned speeches, Alfieri enters the room, casts a glance of surprise and hauteur at the pair, and lets fall some expression that discloses to the humbled Princepessa the shoking mistake she has made. The poor secretary (for such he was) is blamed by the lady, while he declares his innocence, finding himself, as he says, in the embraces of a lady who never allowed him even a moment to interrupt her, by the simple question of what she meant! Alfieri retired in offended dignity, shocked that any one should be mistaken for him, while the Principessa had to retrace her steps, her enthusiasm somewhat cooled by the mistake and its consequences."

(93)

OLE BULL.

December 1868.
Last evening I enjoyed the pleasure of hearing the famous violinist Ole Bull; never having heard him before, I was at once delighted and surprised. He came forward upon the stage, and was greeted ~~by~~with the most enthusiastic applause. His age I should judge to be between sixty and seventy; but though old he is still handsome—tall straight and robust. His countenance is excessively pleasing; his ~~hair~~ of an iron gray; and his whole appears ~~is~~ that of ~~an~~ gentleman of the old school. He handles his instrument, as I thought, tenderly, as though it were something he loved, and in his performance is perfectly at ease—displaying nothing of that exagerated style most usually seen in fine violinists. His selections were mostly those of his own composition, and these I prefered to his borrowed pieces.
To describe the effect whis his music had upon me would be

impossible. It seemed the very perfection of the art, and while listening to him, I

(94)

for the first time longed to be blind, that I might drink it all in undisturbed and undistracted by surrounding objects. I presume I have heard him for the first and last time, as he is now old, and returning to Europe without the intention, I understand, of ever revisiting the United States.

New Year's Eve Dec 31st 1868

Rain! Rain! Rain!—I am going to receive calls tomorrow—My first winter I expect a great many visits. I trust the weather will change this rain is intolerable.—What a nuisance all this is—I wish it were over. I write in my book to day the first time for months; parties, operas, concerts, skating and amusements ad infinitum have so taken up all my time that my dear reading and writing that I love so well have suffered much neglect.

(95)

BILDERBUCH OHNE BILDER
VON
HANS CHRISTIAN ANDERSEN
ERSTER ABEND
"In der vergangenen Nacht, das sind des Mondes eigene Worte 'glitt ich durch die klare Indiens; ich spiegelte mich in dem Ganges und meine Strahlen machten den Versuch, durch das dichte Geflechte der wie eine Schildkrötenschale gewölbten Blatanen zu drinken. Da hüpfte aus dem Dickicht ein Hindu Mädchen leicht wie ein Gazelle, schön wie Eva. Es war eine so lustige und doch so anmutif und scharf ausgeprägte te Erscheinung, diese Tochter Indiens: ich konnte durch die zarte Haut den Gedanken sehen. Die dornigen Lianen zerrissen ihre Sandalen, aber schnell schritt sie vorwartz; das Wild, vom Flusse kommen, wo es seinen Durt gestillt hatte, sprang scheu vorrüber, denn das Mädchen hielt in der Hand

(96)

eine brennender Lampe, ich konnte das frische Blut in den feinen Fingern gewahren, die sie zu einem Schirm über der Flamme wölbte.

Sie näherte sich dem Flusse, setze die Lampe auf den Strom und
sie glitt dahin, die Flamme flackerte, als wollte sie erlöschen,
aber sie blieb doch brennen und des Mädchens schwarze, funkelnde
Augen hinter der Augenlieder langen Seindenfransen folgten ihr
mit seelenvollem Blick. Sie musste, dass, wenn die Lampe
fortbrannte, so weit sie dieser mit den Augen folgen konnte, ihr
Geliebter noch lebte; erlosch sie aber früher, so war er todt.
Und die Lampe brannte und flammte! Sie sank auf die Kniee und
betete. Neben ihr im Grase lag eine glatte Schlange, sie aber
dachte nur an Brama und ihren Bräutigam. Er lebt', jubelte sie;
'er lebt' hallte es von den Bergen wieder, 'er lebt!'"

(97)

GEFUNDEN.
Von Göethe.

Ich ging im Walde so für mich hin,
Und nichts zu suchen, dass war mein Sinn.

Im Schatten sah ich ein Blümchen steh'n
Wie Sterne leuchtend, wie Aeuglein schön.

Ich wollt es brechen, da sagt es fein
Soll ich zum Welken gebrochen sein?'

Ich grub's mit allen den Würzlein aus;
Zum Garten trugs ich am hübschen Haus.

Und pflanzt' es wieder am stillen Ort
Nun wächst es wieder und blüht so fort.

<u>Schlaf ein mein Herz.</u>

"Schlaf ein, mein Herz in Frieden!
Den müden Augenlieden
Der Blumen hat gebracht
Erquickungsthau die Nicht.

Schlaf ein, mein Herz in Frieden!
Das Leben schläft hinieden
Der Mond in stiller Pracht
Ein Auge Gottes, wacht.

(98)

Schlaf ein mein Herz, in Frieden!
Von Furcht und Gram deschieden;
Der Welten fort bedacht,
Nimmt auch ein Herz in Acht.

Schlaf ein mein Herz, in Frieden!
Von bösem Traum gemieden,
Gestärkt von Glaubensmacht
Von Hoffnung angelacht.

Schlaf ein mein Herz, in Frieden!
Und wenn dir est in Frieden
Der Tod hier in der Nacht,
So bist du dort erwacht.
                                    Rückert

THE KNIGHTS OF THE GARTER.

A military order instituted by Edward III, consisting
originally of twenty six members of high rank having the King of
England as Sovereign. The number was increased to thirty two in
1786. The habit and ensign of the order are a garter, mantle, cap
and collar. The first three were assigned to the knights of the
founder, and the other two by Henry VIII. The garter is worn on
the left

(99)

leg just below the knee, and is of dark blue velvet edged with
gold, bearing the motto in golden letters "Honi soit qui mal y
pense." The mantle is of blue velvet lined with white taffety
and having on the left breast the star which is the cross of St
George irradiated with silver, and encircled with the garter. The
collar is composed of twenty two pieces of gold each in the form
of a garter, and the ground enameled with blue has appended to it
the figure of St George on horse back, encountering the dragon.
The origin of the order is said to be this. At a court ball the
countess of Salisbury dropped her garter; the King Edward III
picked it up and presented it to her remarking at the time as he
observed some of his courtiers smile intimating they thought the
affair not accidental—"Honi soit qui mal y pense," adding that

shortly they should see that Garter advanced to so high an honor and renown, as to account themselves happy to wear it.

---

(100)

BLUE STOCKINGS.

A title which originated in England in the time of Dr Johnson for ladies who cultivated learned conversation. Boswell relates that in 1781 it was fashionable for ladies to form evening assemblies where they might converse with literary and ingenious men. One of the most eminent talkers on these occasions was a Mr Stillingfleet who always wore blue stockings, and whose absence at anytime was so much regretted that it used to be said—"We can do nothing without Blue Stockings." "Blue Stockings" soon became a title for pedantic or ridiculous literary ladies. One of the most famous of the accounts was of that which met at the house of Mrs Montaigu which was sometimes honored with the presence of Johnson and the principal members of which have been sketched by Hannah Moore in her poem the Bas Bleu.

ABBOTSFORD.

The seat of Sir Walter Scott, from which his baronets' title is taken. It is

(101)

situated on the right bank of the Tweed and in the neighborhood of the Abbeys of Melrose, & Jedburgh. Sir Walter purchased the estate in 1811 and gave it its present name. It is surrounded by beautiful natural scenery, and is rich in historical recollections. Like so many old cloisters it lies on flat ground near the river, with a lofty overhanging bank in the rear. The ground and present house are entirely the creation of its late illustrious owner.

The house is irregular and after the pattern of the old English manor-houses—flourishing plantations hem it around, and a beautiful meadow on the opposite side forms its immediate prospect. The external walls of the house are intercalated with antique carved stones taken from the old castles and Abbeys. The interior is decorated with beautiful paintings and a Library of

curious works and British antiquities. Abbotsford is now (1857)
occupied by James Hope Scott Esq, and his wife the sole surviving
granddaughter of Sir Walter.

(102)

*Yesterday—Feb 24th—I made my first appearance at the
"German Reading club, and from this day I hope to be able to
speak the language more and more fluently.- - - - Heigh ho! This
is one of my blue days; Reading music, German, walking,
skating—all of which are this morning within the range of my
ability—have no attractions for me.*

LE LAC.
Lamartine.
Ainsi toujours poussés vers de nouveaux rivages,
Dans la nuit éternelle emportés sans retour,
Ne pourrons nous jamais sur l'ocean des âges.
    Jeter l'ancre un seul jour?

O lac! l'année à peine a fini sa carrière,
Et près des flots chéris qu'elle devait revoir,
Regarde! je viens seul m'asseoir sur cette pière
    Où tu la vis s'asseoir!

Tu mugissait ainsi sous ces roches profondes,
Ainsi tu te brisais sur leurs flans déchirés,
Ainsi le vent jetait l'écume de tes ondes
    Sur ses pieds adorés.

(103)

Un soir, t'en souvient-il? nous voguions en silence,
On n'entendant en loin, sur l'onde et sous les cieux,
Que le bruit des rameurs qui frappait en cadence
    Les flots harmonieux.

Tout à coup des accents inconnus à la terre
Du rivage charmé frappèrent les échos:
Le flot fut attentif, et le voix qui m'est chère
    Laissait tomber ces mots:

"O temps! suspends ton vol; et vous heures propices!

Suspendes votre cours:
Laissez-vous savourer les rapides delices
    Des plus beaux de nos jours!

"Assez de malheureux ici-bas vous implorent,
    Coulez, coulez pour eux;
Prenez avec leurs jours les soins que les dévorent,
    Oubliez les heureux.

"Mais je demande en vain quelques moments encore,
    Le temps m'échappe et fuit;
Je dis à cette nuit; sois plus lente: et l'aurore
    Va dissiper la nuit.

"Aimons donc, aimons donc; de l'heure fugitive,
    Hâtons-nous, jouissons!

(104)

L'homme n'a point de port, le temps n'a point
        de rive;
    Il coule et nous passons!"

Temps jaloux, se pent-il que ces moments d'ivresse,
Où l'amour à longs flots nous verse le bonheur,
S'envolent loin de nous de la meme vîtresse,
    Que les jours de malheur?

Eh quoi! n'en pourrons-nous fixer au moins la trace?
Quoi! passés pour jamais? quoi! tout entiers perdus?
Ce temps qui les donna, ce temps qui les efface,
    Ne vous les rendra plus!

Eternité, néant, passé, sombres abîmes,
Que faites vous des jours que vous engloutissez?
Parlez: nous rendrez-vous ces extases sublimes
    Que vous nous ravissez?

O lac! rochers muets! grottes! forêt obscure!
Vous que le temps épargne ou qu'il peut rajeunir,
Guardez de cette nuit, gardez belle nature,
    Au moins le souvenir!

Qu'il soit, dans le Zéphyr qui frémit et qui passe
Dans les bruits de tes bords partes bords répétés,
Dans l'astre au front d'argent qui blanchit ta surface

(105)

De ses molles clartés!

Que le vent qui gémit, le roseau qui soupire,
Que les parfums légers de ton air embaumé,
Que tout ce qu'on entend, l'on voit ou l'on respire,
　　Tous dise: ils ont aimé!

Lamartine having passed a happy summer with a friend who resided near the lake of Geneva, and with whose daughter—a beautiful girl—he was accustomed to walking on its banks—wrote the above piece, on finding, when he returned the next summer—that the girl had died.

LA PETITE MENDIANTE.
Boucher de Perthes.

C'est la petite mendiante
Qui vous demande un peu de pain;
Donnez à la pauvre innocente,
Donnez, donnez, car elle a faim;
Ne rejettez pas ma prière!
Votre coeur vous dira pourquoi
J'ai six ans, je n'ai plus de mère;
J'ai faim, ayez pitié de moi!

(106)

Hier, c'était fete au village,
A moi personne n'a songé;
Chacun dansait sous le feuillage,
Hélas! et je n'ai pas mangé.
Pardonnez moi si je demande,
Je ne demande que du pain;
Du pain! je ne suis pas gourmande;
Ah! ne me grondez pas, j'ai faim.

N'allez pas croire que j'ignore
Que dans ce monde il faut souffrir;

Mais je suis si petite encore!
Ah! ne me laissez pas mourir.
Donnez à la pauvre petite
Et pour vous comme elle priera!
Elle a faim, donnez, donnez vite,
Donnez, quelqu'un vous le rendra.

Si ma plainte vous importune,
Eh bien! je vais rire et chanter;
De l'aspect de mon infortune
Je ne dois pas vous attrister;
Quand je pleure l'on me rejette,
Chacun me dit: "Eloigne-toi!"
Ecoutez donc ma chansonnette;
Je chante, ayez pitié de moi!

(107)

ESPOIR.

Victor Hugo.

Espère, enfant! demain! et puis demain encore!
Et puis toujours demain! croyons dans l'avenir,
Espère! et chaque fois que se lève l'aurore,
Soyons la pour prier comme Dieu pour benir!

Nos fautes, mon pauvre ange, ont causé nos souffrances.
Peut-être qu'en restant bien longtemps à genoux,
Quand il aura béni toutes les innocences,
Puis tous les repentirs, Dieu finira par nous!

JOHANN WOLFGANG VON GOETHE.
BIOGRAPHICAL SKETCH OF HIS LIFE.

This world renowned author and poet-prince of Germany, was born at Frankfort on the Mayne, the 28th of August, 1749. His father was a sollicitor and held the rank of Imperial Councillor. He was a man of culture, possessed a good library and splendid collections of paintings and engravings and spared neither means nor pains to unfold the abilities of his son, which were in early youth of peculiar promise. At the breaking out of the seven years' war, a French army marched into Germany, and Count of Thorane, the commander of the French forces, established

(108)

his head quarters in Goethe's house. The count was a man of taste and lover of the fine arts and, made himself the centre of the artistic circle of Frankfort. Young Goethe, being allowed to be present at these conversations, seized the opportunity of learning the French language, and the privilege exercised a strong influence on his character and on his taste. At the age of sixteen he was sent to the university of Leipzig to study law, but he occupied himself more with the pursuits of general literature, poetry and art. In 17689, he returned to his father's house in a much impaired state of health, and was affectionately embraced by his mother, his sister Cornelia, and a friend of his mother's, a soul-sick lady, named von Klekeberg, who nevertheless influenced his mind, and contributed to his mental and moral improvement. Under her influence he was led to study chemistry and alchimy, the effect of which is seen in "Faust." In 1770, to comply with his father's wishes, he went to Strassburg to finish his study of the Law, but chemistry and anatomy were his favorite pursuits. Here it was that he became acquainted with Herder who exercised a lasting influence on his life. A year later he took the degree of Doctor of Laws, and returned to Frankfort.

(109)

In 1773 appeared "Goetz von Berlichingen," and the next year "Werther." In 1775 he accepted an invitation of the young duke Karl August to the court of Weimar where he received the rank of Councillor of Legation. He accompanied the duke on a journey to Switzerland, the fruit of which was his "Schweizerreise." On his return in 1782 he was made president of the council and ennobled. In 1786 he set out for Italy where he spent two years and after his return the duke made him Prime Minister. Now appeared in succession: "Stella," "Clavigo," "Iphigenia," "Egmont," "Tasso," "Faust," "Gross-Cophta," "Wilhelm Meister's Apprenticeship," "Hermann and Dorothea," "Reineke the Fox," "Truth and Fiction," "Wilhelms M. Wanderings" and his other numerous works. His writings embrace almost every department of literature, and many of the sciences, which have gained for him the surname of "Der Vielseitige" the many sided.

Goethe died in Weimer, in 1833—at the age of 83.

(110)

MIGNON.

Mignon is one of the most interesting characters in "Wilhelm Meister." When a mere child she was kidnapped by strolling jugglers in Italy, and brought to Germany, where Meister fell in with her, and delivered her from her oppressors. A short time after he had become her protector he heard her singing this song, and only then discovered she was from Italy. Mignon died in the bloom of life.

> "Kennst du das Land? wo die Zitronen blühn,
> Im dunkeln Laub die Gold-Orangen glühn,
> Ein sanfter Wind vom blauen Himmel weht,
> Die Myrte still und hoch der Lorbeer steht,
> Kennst du es wohl?
>   Dahin! Dahin
> Möcht ich mit dir, o mein Geliebter, ziehn.

> "Kennst du das Haus? Auf Säulen ruht sein Dach,
> Es glänzt der Saal, es schimmet das Gemach,
> Und Marmorbilder stehn und sehn mich an:
> Was hat man dir, du armes Kind, getan?
> Kennst du es wohl?
>   Dahin! Dahin
> Möcht ich mit dir, o mein Beschützer, ziehn.

(111)

> "Kennst du den Berg und seinen Wolkensteg?
> Das Maultier sucht in Nebel seinen Weg;
> In Höhlen wohnt der Drachen alte Brut;
> Es stürzt der Fels und über ihn die Flut—
> Kennst du ihn wohl?
>   Dahin! Dahin
> Geht unser Weg! o Vater, lass uns ziehn!"

ERLKÖNIG.

The Erl-King . . Goethe having put up one evening at a road side inn, saw a man riding his horse at a sharp trot, and was told that the man, a farmer of the neighborhood was returning from to the city, whither he had carried his sick child for a consultation. He sat down and wrote this ballad in the inspiration of the moment. The Erl-King (Erl is Alder tree) is an evil spirit in northern mythology, which way-lays children. The superstition is still current among nurses and children.

"Wer reitet so spät durch Nacht und Wind?
Es ist der Vater mit seinem Kind;
Er hat den Knaben wohl in dem Arm,
Er fasst ihn sicher, er hält ihn warm.

(112)

"Mein Sohn was birgst du so bang dein Gesicht?
Siehst Vater, du den Erlkönig nicht?
Den Erlkönig mit Kron und Schweif?—
Mein Sohn es ist ein Nebelstreif.

"Du liebes Kind komm geh mit mir.
Gar schone Spiele spiel ich mit dir,
Manch bunte Blumen sind an dem Strand,
Meine Mütter hat manch gülden Gewand."

"Mein Vater, mein Vater, und hörest du nicht?
Was Erlenkönig mir leise verspricht?
Sei ruhig, bleib ruhig, mein Kind;
In dürren Blattern säuselt der Wind.

"Willst feiner Knabe, du mit mir gehen?
Meine Töchter sollen dich warten schön;
Meine Töchter führen den nächtlichen Reihn,
Und wiegen, und tanzen und singen dich ein."

"Mein Vater, mein Vater, und siehst du nicht dort
Erlkönigs Töchter am düsteren Ort?—
Mein Sohn, mein Sohn, ich seh' es genau
Es scheinen die alten Weiden so grau.

"'Ich liebe dich, mich reizt deine schöne Gestalt,
Und bist du nicht willig, so brauch ich Gewalt'-

(113)

Mein Vater, mein Vater, jetzt fasst er mich an
Erlkönig hat mir ein Leids gethn!"

Dem Vater grauset's, er reitet geschwind,
Er hält in Armen das ächzende Kind,
Erreicht den Hof mit Müh and Noth;
In seinen Armen, das Kind war todt.

JOHANN CRISTOPH FRIEDREIG VON SHILLER.

Was born at Marbach Nov. 10th 1759. He manifested early an
ardent imagination and a love for poetry. The poetical passages
of the Old Testament and the works of the pious Klopstock were
his favorite reading. Already when a child he had an ardent
desire to study Divinity, but his monarch, Charles Duke of
Weurtemberg offered to educate him at his military school, known
as the "Karlsschule," an offer which Shiller's father, who was in
the dukes service, did not feel at liberty to decline. Here he
lived in almost monastic seclusion from the world and under a
severe discipline. In addition to the military studies, those of
law and medicine were pursued there, and he selected the latter
for a profession. The classics and poetry especially occupied
part of his time. At

(114)

the age of sixteen he wrote a translation of part of the "Aenied"
in hexameter. The reading of Shakspeare kindled in him an
enthusiasm for the drama, and he began some pieces which were
afterwards burned. His original power first became manifest in
the "Robbers" which he commenced at the age of eighteen, but when
they had been on the stage in Mannheim, he was placed under
arrest, the duke commanding him to confine his writings to his
profession. But Shiller was not the man who could bear such
restraint, he fled from his native state, and threw himself upon
the world. From 1782 to 1789 he lived in several places,
publishing beside minor poems the following dramas: "Cabal and
Love," "Fiesco," "Don Carlos" &c. In 1787 he went to Weimer and
was kindly received there by Wieland, Herder and Goethe. The next
year he wrote the "History of the Revolt of the Netherlands," a
work suggested by the preparatory studies for "Don Carlos." In
1789 he was appointed through the influence of Goethe, Professor
of History at the university of Jena, where he lectured both on
History and aesthetics. For several

(115)

years after, he occupied himself chiefly with history, aesthetics, the Kantian philosophy, and with the composition of his famous historical work—"The History of the Thirty Years war." In 1790 he married Charlotte von Legefeld. In 1793 he formed the plan of publishing the "Horen" (Hours) as a monthly periodical—with the assistance of the greatest names in Germany: Goethe, Herder, Jacobi, Matthisson &c. Soon after this he produced his first ballads, and in 1799 his dramatic masterpiece "Wallenstein" was finished. From this time he lived in Weimer, where in 1800 and 1801 he composed "Mary Stuart" "Lay of the Bell" and the "Maid of Orleans" In 1802 he received from the Emperor of Germany a patent of nobility. The "Bride of Messina" appeared in 1803 and his last dramatic work "William Tell." In 1804 he repaired to Berlin to be present at a representation of "Tell," whither he returned to Weimer in a state of health which caused his friends to fear the worst for him. He continued ill and died May 9th 1805 at the age of 46.

(116)

GOTTFRIED AUGUST BÜRGER.

The father of the German ballad, was born at Wolmerswende near Halberstadt, in 1748. In his boyhood he was very backward in his studies, but began early to write verses. In 1764 he began the study of Divinity at Halle, but thinking himself more fitted for law than for divinity, he changed his profession and studied law at Göttingen. This change so displeased his grandfather upon whom he was dependant, that he withdrew his support, and he was obliged to accept the aid of some of his young college friends. With them he studied French, Italian, Spanish and English, particularly the ballad literature. In 1772 he obtained the small office of baily, still maintaining a close connection with the literary circles known as the "Göthigenb Bardenbund." His first marriage proved unhappy, but after his wife's death he married her sister to whom he had been long attached—the "Molly" of his poems. This union was happy but brief, as she died some months after their marriage. In 1790 he received the appointment of Professor Extraordinary at at the University of Göttingen, but with little or no salary. All his little property was

(117)

gone, and the great poet earned a poor living by translating books for the publishers. To complete his misfortune he married again, "The Swabian Girl" who under this name in a poem had offered herself hand; two years later they were divorced. Shortly before his death he received assistance from the the government of Hanover, but on the 8th of June 1794 he died of disease of the lungs—a disease brought on by poverty and wretchedness. Schlegel calls him a true poet of the people; and his style, though sometimes coarse, is clear, vigorous and fresh. His works are "poems" "Macbeth," "Münchhausen's Travels," a translation of the 6th book of the Illiad and a prose version of "Ossian." A marble monument has been erected to his memory in the gardens of Goettingen.

LUDWIG UHLAND.

Born at Tübingen in 1787—is the greatest of modern lyric writers.

Das Schloss am Meere.

"Hast du das Schloss gesehen,
das hohe Schloss am Meer?
Golden und rosig wehen
die Wolken drüber her.

(118)

Es möchte sich niederneigen
In die spiegelklare Fluth
Es möchte streben und steigen
In der Abendwolken Gluth.

Wohl hab' ich es gesehen,
das hohe Schloss am Meer,
Und den Mond darüber stehen,
Und Nebel weit umher.

Der Wind und des Meeres Wallen,
Gaben sie frischen Klang?
Vernahmst du aus hohen Hallen
Saiten und Festgesang?

Die Winde, die Wogen alle
Lagen in tiefer Ruh,
Einem Klagelied aus der Halle

Hört ich mit Thränen zu.

Sahest du oben gehen
Den König und sein Gemahl?
Der rothen Mäntel Wehen,
Der goldnen Kronen Strahl.

Führten sie nicht mit Wonne

(119)

Eine schöne Jungfrau dar,
Herrlich wie eine Sonne,
Stahlend im goldnen Haar?

Wohl sah ich die Eltern beide
Ahnen der Kronen Licht,
Im schwarzen Trauerkleide;
Die Jungfrau sah ich nicht."

HEALING OF THE DAUGHTER OF JAIRUS.
N. P. Willis.

Freshly the coole breathe of the coming eve
Stole through the lattice, and the dying girl
Felt it upon her forehead. She had lain
Since the hot noontide in a breathless trance
Her thin pale fingers clasped within the hand
Of the heart-broken Ruler, and her breast,
Like the ~~white~~ dead marble, white and motionless,
The shadow of a leaf lay on her lips,
And, as it stirr'd with the awakening wind,
The dark lids lifted from her languid eyes,
And her slight fingers moved, and heavily
She turned upon her pillow. He was there—
The same, loved, tireless watcher, and she looked
Into his face until her sight grew dim

(120)

With the fast falling tears; and with a sigh
Of tremulous weakness murmuring his name
She gently drew his hand upon her lips
And kissed it as she wept. The old man sunk

Upon his knees, and in his drapery
Of the rich curtains buried upon his face;
And when the twilight fell, the silken folds
Stirr'd with his prayer, but the slight hand he held
Had ceased its pressure—and he could not hear,
In the dead, utter silence, that a breath
Came through her nostrils—and her temples gave
To his nice touch no pulse and, at her mouth
He heald the lightest curl that on her neck
Lay with a mocking beauty, and his gaze
Ached with its deadly stillness . . . .
                  It was night—
And; softly o'er the sea of Galilee,
Danced the breeze-ridden ripples to the shore,
Tipped with the silver sparkles of the moon.
The breaking waves played low upon the beach
Their constant music, but the air beside
Was still as starlight, and the Savior's voice,
In its rich cadences, unearthly sweet,
Seemed like some just-born harmony in the air,
Waked by the power of wisdom. On a rock,
With the broad moonlight falling on his brow,

(121)

He stood and taught the people. At his feet
Lay his small scrip and pilgrim's staff
For they had waited by the sea
Till he came o'er from Gaderene, and pray'd
For his wont teachings as he came to land.
His hair was parted meekly on his brow,
And the long curls from off his shoulders fell,
As he leaned forward earnestly, and still
The same calm cadence—passionless and deep—
And in his looks the same mild majesty—
And in his mien the sadness mix'd with power—
Filled them with love and wonder. Suddenly,
As on his words entrancedly they hung,
The crowd divided, and among them stood
Jairus the Ruler. With his flowing robe
Gathered in haste about his loins, he came,
And fixed his eyes on Jesus. Closer drew
The twelve disciples to their master's side;
And silently the people shrunk away,

And left the haughty Ruler in the midst
Alone. A moment longer ~~he kept his gaze~~ on the meek face
Of the meek Nazerene he kept his gaze,
And as the twelve looked on him by the light
Of the clear moon, they saw a glistening tear
Steal to his silvery beard; and drawing nigh
Unto the Savior's feet, he took the hem

(122)

Of his coarse mantle, and with trembling hands
Press'd it unto his lips, and murmur'd low
"Master! my daughter!"
                  The same silvery light
That shone upon the lone rock by the sea,
Slept on the Ruler's lofty Capitals,
As at the door he stood, and welcomed in
Jesus and his disciples. All was still.
The echoing vestibule gave back the slide
Of their loose sandals, and the ~~arrowy~~ beam
Of moonlight, slanting to the marble floor,
Lay like a spell of silence in the rooms,
As Jairus led them on. With hushing steps
He trod the winding stairs but ere he touched
The latchet, from within a whisper came,
"Trouble the master not for she is dead!"—
And his faint hand fell nerveless at his side,
And his steps faltered, and his broken voice
Choked in its utterance; but a gentle hand
Was laid upon his arm, and in his ear
The Saviors voice sank thrillingly and low,
"She is not dead but sleepeth!"
~~He sp~~   They passed in
The spice lamps in the alabaster urns
Burned dimly, and the white and fragrant smoke
Curled indolently on the chamber walls.

(123)

The silken curtains slumbered in their folds,
And as the Savior stood beside the bed,
And pray'd inaudibly, the Ruler heard
The quickening division of his breath—

As he grew earnest inwardly. There came
A gradual brightness o'er his calm, sad face;
And, drawing nearer to the bed, he moved
The silken curtains silently apart,
And looked upon the maiden.
                       Like a form
Of matchless sculpture in he sleep she lay—
The linen vesture folded on her breast,
And over it her white transparent hands,
The blood still rosy in her tapering nails.
And in her nostrils, spiritually thin,
The breathing curve was mockingly like life;
And round beneath the faintly tinted skin
Ran the light branches of the azure veins;
And on her cheek the jet-lash over lay
Matching the arches pencilled on her brow.
Her hair had been unbound, and falling loose
Upon her pillow, hid her small round ears.—
In curls of glossy blackness, and about
Her polished neck, scarce touching it, they lay,
Like airy shadows as they slept.
'Twas heavenly beautiful. The Savior raised

(124)

Her hand from off her bosom, and spread out
The snowy fingers in his palm, and said,
"Maiden! arise!" And suddenly a flush
Shot o'er her forehead, and along her lips
And through her cheek the rallied color ran;
And the still outline of her graceful form
Stirrd in the vesture; and she clasped
The Saviors hand, and fixing her dark eyes
Full on the Saviors countenance—Arose!

"What is it makes a house bright? pleasant to go to—to
stay in—even to think of, so that even if fate totally
annihilates it we recall tenderly for years its atmosphere of
peace, cheerfulness, loving-kindness—nay, its outside
features—down to the very pictures on the walls, the pattern of
the papering, the position of the furniture? While other
houses—we shiver at the remembrance of them, the dreary days we

spent in them—days of dullness, misery or strife—these houses we would not revisit for the world.

Why? If a house with fair possibilities of home comfort is ~~thorsoughtessly~~ thoroughly

(125)

comfortless—if within it there is a reckless impossibility of getting things done in the right way or at the right time—or if, on the contrary, it is conducted with a terrible regularity, so that an uninvited guest—or an extempore meal sends a shock throughout the whole abode—if the servants never keep their places long—and the gentlemen of the family are prone to be "out of evenings"—who is to blame?

Almost invariably, the woman of the family. The men make or mar its outside fortunes; but its internal comfort lies in the woman's hands alone. And until women feel this—recognize at once their power and their duties—<u>it is idle for them to chatter about their rights</u>." Men may be bad enough out of doors; but their influence is limited and external. It is women who are in reality either the salvation or the destruction of a household."

"The Woman's Kingdom"
Miss Mulock.

(126)

Thursday, March 25th 1869.—

Holy Thursday,—and no sun—no warmth—no patch of blue sky, nothing to make one's heart feel glad; nothing but mud in the streets, and ~~and~~ an incessant rain pattering against the pavements ~~and~~ making the passers-by look blue, and cold, and miserable. I feel in a very idle humor to day—and a little cross at thinking that my proposed visit to the churches by moonlight, has been so disagreeably interrupted.

In three more days Lent will be over—and then commence again with renewed vigor—parties—theatres, and general spreeing. I feel as though I should like to run away and hide myself; but there is no escaping—I am invited to a ball and I go.—I dance with people I despise; amuse myself with men whose only talent lies in their feet; gain the disapprobation of people I honor and respect; return home at day break with my brain in a state which was never in-

(127)

tended for it; and arise in the middle of the next day feeling
infinitely more, in spirit and flesh like a Liliputian, than a
woman with body and soul.—I am diametrically opposed to parties
and balls; and yet when I broach the subject—they either laugh
at me—imagining that I wish to perpetrate a joke; or look very
serious, shake their heads and tell me not to encourage such
silly notions.

I am a creature who loves amusements; I love brightness and
gaiety and life and sunshine. But is it a rational amusement, I
ask myself, to destroy one's health, and turn night into day? I
look about me, though, and see persons so much better than
my self, and so much more pious engaging in the self same
pleasures—however I fancy it cannot have the same effect upon
them as it does upon me.— Heigh ho! I wish this were the only
subject I have doubts upon. One does become so tired—reasoning,
reasoning, reasoning,

(128)

from morning till night and coming to no conclusions—it is to
say the least slightly unsatisfactory.

A friend who knows me as well as anyone is capable of knowing
me—a gentleman of course—told me that I had a way in
conversation of discovering a persons characteristics—
opinions—and private feelings—while they knew no more about me
at the end than they knew at the beginning of the conversation.
Is this laudable? Bah! I'll not reason it, for whatever my
conclusion I'll be sure to follow my inclination.

What a dear good confident my book is. If it does not
clear my doubts it at least does not contradict and oppose my
opinions.—You are the only one, my book, with whom I take the
liberty of talking about my self. I must tell you a discovery I
have made—the art of making oneself agreeable in conversation.
Strange as it may appear it is not necessary to

(129)

possess the faculty of speech; a dumb person, provided they be
not deaf, can practice it as well as the most voluable. All
required of you is to have control over the muscles of your
face—to look pleased and chagrined, surprised indignant and

under every circumstance—interested and entertained. Lead your antagonist to talk about himself—he will not enter reluctantly upon the subject I assure you—and twenty to one—he will report you as one of the most entertaining and intelligent persons,—although the whole extent of of your conversation was but an occassional "What did you say—""What did you do—""What do you think"—On that principal you see, my friend you are very entertaining; but I must admit that for want of a sympathizing countenance tu es non peu ennuyant (what I would never dare tell a mortal) so I will leave you for my new friend Mr "Harry Lorrequer"; not as edefying a book, I grant you, as would

(130)

be advisable for Holy Week, but Gott in Himmel! were I to resume the thread of Sister Mary Catherine Macaulay's life—which in a devout mood the other day I began—that, together with the rain and sky, would by evening throw me into such a fit of blue moralizing and contempt of the species as to render me unbearable to the rather large household for weeks to come—a situation not "devoutely to be wished."

        Saturday May 8th   *l869.*
What a bore it is to begin a story—become interested in it and have to wait a week—a full round week before you can resume it. Thus have I devoured in Appleton's Journal (a new paper by the way) "The Man Who Laughs" by V. Hugo devoured it to the very last word of the last number and must wait till next saturday to satisfy in a small degree my ravenous appetite.

(131)

    O what a lovely pen—how I adore this quality. Can any one explain to me how hairs and such rubbish get at the point of a pen and make one's writing—not already perfect—look like the trail of a spider with his legs dipped in ink. I see no hairs in the ink bottle none on the paper or pen—and still here are visible proofs of them. They are like Topsey they "growed."
    March 25th and May the 8th quite a span. Let me see what have I been doing with myself. Three weeks were consumed in going to New Orleans and coming back again, and what a trip it was! Mother Miss Rosie (poor Rosie), Mrs Sloan, Mamie, Nina—and myself formed the party. Not remarkably gay for me when one reflects

*that Mother is a few years older than myself—Rosie and
invalid—Mrs Sloan a walking breathing nonentity—Mamie a jovial
giggler and Nina a child.—N. Orleans I*

(132)

*liked immensely; it is so clean—so white and green. Although
in April we had profusions of flowers—strawberries and even
black berries.*

*One evening I passed in N. O. which I shall never forget—it
was so delightful and so noval. Mamie and myself were invited to
dine and spend the evening with a Mrs Bader—a german lady. She,
her husband and two brothers in law lived in a dear little house
near Esplanade St. a house with an immensity of garden. One of
the brothers was a gay, stylish and very interesting fellow—with
whom Mamie fell very much inamorata. I quaffed all sorts of ales
and ices—talked French, and German—listened enchanted to Mrs
Bader's exquisite singing and for two or three hours was as gay
and happy as I ever have been in my life. Mrs Bader had been but
a year married, she was the famous*

(133)

*Miss Ferringer—Singer and Shauspielerin, who in order to support
indigent parents went upon the stage thereby not only retaining
respect, but gaining it from every quarter. Her talents and
womanly attractions won her a kind and loving husband—Mr
Bader—one of the first merchants of New Orleans and a man worth
$600,000.*

EXTRACTS FROM "GRAZIELLA."
Lamartine.
"Le preuve que la liberté est l'idéal divin de l'homme,
c'est qu'elle est le premier rêve de la jeunesse, et qu'elle ne
s'evanouit dans notre âme que quand le coeur se flétrit et que
l'esprit s'aviltit—ou ce décourage. Il n'y a pas une âme de
vingt ans qui ne soit républicaine. Il n'y a pas son coeur usé
qui ne soit servile."
Le Tasse—"Quand l'horison du matin était limpide, je voyais
briller la maison blanche du Tasse, suspendue comme un nid de
cygne au som-

(134)

met d'une falaise de rocher jaune, coupé à pic par les flots.
Cette vue me ravissait. Le lueur de cette maison brillait
jusqu'on fond de mon âme. C'etait comme un éclaire de gloire qui
étincelait de loin sur ma jeunesse et dans mon obscurité. Je me
souvenais de cette scène homérique de la vie de ce grand homme,
quand, sorti de prison, poursuivi l'envie des petits et par la
calomnie de grands, bafoué jusque dans son génie, sa seule
richesse, il revient a Sorrente chercher un peu de repos, de
tendresse ou de pitié, et que, déguisé en mendiant, il se
presente à sa soeur pour tenter son coeur et voir si elle, au
moins, reconnaitra celui qu'elle a tant aimé.

'Elle le reconnaît à l'instant, dit le biographe naïf, malgré sa
pa-pâleur maladive, sa barbe blanchissante et son manteau
déchiré. Elle se jette dans ses bras avec plus de tendresse et de
miséricorde que si

(135)

elle eût reconnu son frère sous les habits d'or des courtisans de
Ferrare. Sa voix est etouffeé longtemps par ses sanglots; elle
presse son frère contre son coeur. Elle lui lave les pieds, elle
lui apporte le manteau de son père, elle lui fait préparer un
repas de fête. Mais ni l'un ni l'autre ne purent toucher aux mets
qu'on avais servis, tant leurs coeurs etaient pleins de larmes;
et il passerent le jour à pleurer, sans se rien dire, en
regardant la mer et en se souvenant de leur enfance.'' . . . . . .
Grazielle . . ''Nous entendîmes une voix mal éveillée, mais claire et
douce, qui jetait confusement quelques exclamations de surprise
du fond de la maison. Puis le battant d'une des fenêtres s'ouvrit
à demi, poussé par un bras nu et blanc qui sortait d'une manche
flottante, et nous vimes, à la lueur de la torche que l'enfant
élevait vers la fenêtre, en se dressant sur la pointe des pieds,
une ravissante figure de jeune fille apparaitre entre

(136)

les volets plus ouverts.

Surprise au milieu de son sommeil par la voix de son frère,
Grazielle n'avait eu ni la penseé ni le temps de s'arranger une
toilette de nuit. Elle s'était élancée pieds nus à la fenêtre,
dans le désordre où elle dormait sur son lit. De ses longs
cheveux noirs la moitié tombait sur l'une de ses joues; et

l'autre moitié se tordait autour de son cou, puis, emportée de l'autre côté de son épaule par le vent qui soufflait avec force, frappait le volet entr'ouvert et revenait lui fouetter le visage comme l'aile d'un corbeau battue du vent.

Du revers de ses deux mains, la jeune fille se frottait les yeux en élevant ses coudes et en dilatant ses épaules avec ce premier geste d'un enfant qui se reveille et qui vent chasser le sommeil. Sa chemise, nouée autour du cou, ne laissait apercevoir qu'une taille élevée et mince où se modelaient à peine sous la toile

(137)

les premieres ondulations de la jeunesse. Ses yeux, ovales et grands, etaient de cette couleur indécise entre le noir foncé et le bleu de mer qui adoucit le rayonnement par l'humidité du regard et qui mêle à proportions égales dans ses yeux de femme la tendresse de ~~dfass~~ l'âme avec l'energie de la passion, teinte céleste que les yeux des femmes de l'Asie et de l'Italie im-pruntent un feu brûlant de le jour de flamme et à l'azur serein de leur ciel, de leur mer, et de leur nuit. Les joues etaient pleines, arrondies, d'un contour ferme, mais d'un teint un peu pale et un peu bruni par le climat, non de cette pâleur maladive du Nord, mais de cette blancheur saine du Midi qui ressemble à la couleur du marbre exposé depuis des siècles à l'air et aux flots. La bouche, dont les lèvres etaient plus ouvertes et plus épaisses que celles des femmes de nos climats, avait les plis de la candeur et de la bonté. Les dents courtes, mais eclatantes, brillaient aux lueurs flottantes

(138)

de la torche comme des écailles de nacre aux bords de la mer sous la moire de l'eau frappée du soleil.

Tandis qu'elle parlait a son petit frère, ses paroles vives, un peu âpres et accentuées, dont la moitié etait emportée par la brise, résonnaient comme une musique à nos oreilles. Sa physionomie, aussi mobiles que les lueurs de la torche qui l'éclairait, passa en une minute de la surprise à l'effroi, de l'effroi à la gaieté, de la tendresse au rire; puis elle nous aperçut derrière le tronc du gros figuier, elle se retira confuse de la fenêtre, sa main abandonna le volet qui battit librement la muraille; elle ne prit que le temps d'éveiller sa grand'mere et de s'habiller à demi, elle vint nous ouvrir la porte sous les

arcades et embrasser, tout émue, son grand-père et son frère."
A Picture "Même quand la jeune fille, sollicitée, par nous, se
levait modestement pour danser la tarentella aux sons

(139)

du tambourin frappé par son frère, et, qu'emportée par le
movement tourbillonnant de cette danse nationale, elle tournoyait
sur elle-même, les bras gracieusement élevés, imitant avec ses
doigts le claquement des castagnettes et précpcipitant les pas de
ses pieds nus, comme des gouttes de pluie sur la terasse; oui,
même alors, il y avait dans ce deluire, dans les attitudes, dans
la frénésie meme de ce délise en action, quelquechose de serieux
et de triste, comme si toute joie n'eût été qu'une demence
passagère, et comme si, pour saisir un eclair de bonheur la
jeunesse et la beauté même avaient besoin de s'etourdir jusqu'au
vertige et de s'enivrer de mouvement jusqu'au la folie! vertige
et de s'enivrer _ _ _ _ _ _ _

Le sublime lasse, le beau trompe, le pathétique seule est
infaillible dans l'art. Celui qui sait attendrir sait tout. Il y
a plus de génie dans une larme que dans tous les musées et dans
toutes les bibliothèques de l'univers. L'homme est comme l'arbre
qu'on n'ebranle secoue pour en faire tomber

(140)

des fruits: on n'ebranle jamais l'homme sans qu'il en tombe des
pleurs."

───────── ────────────── ───────────── ──────────────

"'Je me sens bien! me dit-elle en partant tout bas, d'un ton
doux, égal et monotone, comme si sa poitrine eût perdu à la fois
toute vibration et tout accent et n'eût plus conservé qu'une
seule note de sa voix.
J'ai voulu en vain me le cacher a moi-même, j'ai voulu en
vain te le cacher toujours, à toi. Je peux mourir, mais je ne
peux pas aimer une autre que toi. Ils ont voulu me donner un
fiancé, c'est toi qui est le fiancé de mon âme! Je ne me donnerai
pas à un autre sur la terre, car je ne suis donnée au secret à
toi! Toi sur la terre, ou Dieu dans le ciel! c'est le voeu que
j'ai faits le premier jour où j'ai compris que mon coeur était
malade de toi. Je sais bien que je ne suis que qu'une pauvre

fille indigne de toucher tes pieds pur sa penseé. Aussi je ne t'ai jamais demandé de m'aimer.

(141)

Je ne te demanderai jamais si tu m'aimes. Mais moi, je t'aime, je t'aime, je t'aime! Et elle semblait concentrer toute son âme dans ces trois mots. Et maintenant, méprise moi, raille-moi, foule-moi aux pieds! Moque toi de moi, si tu veux, comme d'une folle qui rêve qu'elle est reine dans ses haillons. Livre-moi à la risée de tout le monde! Oui, je leur dirai moi-même: Oui, je l'aime! et si vous aviez t à une place, vous auriez fait comme moi, vous seriez mortes ou vous l'auriez aime!

———— ———— ———— ———— ———— ————

"Je lui disait quelquefois: 'Graziella, qu'est-ce que tu regardes donc ainsi là-bas, là-bas, au bout de la mer, pendant des heurs entieres? Est-ce que tu y vois quelque chose que nous n'y voyons pas, nous?'—'J'y vois la France derrière des montagnes de glace' me repondait-elle.—'Et qu'est-ce que tu vois donc de si beau en France?' ajoutais-je—'J'y vois quelqu'un qui te ressemble' repliqu-

(142)

alt-elle, 'quelqu'un qui marche, marche, marche sur une longue route blanche qui ne finit pas. Il marche sans se retourner, toujours, toujours devant lui, et j'attends des heures entières, espèrant toujours qu'il se retournera pour revenir sur ses pas. Mais il ne se retourne pas!' Et puis elle se mettait le visage dans son tablier, et j'avais beau l'appeler des nomoles plus caressants, elle ne relevant plus son beau front."'

— — — ———————————— ————————

"Pauvre Graziella! Bien des jours ont passés depuis ces jours. J'ai aimé, j'ai été aimé. Dautres rayons de beauté et de tendresse ont illuminé ma sombre route. Dautres âmes se sont ouvertes à moi pour pour me révéler dans ces coeurs de femmes les plus mystérieux tresors de beauté, de sainteté, de pureté que Dieu ait animés sur cette terre, afin de nous faire comprendre, pressentir et désirer le ciel. Mais rien n'a terni ta première apparition dans mon coeur. Plus j'ai vaiçu, plus

(143)

je me suis rapproché de toi par la penseé. Ton souvenir est comme ces feux de la barque de ton père, que la distance dégage de toute fumée et qui brillent d'autant plus qu'ils s'éloignent davantage de nous. Je ne sais pas où dort ta depouille mortelle, ni si quelqu'un te pleure encore dans ton pays; mais ton véritable sépulcre est dans mon âme . . . Il y a toujours au fond de mon coeur une larme qui filtre goutte à goutte et qui tombe en secret sur ta memoire pour la rafraichir et pour l'embaumer en moi." 1829.

"Mais les [   ] âmes pardonnent là-haut. La sienne m'a pardonné. Pardonnez-moi aussi, vous! J'ai pleuré.

––––––––––––––––––––––––––

"Poor Graziella?"— No rich Graziella! ~~and~~ *happy Graziella! To have won not only the tears—the remembrance of Lamartine, but an offering of his rich and rare talents to the shrine of her memory. — The story is doubly*

(144)

enhanced when we think that it is really an episode, and ~~an~~ *cherished one in the life of the gifted writer. What tears of grief of indignation does one not shed over its pages—tears all ending in forgiveness. For at the end we feel an assurance that Graziella has conquered—since her heart's Idol—years after her death—weeps at her remembrance.*

––––––––––––––––––––––––––

~~Extracts from "The Fisher Maiden"~~

by ~~Björnstjerne Björnson~~

(145)

THE SIEGE OF CORINTH.

"Many a vanquished year and age,
And Tempest's breath and battle's rage
Have swept o'er Corinth; yet she stands,
A fortress formed to Freedom's hands.
The Whirlwinds wrath, the earthquake's shock,

Have left untouched her hoary rock,
The keystone of a land, which still
Though fall'n looks proudly on that hill;
The landmark to the double tide
That purpling rolls on either side,
As if its waters chafed to meet,
Yet pause and crouch beneath her feet.
But could the blood before her shed
Since first Timoleon's brother bled,
Or baffled Persia's despot fled,
Arise from out the earth which drank
The stream of slaughter as it sank,
That sanguine ocean would o'er flow
Her isthmus idly spread below:
Or could the bones of all the slain,
Who perished there, be piled again,
That rival pyramid would rise
More mountain-like through those clear skies,
Than yon tower-capp'd Acropolis
Which seems the very clouds to kiss."

——— ——— ——— ——————— ———————

(146)

SHORT EXTRACTS FROM
DIFFERANT AUTHORS.

"A man who knows the world, will not only make the most of
every thing he does know, but of many things he does not know,
and will gain more credit from his adroit mode of hiding his
Ignorance, than the Pedant by his awkward attempt to exhibit his
Erudition"   Colton
Adversity. "Sweet are the uses of adversity;
    Which, like the toad, ugly and venemous,
    Wears yet a precious jewel in his head
            Shakepeare.
"The good are better made by ill;—
As odors crushed are sweeter still.'
Affection. "~~In~~   Rogers.
    "In the intercourse of social Life, it is by little acts of
watchful kindness, recurring daily and hourly,—and
opportunities of doing kindness if sought for, are ever starting

up,—it is by Words, by Loves, by Gestures, by Looks that
affection is ~~won~~ and preserved. He who neglects these trifles,
yet boasts that, when ever a great sacrifice is

(147)

called for, he shall be ready to make it, will rarely be loved.
The likelihood is he will not make it: and if he does, it will be
much rather for his own sake than for his neighbors." Anon.
Age— "When men grow virtuous in their old age, they are
merely making a sacrifice to God of the Devil's leavings"
Swift.

"It is difficult to grow old gracefully
de Stael.

"It is shameful for man to seat in ignorance of the
structure of his own body, especially when the knowledge of it
mainly conduces to his welfare, and directs his application of
his own powers."   Melancthon.
Art. "It is the height of art to conceal art." From the Latin.
"The enemy ~~fo~~ Art is the enemy of nature; Art is nothing
but the highest sagacity and exertions of Human Nature; and what
nature will be honour who honors not the human?" Lavater.

(148)

Artifice—"There is a certain artificial polish—a common place
vivacity acquired by perpetually mingling in the beau Monde,
which, in the commerce of the world, supplies the place of
natural Suavity and good humor, which is purchased at the expense
of all original and sterling traits of character: by a kind of
fashionable discipline, the Eye is taught to brighten, the Lip to
smile, and the whole countenance to emanate with the semblance of
friendly Welcome, while the Bosom is invaided by a single
Spark of genuine Kindness and goodwill."   Washington Irving
Atheism.   'There is no being eloquent for Atheism. In that
exhausted receiver the mind cannot use its wings,—the clearest
proof that it is out of its element."   Hare.
Beauty   "An Eye's an eye, and whether black or blue,
Is no great matter, so 'tis in request;
"Tis nonsense to dispute about a Hue,—
The Kindness make be taken as a Test.

(149)

The fair sex should be always fair;
    and no man,
Till thirty, should perceive there's a
    plain woman." - - Byron.

"She gazed upon a world she scarcely knew,
As asking not to know it; silent, lone,
As grows a Flower, thus quietly she grew,
And kept her heart serene within its home.
There was Awe in the homage which she drew;
Her Spirit seemed as seated on a throne
Apart from the surrounding world, and strong
In its own strength—most strange in one so young!"
                      Ibid.

    "Her glossy hair was clustered o'er a brow
Bright with intelligence, and fair and smooth;
Her eye-brow's shape was like the aeriel bows
Her cheek all purple with the beam of youth,
Mounting at times to a transparent glow,
As if her veins ran lightening."   Ibid.
    "Her glance how wildly beautiful!
    how much
Hath Phoebus woo'd in vain to spoil her cheek
Which grows yet smoother from his amorous clutch
Who 'round the north for paler dames would seek
How poor their forms appear! how languid, wan,
    and sick!"   Ibid.

(150)

"There was a soft and pensive grace,
A cast of thought upon her face,
That suited well the forehead high,
The eyelash dark and down-cast eye:
The mild Expression spoke a mind
In duty firm, composed, resigned."
                      Scott.

"Give me a look give me a face,
That makes simplicity a grace;
Robes loosely flowing, Hair as free!

Such sweet neglect more taketh me,
Than all the adulteries of art;
That strike mine eyes but not my heart."
                                        Ben Jonson.

'That is not the most perfect beauty which in public would
attract the greatest observation; nor even that which the
statuary would admit to be a faultless piece of clay, Kneaded up
with blood. But that is true beauty which has not only a
Substance but a Spirit,—a beauty that we must intimately know,
justly to appreciate,—a beauty lighted up in conversation where
the mind shines as it were through its casket where, in the
language of the poet:- "The eloquent blood spoke in her cheeks,
and so distinctly wrought, that we might almost

(151)

say her body thought. An order and a mode of beauty which, the
more we know, the more we accuse ourselves for not having before
discovered those thousand graces which bespeak that their owner
has a soul. This is that beauty which never cloys, possessing
charms as resistless as those of the fascinating Egyptian, for
which Antony wisely paid the bauble of a world, a beauty like the
rising of his own Italian Suns, always enchanting, never the
same" Colton
Books.-   "Thou mayest as well expect to grow stronger by
always eating, as wiser by always reading. Too much overcharges
nature, and turns more into disease than nourishment. 'Tis
thought and digestion which makes books serviceable, and gives
health and vigor to the mind."   Fuller.
    "I have always gained the most profit and most pleasure also
from the books that have made me think the most; and, when the
difficulties have once been overcome, these are the books which
have struck the deepest root, not only in my memory and
understanding but also in my affections.—   Anon.

(152)

"Books like friends should be few and well chosen." [   ].
    "As good almost kill a man as kill a good book. Many a man
live lives a burthen to the earth; but a good book is the
precious life blood of a Master-Spirit, embalmed and treasured up
on purpose, to a life beyond life."   Milton.

"Many readers judge of the power of a Book by the shock it
gives their feelings—as some savage tribes determine the power
of muskets by their recoil; that being considered best which
fairly prostrates the purchaser."   Long fellow.

Character. "The best rules for a young man are, to talk little,
to hear much, to reflect alone upon what has passed in company,
to distrust ones own opinions, and value others that deserve it."
Sir Wm Temple.
          "Actions, looks, words, steps, form the alphabet by which
you may spell characters."   Lavater.
          "You may depend upon it that he is a good man whose intimate
friends are all good.   Ibid.
               "Character is a perfectly educated will."   Novalis.

(153)

"A man's character is like his shadow, which sometimes follows
sometimes precedes him, and which is occasionally longer,
occasionally shorter than he is." — From the French.
               "Best men are moulded out of faults"
                         Shakspeare.
Company—"No man can possibly improve in any company, for which
he has not respect enough to be under some degree of restraint.
                         Chesterfield.
"The freer you feel yourself in the presence of another, the more
free is he."   Lavater.
Conduct. "I will govern my life and my thoughts, as if the whole
world were to see the one and read the other; for what does it
signify to make anything a secret to my neighbor, when to God
(who is the searcher of our Hearts) all our privacies are open"
          Seneca
          *Quite laudable in Mr Seneca—but not as practicable
as possible.*
          "When wes are young we are slavishly employed in procuring
something where by we may live when we grow old; and when we are
old, we perceive it is too late to live as we proposed."
                         Pope.

(154)

Country= "They love their land because it is their own,
          And scorn to give aught other reason why"
                         Halleck

                    "Now from the town
"Buried in smoke and sleep, and noisome damps,
Oft let me wander o'er the dewy fields,
Where freshness breathes, and dash the trembling drops
From the bent brush, as through the verdant maze
Of Sweet-brier hedges I pursue my walk."
                                        Thompson.
"God made the country and man made the town.
What wonder then, that health and virtue, gifts
That can alone make sweet the bitter draught
That life holds out to all, should most abound
And least be threatened in the fields & Groves."
                                        Cowper.
Perhaps thy loved Lucinda shares thy walk,
With soul to thine attuned. Then nature all
Wears to the lovers eye a look of love;
And all the tumult of a guilty world,
Tossed by ungenerous passions, sinks away."
                                        Thompson.

Death=   "The hand that summoned Belshazzar derived its
most horrifying influence from the want of a <u>body</u>; and Death
itself is not formidable in what we <u>do</u> know of it, but in what we
do <u>not</u>."—Colton.

                              (155)

                    "The tongues of dying men
Enforce attention like deep harmony;
Where worlds are scarse, they are seldom
                spent in vain,
For they breathe truth that breathe their words
        in pain."
                                        Shakspeare.
"Nothing can we call our own but death;
And that small model of the barren earth,
Which serves as paste and cover to our bones"
                                        Ibid.
            "To die—to sleep—
No more; and, by a sleep, to say we end
the heart ache and the thousand natural shocks
That flesh is heir to,—'tis a consummation
    Devoutly to be wished."
                                        Ibid.

"Death is the crown of life:
Were Death denied, poor men would live in vain;
Were Death denied, to live would not be life,
Were Death denied e'en fools would wish to die"
Young.

"One may life as a conqueror, a king, or a magistrate; but
he must die as a man. The bed of Death brings ever human being
to his pure individuality; to the intense contemplation of that
deepest and most

(156)

solemn of all relations, the relation of the creature and his
creator. Here it is that fame and renown cannot assist us; that
all external things must fail to aid us; that even friends,
affection, and human love and devotedness cannot succor us."
Webster.

—————————— —————————— ——————————

"There are no circumstances however unfortunate, that clever
people do not extract some advantage from"   La Rochefaucold.
Happiness. "Think ye, that sic as you and I,
Wha' drudge and drive thro' wet and dry,
Wi' never ceasing toil;
Think ye'are we less blessed than they
Wha' scarcely tent us in their ways,
As hardly worth their while?"
Burns.
"They live too long, who happiness outlive"
Dryden.
"The rays of Happiness, like those of light, are colorless when
unbroken."   Longfellow.
Life -   "Who breathes must suffer; and who
Thinks must mourn
And he alone is blessed who ne'er was born."
Prior.

(157)

"Since every man who lives is born to die,
And none can boast sincere Felicity,
With equal mind what happens let us bear,
Nor joy nor grieve too much for things beyond our care.

Like pilgrims to the appointed place we tend;
The world's our inn, and Death the journey's end."
     Dryden.

Why all this toil for triumphs of an hour?
   What tho' we wade in wealth, or soar in Fame?
Earth's highest station ends in "Hear he lies"
And "Dust to dust" concludes her noblest song."
                                              Young.
"The vanity of Human life is like a river, constantly passing
away, and yet constantly coming on."   Pope.

"This is the state of man; to day he puts forth
The tender leaves of Hope, to morrow blossoms,
And bears his blushing honors thick upon him.
The third day comes a frost, a killing frost;
And,—when he thinks, good easy man, full surely
His greatness is a ripening,—nips his Fruit,
And then he falls."
                              Shakspeare.

(158)

"Bestow thy youth so that thou mayest have comfort to remember it
when it has forsaken thee, and not sigh and grieve at the account
thereof. Whilst thou art young thou wilt think it will never have
an end; but behold, the longest day hath his evening, and that
then shall enjoy it but once, that it never turns again. Use it
therefore as the spring time which soon departeth, and wherein
thou mightest to plant and sow all provisions for a long and
happy life.'   Sir Walter Raleigh.

     "Like the baseless fabric of a vision
     The cloud capped towers and gorgeous palaces
     The solemn temples—the great globe itself—
     yea all which it inherits, shall dissolve
     And like this insubstantial pageant fade;
     Leave not a rack behind. We are such stuff
     As dreams ~~of are~~ are made of, and our little life
     Is rounded with a sleep."
                              Shakspeare.

*   "Society a a sphere that demands all our energies, and
deserves all that it demands. He therefore that retires to cells

to Stripes and to Famine, to court a more arduous conflict, and
to win a richer crown, is doubly deceived; the conflict is less,
the reward is nothing:

(159)

He may indeed win a race, if he can be admitted to have done so
who had no competitors because he chose to run alone; but he will
be entitled to no prize, because he ran out of the course."
Colton

> "Nor love thy Life, nor hate; but whilst thou livest
> Live well, how long how short,—permit to heaven."
> > Milton.
> Love   "So Love does raine
> In stouttest minds, and maketh monstrous warre.
> He maketh warre, he maketh Peace again,
> And yett his Peace is but continuall Jarre,
> Oh miserable men that subject to him arre!"
> > Spenser.
> > "Oh! I envy those
> Whose Hearts on Hearts as faithful can repose
> Who never feel the wind—the wandering thought
> That sighs o'er visions such as mine hath wrought"   Byron.
> Lovers and Madmen have such seething
> > brains,
> Such shaping fantasies that, apprehend
> more than cool Reason ever comprehends
> > Shakspeare.

(160)

May 24th 1870   St. Louis.
  *Exactly one year has elapsed since my book and I held
intercourse, and what changes have occurred! not so much
outwardly as within   My book has been shut up in a great immense
chest buried under huge folios through which I could never
penetrate, and I—have not missed it. Pardon me my friend, but I
never flatter you.*
  *All that has trans pired between then and now vanishes before
this one consideration—in two weeks I am going to be married;
married to the right man. It does not seem strange as I thought
it would—I feel perfectly calm, perfectly collected. And how
surprised every one was, for I had kept it so secret!*

(161)

June 8th Wednesday.
    Tomorrow I will be married. It seems to me so strange that I am not excited—I feel as quiet and calm as if I had one or two years of maiden meditation still before me. I am contented—a

(162)

[blank page]

[Note: From here on, the text—the honeymoon diary—is all composed by Kate Chopin.]

(163)

THREE MONTHS ABROAD.

June 9th

    My wedding day! How simple it is to say and how hard to realize that I am married, no longer a young lady with nothing to think of but myself and nothing to do. We went to holy Communion this morning, my mother with us, and it gave me a double happiness to see so many of my friends at mass for I knew they prayed for me on this happiest day of my life. The whole day seems now like a dream to me; how I awoke early in the morning before the household was stirring and looked out of the window to see whether the sun would shine or not; how I went to mass and could not read the prayers in my book; afterwards how I dressed for my marriage—went to church and found myself married before I could think what I was doing. What kissing of old and young! I never expect to receive as many embraces during the remainder of my life. Oscar has since confessed that he did not know it was customary to kiss and that he conferred that favor on only a very few—I will have to make a most sacred apology for him when I get home. It was very painful to leave my mother and all at home; and it was only at starting that I dis covered how much I would miss them and how much I would be missed. We meet several acquaintances on the cars who congratulated us very extensively, and who could not be brought to realize that they must call me Mrs Chopin and not Miss Katy. They joined us however in consuming a few champagne bottles that had escaped the dire destruction of their companions to meet with a more honorable consummation by the bride and groom.

(164)

10th   Cincinnati.
   Reached Cincinnati at 6 this morning and will leave with
quite a pleasing impression of the "Queen City" a title which St.
Louisians must be permitted to dispute. It is a nice cheerful
place, and though we saw very little of it, still we saw enough
to discover that the handsome bridge over the Ohio, deserves all
the admiration which I know the good people wish bestowed upon
it; and that the sole life sustaining article of the inhabitants
is <u>Beer</u>, simply Beer; without it they would cease to
live—"vanish into thin air." In saying so I do not speak from my
own observation, mind, although it was extensive enough to
warrant my saying; but from private information received from a
gentleman—native of the city, whose name it would be treason to
disclose. In our afternoon walk we meet Mr Dobmeyer who was very
much surprised and seemingly pleased to see us. He took us to a
little amateur concert which did not amount to a row of pins, and
afterwards to the rehearsal of the great "Saenger Fest," which I
believe and hope will prove a success. Farewell to Cincinnati and
a fond farewell to its Beer Gardens—may their number never grow
less!
   12th Philadelphia. . Arrived in Philadelphia this afternoon—&
have come to the Continental Hotel. What a long, dusty, tedious
trip; and what a gloomy puritanical looking city! Perhaps it is
owing to the sabbath that every thIng should look so miserable,
for posatively the people all look like Quakers—the streets look
like Quakers—and the very houses resemble them with their odious
red brick fronts, and those everlasting white shutters. Oh! those
white shutters; what rows and rows and miles of them! Why will
not <u>some one</u>, out of spite, out of anything, put up a black
blind, or a blue blind, or a yellow blind—any thing but

(165)

a white blind. Fairmount is pretty though, a very pretty park,
and I hardly think we will see any lovelier view in Europe than
we had from the rising ground of the park, of the Skiulykill
river, bright and sparkling—with its picturesque little boat
houses—the city—like Campbells mountain looking more <u>enchan</u>ting
in the <u>distance,</u> and the full round moon staying the departure of
twilight. It was a <u>lovely</u> night! and I thought of how the

moonlight looked at Oakland. The moon knew better how to honor the sunday than did the people—for it filled us with—happiness and love.

13th   The city looked a little less gloomy to day, the stores being all opened and a great many people on the streets. We saw a few pretty girls on Chesnut. St whose chief beauty consisted in the lovely complexions. We were not sorry to take the 6 P.M. train for New York—the ride in the cars was long, but extremely agreeable, and besides we had the honor and pleasure of making the acquaintance of Miss Clafflin, the notorious "female broker" of New York—a fussy, pretty, talkative little woman, who discussed business extensively with Oscar, and entreated me not to fall into the useless degrading life of most married ladies—but to elevate my mind and turn my attention to politics, commerce; questions of state, &c. &c. I assured her I would do so—which assurance satisfied her quite.—Reached the city at midnight.

25th   New York . . We have passed almost two weeks in New York in an uncertainty about sailing, and without amusing ourselves to any great extent. Oscar thinks it a great den of swindlers, and I have only to follow his opinion. We visited the Park of course, and went several times to hear Theo. Thomas' Orchestra—how I <u>did</u> enjoy it! It has been my chief pleasure in New York. I have heard the "Bulls and Bears of Wall St" bellowing and grunting in the Stock and Gold Boards—proceedings which

(166)

interested me very much, though I was to some extent incapable of understanding their purport. N. York has been dull, dull! and I am glad that to day we sail. Although so late in the season we have succeeded in securing a good cabin on the German vessel the "Rhein"—and now I can only hope that we will have a fortunate passage and no sea sickness.

July 6th   On Board. Already the 6th of July and we will not reach Bremen till tomorrow. How agreeable our passage has been! no sickness whatever and the sea has been as a lake. It is indeed a great pleasure to be on the ocean when one feels well and comfortable. Day before yesterday a faint effort was made to celebrate our national festival, but I am forced to admit that enthusiasm was wanting: the Dutch band scraped out "Hail Columbia" and a few other martial strains, whilst we were occupied in dining, and some, more patriotic than their companions, laid aside knife and fork to give vent to a feeble "bravo"—afterwhich "order was restored." Yesterday we bade good by to some of our fellow passengers at Southampton, who thought they had been long enough on the "briny deep," but they have missed the most beautiful part of the trip, for to night we are on the North Sea. I had studied at school about the atmosphere of these northern regions, but I had not till now realized what it meant. At ten o'clock it was still twilight, and a clear twilight. The moon is out again, full and round like in Philadelphia, but how many thousands of miles closer it looks! it seems so immense too, and the stars appear so huge that one can scarcely imagine them so very, very far off. No more sick complaining people; every one is gay and happy with the prospect of reaching land tomorrow; and with this calm sea, and this magnificent sky, it seemed sinful to leave the deck. But tomorrow—Terra Firma!

(167)

7th Bremen. "The free and independent city of Bremen" as the Germans style it, betcause, from what I can understand, of its being subject to no particular power. Well this "free and independent city" &c pleases me immensely: the private residences are the most exquisite little gems, and the people all look so amiable and happy. On landing this morning at Bremen Harbor we had to wait an hour for the train to bring us to Bremen, and en route, the only things we noticed remarkable were, that the houses were all thatched and the cows all black. We have stopped at the Hillman Hotel, a very lovely house, in company with Mr & Mrs Griesinger from N. Orleans—Whose society will have, I presume all through Germany. Together with some gentlemen acquaintances—natives of Bremen, we visited the Summer Theatre, a nice little place, where we heard a famous commedien of Vienna—Knack; and afterwards finished the evening in the notorious "Rathskeller" the most celebrated wine celler in the world. I cannot say that "the most celebrated wine celler in the world" is the loveliest of places, but you know "handsome is as handsome does" and, this does very well indeed for such as own a partiality for wine. Rath-haus means Council house and the Rathskeller is the celler of the ancient council house. It is under ground, and on entering one is almost stifled by the fumes of wine and the hazy atmosphere of the place. Before seating ourselves for supper we took a look at the great casks of Rhine wine, each of which is named, and most of whice have each an apartment to itself. Twelve which contain the oldest and best

wine are called the "twelve Apostles;" one hughe cask is
dedicated to Bachus, and separated from the others is one, which
together with the room

(168)

in which it stands, bears the name of "The Rose." On the ceiling
of the apartment is painted an immense rose, with underneath a
latin inscription; and we were told that in this chamber were
held the secret meetings of the ancient ruler of Bremen: hence
comes the expression "Sub Rosa" "Under the Rose."

8th Have passed another pleasant day—morning devoted to
to shop seeing and shopping. This afternoon in company with the
G—s—Mr Bechtel and Mr Brantlet; we went ten miles out in the
country to visit the residence of a Mr Knoop, the wealthiest
merchant of Bremen. Although not yet completed, it is the
princliest private residence that I have ever seen—a miracle of
costliness and exquisite taste. We took tea, a regular German tea
in the loveliest spot—in a sort of bower-nook—summer retreat—I
know not what to call it—and all grew merry on cheese and fresh
milk. I am tired tonight and will sleep well.

9th Oscar and I started out alone this morning, and following
the direction of our Guide Book, gracefully wended our way
towards the Cathedral, an old edifice founded by Charlemagne in
800—now a Protestant temple. The chief interesting object was
the Blei Keller—Lead celler—which possesses the power of
preserving bodies from total decay. In order to convince us that
there was no hoax in the story, and old woman—fit keeper for
such treasures, displayed to us several dried up remains—the
mummies they call them—ghastly old thing that would have been
infinitely more discreet in crumbling away hundreds of years
ago.—To night we leave for Cologne. Bremen being my first
European city I cannot compare it. I think it a lovely place
however—the private houses especially struck me as being
exquisite—so white

(169)

so neat and so ornamented with flowers. The people are
exceedingly polite and obliging.

Cologne.

10th We left Bremen last night by the 10 o/clock train, and were fortunate enough Mr & Mrs G. and ourselves to get a coupe all to ourselves; it is needless to mention that a few thalers went a great way towards assisting us. Travelled till 12 & had to wait two hours for a connection. Is there any greater agony than waiting for a connection in the middle of the night? I know of none, & prefer passing over those two hours in silence. A sleepless night of course, and reached Cologne only at 8 o/clock this morning. We have come to the Hotel du Nord—a very lovely house. The first thing we did was to take a good bath, and then march over to the Cathedral, its being sunday, where we heard an eleven o'clock mass. I found it extremely odd that the people sing during service & seem to sing with great taste and keep very good time. We will not visit the cathedral regularly till tomorrow.—Dear me! what a hot scorching day it has been—and what wild unheard of things we do in travelling that at home we would shudder to think of. At three o'clock, under a broiling sun we (the quartette) got on a Rhine boat and went a mile down the river to visit the Zoological Gardens. I hate Zoological Gardens of a hot Sunday afternoon. This was a very fine one though, and we saw any number of wild beasts that showed their teeth in the most wonderful manner—but we were'nt at all frightened, which I set down as an instance of bravery on our part. There was plenty of music—lots of it, and such a marvelous number of girls in white waists and variegated skirts, who seemed to be casting longing glances towards a certain house—en-

(170)

closure—whatever one might call it, which I afterwards learned was set aside every sabbath evening for the pious purpose of dancing. At sunset we tore ourselves away, not from the animals, from the scene, and after a repetition of the crushing on the boat, reached our hotel in comparative safety. Lina and her husband have left us; we will meet them again in Bonn.

11th Well! we have visited the cathedral. I do not know much about architecture but I have sufficient taste to feel that it is a marvelous conception and exquisite piece of work; it is still incomplete, and they say will not be finished for ten years. Whilst stroling through one of the Passages this morning, whom should we come suddenly upon but Bunnie Knapp. To say he was surprised to see us would be using a very feeble term—he was astounded! Tomorrow we meet him again in Bonn, where he is following a course of lectures. I find nothing particularly attractive in Cologne: of course we have in vested in sundry

bottles of its famous water. This evening we went to the Belle
Vue Garden the river and were caught in a drenching rain for our
pains. Tomorrow we bid farewell to the city with its narrow ugly
streets, and pass on.   <u>Bonn</u>.
12th
     We left Cologne this morning at 8 o'clock by a Rhine
boat—saw no particularly nice scenery and reached Bonn at 11. We
have stopped at the Kley hotel which possesses the advantage of
having a very fine garden leading down to the river. I slept away
half the day and arose at 6 to go out for a drive. How I did
enjoy

(171)

it! the afternoon was lovely—the country was lovely and indeed
every thing was charming. Our driver rejoiced in a very amiable
disposition, and endeavored to explain all the objects of
interest which we encountered; we understood one half of his
communication and guessed at the other. The house in which the
great Beethoven was born was pointed out to us—and resembled
very much all the other houses in the neighborhood. Bonn is very
nice; and it is very late; and I am very sleepy. Wrote to mother
to night.
     13th. How like a dream this whole day has been! Let me think for
a moment.—As usual we arose very late this morning, and after
enjoying a good breakfast, started out for a strole. We took into
our heads that we should like to visit the University; and after
gazing up at all the windows, and knocking ineffectually at
several doors we came upon an amiable sprightly woman who spoke
French and offered to "show us around." We saw nothing remarkably
interesting—only a mass of copies from famous pieces of
sculpture. The good dame would not take us through the hall in
which the students were gathered, "for," she said "the young
gentlemen are not sorry when a young lady passes through their
room." I ventured to suggest that my being married might in a
manner abate the interest with which they might otherwise regard
me; but my argument proved weak, and failed utterly.—We met
Bunnie again, whom we encountered diligently occupied in playing
cards in a "Bier Halle", and upon seeing us he came forward and
insisted upon our giving him the rest of the day. We delivered
ourselves into his hands and were not sorry to have been so
pleasantly captured. We took the 3 o'clock train and went about a
half hour's ride up the Rhine, to obtain one of the finest views
on the river. It was indeed lovely! The Drachenfels—black and in

bold relief against the sky;

(172)

below it and nearer to us the island of Nonnenwerth,—half burried in the Rhine waters—with Rollensecke keeping guard in the distance. The legend attached to the spot is romantic, & I have no doubt perfectly true. It is related that during the first Crusade, Rollen, a brave and generous youth, fired with holy enthusiasm, took himself off to fight in the good cause, leaving behind him disconsolate friends, and a weeping sweet heart. Time went on, and in an evil hour a report reached the quiet neighborhood that Rollen had met his death in Palestine. Fancy the wild grief of the maiden! In her utter despair she fled from friends and family & entered the convent still to be seen on the island of Nonnenwerth—intending there to bear with her grief, and in the course of human events, to die. But listen! On a warm summer's day a solitary horseman entered the small town which has since been demolished, and the lone traveller was none other than Rollen. He hastens to the house of his beloved filled with expectant happiness. He enters—"Where is Gretchen?" he cries! "Mein Gott! We thought you were dead—she has gone to the convent." Grief and rage mingle in the bosom of the hero to render the scene terrible: Moved by contending emotions, he flies to the top of a distant mountain and builds himself the castle of Rollensecke, from the windows of which he watches the convent night and day, catching occasional glimpses of a form which he loved alas! too well. Thus ended his live—a wreck—the fruits of a false report.

We stopped at a very attractive and nicely situated house—commanding a lovely view of surrounding objects—and with the people of which B. seemed to be very familiar. He speaks German astonishingly well. We

(173)

were treated with a delightful beverage composed of Rhine wine and straw berries and known as "Ende berren Boule." At 5 o'clock we took the train returning to Bonn, and arrived here to find Mr and Mrs G. awaiting us in the Garden; so there we were a nice little party at once, and knowing that once companion ship was to be of short duration, we made excellent good use of our time. There was a concert in the Garden which of course we attended—but did not pay much attention to. What quantities of that maddening Rhine wine I have drunk to day. The music—the scenery—the bright waters—the wine—have made me ex cessively gay. In fact we all gave play to our spirits more or less, and I fear these phlegmatic Germans will consider our American sociability as somewhat too loud. During the tableax which followed the concert there was a little encounter between a citizen and a student; brought about by some fancied slight on the part of the citizen. Bunnie fears it will end in a duel— which, he tells me are of frequent occurrence.—Dear me! I feel like smoking a cigarette—think I will satisfy my desire and open that sweet little box which I bought in Bremen. Oscar has gone to some Halle to witness these Germans' interpretation of a galop—a waltz & c. Tomorrow we take the boat far up the Rhine—perhaps B. will accompany us. I must not forget to note that we travelled on the same

(174)

train this afternoon with the queen of Prussia, who was going to attend a concert in Rollensburg. I am enchanted with Bonn, and sincerely hope I have not

14   "The Rhine! the Rhine! A blessing on the Rhine" so says Long fellow & so say I. It seems like an exquisite panorama—as I close my eyes, and pass again in fancy Drockenfeld, Godes berg, and the Rolans's ecke. Shall I ever forget the beauties of the beautiful Rhine? The gray & stately ruins,—the churchs peeping out of the dense foliage, & those vineyards upon vineyards sloping to the waters edge.
                    Wiesbaden.
15th We left Mayence this afternoon & arrived in Wies baden. What an unpleasant souvenir I retain of Mayence. Let it dwell only in my memory—and I trust even there, not too long. We stroled into the Cursaal to night and watched intently the gambling. It is all as I had pictured—the sang froid of the croupier—the eager, greedy, and in some instances fiendish look upon the faces of the players. I was tempted to

(175)

put down a silver piece myself—but had not the courage.
16— Walked about town rather listlessly to day. In the morning went to the boiling springs tasted the water and thought it shocking; Oscar of course found it delicious. Dined at 6. and afterwards went to the Opera to hear the in comparable Wachtel in

Wm Tell. How I could & how I would have enjoyed it, had I felt
better; but have been feeling badly all day. To morrow en route
for Frankfurt.
17th What an uproar! What an excitement! I do not see how we got
out of Wiesbaden alive. News reached us last night of the
declaration of war between France & Prussia; so this morning all
the hotels emptied their human contents into the various dépôts.
French women with their maids, their few children, their laces
and velvets hastening to get started on their homeward
journey—every other nationality equally anxious to get back to
their respective domiciles.

(176)

The depot from whence we took the train for Frankfurt, presented
a scene of fashionable excitement, that I shall never forget. We
reached Frankfurt at 1 o'clock. I was struck in the way by the
familiarity of an otherwise very refined German lady, with her
maid. They seemed more like sisters, than mistress and maid.
Remained in F. only four hours. Took a good dinner & then started
out to see the objects of interest. It seems to be the city of
statues: Gottenberg is remembered in a magnificent
representation, nor is Goethe & Shiller forgotten. We visited the
house the founder of the great family of Rothschild was born, it
is in the jewish quarter of the city and looks shabby. A much
better edifice is the house in which Goethe was born—it is kept
in repair by the people. The house from which Luther addressed
the people is held in great reverance. Left at 7 1/2 and reached
Heidelberg after II. Have taken rooms at the Victoria Hotel.

(177)

18th   Heidelberg.
Arose at 12. this morning, breakfasted & started out on foot for
the Schloss. It was rather hard at first with our imperfect
knowledge of german to get into the right path; but that point
secured, we started off like true mountaineers. I have thought
and talked a great deal of Heidelberg, and for once in my life
have not been disappointed by the real versus the ideal. It is a
magnificent old ruin: the scenery surrounding it being well worth
walking miles to see. And what a glorious day! And glorious walk
to the very top of the Berg where we dined with hungry appetites
on eel & necker wine, enjoying at the same time, the exquisite
view through the soft summer land scape.

How unfortunate is this war! We cannot go as was our intention to Baden and it is even probable we may not visit France. That would indeed be deplorable; for what is Europe out side of Paris? So say tourists.

(178)

Tomorrow we see a little more of Heidelberg, then leave for Stuttgart where, Heaven be praised, our tents shall be pitched for a breathing space.
July 19th. Stroled about town all morning making a few purchases of books and music & left the hotel at 4, having some difficulty in securing comfortable rail way accommodation, owing to the large number of soldiers in movement. Passed through a lovely country, picturesque in the extreme and reached Stuttgart at 10 P.M. Have come to the Marquart Hotel.
20th Rose late—feeling not well & staggered at the amount of unpacking and washing to be given out: which interesting occupation engaged my time till 5 in the afternoon. Dined at a restaurant—took a cab & visited Herman where we met the Griesingers, came back about 10—read and went to bed late after an uneventful day.

(179)

21st Have done nothing but lounge—took a ride in the afternoon and retired early.
22d—Went out this morning in company with Lina G. and her mother in law—who, speaking neither french nor english, does not converse much with me; unless when Lina acts as interpreter. A delightful lady. Bought a black lace shawl—some brussels and valenciennes lace—table and bed linnen &c in anticipation of that house keeping which awaits me on the "other side". Do not like Stuttgart. "The reason why I cannot tell" but the blame must rest with me & not with the no doubt charming city.—There is such movement—especially about the hotel—such an influx of troops. I met the commander in chief Von Moltke face to face on the stair way. What an iron countenance; the French I fancy will meet their equal when they encounter the rugged old general—and his troops.

(180)

Ulm

27th   Left Stuttgart this morning—arriving at Ulm in two hours
time; having barely time to dine & visit the handsome Cathedral
and fine fortifications, and left for Friedrickshafen which we
~~lef~~ reached late at night. Took lodgings for a nights rest, and
started early in the morning for Constanz. We are anxious to get
into Switzerland.
28th Took the boat at 10 this morning—day cloudy—but I was
glad we had no sun. The "blue lake of Constanz" looked bluer than
ever through the mist. Just as we were starting out, a child
playing near the boat, fell in the water: we had not time to wait
& see if he was rescued, but I fear not as he must have been
caught in some of the numerous net work of wooden piles. The
scenery was exquisite along the shore, and the hour glided away
only too fast.
          at   Constanz
We set out immediately to "see the

(181)

town;" taking in the beautiful church of St. Stephens, which
belongs to the severe gothic order; saw some beautiful paintings
not the less lovely for being new, and then went to the
Cathedral—ascending some 5000000 steps (more or less) to reach
the tower, but were repaid for our fatigue by the view. I should
fancy such scenery—such a beautiful side of nature, would
influence these people only for good deeds. Left Constaz at 4
1/2, reaching Schaufhausen at a 7.   Schauf hausen.
     The Blue bien Hotel; where we have taken quarters seems to be
entirely at our disposal; the war having frightened off all
visitors. I trust the landlord will not attempt to make his
accounts balance at our expense. We command a charming view of
the Rhein falls (the largest in Europe) and will remain here some
time, if only our impatient spirits permit.
29th Rain! All the day rain. So we could not venture out, and
have amused ourselves all day, making mental photographes of the
falls.

(182)

30th Still cloudy and raining, so we did little more than
lounge. The landlord has transferred us bag and baggage, to the
small hotel adjoining which we like infinitely better, having
gained a large room by the exchange
31st Sunday! Intended to go to church—but what is it they say of

the paving stones of the lower realm? Did not rise till ten and
the church is three quarters of an hour from here. As the morning
looked bright Oscar and I started out to tmake our long delayed
personal acquaintance with the environs. A precipitous path leads
down to the falls which we had no difficulty in <u>descend</u>ing;
looked into the mysteries of a camera obscura which graces the
shore, drank some "bier" to the delicious accompanyment of a
zither, and seeing clouds gathering, started for home. Talk of
the flood gates of Heaven! I think Heaven and hell were combined
to our discomfiture. Never had I felt such rain with a sprinkling
of hail. We scrambled

(183)

as best we could up the slippery path which a moment before had
seemed so idylic—drenched to the skin. My grenadine I fear is
ruined. The remainder of the day I devoted to the perusal of
Dickens.

August 1st. Every thing stupidly quiet a l'ordinaire." No one
remains in our hotel save two families. Nearly all the domestics
are being discharged. There is a Russian family, consisting of
husband wife & little boy, to whom we have taken a great fancy.
The lady is a lovely blond, full of spirits and speaks charming
french: What linguists are the Russians! The husband seems
delicate and the boy very pleased with us; he calls me <u>die schöne
Dame</u>, not being able to master the intricacies of Chopin. A long
walk to Schafhausen, and retired early.
2d A walk after dinner is about the only distraction. A beautiful
afternoon, so we went again to Schaffhausen, about 3/4 of an hour
from here, returning at 9 oclock in the hotel stage, which
returns—always empty.

(184)

3d Day cloudy, much rain—could not go out—it is impossible to
venture out here when it rains—the walking is something
execrable. Must remember a good anecdote Mrs Kendensky related at
dinner. "Il y avait un jeune homme qui etait fort amoureux d'une
jeune fille, mais il etait tellement timide et tellement bête,
qu'il ne savait ce qu'il fallait lui dire. Il avait un ami intime
que etait aussi son confident, Il lui chercha un jour et lui dit.
A mon ami, aide moi, dite moi ce que je puis dire a Mlle—tu
connais mon passion, qui est d'un telle charactere, que dans sa

présence, je ne parle plus! A bah! qu'est-ce qui cela
fait—dite-lui n'importe quoi" Mais, aide moi d'abord! " Eh,
bien, à quelle heure va tu generalement la voir? "le soir" Alors
quand elle t'offrira du thé, dit-lui "Mademoiselle, vous est
comme cette tasse, pleine de bontée (bon thé). A la bonne heure,
le pauvre bête etait joyeaux. Malheuresement sa a fait, la
prochaine fois qu'il alla

(185)

voir sa belle c'etait le matin, et elle lui offra du café—ne
voila pas que le stupide qui dit de haute voix "Mlle vous etes
comme cette tasse" "Comment?" repondit-elle avec etonnement.
"Vous etes pleine de bon café!
9th   Nothing now claims the attention but war news. We
learned to day of the defeat, on every side, of the French. The
Prussians have retaken Saarbruck—defeated the enemy at
Wissunburg—Mc Mahon has suffered a severe defeat, and we hear
that Paris is in revolution. We place no reliance on the last
intelligence. We leave the Rhein fall tomorrow for Lucerne. Two
weeks have we rested here quietely—no excitement, ex cet such as
caused by the imperfect "rumors of war" which reach us now and
again. Yesterday we crossed the bridge and visited Lauffen castle
from whence the finest view of the Falls is obtained. So closely
did we approach them that the spray fell upon us like rain. Such
a delicious, indescribable feeling of moistness. Yesterday our
friends the Kendenskys bade us "auf wiedersehen." We

(186)

meet at Lucerne. Rcd a letter from Lil Chouteau to day, written
on the 29 of June.

Aug 11th Have not yet left the Falls. The weather was so
inclement yesterday that we could not leave, and today the rain
is pouring in torrents. I wish to leave at all events on the 2.30
train. It is 10 o'clock and Oscar is still asleep. I woke him a
moment ago and said something about going—but he turned over
mumbling weather too bad—go to morrow. Up at last changesd his
mind—thinks we will go. Impossible to get news of the war. I
fancy the Germans must have suffered somewhat: when the French
are defeated, we are always sure to hear of it. To night we sleep
at Zurich "On the banks of the blue Zurich's waters" Blue enough
I fancy, this dull day.

What reluctance I feel in leaving the Rhein—so green and beautiful! propally never to see it again. But our stay in Europe is so limited we can not give longer

(187)

than two weeks even to so idylic a spop as the "Rhein Fall." 11th Reached Zurich at half past four after a two hour's ride by rail: which would have been more agreeable had the weather been so. Came to the "Baur au Lac" which cannot be recommended on the score of economy. I have yet seen no more bautiful situation than that possessed by Zurich. The white houses gleaming on the hills—the mountains surrounding the landscape like a frame work—and more than all—the clear green waters like a mirror reflecting back the hills—the trees that surround it. We went in the evening to the Ton Halle to hear some music, which was only tolerable.
12th Awoke this morning to find a disagreeable rain falling, which had stopped however when we finished our 10 o'clock breakfast. The sun came out brilliantly and we ventured on a row on the lake. I

(188)

find myself handling the oars quite like an expert. Oscar took a nap in the afternoon and I took a walk alone. How very far I <u>did</u> go. Visited a panorama which showed the Rigi Kulm in all its grandeur—the only audience being myself and <u>two</u> soldiers. I wonder what people thought of me—a young women strolling about alone. I even took a glass of beer at a friendly little beer garden quite on the edge of the lake; and amused myself for some time feeding the importunate little fish who came up to the surface as tame as chickens to receive their crumbs.

No news of the war. Lelft Zurich at half past seven by boat on the lake for Horgen, where I am now preparing to retire. Admired very much the scenery on the lake and the lights of the town in the distance that seemed to touch the waters edge. We leave in the morning by 7 o clock stage for Zug.

(189)

13th Started at seven o'clock this morning only half awake from Horgan. Got into a delightful little stage, with no one but a delightful old lady, who did not in the least object to

smoking—on the contrary, rather liked it, and gave us to
understand that she indulged herself in an ocassional weed. The
drive from Horgan to Zug was charming in the early fresh morning.
At Zug we breakfasted, and took the boat at half past eleven for
Guda. Met a party of America—gent and wife two young men, and a
young German, the last of whom was very nice, the rest, perfect
Yankees.

At 3 commenced the ascent of the Rigi: the lady, her husband,
the german and myself on horse back. My husband and the two
others walking. What views we had coming up the mountain! Can
there be anything finer in Switzerland? Reached the summit at 6,
but too cloudy to see much. Had one of my fearful head aches,
which took me directly to

(190)

bed—knowing that sleep alone would come to my relief.
14th The blowing of the horn awoke us at 4 this morning, and
dressing in all haste, we started out—a set of shivering, half
awakened mortals—and half clad, to see the sight of sights! We
had been favored—I might almost say blessed, with a grand
morning. Standing on the summit of the Rigi, we see this mass of
white, soft, floating clouds, and the snow covered mountains,
rearing their heads above. Grim Pilatus with his rugged top
looking blacker amid the clouds, and the sun just tipping with
red the white mountains.

Started down at 8 for Küssnach—pretty much in a
fog—breakfasted and took a hack for Lucerne. En route visited
Tell's chapel: the spot where Tell is said to have killed Gesler.
Hot ride—reached Lucerne at 3. Have taken rooms at the Keble
Vieu—and parted with our Yankee acquaintances.
Oscar is very tired from

(191)

his walk up and down the mountain.
15 The "Fête de l'Empereur" but very little celebration will
there be I fancy in Paris. We all presume a great battle has been
fought to day—but whether the Prussians or French were
victorious, there is no telling. It is also the feast of the
Assumption, which fact I discovered when it was too late to
attend mass. Went in the afternoon to see the famous Lion, with
our Russian friends who have again turned up. It impressed me as a
grand piece of art. Took a row on the lake—and handled the oars

with marked improvement. Indulged in ices which are far from approaching our home ices—& came back to the hotel feeling decidedly tired. Mrs K. told an anecdote of an old priest who made such an impressive sermon to his congregation of the sufferings of Christ, as to excite them all to tears. Seeing the affliction into which he had thrown his good people, he exclaimed: "Do not cry thus my good children, for after all, it may not

(192)

be true."—Received a letter from Nina to day. Nothing unusual has occurred since my absence.

16   Went down town with our Yankee acquaintances, whom we leave to day. Heard the great organ play—Beautiful music—wonderful imitation of the human voice—and a storm. Took a row on the lake! our last on the beautiful lake of Lucerne. Tomorrow we leave early, in a coach with the Kendenskys for Brienz, whe I suppose we part. Oscar has gone out to gather some war news.
Interlaken

17th All day in a coach & four, travelling through this beautiful country. During the morning along the lake of Lucerne and in the afternoon through the valley of the Arr and along the lake of Brienz until Interlaken.
18.   Spent the morning in looking into the pretty shops, which seem to be filled with curious wood carving. The afternoon was past in contemplating the rain fall, and gazing

(193)

through the mist at the Young Frau. Wrote to Nina.
19th Rain still falling, so Oscar went out alone this morning, & returned with very sad news of the war. Never have the French Armies suffered such repeated mortifications: Saarbruk - Wirth - Metz - Wiessenburg have followed in quick & inglorious succession. - Took leave of the Kendenskys at 5 o'clock, and started for the boat. Passed an agreeable hour on the lake of Thun, from which many glaciers are visible. Reached Berne at 9 oclock. Have a pleasant room at the Hotel Boulevard, but will leave tomorrow.
Fribourg.

20 Have passed the day in visiting object interesting and otherwise of Berne. It is the largest city in Switzerland and is

besides so quaint and old, and has so perfectly retained its
ancient manners and customs. It may be called, essentially the
city of Bears

(194)

deriving its name from the animal. We of course looked into the
Bears' cave, enjoying their curious antics for a moment—stroled
leisurely through the quaint streets; and at 8 o'clock find
ourselves in Fribourg, where, at last! "on parle le français."
What a rest it will be! Not that we ever succeeded in talking
german; but what excrutiating efforts have we not made. How short
the distance seems to us here, from one city to another; in
comparison with those interminable miles and miles of day and
night travelling in America.

Ouchy

21st Attended mass this morning at the cathedral of Fribourg,
where we heard, what is considered, the finest organ in the
world. Left at noon, and it has taken but three hours to reach
Ouchy. We are installed at the beautiful hotel of the Beau
Rivage. Americans

(195)

seem to have bodily posession. Amongst others we chanced across
the Hoyles this morning afternoon. Mrs Hoyle, Ella and Charlie,
whom we tried to induce or to inveigle into a row on the lake,
but sunday, taken into connection with some rather menacing
looking waves, was enough to deter them. I did not believe, that
Switzerland had any thing so enchanting in reserve for us, as the
lake of Geneva. How indescribably lovely

22 it was this morning as we glided over its blue waters! Saw in
the distance the castle of Chillon - and gave a tender thought to
Byron, en passant. Will go to Chamounix tomorrow. What a dull
place is this Martigny.

Argentère.

23—Although the middle of August, I am sitting at a country
hotel, before a blazing wood fire, trying to thaw my frozen
corporosity. We left Martigny this morn-

(196)

ing at 6 o'clock on horse back, with a guide, en route for
Chamounix. All went well, until about 2 o'clock we had passed the

mauvais pas, and the Tête Noir (where the sun was never known to shine) and were far from the shelter of a hotel, when the rain commenced to fall in torrents. A peasants hut, presenting itself on the way, we did not hesitate to enter; nor was I sorry of having done so; the place & people, forming quite an interesting study to me. Oscar conversed with them freely. The family consisted of the old man, aged 82 years—the old grandfather, who had never in his life been farther than Geneva. a distance of 9 miles: the father, a handsome man, mother and four daughters, the eldest but fourteen. What surprised me was that in a cabin where there was barely a chair to sit on, the eldest girl was going to school (in winter only when she did not work)

(197)

and showed us her exercises which were written correctly, and in one of the most beautiful hands I have ever seen. I really believe, it is to the thrift and intelligence of her lower classes, that France owes her greatness, and even should she suffer defeat, it is mainly that quality of endurance & pride in her people that will enable her to rise again. These peasants were catholics; the only ornaments in their house being holy pictures. Oscar presented the delighted children with small coin. And when about to leave, the mother called them all to look and feel of my dress (an old black silk) something they had never seen before. We continued our journey, hoping the rain would cease or moderate; but it poured on in torrents—and such a cold rain. Oscar's southern blood felt it more keenly than I, and he would alternately walk in hopes

(198)

of stirring up a little warmth. We arrived an hour ago—with hands and feet almost frozen—and our persons beautifully festooned with icicles. In the morning we continue our way to Chamounix.- An appeal has just been received from head quarters, calling on all men capable of bearing arms, to try to save France. Vain appeal, I fear.

 24th   Chamounix

 Kitty Garesché's birthday: I had not forgotten her. We left Argentere this morning at 7—in a sort of little barouche, driven by rather an amiable specimen of the genus homo. It was a beautiful morning—so cold and bracing. We drove to the mer de glace and ventured into a glittering fairy like cavern which has

only recently been dug under the "mer". Were pointed out the
place where Mrs Mark and her guide perished not long since in
ascending Mont Blanc. On the way to Chamounix, met Mr &

(199)

Mrs Knapp and Miss Harrison in a carriage en route to Martigny.
Bunnie ~~and~~ Miss Belsonver and Andy had gone on ahead on mules, so
we missed them; being at the mer de Glace when they passed. Oscar
and I took a modest tramp up the mountain of the Glacier de
Bosson - not <u>on</u> the Glacier - no thank you! Enjoyed the descent -
going up was too warm. We are obliged to sleep at Chamounix to
night having missed the stage this morning. Leave tomorrow at
seven for Geneva.

Geneva

25   Left Chamounix this morning at seven and travelled through
a beautiful mountains country in a lumbering old coach and six,
which had every appearance of being a relic of the days of Louis
XIV. Reached Geneva at 2. What a beautiful City - The loveliest
we have visited yet. Face burned again - great nuisance.

(200)

Neuchatel.

26th
    We have taken our usual desultory stroll through the streets
of Geneva - admiring the glittering white house, indulging in an
occasional purchase. Amongst other things, bought a cute,
diminutive little watch. We left Geneva at +1 1/2 and only
reached Neuchatel at 11. Have taken our last view of the Alps at
Lausane. How grand they were in the deepening twilight.
It is very hard to get to Paris: tomorrow, let us hope we start.

Paris

Sunday Sep 4th 1870
    What an eventful day for France - may I not say for the world?
And that I should be here in the midst of it. This morning my
husband and myself rose at about eleven, and after taking our
coffee, started of in the direction of the Madelein for mass.

(201)

Very sad and very important news had reached Paris during the

previous night, from the seat of war. The Emperor was prisoner in
the hands of the Prussians - McMahon either wounded or dead, and
forty thousand armed men had surrendered! What did it mean? The
people on the streets looked sad and preoccupied. It was now
nearly one, & we entered church where mass had not yet commenced.
It was also the hour when the Corps Legislativef was going to
meet to decide on an important affair of state, and already there
were determined looking people marching towards the Chambre. The
short mass was soon over. We hastened out and stationed ourselves
on the Church steps, from which position we commanded a splendid
view of the entire length of the street up to the Chamber of the
Corps Législatif. There were thousands of people forming one
great human

(202)

mass. In the Chamber was an all important question being decided,
and, without, was an impatient populace ~~learning~~ waiting to learn
the result. Scarcely an hour passed, when down they came, when
down they came, the whole great body, and at once it seemed to
pass like an electric flash from one end of Paris to the other -
the cry "Vive la Republic"
    I have seen a French Revolution! And astonishing - no drop
of blood has been shed - unless I take into account the blood
that has paid sad tribute to the Prussian.
    The Gens' D'Armes have been dispersed, and the Garde National
has taken under its care the public buildings and places of the
city. Oscar has gone to night on the Boulevards, where men women
and children are shouting the Marseilles with an abandon and
recklessness purely <u>french</u>. Now, whilst I write, comes to me that
strain from the mar—

(203)

tial air " Aux Armes, Citoyens!
    Formons nos Batallions!"
If now they will form their batallions against the Prussian &
cease their cry of "A bas l'Empereur."
    All day they have been tearing down and casting in the dust
the Imperial eagles that have spread their wings so proudly over
Paris. It cannot but make one sad. We have seen the rude populace
running & strutting through the private grounds of the
Tuilleries: places that 24 hours ago were looked upon as almost

sacred ground. What a nation.

Our stay in Paris was short and of course offered none of those attractions - fascinations - usually held out to visitors. We left on the 10th sep and proceeded to Brest, from which point we took the steamer "Ville de Paris" for New York, where we arrived after a very stormy & threatening passage; nor did we tarry on our way to St. Louis - where once again I have embraced those dear ones left behind.

(204)

LIST OF BOOKS.

Chateaubriand—Génie du Christianisme.
Edmund Burke—On the Sublime and Beautiful.
Addison's Spectator.=
The Friend—S. T. Coleridge.
Anecdotes of Literature—W. Beloe.
Amenities of Literature—J. D. 'Israeli.
Curiosities "   "   —"   "
Miscellanies "   "   — "   "
Literary Portraits—G. Gilfin
Prose Writers of Germany = F. Hedge.
Student Life in "   —W. Howitt.
Homes and haunts of the British Poets—W. Howitt.
German Literature—W. Menzel.
Influence of Literature on Society—De Stael.
Memoirs of the Reign of Geo III—Horace Walpole.
Thomas Carlyle's Essays.
Chas Lambs Essays of Elia.
Thoughts on the Poets—H. L. Tuckerman.
Jerusalem Delivered—Tasso.
The Vision—Dante.
Oeuvres de Corneille.
   "   " Molière.
   "   " Racine.
Théatre Classique des Francais.

(205)

Pride and Prejudice = J. Austen.
Shirley—A. Bell
Ernest Maltrevers—Bulwer

Don Quixote.
D'Israeli—Coningsby =
Contarini—Fleming =
Sybil = Tancred
<u>Vivian</u> Grey—Young Duke =
Undine = Grantly Manor.
Diary of a Desennuyée—Gore.
Stories from the Italian Poets—A. L. Hunt.
Heidelberg—James = Kavanagh—Longfellow
Charms and Counter Charms = McIntosh.
Dictionary of Quotations—H. Moore.

1871–1884

Kate O'Flaherty Chopin

In the last entry in her New Orleans diary, Kate Chopin describes a "journey with Oscar through the district of warehouses where cotton is stored and when sold passes under presses of immense power, reducing bales to half their size for better storage aboard ship." The Chopins also visited the "pickeries where damaged cotton is bleached and otherwise repaired. The whole process of weighing, sampling, storing, compressing, boring to detect fraud, and the treatment of damaged bales is open to public view." But there were problems: everywhere she heard about "too much rain for cotton." Everyone complained that the "cotton was shedding."

These lines, quoted by Daniel Rankin in his 1932 biography, are the only words we have from Kate Chopin between 1871 and 1884—the years of her marriage, motherhood, and widowhood in Louisiana. And even that diary was lost, probably by Rankin.

We do know that Kate O'Flaherty Chopin never lost her youthful love of writing. Besides her diaries, she wrote many letters home to St. Louis—letters so lively and engaging that a friend, Dr. Frederick Kolbenheyer, later suggested that she try professional writing.

But in the 1870s, Kate Chopin was otherwise occupied and almost continually pregnant, for between May 1871 and December 1879, she gave birth to five boys and one girl. Jean Baptiste (1871), Frederick (1876), and Felix Andrew (1878) were born in New Orleans, while Oscar Charles (1873) and

George Francis (1874) were born in St. Louis. Lélia (1879) was born in Cloutierville, the tiny French village in northwestern Louisiana where the Chopins had moved earlier that year.

Kate Chopin does seem to have enjoyed New Orleans. Rankin, our source for those years, says she treasured her long, solitary strolls all over the city, much like the walks Edna takes in *The Awakening*. (Rankin, though, seems not to have considered the intense heat of New Orleans, nor the taboos on public appearances by pregnant women.)

The Chopins did live in New Orleans during interesting times. The first modern Mardi Gras, with organized krewes and parades and a Queen of Carnival, was put on in 1871. The New Orleans French Opera, in its prime, was flourishing, and was the first in the United States to stage *Lohengrin* and *Tannhäuser*. It was, as always, the site of romance and scandal, as the gossipers note in Kate Chopin's *The Awakening* (1899).

Although Oscar's parents had died and he had no close relatives in New Orleans, he had many friends in the old French-speaking (Creole) community. As a commission merchant and cotton factor, the gentlemanly middle-man between planters and purchasers, Oscar belonged to the "Société Française de Bienfaisance et d'Assistance Mutuelle," a mutual aid society. He also almost certainly knew Edgar Degas, the French Impressionist who painted his "Bureau de Coton" (The Cotton Office) in New Orleans in 1873.

Kate Chopin may have been even better acquainted with Degas, at least by reputation, for there are striking parallels with *The Awakening*. Like Chopin's main characters, Degas lived on Esplanade Street in the French Quarter, in a large double cottage. A few years before he came to New Orleans, Degas had been especially close friends with the painter Berthe Morisot, whose closest confidante was a beautiful blonde woman named Adèle. But the most intriguing similarity is with another Degas friend, Morisot's sister, a talented artist who gave up her painting once she married. She was forever frustrated, like Chopin's Edna Pontellier—and her name was Edma Pontillon.

Oscar also associated with "Americans" (English speakers) in Company B of the First Louisiana Regiment, a militia outfit allied with the White League, which was formed in 1874 to combat the "pride and ambition" of "the African race." Yet the League was not just a refuge for racists. Its members, smarting from defeat and humiliation in the Civil War, also resented white outsiders (Yankees) telling Southerners what they must do. The White Leaguers enrolled many of the aristocrats and Confederate veterans of New Orleans, all opposed to the violence and corruption of Reconstruction.

During the summer of 1874, while Kate was in St. Louis awaiting the birth of her third son, George, the White League and associated companies were drilling. On September 10, the militias—including Oscar Chopin—attacked the Metropolitan Police on Canal Street, New Orleans's city center and the dividing line between the "Americans" and the "French." Nearly thirty men were killed and over a hundred wounded, but the White League attack-ers were praised as great heroes. Later the skirmish was lauded as "The Battle of Liberty Place."

Oscar Chopin survived and remained loyal to the lost cause. By early 1877 he was a private in Company A of the Ogden Guards in the Crescent City White League, but evidently took no part in any more public activity.

[Whether Kate Chopin shared Oscar's political opinions cannot be known: her sons said she disapproved of slavery. In her later stories, the mature Kate Chopin wrote sympathetically about African American women, especially those with strong motherly feelings, in "La Belle Zoraïde," "Beyond the Bayou," "Tante Cat'rinette," and other stories. She also wrote several stories (including *At Fault*, "In and Out of Old Natchitoches," and "Ti Démon") in which hot-headed young men bring sundry and terrible troubles upon themselves.

Kate Chopin herself was motherless for the first time in New Orleans. Oscar's orphaned nine-year-old sister, Marie, stayed with the Chopins, but we know virtually nothing about any other women friends. A Mrs. L. Tyler was interviewed by Rankin, and a Mrs. Tritle by Seyersted—but they could not take the place of Chopin's St. Louis circle, which included her mother and grandmother, her aunts and cousins and relatives, and Sacred Heart nuns and classmates. Her mother came to visit for the birth of the first child, and Chopin also spent months at a time visiting in St. Louis: in some ways she never fully lived in New Orleans. She never, for instance, joined the Children of Mary Sodality in New Orleans, although Sacred Heart honors graduates were expected to do so.

Between household duties, the young Mrs. Chopin no doubt thought about love and loneliness and varying destinies for women. Her best friend, Kitty Garesché, was now a Sacred Heart nun.

The Chopins kept two live-in servants, a cook and a laundress, in their New Orleans homes at 443 Magazine Street, on the northeast corner of Pitt and Constantinople, and finally at 1413 Louisiana Avenue. (Only the last home still exists, and is privately owned.) The Chopins never lived in the French Quarter, and in fact, each of their moves took them farther away from the French part of town.

Kate and Oscar were often apart for long stretches. After the birth of their first child, Oscar spent several months in France settling his late father's estate. (Oscar's hotel bills showed that he liked treats: he ordered cigars, oranges, and chocolate.) Kate often spent summers either with her mother in St. Louis (where her brother died in 1874), or with the children on Grand Isle, then becoming a popular Creole resort. New Orleans was an unhealthy city in the summer, full of cholera and yellow fever, while Grand Isle was a tropical paradise of water and birds and flowers—much as it is described in *The Awakening*.

For Kate and Oscar Chopin, living apart was also the most effective form of birth control.

But by the late 1870s, the cotton crop had been poor for several years. Oscar Chopin's business failed, and he, Kate, and the children moved to his family land in Cloutierville ("Cloochyville"), a French-speaking village in Natchitoches "*Nack*-i-tosh") Parish, in northwest Louisiana. (Louisiana has parishes instead of counties.)

Living in a big white house toward the end of Cloutierville's one dusty street, Kate Chopin presumably kept diaries and letters, and there are bills and receipts in her handwriting. She also read new scientific books and was interested in the ideas of Charles Darwin, Thomas Huxley, and Herbert Spencer. But thanks to her big city ways, cigarette smoking, flamboyant fashions, and tendency to flirt with other women's husbands, Kate Chopin was a Cloutierville scandal.

Unfortunately for the researcher, no truly private papers survive from those years, and we know about her activities only through oral histories and legal documents. She and Oscar evidently spent more and more time apart. She would go to St. Louis; he would go to Hot Springs to recover his health. In the fall of 1882, he was taken with "swamp fever," which seems to have been misdiagnosed by the village doctors. On December 10, 1882, racked by malaria, Oscar Chopin died.

The widowed Kate Chopin was left with six young children, ranging in age from eleven to just under three. She inherited $12,000 in debts from Oscar's general store and his failure to pay taxes on New Orleans property. And she was immediately offered help and comfort by Albert Sampite (pronounced "SAM-pi-tay"), a handsome Cloutierville planter—married—who liked to console widows and was famous for pursuing other women.

He did help with her financial affairs: a century later, some of her bills turned up in his records. Kate Chopin and Albert Sampite were also romantically linked, although what they actually "did" cannot be determined. His wife often said that Kate Chopin had broken up her marriage, while Chopin, for her part, later wrote a short story about a disagreeable, ugly female character and named it after Albert Sampite's wife ("Loka"). Sampite himself is mentioned in "Loka," the name spelled "Sambite."

He also partially inspired the Chopin characters named Alcée in *The Awakening*, "At the 'Cadian Ball" and "The Storm." Chopin's Alcées are always earthy and sensual, and their name is a clue to their origins: "Al. S——é," an abbreviated form of Albert Sampite's name, is pronounced "al-say," the same as "Alcée." (Chopin's character Calixta in "At the 'Cadian Ball" and "The Storm" also closely resembles Maria Normand DeLouche, the Cloutierville woman who took up with Albert Sampite after Kate Chopin's departure.)

The Chopin-Sampite romance was a scandal without a future. Divorce, then remarriage was not possible, and Albert was a dangerously violent man. As court records show, he frequently beat his wife with a leather strap—once so badly that she could not work for a year. Meanwhile Kate's mother, like the loving mother in the Chopin story "Désirée's Baby," urged her to come home, to St. Louis—where there were also better schools for her children. Like Edna in the last part of *The Awakening*, Kate Chopin left a lover to be with a mother-woman. By the middle of 1884, Kate Chopin was a handsome widow of thirty-four, living with her children and her mother in St. Louis.

But Chopin never fully left Louisiana. She returned numerous times for visits: it was an easy trip by boat or train from St. Louis. The dates of her visits suggest that she could easily have seen Albert Sampite. (After several attempts, his wife was finally granted a legal separation in 1891.) Kate Chopin did not finally sell her Cloutierville house until 1898, fourteen years after moving away.

Louisiana always lingered in her mind. She began her writing career in the late 1880s with the short story "Euphrasie" (later called "A No-Account Creole"), set in Louisiana, and eventually she created an entire fictional world around the Cane River country of Natchitoches Parish. She loved Louisiana as a place of languor and lust, food and festivities, drama and delight, music and madness—yet none of the private writings from her fourteen years in New Orleans and Natchitoches Parish survive.

All we know is that once she began writing in St. Louis, Kate Chopin wrote as a mature woman who had studied life's possibilities and knew women and men, passion and pride. She could have chosen a life of love and scandal—but instead chose ambition.

By the time she returned to St. Louis, Kate Chopin had been an honor student, a debutante, a bride, a wife, a mother, a widow, and a scandalous woman.

It was time to choose her own identity. In St. Louis, just a little before she turned forty, Kate Chopin became a professional author.

1885–1904

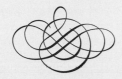

Kate Chopin

When Kate Chopin moved back to St. Louis in 1884, she was a daughter returning to the family nest. The home at 1122 St. Ange Avenue was a grown-up version of the world of her childhood—a houseful of widows and children. Kate and her five sons and a daughter rejoined her mother, Eliza O'Flaherty; her mother's sister Amanda McAllister; and Amanda's grown children Nina and Andrew.

But their ménage lasted for barely a year. When Eliza O'Flaherty died of cancer in June, 1885, she left her thirty-five-year-old daughter Kate "literally prostrate with grief."

Within a few months, however, Kate Chopin took a decisive step. She paid $18,000, a significant sum, for a new two-story house at 3317 Morgan Street (now Delmar). The house was built in the Lafayette Square (Federal) style, with limestone facing and a low mansard roof—but most important, it was her own. From there, she set about creating a new life for herself.

Dr. Frederick Kolbenheyer, a family friend and obstetrician, provided the crucial spark. A writer himself and an associate of Joseph Pulitzer, editor of the *Post-Dispatch*, Kolbenheyer had read the lively letters Kate Chopin sent home from Louisiana. Now he recognized a talent that could be put to use. Why not try writing for publication?

Chopin soon found herself a literary role model in Guy de Maupassant, the great French author who was exactly her age. (He was already going insane from syphilis, and would die in 1893.) Maupassant had been an early success with his pointed, amoral stories of women and men, divorce, suicide, and madness. When Chopin discovered him in the early 1890s, she found an author who told stories the way she wanted to: without creaking, old-fashioned machinery, and with a clear-eyed and unsentimental focus on reality.

Three years after her mother's death, Kate Chopin became a published author. Her first work was a piano polka named for her daughter, "Lilia" (1888); the second was a love poem, "If It Might Be" (1889). In mid-1889 her short stories began seeing print, the first one in the *Philadelphia Musical Journal* ("Wiser Than a God"). A year later she published her first novel, *At Fault*, in which she contrasted St. Louis and Louisiana—to St. Louis's detriment.

By 1891, Kate Chopin's byline was appearing in national magazines. Over a period of a dozen years, she published two novels, wrote nearly a hundred short stories, and produced poems, essays, translations, and even one play (never produced).

For most of those years Chopin wrote prolifically—until critical disapproval of *The Awakening* (1899), poor health, and family concerns slowed her down. Still, she was one of the first St. Louisans to get a telephone: in 1902 her phone number was Lindell 1594M. Her last address was 4232 McPherson, in the city's West End. (The McPherson house, now a private home with an exquisite Victorian staircase, is the only Chopin residence still extant in St. Louis. It has national landmark status.)

When Kate Chopin died of a cerebral hemorrhage in her home on August 22, 1904, two days after visiting the St. Louis World's Fair, she was on her way to being considered a minor local color writer and a bit of a has-been. Yet for a little more than a decade, Chopin had been a nationally acclaimed writer, and the private writings surviving from her last twenty years give tantalizing glimpses of her life in St. Louis.

By the early 1890s, Kate Chopin was the hostess of a literary salon, and her "Thursdays" were the place to be for authors, artists, and visiting creative people. Her writer friends and regular visitors included Sue V. Moore, editor of *St. Louis Life*; Dr. Kolbenheyer, an Austrian-born anarchist and freethinker who enjoyed expressing outrageous opinions; Charles Deyo, an ethereal and self-important *Post-Dispatch* journalist; and George Johns, a *Post-Dispatch* reviewer, married, who admired Kate Chopin enormously.

Other Chopin friends, admirers, and habitués of her salon included William Marion Reedy, the raffish editor of the *St. Louis Mirror* (later called "Reedy's Mirror"); Carrie Blackman, an enigmatic painter who may have inspired the Chopin story "Her Letters"; Florence Hayward, a humorous feature writer who sneaked cigarettes with Kate Chopin and resembled "Fedora" in the story of that name; and William Schuyler, a schoolteacher, novelist, and composer who set several Chopin poems to music. Together, Chopin's salon friends formed what her son Felix later called "a liberal, almost pink-red group of intellectuals, people who believed in intellectual freedom and often expressed their independence by wearing eccentric clothing."

Kate Chopin herself was something of an enigma, a mysterious and fascinating woman whose manner, according to one friend, was "extremely quiet, and one realizes only afterward how many good and witty things she has said in the course of the conversation."

Chopin also belonged to women's groups. She joined the St. Louis Children of Mary Sodality, and was a charter member of the prestigious Wednesday Club, founded by the biographer, poet, and social reformer Charlotte Stearns Eliot (now best known as the mother of T. S. Eliot). Chopin left the Wednesday Club when it became more structured, but the club remained loyal to her. In late 1899, after *The Awakening* had been condemned by most male reviewers, the Wednesday Club invited Chopin to give a reading, and over 300 women turned out to applaud and praise her.

Meanwhile, Chopin took country excursions with women's groups and always belonged to at least one card-playing club: she called herself "something of a euchre fiend" (see diary entry for May 28, 1894, pp. 183–85). Still, she could not resist making fun of women's clubs in several stories, notably *At Fault* and "Miss McEnders." With women as with men, she was an amused and curious observer.

In her 1894 diary, reprinted here, Chopin wrote judicious, rarely sentimental, comments about people she knew, including her salon friends, a neighbor who yearned to be an author, and various "philistines" who claimed to appreciate Chopin's writing (but lacked the wit). Sometimes she berated herself for her "commercial instinct"—but in fact she was never able to earn a living from her writings. She supported herself and her children with income from real estate in Louisiana and St. Louis.

Kate Chopin's surviving writings, public and private, show a woman with humor and an appreciation for gossip. But she was also a highly disciplined, ambitious writer whose aims sometimes conflicted with expectations for women, and especially for mothers. In real life, she seems to have embodied the contradiction she describes in chapter VII of *The Awakening*: "the dual life—that outward existence which conforms, the inward life which questions."

Kate Chopin claimed, for instance, to be a spontaneous writer who rarely revised. But those manuscripts which survive in more than one draft (notably "Charlie") show that she did indeed revise, change, and rework. Further, like so many women of her era and ours, she presented herself as first and foremost concerned with family and home and not serious about her career. She wrote her stories, she declared in an 1899 essay, only if sewing or polishing a table leg did not attract her attention first. She always described herself as more involved with her children than with her writing.

But by the late 1890s, Chopin's children were already in their twenties and occupied with their own friends, and they had no need to swarm about her. Her daughter later insisted that Chopin would never shut herself off from the family—but in fact she kept her own writing room, furnished with bookcases, a comfortable Morris chair, and a very naked Venus on the bookshelf. Kate Chopin obviously knew the art of contriving one's public image. Or perhaps those who wrote about her knew that the public would take more kindly to a woman who seemingly was a mother first, and an artist only in her spare time.

Her children did indeed adore her, and she never pushed them to get jobs or leave home. Only one, her eldest son Jean, married before her death, and he was already thirty-one. After his wife's death, he moved back with his mother.

The most accurate picture of Kate Chopin's 1890s may be in the private writings she left behind, those reprinted here. Her manuscript account books show that she was a thorough professional who diligently recorded the dates, word counts, and magazine submissions for each of her short stories. Yet she also rebelled against being thoroughly systematic. The long, tall account book (which we are calling the Bonnell Manuscript Account Book) begins with a record of Chopin's 1899 poems, yet later pages list stories from 1888 on. In the square, smaller account book (which we are calling the Wondra Manuscript Account Book) Chopin skips pages, scrawls entries over each other, and generally resists being linear and orderly.

Her poems, too, exist in various versions, some scrawled on the backs of others. Since very few were published, it is impossible to know which—if any—she considered the final copies.

The final copies of other works, such as her translations from Guy de Maupassant, are written carefully, in a clear and definite hand. But the drafts, especially the pencil version of "Father Amable," are virtually unreadable. (Thomas Bonner somehow deciphered them for his edition in *The Kate Chopin Companion*, for which all Chopin scholars are grateful.) Chopin did employ a typist named in the account books, a Miss Keleher, and presumably gave her the "final" ink drafts to copy.

In some cases, however, we have no idea what Kate Chopin planned, for she did have false starts. The recently recovered fragments called "Doralise" and "Melancholy" in this volume do not resemble any of her known works, and they do not seem to be listed in her notebooks. Possibly she started, then abandoned them.

She also seems to have abandoned, fairly early in her career, the practice of responding to her critics. When reviewers in the *St. Louis Republic* and *Natchitoches Enterprise* misconstrued her first novel *At Fault*, she wrote blistering retorts (reprinted in this volume, p. 201–202). But when, nine years later, *The Awakening* was savagely reviewed in many papers across the country, she deigned to answer her critics only once, in the *Book News* "Statement on *The Awakening*," reprinted here (p. 296).

The fierce 1890s condemnation of *The Awakening* was, of course, one of the major reasons it was revived some seventy years later. After Per Seyersted's Chopin biography appeared in 1969, calling her "A Daring Writer Banned," rebellious readers raced to find the forbidden book—which is now securely in the American literary canon.

But *The Awakening* was not, in fact, ever banned. Nor, contrary to legend, was Chopin ever denied membership in any literary societies. Nor was she widely shunned in St. Louis. The Wednesday Club hosted her reading, and she received fan letters and warm congratulations from women, and some favorable notices. Copies of *The Awakening* were taken from St. Louis library shelves only years later—after they were worn out.

By the early 1900s, though, Kate Chopin's literary career was waning. Her third short-story collection, *A Vocation and a Voice*, had been cancelled by the contracted publisher, and her health was failing. "Charlie," a long short story, went through many drafts (including at least one called "Jacques") before Chopin deemed it fit to send out—but no one wanted to publish it. In 1903 Chopin moved to the smaller, rented house on McPherson, close to the home of her son Jean and his wife, who was expecting her first child. But when Jean's wife and child died in childbirth, Jean suffered a nervous breakdown. Other Chopin relatives and friends were also struggling with serious, even terminal illnesses.

And so motherhood and family responsibilities did finally take precedence with Kate Chopin, although obituaries reported that she had another story collection ready for publication. That may have been *A Vocation and a Voice*—which was not actually published until 1991, eighty-seven years after her death.

Then, in 1992, there was a remarkable find.

In Worcester, Massachusetts, Linda and Robert Marhefka had purchased, as an investment, an old warehouse building on 3 Chestnut Street. Formerly the Worcester Moving and Storage Company, it was slated to be torn down for a high-rise. But when that fell through, the building was turned into a self-storage facility. It fell to the Marhefkas to clean out the old, abandoned contents stored there for generations.

One locker was full of "literary stuff," according to Linda Marhefka: fragile manuscripts written in pencil on newsprint. She thought they might be important, especially since the cache included a 1932 letter from Professor Arthur Hobson Quinn of the University of Pennsylvania to one Father Daniel Rankin, praising Rankin's *Life of Kate Chopin*. (Quinn, who later in his letter declared that "Readers are stupid!" evidently meant Rankin's *Kate Chopin and Her Creole Stories*.)

Linda Marhefka, who had never heard of Kate Chopin and was well aware that sixty years had passed, nevertheless contacted the University of Pennsylvania. There Daniel Traister, the Penn Library's Curator of Special Collections, leaped to tell her that yes, Kate Chopin's papers would be extremely valuable. Trying to avoid any more damage, Marhefka carefully wrapped and

mailed the crumbling papers to Traister (who later admitted to a brief temptation to keep them: they'd be a *coup* for his library). But Traister did what a
librarian must, and forwarded the unopened package to the Missouri Historical Society, repository for Chopin's other manuscripts. The Rankin-Marhefka
papers have since been photocopied, and can now be read at the Society's
library in St. Louis. The originals are safely kept in a vault.

Meanwhile, Peter Michel of the Missouri Historical Society was piecing
together the story of Father Rankin's questionable conduct. A Marist priest,
Rankin had written the first Chopin biography, *Kate Chopin and Her Creole
Stories*, as his doctoral dissertation at the University of Pennsylvania. It was
published under the university imprint in 1932.

But while he was doing that research, Rankin—a red-haired fellow in his
mid-thirties who resembled the entertainer Arthur Godfrey—had taken some
liberties for a biographer. He'd moved in, possibly unasked, with some of
Chopin's descendants in St. Louis. He said he'd stay for just a week, but
Chopin's grandson George later remembered it as three weeks—or maybe
more. Rankin even induced the family to chauffeur him about town.

During that very hot summer of 1929, Rankin also wheedled Lélia
Hattersley, Chopin's daughter, into lending him her mother's manuscripts. In
a 1961 letter to Per Seyersted, Rankin said he'd received the manuscripts in
old, rat-gnawed cardboard boxes and suitcases that had been carelessly stowed
in an attic. (Rankin also wrote that some of the family members were quite
eccentric, especially Chopin's son Felix: he reportedly stole Rankin's thesis
from the library in order to commune better with his late mother.)

In any case, Rankin never returned the manuscripts, although he lived
another forty years. He had placed all of them, he claimed, "on loan" at the
University of Pennsylvania library—an arbitrary and unilateral decision that
the Chopin children vigorously disputed. It took eight years (1947–1955) for
that library to track down the elusive Rankin and get his permission to transfer the materials to the Missouri Historical Society.

Father Rankin evidently told no one at Penn or the Missouri Historical
Society about the other manuscripts he'd stashed in the locker in Worcester,
Massachusetts.

Even in the 1930s, Chopin's descendants had not been pleased with his
biography. Her daughter Lélia called it "a milquetoast," a whitewash, and
referred to Rankin as "that horrible man" (others called him "a fat liar").
Although he wrote in a lively, energetic style, he was careless with dates and
facts, and did not consult people still alive who had known Kate Chopin and
could have contributed insights and details. (For her Cloutierville years, in
particular, virtually his only source was Kate Chopin's young sister-in-law
Fannie Hertzog Chopin, who had been a child when the Chopins were her
neighbors—and by the time Rankin interviewed her, she had become somewhat senile.) Moreover, Rankin was vague if not slippery with sources: his

book is only lightly footnoted, and there is no telling what other materials he may have lost or squirrelled away.

In what we are calling the Rankin-Marhefka Fragments, drafts of later-revised or published material include "Charlie," "Alexandre's Wonderful Experience," "The Gentleman from New Orleans," "A Little Country Girl," "A Vocation and a Voice" (here called "The Boy") and the fragment we are calling "Misty." There are also two thoroughly unknown works, which we are calling "Doralise" and "Melancholy." The handwriting in the Rankin-Marhefka Fragments is extremely difficult to read, and the renderings here represent months of often tedious work by a group of Louisiana State University graduate students (they are listed with the transcriptions).

They, and we, think it unlikely that anyone else will want to do that work again.

We cannot know, of course, what other kinds of writing Kate Chopin also attempted. Her now-famous "The Storm," for instance, may be only one of many very racy, and thoroughly unpublishable, pieces of erotica.

Kate Chopin was not easy to know, for while she liked social life—including "al fresco suppers in the summertime" with close friends—she was often truly "a lone wolf." Although she evidently enjoyed motherhood and the opportunity to encourage and mold youngsters, she also had the writer's need to be alone, to observe, and to think. (The word "alone," after all, appears in positive contexts throughout *The Awakening*.)

Future readers may have much more to say about what Kate Chopin's private papers from the last years of her life reveal. We look forward to their insights.

MANUSCRIPT ACCOUNT BOOKS

Kate Chopin's two surviving manuscript account books show two sides of the author: the brisk businesswoman, meticulously noting her output and earnings; and the artistic author, impatient with the drudgery of recording articles submitted, rejected, and accepted.

The brisk businesswoman seems most evident in the long, thin (5½" x 11½") brown, gold-bordered, leather-covered account book embossed with the name "KATE CHOPIN," here called the Bonnell Manuscript Account Book, since Cheyenne Bonnell transcribed it. The Bonnell Book is currently in fair condition: the pages, probably originally cream or white with red vertical lines, are now brownish; some pages are slightly torn. Only about a third of the notebook is used. Kate Chopin made her notations in black ink, which has sometimes faded to brown.

In this notebook Chopin recorded some submissions of stories, but most entries trace her output and earnings: stories written, number of words, monies earned. At the end of the book, evidently for reference, she included records of the real estate properties that supported her and her children.

Chopin's other account book, in which she noted most of her story submissions, is much more casual. The Wondra Manuscript Account Book (named for its transcriber, Janet Wondra) also has a brown leather cover with gold border and the name "KATE CHOPIN" embossed in capitals. It is in good condition, white- or cream-colored pages only slightly browned; the black ink, on lined pages, has sometimes faded to brown.

The account book itself is a squarish (8" x 7") mass-produced school notebook, called (on the inside) Patterson's Complete Composition Book, published by Potter, Ainsworth & Co. The notebook apparently once belonged to the author's eldest son, Jean Baptiste: the name "J. B. Chopin" is twice crossed out on the first page and replaced with "Kate Chopin," in the author's handwriting. (Whether Jean objected to his mother's commandeering his notebook cannot be known.)

The Wondra Book is sometimes almost slapdash: Chopin's handwriting varies from entry to entry, as do her abbreviations for months and magazines. She seems to have jotted down information quickly and informally, rather than precisely, and sometimes she is incorrect. For instance, she lists "A Study in Heads," "The Revival of Wrestling," and "Cut Paper Figures" (a translation also called "How to Make Manikins") for 1892, but they were actually sold and published in 1891. (The articles are reprinted in this volume).

In the Wondra Book, Chopin's handwriting varies in size, and she sometimes crosses out items or writes words across pages at a slant. The word "Published," listed at the end of many entries, is actually written in a diagonal across the pages where it appears.

Chopin's handwriting is generally legible, but more so in the Bonnell Book, where she kept records more carefully.

For ease in reading, the transcriptions here have simplified Chopin's idiosyncrasies. The lengths of her dashes, which vary greatly, have been standardized, as have her abbreviations for months. Her ditto marks have mostly been replaced with words, and a few obvious misspellings have been silently corrected. In a few cases, the items in entries have been slightly rearranged for readability. The many squiggles and doodles and mysterious numbers have not been reproduced, since they are probably the work of her grandchildren. Occasionally they seem to be scorekeeping for a game.

Both manuscript account books are housed at the Missouri Historical Society in St. Louis, and those who want to analyze Chopin's handwriting, spacing, and other orthographic features should consult the originals. A textually correct transcript of the Wondra Book, with all idiosyncrasies reproduced, is also available from Janet Wondra, assistant editor of the *Georgia Review*.

In the transcriptions below, the Bonnell Book appears first, followed by the Wondra Book.

[The Bonnell Manuscript Account Book]

VERSES

To Century   Jan. 6 — '99

Old Nat — R.
By the Mead. Gate — R.
Abide with me — Accepted
An Hour — R.
The New Year — R.
A Document in Madness — R.

The Roses — R.
Ome - Omy — R.
The Rubaiyat — R.   Feb. 6 — '99

TYPICAL GERMAN COMPOSERS

To Atlantic —   Jan. 10, '99
  R —   Jan. 17 —
  ~~To Century~~   ~~Jan. 17~~

~~Ti Fre~~
A VOCATION & A VOICE
COLLECTION

To Atlantic   Nov. 24 '96
  R —   Jan. 2 '97
To Bodley Head —   Jan. 5 '97
  R —
To F. Tennyson Neely   Mar. 14 '97
  R —   Apr. '97
To Way & Williams   — '98
  Accepted —
Transferred to H. S. Stone   —   Nov. '98
  R —   Feb. 1900

1888

                                                     $ cts
July- "If it might be" (poem) America —   2.50

1889

Oct.- A Point at Issue—P. Dis.—   16.00
Dec.- Wiser than a God—Musical J—   5.00

1891

Jan.— At Fault—(Novel)   11.60
     At Fault   5.00

Mar.—	At Fault	30.00
"	A Red Velvet Coat (Companion)	15.00
"	A Study in Heds-Trans. (Post Dis	6.00
	Wrestling-Trans. (Post Dis	8.00
Apr.	Manikins-Trans. (Post Dis	5.00
"	For Marse Chouchoute (Companion)	35.00
June	At Fault	2.00
"	A Wizard from Gettysburg (Comp)	35.00
Aug.—	A No-Account Creole (Century)	100.00
"	A Rude Awakening (Companion)	40.00
Nov.	A Very Fine Fiddle (Young Peo)	5.00
"	Boulot & Boulotte	5.00
Dec.-	Beyond the Bayou (Comp)	30.00

1892

Jan.-	Love on the Bon Dieu (Two Tales)	40.00
"	After the Winter (Comp)	50.00
"	The Benitous Slave (Young P)	7.00
"	A Turkey Hunt (Young P)	7.00
"	Old Aunt Peggy (Young P)	3.00
May	Loka (Comp)	40.00
July-	At Fault	2.40
"	At Fault	1.60
Aug.	Mons Pierre Trans. (P.Dis)	5.00
"	At the Cadian Ball- (Two Tales)	40.00
Oct.	The Maid of St. Phillippe—(Short	
	Stories)	10.00
Nov.-	A Visit to Avoyelles- (Vogue)	15.00
Dec.-	Desiree's Baby- (Vogue)	25.00
" -	The Christ Light (Syn)	6.00

608.10

1892-CON

$ cts

608.10

Dec.-	The Return of Alcibiade (Life)	15.00

1893

March	Mamouche (Companion)	40.00
Apr	In & Out of Old Natchitoches (Two Tales)	50.00
"	Caline (Vogue)	9.00
"	The Lilies (Wide Awake)	10.00
May	A Shameful Affair (Times-Dem)	5.00
"	Mrs. Mobry's Reason (Times-Dem)	5.00
July	A Matter of Prejudice (Comp)	25.00
Aug.-	Ripe Figs (Vogue)	3.00
Sept.	Dr Chevalier's Lie (Vogue)	4.00
"	A Lady of Bayou St. John (Vogue)	15.00
Nov.-	La Belle Zoraïde (Vogue)	23.00

1894

Jan.-	Ma'ame Pelagie (Times-Dem)	5.00
Feb.-	Azélie (Century)	50.00
" -	A Respectable Woman (Vogue)	15.00
Aug.-	Good By (poem) (Times-Dem)	2.50
Sept.-	Tante Cat'rinette (Atlantic)	40.00
Nov.-	Regret (Century)	30.00
"	Ozeme's Holiday (Century)	45.00

1895

Jan.-	Tonie (Times-Dem)	5.00
"	Dream of an Hour Vogue	10.00
"	The Kiss Vogue	10.00
Feb.	Reprint Am Press-Bayu F-	21.10
"	A Dresden Lady in Dixie (House J)	60.00
Mar.	Her Letters Vogue	25.00
Apr.	Polydore (Comp)	35.00
"	Cavanelle (Am. Jewess)	10.00
Aug.	Bayou Folk (Collection)	1.75
Oct.	The Unexpected (Vogue)	10.00

1896

Jan.-	A Sentimental Soul Times Dem	10.00

Feb.	Mme Martel's Chris Eve - Comp	50.00
		1247.45

1896 (CON)

Feb.	Bayou Folk		6.37
May	After the Winter	Times Dem	5.00
"	The Recovery	(Vogue)	10.00
July	Athenaïse-Part I	(Atlantic)	75.00
Aug.	Aunt Lympy's Interference (Comp)		50.00
"	Athenaïse Part II	(Atlantic)	80.00
"	Bayou Folk		2.25

1897

Jan.-	Lilacs	(Times Dem)	10.00
Feb.-	Dead Men's Shoes	(Independent)	20.00
"	As You Like It	Criterion	5.00
"	Fedora	Criterion	5.00
Mar.	As You Like It	Criterion	5.00
"	Bayou Folk - Aug. - 137		4.50
"	Miss McEnders	(Criterion)	10.00
"	Ti Frère	(Companion)	65.00
"	As You Like It		5.00
July	Nég Créol	(Atlantic)	30.00
"	Easter Story	(Criterion)	13.00
"	The Blind Man	(Vogue)	5.00
"	A Pair of Silk Stockings	(Vogue)	5.00

1898

Jan.-	A Family Affair	Am. Press. Ass.	78.00
Feb.-	Reading at St George's Guild		25.00
Mar.-	Bayou Folk - 350 Aug.		4.88
Sept.-	Bayou Folk		3.50
June -	Translation - Republic		4.00
	Suzette		10.00

1899

Jan.	Contributors Club Atlantic	10.00
	A night in A - Stone -	3.25
	Abide with me (Poem) Century _ _	5.00
	Bayou F - H & M ____	3.12
	A Little Country Girl - (Companion)	50.00
		1843.45
		3.80
		1848.32

		1848.32
	A Family Affair/additional	5.00
	A Reading at Wed. Club	15.00
Dec. -	Royalties on The Awakening	102.00

1900

comp

Feb. 18 -	Alexandre's Wonderful Experience	50.00
Mar. -	Bayou Folk	3.25
" -	One Day in Winter - Companion	10.00
" -	The Gentleman from New Orleans	40.00
Apr-	An Egyptian Cigarette	6.25
May -	The White Eagle	4.55
June -	Royalties Awkning - Nght in A-	35.00
Sept. -	Royalties Bayou F-	1.37
Dec.	Awakening & Night in A	10.15
"	Republic article —	12.00

1901

Feb. -	Bayou Folk	2.13
Aug. -	Bayou Folk	2.50
Dec. -	Stone & Co	3.69
" -	The Wood Choppers (Compn)	40.00
"	Millie's First Party —	30.00

1902

Jan.	The God Mother - (Mirror)	30.00
Feb. -	Polly's Opportunity - Companion	35.00

"   Bayou Folk   3.35
Mar. - A Vocation and a Voice (Mirror)   40.00

A MENTAL SUGGESTION

Scribners	Dec. 19 '96
R—	Jan. 7 '97
Vogue Jan. 7	
R—	Feb. '97
McClure	Feb. 23
R—	Mar.
Cosmopolitan	Mar.
R—	Mar.
To Lippincott	Apr. 19
R—	Apr.
To Black Cat	Mar. '98
R—	
To Sat Eve. Post	Feb. 14 1900
R—	Feb. 22 1900

THE LOCKET

To Companion	Mar. 19 '97
R—	
To Century	Apr 12
R—	Apr.
To Polyglot	Apr.
R—	
To Times-Dem	Dec. 8
R—— (Too Late)	
To Amer. Press Ass. —	Jan. '98
R—	Jan.
To Independent	Apr. '98
R—	Apr.
To Chap Book	
R—	
To RepAug. 5	
R—	
To Sat Ev. Post —	Dec. 1
R—	Dec. 15

AN EGYPTIAN CIGARETTE

To Lotus — (never arrived)	
To Chap Book —	Apr. '98
R—	

To Rep —	Aug. 5 '98
R —	
To Criterion	Jan. 6 '99
R —	
~~To Vogue~~	~~Mar. 6 '99~~
To Vogue	Feb. 14 1900
Accepted	Apr. 1900

ELIZABETH STOCK'S ONE STORY

To Century____	Mar. 22 '98
R —	Apr. '98
To Atlantic	Apr. '98
R —	Apr. '98
To Harpers	Aug. 5, '98
R —	
To Scribner's	Jan. 11, '99
R —	Feb. '99

HORSE STORY

<u>CHANGE TITLE</u>

~~**TI DÉMON**~~

To Century	Mar. 31 '98
R —	
To Companion	Apr. '98
R —	
To Atlantic	Aug. 5, '98
R —	
To Cosmopolitan	Jan. 11, '99
R —	
To Sat Eve Post	
R —	

NIGHT (TRANS)

To Times Dem	Apr 15 '98
R —	May '98
To Rep	Aug. 5, '98
R —	

THE AWAKENING —

A Solitary Soul (novel)

To Way & Williams —	Jan. 21 '98
Accepted	

Transferred to H. S. Stone —   Nov. '98
Accepted —   Jan. 1899

VAGABONDS -

To Chap Book   Dec. '95
  R —
To Vogue   Dec. '95
  R —   Dec. '95
To Short Stories   Jan. '96
  R —   Apr. '96
To Philistine   May 6, '96
  R —   July, '96
To Wayside Press   —   Jan. 5, '97
  Accepted
  R — Suspended —
To Times-Dem   —   Apr '98
  R —   Apr. '98
To Rep   Aug. 5 '98
  R —
To Times Herald   Jan. 11, '99
  R —   Feb. '99

$10 —

ONE DAY IN WINTER
A WINTER DAY IN DIXIE —
A REFLECTION

To Times - Herald -   Jan. 17 '99
  R —   Feb. '99
To Companion   Feb. 15 - 19
  Accepted —   Mar. 8   19

                                        Feb. 6, '99

The Unwritten Law

To Century —   Feb. 6, '99
  R —   Mar. 3, '99
To Atlantic   Mar. 4, '99
To Cosmopolitan   May 18, '99

R —
To Saturday Ev Post —   Dec. —
R —
~~To Scribners —~~   ~~Feb. 15, 1900~~
To Scribners —   Sept. 11, 1900
"Godmother"
Mirror $35
  Accepted   Dec. 1901

2650 words   Feb. 11, '99

A LITTLE COUNTRY GIRL

To Companion —   Feb. 11 , '99
  Accepted —   Mar. 6th, '99
$50

TI DÉMON (2)   **99**

To Century —   Dec. 1
  R —   Dec. 28
To Atlantic —   Jan. 8, 19—
  R —   Jan. 19
To Scribner's —   Feb. 19
  R —   Mar. 19
To Boston Brown Book —   May 24
  R —   May

3302 words   Jan. 24, 19~~99~~
  $50

THE WONDERFUL EX- OF ALEXANDRE -

To Companion —   Jan. 24, 19
Accepted —   Feb. 18 , 19-

3000 $40.00   Feb. 8, 19—

THE GENTLEMAN FROM NEW ORLEANS

To Century   Feb. 9
  R —   Feb. 21
To Companion —   Feb. 21
  Accepted —   Mar. 12, 19—

15,000   Apr. 1900

CHARLIE

To Companion —   Apr. 24, 1900
   R —   May —
To Century   May — 18
   R —   May

900   4–55   May 9, 1900

THE WHITE EAGLE

To Vogue —   May 9 —
   Accepted —   May 21

TOOTS' NURSES —

To Companion —
   Returned —
To Mirror — Returned

1901   Oct. 16 - 17 - 18
                                              1901

Millie's First Ball ——   1663   wds
The Wood Choppers ——   1636   wds
~~Toots's Nurses~~   ~~1440   wds~~
To Youths Companion

OCT. 18, 1901

   Accepted — $30.00
   Accepted —   40.00

                                              Jan. 14 1902
2000
words
                                              $35

POLLY'S OPPORTUNITY

To Companion —   Jan. 14, 1902
   Accepted —   Feb. 8, 1902

1888

Euphrasie   30.000

1889

Unfinished Tale (Destroyed)	30.000
May — A Poor Girl (Destroyed)	7.000
June - Wiser Than a God - Musical Journal	2.500
Aug. - A Point at Issue — Post. Dis.	3.000
Nov. - Miss Witherwell's Mistake — Fashion & Fancy	4.000
Dec. - With The Violin — Spectator Pub	1.800

1890

At Fault Pub - self.	60.000
Young Dr Gosse (Destroyed)	50.000
A Red Velvet Coat— Comp.	1.800

1891

Pub

Jan. - Mrs Mobry's Reason - Times-Dem.	3.500
Feb. - A No Account Creole - Century - B. F.	10.000
Mar. - Roger and His Majesty (Destroyed)	900
" - For Marse Chouchoute - Companion B. F.	3.000
Apr - Liza Jane - Synd. Pub	2.300
" - The Maid of St. Phillippe - Short Stories	2.800
May - A Wizard From Gettysburg - Comp. B. F.	2.600
June - A Shameful Affair - Times Dem Pub	2.300
July - A Rude Awakening - Comp - B. F.	3.000
Sept. - A Harbinger - St Louis Mag Pub	400
" - A Very Fine Fiddle - Young People B. F.	500
" - Boulot & Boulotte - Young People B. F.	680
Oct. - Love on the Bon Dieu - Two Tales B. F.	4.600
—— An Embarrassing Situation - Mirror . Pub	4.000
Nov. - Beyond the Bayou - Companion - B. F.	300
Dec. - After the Winter - Times. Dem. N.I.A.	3.300

1892

Jan. - The Benitous Slave - Young People B. F.	700
" A Turkey Hunt Young People B. F.	700
" Old Aunt Peggy Young People B. F.	300
" Lilies Wide Awake N.I.A.	2.000
Feb. Mittens - (Destroyed)	700
" Ripe Figs - Vogue - N.I.A.	300
	241.150

1892

Feb. - Croque Mitaine	700
" A Little Free Mulatto	400
Mar. - Miss McEnders - *Criterion* - Pub	3.600
Apr - Loka - *Comp.* B. F.	2.600
May - Bambo Pellier -	13.000
July - At the Cadian Ball - Two Tales - B. F.	4.000
Aug. - A Visit to Avoyelles - Vogue - B. F.	1.500
Aug. - Ma'me Pelagie - Times Dem. B. F.	3.300
Nov. - Desirée's Baby - Vogue - B. F.	2.200
Dec. - Caline - Vogue N.I.A.	900
Dec. - The Return of Alcibiade - St. L. Life - B. F.	2.300

1893

Feb. - In And Out of Old Natchitoches - Two Tales -N.I.A.–5.000	
Feb. - Mamouche - Comp. - N.I.A.	2.800
May - Madame Celestin's Divorce - B. F.	1.300
June - An Idle Fellow	400
June - A Matter of Prejudice - Comp - N.I.A.	2.600
July - Azélie - Century - N.I.A.	3.680
July - La Belle Zoraïde - Vogue - N̶ B. F.	2.200
Aug. - A Lady of Bayou St. John - Vogue B. F.	1.700
Oct. - Chenière Caminada - Times D - N.I.A.	4.275
Nov. - A Gentleman of Bayou Teche. B. F.	2.400
Nov. In Sabine B. F.	3.400

1894

Jan. A Respectable Woman - Vogue. N.I.A.	1.500
Feb. - Tante Catrinette - Atlantic. N.I.A.	3.200
Mar. - A Dresden Lady In Dixie - Home Journal N.I.A.	3.000
Apr - Dream of An Hour. Vogue Pub	1.000
May A Lady of Shifting Intentions	1.600
May Lilacs - Times-Dem. Pub	4.820
July - Cavanelle - Am. Jewess. N.I.A.	2.500
July - Night - Juanita - Moods - Pub	1.000
Sept. - Regret - Century - N.I.A.	1.500
Sept. - The Kiss - Vogue Pub	1.000
	———————
	85.370

1894 -

Sept. Ozème's Holiday - Century - N.I.A.	2.800
Nov. A Sentimental Soul - Times Dem - N.I.A.	4.000
Nov. Her Letters - Vogue Pub	3.000

1895

Jan. - Odalie Misses Mass - Shreveport T. N.I.A.	1.870
Feb. - Polydore - Comp. N.I.A.	2.800
Feb. - Dead Men's Shoes - Independent - N.I.A.	3.000
Apr - Athénaïse - Atlantic - N.I.A.	13.760
July - Two Summers & Two Souls - Vogue. Pub	900
July - The Unexpected Vogue Pub	1.250
Aug. - Two Portraits	2.000
Nov. - Fedora - Criterion - Pub	1.000
Dec. - Vagabonds -	1.200

1896

Jan. - Madame Martels Christmas Eve - Comp.	3.000
Feb . - The Recovery - Vogue Pub	1.300
Mar. - A Night In Acadie - N.I.A.	6.860
Apr - A Pair of Silk Stockings Vogue	2.000
Apr.- Nég Créole - Atlantic N.I.A.	2.650
June - Aunt Lympy's Interference. Comp. Pub	3.000
July - The Blind Man - Vogue Pub	780
Sept. Confidences - Atlantic - Pub	2.000
Sept. - Ti Frère - Comp Returned (accepted)	3.600
Nov. A Vocation and a Voice Mirror Pub	13.000
Dec. A Mental Suggestion	4.000

1897

Feb. - Suzette - Vogue Pub	1.000
Mar. - The Locket	3.000
Apr - A Mornings Walk - Criterion Pub	1.350
Apr.- An Egyptian Cigarette Vogue Pub	1.200
The Awakening - Stone, tc.	30.000

1898

The Awakening	20.000

	136.420

1898

A Family Affair - Sat Eve. Post Pub	5.200
Elizabeths Stock's One Story	2.700
The Pony	3.000
The Storm	2.000

1899

Jan. ~~The Unwritten Law~~ The God Mother Mirror	10.000
Feb. - A Little Country Girl Comp comp	2.700
Ti Démon -	2.000

1900

One Day in Winter Comp	1.000
Jan. - Alexandre's Wonderful Experience Comp	3.300
Feb. - The Gentleman from New Orleans Comp	2.880
Apr. - "Charlie"	15.000
May - The White Eagle Vogue P.	1.000

1901

Oct. - The Wood Choppers Comp P.	2.000
Oct. - Millie's First Party Comp	2.000
Oct.- Toot's Nurses —	1.500

— 1902 —

Jan. - Pollys Opportunity com.	2.000

BUSINESS MEM -
1898 -

Feb. - Transferred business from Rutledge & Kilpatrick to John McMenany —

— $9500 - deeds of trust on following property:

Morgan St- Feb. 9 - 1897 - 3 years loan - (renewal) with R & K —	3–500
7th St - Mar. 1896 3 years loan with R & K	2–000
" " - May 1897 3 years loan with R & K	2–000

Gamble St — May 96 - 2 years loan

with McMenany   1–000

N. 3d St. - Feb. 1898 2 years loan
   with McMenamy   1–000

Cloutierville Plantation rented for '98
to Edmond deLacerda for $240.00

Oakland Plantation rented to Abraham Rachal for '98 for $300.00

7th St rented to W. S Parr - $900.00 - behind about $400 - has
   promised to make it good in the next few months.

2708 Gamble rented to - Biering — $20.00 per month

2710 - Gamble to - Sheridan — $20 per month

Atlantic -
Century -
Scribners -
Cosmopolitan -
Munseys -

23— IN BAYOU FOLK

Ready —

[The Wondra Manuscript Account Book]

~~J B Chopin~~

~~J. B. Chopin~~

~~S E~~

K. Chopin

EUPHASIE
1888—

abt 30,000 words
   Gave to Dr Kolbenheyer — April
Returned — June 1890
Started to Revise Jan. 24 — 1891 — (evolved A No-
                Account Creole)
Unfinished Story — Grand Isle —
30,000 words — 1888–89

FROM THE FRENCH OF GUY DE MAUPASSANT (MAD STORIES)

"A Divorce Case" — July 11, '94
"Mad" — Sept. 4 '94
"It" — Feb. '95
"Solitude" — March 5 '95
"Night" — March 8 '95
"Suicides" — Dec. 18 '95

1892   NOV. 24 — 1892
THE FATHER OF DÉSIRÉE'S BABY

2200 words
To Vogue — Nov. 26
Accepted — Dec. 11 — $25
Pub — Jan. 14, 1893
Published

SIX POEMS TO VOGUE — JUNE 9, '93

The Song Everlasting — You and I — A Message — If The Woods Could
talk — A Sentimental Serenade — It Matters All

R — 5 — Retained "It Matters All"
Song Everlasting
To Century — Aug. 6
R — Aug. 12

ODALIE MISSES MASS
Atlantic — Century —
To companion — March ~~25~~ 31 '92
R — April
To Shreveport Times by request — Pub July 1895

1889
A POOR GIRL
abt 7,000 words   May 1889
Returned
from Home Mag Dec. 1 — objection to incident not
desirath to be handled
remarks "well written full of interest" if changed, would
reconsider
Gave to John Dillon to read Dec. 11.
Sent to New York Ledger May 1890
Returned from New York Ledger June 5
destroyed

Sent In and out of Ol Nat— & In Sabine to American Press Ass for
reprint — Jan. 2 '95
Accepted — Jan. 12, '95
              $42.10

ODALIE MISSES MASS
1875 words   Jan. 28
To Atlantic — Jan. 31, '95
R — Feb. 15, '95
To Century Feb. 16
R — March 23
Pub

1892
POOR MA'AME PÉLAGIE
~~IN THE SHADOW OF THE RUIN~~
3300 words   Aug. 27/28, 1892
To Century Mag — Aug. 30—
R — Sept. 14
To Harpers — Sept. 15

R — Sept. 27
To Atlantic — Oct. 1
R — Oct. 8
To Scribners — Oct. 9
R — Nov. 2
To Vogue — March 9
Returned — March 20
To Times-Dem — March 21
Accepted — April 3 '93
Published — Dec. 24, 1893
Published

POLYDORE

2810 words   Feb. 17—95
To Companion — ~~Prize Contest~~
Feb. ~~18~~ 25 95
Accepted — March 28 —
$35

1889
"WISER THAN A GOD"

abt 2,500 words   June 1889
Sold to "Phil Musical Journal" — $5.00
Published Dec. 1889
Published

1892 CALINE

900 words   Dec. 2, '92
$9.00   To Vogue —   March 9, '93
Accepted   March 20
Published   May 20, '93
Published

A SENTIMENTAL SOUL — CON

Century —
To Atlantic — Jan. 23, '95
R — Feb. 9, '95
To Harper's   Feb. 15, '95
R — March 6
continued
Pub —

1892
THE LOVER OF MENTINE
A ~~THE VISIT~~ TO AVOYELLES

1300 ~~2000~~ words   Aug. 1, 1892
To Cosmopolitan — Aug. 2
R — Sept. 22
~~To Harpers Mag — Oct. 9~~
To Vogue — Oct. 22 '92
Accepted by Vogue — Nov. 4 — $15
Published — Jan. 14, '93
Published

1892
THE RETURN OF ALCIBIADE DEC. 5/6 1892

2300 words
St Louis Life — by request
Published — Dec. 15, '92
$15
Published

DEAD MEN'S SHOES

3000 words   Feb. 21/22 95
To Companion ~~Prize cnt.~~ Feb. 24
R — Jan. 2
To Century — Jan. 2
R — March 12

"A POINT AT ISSUE"

1889   abt 3,000 words
Aug. 1889
Sold to Post Dispatch — $16.00
Published Oct. 27, 1889
Published

1893

5000 words   In And Out of Old Natchitoches
Feb. 1/3, '93
To Two Tales — Feb. 6, '93
Accepted — April 8, '93
$50
Published April 8, '93
Published

SENTIMENTAL SOUL

Century — Atlantic — Harpers
Scribners — March 6, '95
R — March 31 '95
To McClure's Mag — June 18, '95
R — July 15, '95
To Times Dem — Dec. 4 '95
Accepted
Pub

1892
AT THE CADIAN BALL

July 15/17 1892   4000 words
To Two Tales — July 18, '92
Accepted by T. Tales — Aug. 28
Pub Oct. 1892 — $40
Published

~~A ROMANTIC ATTACHMENT~~ MAMOUCHE

2800 words   Feb. 24/25, 1893
To Youth's Companion — Feb. 27
Accepted — March 23
$40
Published April 19, 1894
Published

~~ODALIE MISSES MASS~~
~~To Atlantic Century~~

900 words   Two Summers & Two Loves — July 14 '95
To Vogue — July 15
Accepted
Published

1889
MISS WITHERWELLS MISTAKE

abt 4000 words   Nov. 1889
Sent to Harper's Dec. 16
Ret from Harper's Dec. 23
Sent to Scribners Dec. 28
Rt from Scribner's Jan. 18
Sent to Drakes Mag Jan. 20
Rt from Drakes Mag 30   Letter — too spun out — clever story —
— excellent character sketching —

Sent to ~~Scribe~~ Century   April 22
Returned from Century   May
Sent to Home Mag   July 4
Published in Jan. 189~~0~~1 Fashion and Fancy
Published

MADAME CELESTINE'S DIVORCE
1300 words   May 24/25 1893
1893 To Century — May 28
R — June 1
Placed in collection of Short Tales
Published

1892

BAMBO PELLIER
13,600 words   May 25 '92
To Youth's Companion Contest — May 25 '92
R — Nov. 4, 1892

FEDORA
1000 words   Nov. 19, '95
To Vanity   Nov. 25
R —

Collection Tales to Stone & Kimball Nov. 14

1889
"WITH THE VIOLIN."
"The Story That Papa Konrad Told on Chris. Eve"
abt 1500 words   Dec. 11, 1889
Sent to Youth's Companion Dec. 14
Ret from Youth's Companion Dec. 23
Sent to Harper's Dec. 24
Rt from Harper's Dec. 30
Sent to ~~Scribners~~aint Nicholes Jan. 2
Rt from Saint Nicholas 20 (written letter)
Sent to Wm Burnett's Youth Dep. Jan. 20
Rt from Wm Burnett's Youth Dep Jan. 27
"With The Violin" — Published in Spectator Dec. 6, 1889
Published

AN IDLE FELLOW

400 words   June 9 '93
To Vogue — June 9 '93
R — Aug. 6
To Century — Aug. 6
R — Aug. 6
To Short Stories — Aug. 17
R — Sept. 3 —
                    (continued)
To Romance — Sept. 25
R — ~~Sept.~~ Oct. 1, '93

1892
LOKA

2600 words   April 9/10, 1892
To Youth's Companion April 11, '92
Accepted May 14, '92 — $40
Dec. '92 Published
Published

A MATTER OF PREJUDICE

2600 words   June 17/18 1893
To Youth's Companion June 20
Accepted — July 13
$25
Pub 95

AN IDLE FELLOW (CONTINUED)

To Harper's Bazar — May 4, '94
R from Harper's Bazar — May 12, '94
To Times-Democrat — May 12 '94
R — Times-Democrat — May 28 '94
To Chap Book — Oct. 2 '94
R — Chap Book Oct. 26

1890
"MONSIEUR PIERRE"
~~The Sentinel~~ — (Translation)

abt 1300 words — April 1890
Sent to Post Dis April 29
Published — Aug. 8, 1892
Published

MÉLANIE-AMELITE AZÉLIE
POLYTE'S MISFORTUNE

3686 words   July 22/23 '93
To Century Mag July 25
Accepted — Sept. 9, '93
$50
Published Dec. 1, 1894
Published

OZÈME'S HOLIDAY

2800 words
To Century — Sept. 26, '94
Accepted — Oct. 28, '94

A SENTIMENTAL SOUL

4000 words   Nov. 18 — 22 '94
To Atlantic Century Nov. 24 —
R — Jan. 23, '95

---

106 copies at Fault in my possession
Sept. 27 — 1 To John A. Dillon — Ed P. Dispatch
           1 To Dr. Kolbenheyer
           2 To Mercantile Library
           1 To Books Lady at Crawfords
Sept. 29   1 To Ledlie — P.D. — 1 to Dr Scott — 1 Aunt H —
           1 To Aunt Amanda — Jones Rep — 1 Writer — Boston
Oct. 1   1 To Dinmock — Howells — AT — 1 McCullough —
Oct. 2   1 To St.L. Life — Fashion & Fancy —
Oct. 3   1 To Star Sayings — 1 Meysenburg Chicago —
Oct. 3   1 To N. O. Times Dem — N. O. Picayune —
Oct. 3   1 To N. O. L'Abeille-
Oct. 4   1 To Literary World Bos — Critic N.Y. —
Ocr 4   1 To Nation — 1 Miss Keleher —

ATHÉNAÏSE

April 10/28 '95   12,675 words
To Century — May 2, '95
R — May 19, '95
To Chap Book — May 21, '95
R — May 21, '95
To Atlantic — June 18
Accepted — July 15

1890
AT FAULT

Abt 60,000 — July 5 — Finished April 20, 1890
Gave Deyo to read ~~Apr~~ May 2
Gave Miss Keleher first 7 chapts to typewrite June 11
~~Aug.~~ July 29 Sent to Belford Chicago —
Aug. 5 Returned from Belford —
Aug. 19 Gave to Nixon & Jones for Publication —
Sept. 27 — Pd Nixon & Jones for pub 1000 — At Fault
250 copies to Book and News Co —
100 — Sent home —
1 To Mrs Johnson Ed. Spectator
25 To Wm. Barr —
6   Given to me personally at office —
5   To Crawford's —
3   To Self —
Published

A LADY OF SHIFTING INTENTIONS.

1680 words   To Vanity — per pcs. St. Pub. Co. May 4, '95
　　　　　　　May 6

MISS MCENDERS
1892

　　　3600 words　　　　　　March 7, '92
To Two Tales — March 7 —
R — April 13
To Arena — April 14
R — April 20
To New England Mag — April 21
R — April 1893
To Times-Dem — April 22, 1893
To Vogue — June 9, 1893
R — Aug. 6

VAGABONDS

1200 words　　　　　　Dec. '95
To Chap Book　　Dec. 4
R — Dec. 19
To Vogue — Dec. 19
R — Jan. 8

1890

Young Doctor Gosse   abt 50,000 words
commenced May 4, 1890 — Finished Nov. 27, 1890
Sent to A.C. McClurg & co Chicago Jan. 10, 1891
R — Feb. 17 —
Sent to Lippincott's — Feb. 18 — R — March 21
Sent to Belfords March 23 — R
R — Aug.
Sent to Benj R. Tucker — Sept. 17
   45 Milk St — Boston
R — Jan., '92
To Cassett Pub Co N.Y — May 11, '92
R — July
To Schulte & Co Chicago — July 6 —
R — July 20
~~To Arena, Pub Co., Copley Sq., Boston~~
_____ June
To Appletons — May ~~R~~ '93
R — June '93

1892

700 words   "Mittens"   Feb. 25
384 words ~~Ripe Figs Babette's Visit~~ — Feb. 26 to Stub   R
560 words Croque-Mitaine — Feb. 27 to Picayune April 23/25
400 words A Little Free Mulatto —Feb. 28 to M   April 25 R
To Harpers Young People   Feb. 28
R — March 16
To Wide Awake — March 16
R — March 30
"Ripe Figs"
To Cosmopoli — Aug. 2 —
R — Sept. 22
Pub

RIPE FIGS

300 words   To Vogue — May, 1893
$3.50 Accepted June, 1893
Published Aug., '93
Pub

1890

A Red Velvet Coat —1800 words
Dec. 1—8, '90

Dec. 9 — Sent to St. Nicholas
Dec. 30 — Returned
Jan. 3 — Sent to Youth's Companion
Feb. 6̶ 7, '91 — Accepted by Youth's Companion — $15.00

YOUNG DOCTOR GOSSE (CON)

To Arena Pub co — June 6, 1893
R — July —
To Stone & Kimball (Chicag)   Sept. 10, 1894
R — Jan. 12, '95
To Transatlantic Pub co N. Y — March '95
R — March 23

1892

2000 words   How The Lilies Work   Jan. 27/28 '92
To Harpers Young People   Jan. 28
R — Feb. 15
To St Nicholas Feb. 15
R — Feb. 27
To Wide Awake — F̶e̶b̶.̶ ̶2̶8̶ 9
Accepted by Wide Awake — March 4, '92
Pub. April, 1893
$10 Published

A LADY OF BAYOU ST. JOHN

1700 words   Aug. 24/25
To Vogue — Aug. 25, '93
Accepted A̶u̶g̶.̶ — Sept. 2, '93
Pub — Sept. 17 — $15
Sept. 21
Published

THE UNEXPECTED — JULY 18, '95

1258 words
To Vanity — July 20, '95
R — July 25, '95
To Vogue — July 25 '95
Published Sept. '95

1891

A̶ ̶C̶O̶M̶M̶O̶N̶ ̶C̶R̶I̶M̶E̶

A Taint in the Blood. Mrs. Mobry's Reason
"̶T̶h̶e̶ ̶E̶v̶i̶l̶ ̶T̶h̶a̶t̶ ̶M̶e̶n̶ ̶D̶o̶   At 3000 words
Under An Apple Tree   Jan. 10

Sent to Century Jan. 12 — R — Jan. 24 12 days
Sent to Scribners Jan. 24 — R — Feb. 5 12 days
Sent to ~~Lippincotts~~ Arena Feb. 6 — R — Feb. 16 10 days
Sent to Belfords Feb. 17 — R Feb. 23 6 days
Sent to Lippincotts Feb. 23 — R — March 9   17 days
Sent to Atlantic   March ~~9+~~ 11 R March 28   18 days
~~Cosmopolitan~~ To N. Y. Ledger March 28   R April 9
Cosmopolitan April ~~16~~ 11 —
R April 17 —
To Overland Monthly April 18 —
R — June 1
To Harpers Sept. 17
R — Oct. 5   18
To K. Field's Washington Oct. 13
R — Oct. 20
To Two Tales — April 14, '92
R — May 7
To N. Eng Mag — July 26, '92
R — Dec. 12, '92
Returned Nov. 1892
To Vogue — March 9, 1893
Returned — March 20
To Times Dem March 21, '93
Accepted April 3, 1893
Published

1892

A Study in Heads — P. D. Pub —Jan. 25
Pub

A Visit To The Planet Mars — Sent to
Sent to Chicago Times — March 8
R — June, '91

A Trip to Portuguese Guinea P. D. Feb. 27

Wrestling — Pub. in P. D. March 8 —
Transfusion of Goats blood — sent to P. D. March 23
R — To Rep —
Published

A NO ACCOUNT CREOLE

Feb. 24   1891
               ~~Euphrasie's Lovers.~~
~~A Maid and Her Lovers~~ — 10,000 words
Sent to Belfords — Feb. 28
R — March 27 — Letter: too long — if I cut it
  to 5 or 6000 may prove acceptable.
To Harpers   March 28
R — April 7
~~To Mrs. J. A Logan Home Mag April 8~~ —
To Chaperone — April 9 — Too long   R — ~~198~~
To Mrs. JA Logan — April 11 —
R April 14 — Letter — too long
To Scribners — April 18
R — May 1
To Cosmopolitan   May 3
R — May 8
To Century — May 28
July 5 — Returned for revision — with flattering letter —
Revised & sent back on July 12 —
Aug. 3 '91 accepted by Century — $100.00
Pub — Jan. 1894
Published

1892
CUT PAPER FIGURES

600 words   March 29, 1892
To P. Dispatch — March 30
Published   — April 5
Pub

~~LA BELLE~~

2260 words   ~~Li Mouri~~ — Sept. 21 '93
~~One of Man Loulou's Stories~~ —
La Belle Zoraïde
To Vogue — Sept. 26 — '93
Accepted — Nov. 20 — $23.00
Published — Jan. 4, 1894
Published

A RESPECTABLE WOMAN
          1500 words   Jan. 20, '94
To Vogue — Jan. 20
Accepted — Jan. 30

Published   ~~Feb~~ $15.00
Published

1891
ROGER AND HIS MAJESTY
March 1, 1891   —   900 words
Bok Syndicate   March 2 — R March 9
To Once a Week   March ~~10~~1 R — 21
To Argonaut — March 22
R — April 8

THE KISS
1000 words   Sept. 19, 1894
To Vogue — Sept. 21
Accepted — Jan 8, '95
     $10.00
Published

CAVANELLE
Cent — Atlantic — Harper's — Chap B —
Scribner's — Jan. 9, '95
R — Feb. 10, '95
American Jewess — Feb. 13
Accepted — Feb. '95
Published April '95

TWO SUMMERS & TWO SOULS
900 words   July, 1895
To Vogue — July, 1895
Accepted — Aug. 8, 1895
Published

1892
"THE BENITOU'S SLAVE"
700 words — Jan. 7
600 words — "A Turkey Hunt" — Jan. 8
325 words — "Old Aunt Peggy" — Jan. 8
To Harpers Young People   Jan. 8, 1892
Accepted — Jan. 28, '92
Pub Feb. 16 — 16 — 23, '92
Published

TONIE

4275 words   —   Oct. 27/23 '93
To Atlantic Monthly — Oct. 25, '93
R — Nov. 10
To ~~Scribners~~ Century — Nov. 11
R — Dec. 20
To Scribners — Dec. 21
R — Jan. 6, '94
To Harpers Monthly — Jan. 15
R — Jan. 26
To Cosmopolitan — May 4
R — July 24
To Southern Mag — Aug. 27~~5~~
R — Oct. 6
To Times Democrat — Oct. 7
Accepted — Oct. 12
Pub Dec. 23, 1894
Published

1891

For Marse Chouchoute   March 14, 1891
~~"Say, We Read Lectures to You"~~   3000 words
Sent to Youths comp. March 16 —
Accepted — April 20, '91 $35.00
Published — Aug. 20, 1891
Published

A GENTLEMAN OF BAYOU TECHE

2400 words   Nov. 5/7, 1893
To Youths Companion   Nov. 8 —
R — Dec. ~~6~~ 7
To Atlantic — Dec. 7
Placed in collection
Published

TANTE CAT'RINETTE

3200 words   Feb. 23, '94
To Atlantic Feb. 25, '94
Accepted — March 19, '94
Published — Sept., '94
Published

1891
AFTER THE WINTER
3500 words   Dec. 31, 1891
To Youth's companion (by request for Easter story)
Jan. 4, 1892
Accepted by Companion   Jan. 22, '92 — $50

IN SABINE
3400 words   Nov. 20/22, '93
To Atlantic — Nov. 23
Placed in collection
Published

A DRESDEN LADY IN DIXIE
3000 words   ~~Fe~~ March 6, '94
To Atlantic — March 8
R — March 19
To Century — March 26
R — May 13
To Scribners — May 14
R — June 8
Catholic Home
Accepted
Published March '95

1891
THE CHRIST LIGHT
2300 words   April 4, 1891
"~~The Going And Coming of Liza Jane~~"
Sent to Belfords   April 5 —
R — July
Sent to Century   Aug. 1
R — Sept. 14 — 44 days -
To Scribners — Sept. 16
R — Oct. 7 — 21 days
To Atlantic — Oct. 12
R — Oct. 28 16 days
To N. Y. Herald Oct. 31
R — Nov. 7   7 days
To Cosmopolitan Nov. 11
R — Jan. 11, '92
To Lippincott — Jan. 15
R — Jan. 25

To Overland — April 12
R — June 1
To N. Eng. Mag — June 20
R Aug. — Aug. 22
To Short Stories competition — Sept. 16
R — Oct. 1
To K. Fields Wash — Oct. 9
R — Oct. 14
To Harpers Weekly — Oct. ~~18~~ 21
R — Nov. 14
Syndicated by self
Dec. 1892
Published

1891
BEYOND THE BAYOU
2300 words   Nov. 7, 1891
To Youth's Companion   Nov. 7
Accepted Dec. 11, '91 $30.00
Pub — June 15, '93
Published

THE STORY OF AN HOUR —
1000 words   April 19, 1894
To Vogue — April 20
R — April 28
To Century — April 30
R — June 9
~~To Short Stories — June 15~~
To Short Stories — June 24
R — July 5
To Chap Book — Oct. 2
R — Oct. 27
~~To Town Topics~~ — Oct. 27
To Vogue — Oct. 27
Published — Dec. 6, 1894
          $10.00
Published

THE MAID OF SAINT PHILLIPPE.
2850 words   1891   April 19, 1891
April 30 Sent to Youth's companion Folklore contest.
R — Dec. 1891
To — Scribner Dec. 15

R — Jan. 27
To Post Dis — Feb. 16
R — Feb. 29
To Century — March 3
R — April 6
To Short Stories — April 14
Accepted — May 1, '92
   published Nov., 1892
Short Stories
Published

LILACS

4828 words   May 14, 15, 16, '94
To Century — May 19
R — July 24
To Atlantic — July 25
R — Aug. 8
To Scribners — Aug. 13
R — Sept. 12
To Chap Book —

AN EMBARRASSING SITUATION.

1891   Oct. 22, 1891
~~Evening~~. A Social Dilemma
~~An Little Comedy At Parkhams~~
4000 to 5000 words begun Oct. 15, finished Oct. 22
Comedy - Drama in I Act & I Scene.
To N. Y. Herald for Dramatic Contest Nov. 5, 1891
R — March, 1892
To Century — April 4
R — April 18
To Darl Frohman — April 25
R — May 1
To Augustin Daly — May 2
R — May 14
To Harpers Monthly — May 27
R — June 14
To Scribners — July 15
R — Aug. 18
To Short Stories — March ~~9 10~~ 15
R — March 26
To John W. Norton St.L. — Aug. 31, '93
Letter Oct. 14 — will submit it to Felix Morris in a fortnight
To Mirror by request — Accepted

A WIZARD FROM GETTYSBURG

2675 words   1891   May 25, 1891
Sent to Youth's Companion — May 26
Accepted by Youths Comp June 15, '91 — $35.00
Published July 7, 1892
Published

A DRESDEN LADY IN DIXIE — (CONTINUED)

Cent — Atlantic — Scib — R
To Harpers — June 8, '94
R — June 15
To Youths Comp — June 24
R — Aug. 27
To Cosmopolitan — Aug. 28
R — Nov. 24
To Catholic Home Journal — (req.) — Jan. 22, '95
Accepted — Feb. 8, '95
        $60.00
Catholic Home Journal
Published

OCTAVE FEUILLET

1200 words   1891
To Belford Feb., '91
R — by req Oct., '91
To P. Dispatch — Oct. 13

THE WESTERN ASS. OF WRITERS.

325 words   To Critic — June 30
Accepted — July 4
    1 year sub to Critic
Pub July 7 '94
Published

THE NUN ~~THE WIFE~~ & THE WANTON

        2500 words   Aug. 4, '95
To Yellow Book   Aug. 10, '95
R — Nov. 9
To Chap Book — ~~Dec.~~, '9~~5~~6
R —
To Vogue, March 7

1891
"A SHAMEFUL AFFAIR"

~~2783~~300 words   June 5, June 7, 1891
To St L. Chaperone June 8
To Belfords June 10
R — Oct.
To Cosmopolitan — Oct. 12
R — Jan., 1892
To Scribner's — ~~March~~ April 4
R — April 29
To Argonaut — April 29
R — May 11
To Ladies Home Journal May 14
R — ~~May~~ June 6
~~To N. Y. Independent June 9~~
To Frank Leslie's M — June 20
R — July
To Vogue — Oct. 22
R — Oct. 30
To Godey — Nov. 29
R — Dec. 15
To Times Democrat — March 15
Accepted — March 20
Published

"Good by —" poem accepted by Times Dem —
Returned —~~7 Oct~~

1891
LOVE ~~AND EASTER~~ ON THE BON-DIEU

4600 words   Oct. ~~4~~ 3 1891
To Century — Oct. 5
R — Dec. 7
To ~~Scribner~~ Harpers Mag — Dec. 15
R — Jan. 2, 1892
To "Two Tales" Boston   Jan. 4
     Box 3359
Accepted by Two Tales Jan. 22, '92 — $40
Published July 23, 1892
Published

CAVANELLE

2500 words   July 31/ Aug. 6, '94

To Century — Aug. 24
R — Oct. 8
To Atlantic — Oct. 8
R — Nov. 5
To Harpers — Nov. 6
R — Nov. 14
To Chap Book Dec. 15
R — Jan. 8, '95
American Jewess
forward

1891
A RUDE AWAKENING
4000 words   July 13, '91
To Youth's companion July 15 —
Accepted Aug. 27, '91 — $~~3~~40—
Published Feb. 2, '93
Youth's comp
Published

LILACS (CONTINUED)

Century — Atlantic — Scribners — '94
To Harper's — Sept. 1~~2~~3
R — Sept. 26
To Vogue — Sept. 21
R — Dec. 13
To Cosmopolitan — Dec. 15
R — March 15, '95
~~To Chap Book March 16, 95~~
To Yellow Book through Transatlantic P.C. April 8 '95
R — Nov. 9

1891
BOULOT AND BOULOTTE
645 words   Sept. 20 '91
~~To Harpers Young People —~~
To St Nicholas Sept. 20
R — Oct. 5 15 days
To H— Young People — Oct. 12
Accepted by Young People Nov. 15 — 5
Published Dec. 25
Published

COLLECTION OF CREOLE SHORT STORIES

40,000 words
To Century Company May '93
R — May '93
To Appletons — May '93
R — May '93
To L. L Webster — June 5, '93
R — June 29 '93
    request to consider next winter if not placed
    by that time
To Houghton Mifflin & co Boston — July 1 '93
Accepted for Publication — Aug. 11, '93
Published March 24, 1894
Bayou Folk
Published

1891

A ~~Love's~~ Harbinger   Sept. 11, '91
For Mrs. Johnson — St. Louis Magazine
Nov. 1 — Pub Sept. 12
Published

DR CHEVALIER'S LIE

4~~8~~60 words
To Century — Sept. 14
R — Oct. 12
~~To Vogue — June 9~~ '93
Accepted — Sept. 17 — $4
Pub Oct. 5
Published

1891
A VERY FINE FIDDLE

560 words   Sept. 13, '91
To Century Sept. 14
R — Oct. 12
To H — Young People — Oct. 18
Accepted by Young people Nov. 14 — 5 —
Published Nov. 24, '91
Harpers Y. P.
Published

Jan. 14 You & I A Message to K. Field's Washington — R
Jan. 16 Psyches Lam. Scribners Mag
Feuillet Natch to Bed   Feb. 9 —
A Trip to Portuguese Guinea —

REGRET

1500 words   Sept. 17, 1894
To Century   Sept. 18 '94
Accepted by Century   Oct. 17
Published   May 1, '95
Published

HER LETTERS

3000 words   Nov. 29, '94
To Century — Dec. 5, '94
R — Jan. 28, '95
To Vogue — Jan. 30, '95
Accepted — March 1, '95
April 8–15 '95 $25.00
Published

A SCRAP & A SKETCH

1000 words   M '945
To Moods — May 5
Accepted — May 14
Published July 1895

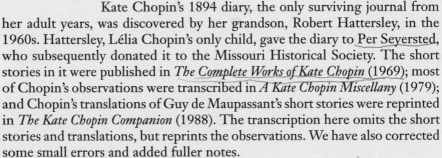

"IMPRESSIONS": KATE CHOPIN'S 1894 DIARY

Kate Chopin's 1894 diary, the only surviving journal from her adult years, was discovered by her grandson, Robert Hattersley, in the 1960s. Hattersley, Lélia Chopin's only child, gave the diary to Per Seyersted, who subsequently donated it to the Missouri Historical Society. The short stories in it were published in *The Complete Works of Kate Chopin* (1969); most of Chopin's observations were transcribed in *A Kate Chopin Miscellany* (1979); and Chopin's translations of Guy de Maupassant's short stories were reprinted in *The Kate Chopin Companion* (1988). The transcription here omits the short stories and translations, but reprints the observations. We have also corrected some small errors and added fuller notes.

The 1894 diary has much in common with Kate Chopin's Commonplace Book, as well as with her short stories. She specializes in the quick and surprising perception, and many of her "Impressions" are exactly that: thoughts about people she encounters, including some very wry and pointed judgments. She is exasperated both by do-gooders (social reformers) and by do-nothings (such as her friend Charles Deyo, who rails about the ills of society while declining to take charge of his own life).

Meanwhile, Kate Chopin the diarist is always aware of outer surfaces and inner realities: her very first entry is an amused sketch of a mild-mannered poet who is secretly an anarchist. Other people seem to puzzle Kate Chopin—among them the enigmatic Carrie Blackman, a painter with exquisite eyes who may have inspired "Her Letters," Chopin's story about a woman with a passionate secret. Dr. Frederick Kolbenheyer, the fiercely radical doctor, also strikes Chopin as continually interesting. He tells stories of filth and bestiality in Poland; he moans about his birthday and growing older. Chopin's tone is warm but not uncritical.

Of course, there were people in the 1890s who thought that Kate Chopin (a dashing widow) and Frederick Kolbenheyer (married to his Austrian childhood sweetheart) were more than friends. "Kolby had eyes for Mom," Chopin's son Felix used to say. But about those eyes, and about any other romances Kate Chopin may have had in St. Louis—we have no private papers.

The 1894 diary shows, nevertheless, both a public and a private Kate Chopin. The public one, the career writer, is irritated by the lack of "a worthy critical faculty" in most reviewers (June 7); by the lack of writing skill in her neighbor's amateur efforts (May 12); and by the tedious society events she must attend to promote *Bayou Folk* (May 4). She has strong opinions about the women writers she admires (Sarah Orne Jewett, Mary E. Wilkins) and deplores (Mary Elizabeth Braddon).

Meanwhile the private Kate Chopin, the solitary soul who seeks escape, also has strong feelings she is not shy about recording. (Of course, she could hardly have expected her diary to be read by strangers a century later). The private Kate Chopin loves nature and warm friendships, and recalls with deep, raw emotion the "animal sensation" of touching her firstborn child (May 22)— a passage that anticipates Edna's thoughts about childbirth in *The Awakening*.

Possibly her lifelong friendship with Kitty Garesché led Kate Chopin to her most extensive meditation in the diary: the entry, also for May 22, about her visit to "Liza," a classmate who had become a Sacred Heart nun. According to Sister Marie Louise Martinez, R. S. C. J., "Liza" was almost certainly Elise Miltenberger, daughter of an old St. Louis French family. Born in 1848, Miltenberger would have been a year or two ahead of Kate O'Flaherty at the Sacred Heart Academy, but she became a Sacred Heart nun a few years after Kitty Garesché. When the nuns decided to open a school in San Francisco in 1889, Elise Miltenberger served on the three-member house council there with Mother Mary O'Meara, Kate's beloved teacher, and Kitty Garesché, who became Mistress General (headmistress) at the new Sacred Heart academy.

By 1894 Elise Miltenberger was back in St. Louis, as the superior at the Sacred Heart's New City House and the founder of Barat Hall, a boys' school associated with the Sacred Heart sisters. As photographs show, Elise Miltenberger had the same narrow eyes with swollen upper lids that Kate Chopin describes (May 22). And eventually, like Kate Chopin, "Liza" was also punished for behavior that was considered too radical.

By 1898–1899 Mother Miltenberger was the superior in the Park Place Academy in Omaha, where there were many Dreyfusard clubs (supporting the Jewish Frenchman accused of treason, whose case had become a *cause célèbre* through the efforts of Emile Zola). But when an order came down from Mother General Mabel Digby that all Jewish students were to be expelled from the Sacred Heart schools, Mother Miltenberger refused to do so. As punishment, she was removed from her post and never again appointed as a superior. Her demotion took place during the same year that *The Awakening* was published.

But in 1894, Kate Chopin could not have known what would become of Liza's career, or of her own. She knew, however, that her diary was not private: school copybooks cannot be locked. And so, when Chopin wrote in the entry about "Liza" that she herself "had loved—lovers who were not divine," she was being carefully mysterious and self-protective.

According to her first biographer, Daniel Rankin, Kate Chopin was considered "a woman of mysterious fascination." The 1894 diary, which Rankin never saw, adds to the mystery, as well as the fascination—for there are so many intriguing, unanswered questions.

What relationship, for instance, is there between the stories Chopin copied into her diary and the diary entries before and after the stories? The stories are definitely not first drafts: they are the kinds of clear copies she gave to her typist. Was Chopin writing simply in chronological order, or was she developing certain themes?

The best way to read the 1894 diary, in fact, is alongside *The Complete Works of Kate Chopin*, dipping back and forth between Chopin's stories and diary entries, and using *The Kate Chopin Companion* for the Guy de Maupassant translations. But despite our interpretive strategies, there are things we will almost certainly never know. What, for instance, did Kate Chopin mean in her June 2 entry, when she wrote, "And then, there are so many ways of saying good night!"?

As with her fiction, she leaves us wondering.

The 1894 diary, entitled "Impressions," is in a 7" x 8" school copybook with a heavy dark brown cover and a rat hole gnawed in the center. The cream-colored lined pages are somewhat faded, as is the black ink Kate Chopin used. There are some stray squiggles and blots, probably jottings by her grandchildren. Housed at the Missouri Historical Society, the diary has been heavily read in recent years and is now in poor condition, its pages falling out. Would-be readers are encouraged to use photocopies.

Kate Chopin's handwriting in her 1894 diary is much easier to read than that in her Commonplace Book, a quarter-century earlier. As a busy single mother, she no doubt had to simplify her life; as a Louisiana widow, she had run Oscar's businesses for awhile, including dealing with bills and letters—tasks which required a simple, readable hand. Her later writing is brisk and businesslike, and her entries read like quick jottings.

Chopin also numbered her own pages, but there are two number 15s. Her numbering ends with p. 113. Her misspellings and odd punctuations are reproduced here: she often, in haste, left out apostrophes.

Where possible, people mentioned are identified in endnotes.

(1)

Impressions. 1894

MAY.

4th—It was at first an amusing figure which very soon became interesting and pathetic—the old gentleman whom I found sitting at Mrs. Moores' elbow today when I went into her office. I at first thought she was engaged in a business transaction and retired to a far corner of the room to await my "turn." He was reading a poem to her on the subject of the commonweal army. One of those endless refrains written on foolscap—pages and pages of it. She is a kinder and gentler woman than I thought for she listened quite patiently. At the close he questioned her as to his chances for having it published. He knew of course that she could not use it in "Life" but—Oh, she was quite sure the Arena might take it. That was hardly kind. He bowed a few words of polite apology to me as he went out, and looking into his gentle old gray bearded

(2)

face I was forced to forgive him. The old fellow it appears is an anarchist! Fancy an anarchist armed with no more serious a bomb than a poem which he carries into the offices of publishers there to accomplish its deadly work. I believe it is not today or tomorrow that this insidious explosive will get in its work on the public—not while there remains the live body of a publisher to stand between.

That woman up at the photographers is interesting. The first sight of her was repellant, with her short fat figure and short brown curly hair. But there is a straightforwardness, a dignity and gentle refinement about her manner that surprises and attracts. She draws me, somehow.

Have missed the euchre club again because Mrs. Whitmore insisted upon having me go to her house to meet Mrs. Ames and her daughter Mrs. Turner, who were anxious to know me and hear me read my stories. I fear it was the commercial

(3)

instinct which decided me. I want the book to succeed. But how immensely uninteresting some "society" people are! That class which we know as Philistines. Their refined voices, and refined speech which says nothing—or worse, says something which offends me. Why am I so sensitive to manner.

My neighbor Mrs. Hull is a delightful little woman; so small—hardly bigger than a child of ten, with a homely irregular face and a forehead of unusual height, debth and bumpiness. She has lived almost next door to me for years and I only know her now. She solicited an interview to talk over a desire which she has to get into print. She says she has known how to write all her life (she is nearly fifty). She knows she can write as good stories as she reads in the magazines (such belief in her own ability is a bad omen). Her life has been interesting, intimately identified with the period of the war, the country life of South

(4)

Missouri and Arkansas. She seems well acquainted with the different types which inhabit this part of the world and talks entertainingly of them. Whether she is able to give these impressions literary form of any value is another thing. She was here tonight for a moment and left two stories in MS for me to read. I never pick up such a MS but with the hope that I am about to fall upon a hidden talent. I read about a thousand words before visitors came. Those thousand words were all employed to tell how a black girl came in possession of her name. It should have been told in five lines.

Ferriss came. I did not see him. I do not quite understand him. Have not got near enough.

The Doctor told interesting stories about the ignorance, filth, beastiality of country life in Poland.

(5)

12th. I read Mrs. Hull's story through this morning. It is upon the theme which Cable has used effectively. A girl with negro blood who is loved by a white man. Possessing a noble character she effaces herself and he knows her no more—she dies of consumption. I have no objection to a commonplace theme if it be handled artistically or with originality. She writes good English, has knowledge of her subject and has evidently received impressions of life but I fear she will not be able to give the literary form which goes to the making of an acceptable story. No freshness, spontaneity or originality or perception. The whole tendency is in the conventional groove. If she were younger I would tell her to study critically some of the best of our short stories. I know of no one better than Miss Jewett to study for technique and nicety of construction. I don't mention Mary E. Wilkins for she is a great genius and genius is not to be studied. We are un-

(6)

fortunately being afflicted with imitations of Miss Wilkins <u>ad nauseum</u>.

I cannot yet discover any serious significance in the present craze for the hysterical morbid and false pictures of life which certain English women have brought into vogue. They appeal to a certain order of mind just as Miss Breddon appeals to another and E. P. Roe to a third.

I have no leaning towards a parrot. I think them detestable birds with their blinking stupid eyes and heavy clumsy motions. I never could become attached to one. I have never in my life heard one talk, though I have waited with sphinx like patience the outcome of the most strenuous efforts and inducements on the part of their owners to make them do so. Perhaps I exercise an adverse influence upon them. It made me positively

(7)

ill today when I had gone to pass a few hours with Blanche, to be forced to divide her society and attention with her own parrot and a neighbor's which she had borrowed. Fancy any sane human being doubling up an affliction in that way. But on the other hand she gave me delicious homegrown strawberries (the first) for luncheon. Their flavor somehow recalled James Lane Allen's exquisite story "A Kentucky Cardinal," begun in the May Harpers. What a refreshing idealistic bit it is, coming to us with the budding leaves and the bird-notes that fill the air.

22nd. I have finished a story of 4800 words and called it "Lilacs." I cannot recall what suggested it. If the story had been written after my visit of last Sunday to the convent, I would not have to seek the impulse far. Those nuns seem to retain or gain a certain beauty with their advancing years which we women in the world are

(8)

strangers to. The unchanging form of their garments through years and years seems to impart a distinct character to their bodily

movements. Liza's face held a peculiar fascination for me as I
sat looking into it enframed in its white rushing. It is more
than twenty years since I last saw her; but in less than twenty
minutes those twenty years had vanished and she was the Liza of
our school days. The same narrow, happy grey eyes with their
swollen upper lids; the same delicious upward curves to the
corners of her pretty mouth. No little vexatious wrinkles
anywhere. Only a few good strong lines giving a touch of
character that the younger Liza lacked perhaps. The conditions
under which these women live are such as keep them young and
fresh in heart and in visage. One day—usually one hey-day of
youth they kneel before the altar of a God whom they have learned
to worship,

(9)

and they give themselves wholly—body and spirit into his
keeping. They have only to remain faithful through the years,
these modern Psyches, to the lover who lavishes all his precious
gifts upon them in the darkness—the most precious of which is
perpetual youth. I wonder what Liza thought as she looked into my
face. I know she was remembering my pink cheeks of more than
twenty years ago and my brown hair and innocent young face. I do
not know whether she could see that I had loved—lovers who were
not divine—and hated and suffered and been glad. She could see,
no doubt the stamp which a thousand things had left upon my face,
but she could not read it. She, with her lover in the dark. He
has not anointed her eyes for perfect vision. She does not need
it—in the dark.—When we came away, my friend who had gone with
me said: "Would you not give anything to have her

(10)

vocation and happy life!" There was a long beaten path spreading
before us; the grass grew along its edges and the branches of
trees in their thick rich May garb hung over the path like an
arbor, making a long vista that ended in a green blur. An old
man—a plain old man leaning on a cane was walking down the path
holding a small child by the hand and a little dog was trotting
beside them. "I would rather be that dog" I answered her. I know
she was disgusted and took it for irreverence and I did not take
the trouble to explain that this was a little picture of life and
that what we had left was a phantasmagoria.

   This is Jean's birthday—twenty-three years old today! How
curiously the past effaces itself for me! I sometimes regret that

it is so; for there must be a certain pleasure in retrospection.
I cannot live through yester-

(11)

day or tomorrow. It is why the dead in their character of dead
and association with the grave have no hold upon me. I cannot
connect my mother or husband or any of those I have lost with
those mounds of earth out at Calvary Cemetery. I cannot visit
graves and stand contemplating them as some people do, and seem
to love to do. If it were possible for my husband and my mother
to come back to earth, I feel that I would unhesitatingly give up
every thing that has come into my life since they left it and
join my existence again with theirs. To do that, I would have to
forget the past ten years of my growth—my real growth. But I
would take back a little wisdom with me; it would be the spirit
of a perfect acquiescence.—This is a long way from Jean, 23
years ago. I can remember yet that hot southern day on Magazine
street in New Orleans. The noises of the street coming through
the open windows; that heaviness with which I dragged myself
about; my

(12)

husband's and mother's solicitude; old Alexandrine the quadroon
nurse with her high bandana tignon, her hoop-earrings and placid
smile; old Doctor Faget; the smell of chloroform, and then waking
at 6 in the evening from out of a stupor to see in my mothers
arms a little piece of humanity all dressed in white which they
told me was my little son! The sensation with which I touched my
lips and my finger tips to his soft flesh only comes once to a
mother. It must be the pure animal sensation; nothing spiritual
could be so real—so poignant.

28th. Mr. and Mrs. Schuyler were here one evening. I never saw
her so attractive, sparkling, scintillant like a charged battery.
But I do not know her, or even think I know her. Mr. S. has
agreed to write a personal sketch of me which "The Writer" has
asked for. He has done it admirably. I don't know who could have
done it better; could have better told in so short a space the
story of my growth into a

(13)

writer of stories.

Mr Dillon has sent me a very frank and enthusiastic letter from New York after reading "Bayou Folk." He sent me a feeble note some weeks ago, a note of faint and damning praise, where he pretended to have read it. It must have been hard for him to set aside the prejudice which I know he has had against my work; and for that reason so much more do I appreciate his frank letter.

A day in the country among the hills of Glencoe. God! what a delight it was—the pure sensuous beauty of it, penetrating and moving as love! Standing on the porch at Mrs. Carr's whose house is on one of the hills, I could look across the tree tops to neighboring hills where cattle were grazing on the sloping meadows. Through the ravine deep down on the other side in a green basin, a patch of the Meramec glistened and sparkled like silver. It was pleasant, too, to be in the company of

(14)

those 20 charming women who for that one day, anyhow, seemed to have thrown every thing but laughter to the winds. We drove out deep among the hills to the "Fermery." There were a few log cabins along the road; ruder and more primitive than the negro cabins of Louisiana; without that little sheltering gallery which all Southern cabins have and which add a certain rude comfort to those humble homes. I could not discover what the people do who live in them, except cut wood for a neighboring lime kiln. There was one rough looking fellow bending over a plow. I said to the woman next me in the back board, that he looked like one of Hamlin Garland's impersonations. She didn't seem to know what I meant and I was glad of it. I hadnt come to the Glencoe hills to talk literature! She is the little woman who calls me Mrs. Chovin and hasn't the slightest idea that I write. Its delicious.
Outside a cabin, there was one man

(15)

as thin as a skeleton, dressed in rough shirt and trousers and a reddish hat. He was patching a piece of gearing and turned his back when he saw us approaching. The half-dozen bare-footed, fat children stared, however, and so did the dog. In the door of the next cabin a mile further a black woman was sitting with a very black round-faced youngster beside her. The woman laughed and bowed pleasantly to us. I have never seen the sky so intensely blue; big patches of it showing through billowing white clouds. Later when we sat at luncheon on the broad porch the storm gathered over across the hills and came ripping in a tempest down upon us almost before we could get within the shelter of the house. It went as suddenly as it came, giving us a sunny hour in which to reach home. I am something of a euchre fiend, but nothing compared with Mrs. Walsh who admits that euchre is the light spot in her existence—"something to live for!" Well—

(15)

after all—something to live for—that is the main thing!

JUNE

2d Mrs. Stone was the most interesting woman I met at Deyo's Wednesday afternoon. Let me see—who were the others? Mrs. Ferriss a frank, wholesome woman, amiable & natural; no doubt a good friend and excellent mother and wife; with nothing of the précieuse offensiveness of manner to which I have become more sensitive than ever. Mrs. Blackman—a woman with the artistic temperament—woefully unballanced I am afraid. Her face is very beautiful and attractive—particularly her large dark eyes. I can understand how her husband gives offense to other women by losing himself in contemplation of his wife when in company. There seems however always an *arrière pensè* with her, which acts as a barrier between us.—Mrs. Sawyer is a harmless poet. She thinks the "Heavenly Twin" a book cal-

(16)

culated to do incalculable good in the world: by helping young girls to a fuller comprehension of truth in the marriage relation! Truth is certainly concealed in a well for most of us. Miss Sawyer is more rusé than her mother. Her speech commits her to nothing. She has the musical gift highly developed but one must discover it. She holds herself with a certain reserve that is admirable; a pleasing woman with a sweet cultivated voice in speaking and no sharp edges to her manner. She has invited me to her home for a musicale.—Mrs. Stone looks like a woman who accepts life as a tragedy and has braced herself to meet it with a smile on her lips. The spirit of the reformer burns within her, and gives to her eyes the smouldering, steady glow of a Savonarolas. The condition of the working classes pierces her soul; the condition of women wrings her heart. "Work" is her watch word. She wants to work to make life purer, sweeter, better

(17)

worth living. She has written a novel and some short stories which I have never read. Her experience with publishers has not been happy, but she does not mind. She does not live for herself but for others and she is just as willing to reach the "world" through her personal work as through the written word. Intentions pile up before her like a mountain, and the sum of her energies is Zero! It is well that such a spirit does not ever realize the futility of effort. A little grain of wisdom gained from the gospel of selfishness—what an invaluable lesson—lost upon ears that will not hear.

What sentimentality over a birthday, oh dear! Let me alone with birthdays—so meaningless. I have known rusé old ladies of 16 and giddy young girls of 35. I am younger today at 43 than I was at 23. What does it matter. Why this mathematical division of life into years? Days

(18)

are what count—not years. My friend whose birthday I remembered with a little gift, a sip of champagne & "wish you luck" looked positively a little sadder on the 31 of May, remembering that he was making his 51st notch. "Ah, if it were only forty one" he sighed. I wonder if I shall ever care if it is 43 or 53 or 63. I believe not.

Last night at an evening party a man in speaking of Felix Morriss and his delicate art remarked that Mr. and Mrs. Morriss aim is to show the world that acting upon the stage can be done by ladies & gentlemen! It took quite an effort to withhold my wrath at such a statement. God A'mighty! Aren't there enough ladies & gentlemen sapping the vitality from our every day existence! are we going to have them casting their blight upon art.

There are a few good things in life—not many, but a few. A soft, firm, magnetic sympathetic hand clasp is one. A walk through

(19)

the quiet streets at midnight is another. And then, there are so many ways of saying good night!

7th. Last night Mr. Deyo spoke of the ecstatic pleasure which he

finds in reading Plato. He seems to have reached the sage by
stages: through Browning then Pater. He feels that there is
nothing for him beyond that poetic height. And when Plato begins
to pall—as he will in a few years, he wonders what life will
have to offer him, and shudders already in anticipation of the
nothingness. This is to me a rather curious condition of mind. It
betokens a total lack of inward resource, and makes me doubt the
value of the purely intellectual outlook. Here is a man who can
only be reached through books. Nature does not speak to him,
notwithstanding his firm belief that he is in sympathetic touch
with the true—the artistic. He reaches his perceptions through
others minds. It is something, of

(20)

course that the channel which he follows is a lofty one; but the
question remains, has such perception the value of spontaneous
insight, however circumscribed.

In looking over more than a hundred press notices of "Bayou
Folk" which have already been sent to me, I am surprised at the
very small number which show anything like a worthy critical
faculty. They might be counted upon the fingers of one hand. I
had no idea the genuine book critic was so rare a bird. And yet I
receive congratulations from my publishers upon the character of
the press notices. Mary Wilkins Pembroke is the most profound,
the most powerful piece of fiction of its kind that has ever come
from the American press. And I find such papers as the N.Y.
Herald—the N.O. Times Democrat devoting half a column to
senseless abuse of the disagreeable characters which figure in
the book. No feeling for the spirit of the work, the subtle
genius which created it.

(21)

Am I becoming more sensitive and susceptible. Things which
bore me and which I formerly made an effort to endure, are
insupportable to me. My love and reverence for pure unadulterated
nature is growing daily. Never in my life before has the Country
had such a poignant charm for me. Yesterday a day at the Kinloch
with the card club.

30—   Provincialism in the best sense . . .
    [Here appears the essay "The Western Association of Writers,"
    on Chopin's pp. 21–23. Full text is in CW.]

(23)

It was a great pleasure for me to walk through the beautiful streets of Anderson at 5 o'clock last Tuesday morning. The yards were green with foliage and crisp with the early due. We stopped for breakfast at an inviting looking boarding house, whose landlady waited herself, upon table—paint, cosmetics and all at that early hour! Northern Indiana at this season

(24)

of the year is really a garden spot.

JULY

5 Deyo talked anarchy to me last night. There is good reason for his wrath against the "plutocrats" the robbers of the public—but there seems too much personal feeling in his invectives. His <u>real</u> grievance is ill health though he doesn't know it—He believes in equal opportunities being afforded to all men, and feels that he has been hampered in the race by the necessity to gain a living. I didn't remind him that his opportunities to follow the direction of his talents have been unusually favorable. He has had a pen in his hand for the past five years or more—what has he done with it?

Critic accepted my paragraph upon "The Western Association of Writers" to be

(25)

to be published this week, and offer me a years subscription to the paper—not bad when I expected nothing for it, and hardly thought it would be used.

6—Received Copy of "Tante Cat'rinette" from Atlantic for correction. Suppose it will appear in September. Read a few delicious comedies of Aristophanes last night

(26)

A DIVORCE CASE—

TRANSLATED FROM THE FRENCH OF G. DE MAUPASSANT BY K. C.

[Here appears the translation of Guy de Maupassant's "A Divorce Case," on Chopin's pp. 26–41. Full text is in TB.]

(41)

July 24th—11. P.M. I am losing my interest . . .
[Here appears the sketch "The Night Came Slowly," on Chopin's
pp. 41–43. Full text is in CW.]

(44)

July 25—What will poor little Dorothea do now, I wonder, since
Mrs. Banhardt is gone. She left to day. Last year Dorothea was
here with her father and mother, two little brothers and a kind
German nurse maid. The children and nurse occupied a room
together. The father and mother a room apart in the cottage
across a narrow strip of lawn and their door opened directly into
the yard. Every morning Dorothea, who was little more than two,
last summer, would toddle out as soon as dressed and make her way
directly to the door of her parents, which always opened, no
matter how early it was, at the first sound of the baby
voice.—In the autumn the family returned to their city home, and
towards the end of winter a third little brother was added to the
family circle. When it came, the mother of these four little ones
died.

(45)

The poor distracted father has sent the baby with little
Dorothea back to the Cedars this year with their devoted German
nurse; and he with the remaining boys has turned his disconsolate
steps elsewhere.—The nurse with the two little ones arrived late
one evening in June and was given the same room she had occupied
the previous year. The following morning when Dorothea awoke she
seemed to faintly recognize her surroundings and evidently felt
at home. And soon as she was dressed, & the nurse was tending her
baby brother, away she went with the most impatient & determined
toddle. She crossed the porch, descended the steps and running
over the strip of grass went unerringly to the door of the room
which her parents had occupied last summer; calling "mama, mama"
and slapping with her two baby hands upon

(46)

the pannel. Mrs. Banhardt opened the door, and with some
astonishment on her fair, motherly face, looked down at the tot,
and Dorothea looked up at her. "Mama, mama" she screamed

joyfully, clasping the lady's knees. Mrs. Banhardt stooped, and putting her arms around the child kissed her tenderly as she is accustomed to kiss her own little ones. And all Summer long Mrs. Banhardt has been Dorothea's "mama." The child has appealed to her when thirsty, hungry or tired; she has nestled beside her in the hammock and climbed into her lap and has often gone to sleep in her arms. But Mrs. Banhardt left this morning. I went a while ago and sat down upon a bench beside Dorothea who was playing with her doll, and put my arm about her. "Will you let me

(47)

be your mama now, Dorothea?" I asked her, lifting her mignonne face up to mine. She did not answer, but stared at me with that unruffled, incomprehensible gaze of very little children. Then she wriggled from my clasp, slid down from the bench and pattered across the grass trailing her doll behind her. She sat herself squarely down on Mrs. Banhardt's door step and looked over at me mistrustfully, even a little defiantly, I thought.

July 26—To all appearances and according to all accounts, Annie Venn . . .
[Here appears the sketch "Juanita," on Chopin's pp. 47–52. Full text appears in CW.]

(52)

July 31   Cavanelle.
[Here appears the story "Cavanelle," on Chopin's pp. 52–69. Full text appears in CW.]

(69)

Aug 6—

MAD?

TRANSLATED FROM THE FRENCH OF DEMAUPASSANT BY K. C.
[Here appears a translation of Guy de Maupassant's "Mad," on Chopin's pp. 69–79. Full text appears in TB.]

(79)

Sep. 4 _____ _____ _____ _____

REGRET

1500 wds.
[Here appears the story "Regret," on Chopin's pp. 79–90. Full text appears in CW.]

(90)

Sep 17th _____ _____ _____ _____ _____ _____

~~REGRET~~

abt 1000 wds   The Kiss.
[Here appears the story "The Kiss," on Chopin's pp. 90–97. Full text appears in CW.]

(97)

Sep 19th

_____ _____ _____ _____

OZÈME'S HOLIDAY.

[Here appears the story "Ozème's Holiday," on Chopin's pp. 97–113, ending with the notation "Sep 23/24." Full text appears in CW.]

Then Wouldst Thou Know?
If some day I, with casual, wanton glance
Should for a moment's space thine eyes ensnare;
Or more, if I should dare
To rest my finger tips upon thy sleeve,
Or, grown more bold, upon thy swarthy cheek;
If further I should seek
With honey-trick of tone thy name to call,
Breathing it soft, in meaning whisper low,
Then wouldst thou know?
Is there no subtler sense, that holds not commerce
With the glancing eyes, the touch, the tone?
Whereby alone
I would convey to thee some faintest gleam
Of what I dare not look, or speak, or dream!
Kate

Aug. 16th '95

Under My Lattice

There's under my lattice at dawn, a bird's song:
  The day is long!
And fair, out of the South the wind blows,
And soft as a maiden's cheek the morn glows.
There are flowers to gather and with them the dew,
Take them or leave them or trample a few.
Some—to pluck them I would not care;
And others—to touch them I would not dare.
At noon the sun beats white and hot;
The winds are gone, the flowers forgot.
But there's rain in the West and a chill it brings;
And there's hail in the West and it bites and it stings,
There's under my lattice at night no bird's song
  And rest is long.
                                        K.C.

Aug 18th
    '95

Christmas Cards - 1895 - Dec-
                    For Mrs. Ferriss.
Five little robbins in a row.
I wonder what they mean!
For now a days as well we know
Things are not what they seem.

Then let each bird a blessing be
That's surely come to stay;
That growling fates, as well we see,
Can never <u>drive</u> away.

                    To Hidee Schuyler
I send a dozen wishes
Let's say the first is "health."
(I send a dozen kisses!)
And the last we'll call it wealth.
                    —-

2
The others you must choose ~~then~~ some
I'm poor at counting wishes.
I'd be pretty sure to lose some
But I double up the kisses!
————-

To "Billy" with a box of cigars.
These may be without question
Rather bad for your digestion.
But the Powers have not sent me
To preach sermons; they've but lent me
A keen desire to please you
Now and always without end,
And a little wish to tease you
With the fondness of a friend.

————
————

To Mrs B————n
Your greeting filled me with distress.
I've pondered long and sore to guess
What 'twould express.

————

Ah, Lady fair! Can you not see:
From gentlemen of high degree
I always flee!

————

To a Lady at the Piano—Mrs. R—n.
I do not know you out upon the street
    Where people meet.
We talk as women talk; shall I confess?
    I know you less!
I hear you play, and touched by ~~the~~ a wondrous spell
    I know you well!

————

To Blanche.
I might have sent you flowers
Or of bonbons sent you showers!

But knowing where your love lies ˎ
Why send what you would <u>dis</u> pise?
So to fill your soul with glee,
Why, I send you puffins three.

————

For Sale
From the French of Guy de Maupassant
[Here appears a translation of Guy de Maupassant's "For
Sale," on Chopin's (unnumbered) pp. 120–134. Full text
appears in *TB*.]

Oct 26—'96

THE "LILIA" POLKA

Kate Chopin was a lover of music all her life. When she was a child at the Sacred Heart Academy, her mother paid for her to take extra piano lessons. As an adolescent, Kate O'Flaherty also attended the St. Louis Academy of the Visitation for extra musical training. She could read music, and could also repeat, by ear, opera music she had heard.

As her Commonplace Book shows in the entry on Ole Bull (December 1868), eighteen-year-old Kate O'Flaherty was struggling to describe the emotional effect of music on souls like her own. Some thirty years later, in *The Awakening*, Chopin's Edna is deeply susceptible to music and also cannot put into words how the glorious piano playing of Mademoiselle Reisz plays on her deepest emotions.

We know nothing, however, about the emotions that may have inspired Kate Chopin to compose the "Lilia Polka," nor do we know why H. H. Rollman & Company happened to publish the piece. The misspelling "Lilia" was often used for the name of Kate's daughter Lélia: Kate's adolescent friend Lélia ("Lil") Chouteau's name was also frequently misspelled the same way. (See note on Lélia Chouteau for the Commonplace Book, p. 317.)

Polkas were quite popular among the Germans and German Americans in St. Louis. H. H. Rollman probably saw a product and a market, and rushed to do business with Kate Chopin.

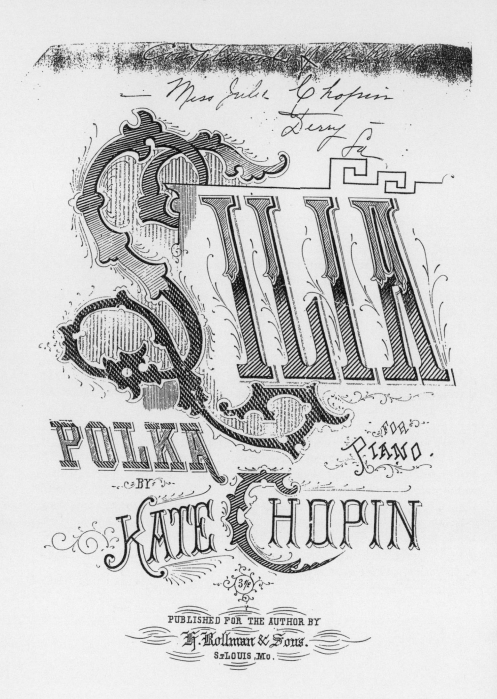

LILIA POLKA.

COMPOSED BY

KATE CHOPIN.

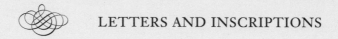 LETTERS AND INSCRIPTIONS

       When she reviewed an edition of the actor Edwin Booth's letters, Kate Chopin found them an inadequate picture of the great thespian's life. They were mostly "expressions wrung from him by the conventional demands of his daily life," not real portraits of his character. Chopin suspected that Booth himself would have disapproved: "I shrink from the indelicacy," she imagined him saying.

       Kate Chopin's letters and inscriptions are not indelicate (a fact which may disappoint her contemporary admirers). Her letters are sometimes private and friendly, sometimes more formal and professional. But like most nineteenth-century letter writers, she was careful, cheerful, and tactful, except when occasionally provoked: her letters answering wrongheaded book reviewers have a distinct edge of asperity.

       Unfortunately for those curious about Kate Chopin's interior life, it is always a matter of chance and randomness which letters—and which inscriptions—survive. Besides the two book autographs quoted here, there are two extant copies of *Bayou Folk* in which Kate Chopin quoted, revised, her own poem "White Oaks" (see this volume, p. 289). But she must have sold or given away, signed, many more copies that have not survived. We know, too, that she wrote colorful and lively letters describing Louisiana to her mother and others in St. Louis—and those, too, are gone.

       The letters and inscriptions here are an inadequate representation of Kate Chopin's autographs and correspondence. They show the conventional demands of her daily life, but—as she said of Edwin Booth—the artist's real character was elsewhere: "The _real_ Edwin Booth gave himself to the public through his art." And so did Kate Chopin.

Dated Letters

TO MARIE BREAZEALE, 1887
Chopin (Louisiana)

June 21st

My dear Marie

Your kind sweet letter, I received yesterday; and I assure you, we shall certainly pay you a visit before returning home: that is as many of us as you can accommodate, for I cannot believe that your house has such unlimited capacity as to receive the whole family. We left St. Louis wednesday morning, and got here thursday night, after rather a tiresome trip. The children are not looking well, & Petsy has been sick since we got here: though he is better now. You know they all had measels lately. I hope they will soon get real strong and well.

We are so anxious to see you. I want to see Phanor and the baby, because I have never seen them, and I want to see you for I hear you have grown extremely stout.

Cora would have written, she says, if I had not been writing. She is looking so well. Nini, I think rather thin, but I suppose it is due to her recent illness.

With love to yourself & Phanor and a kiss for baby.

Your loving sister
Katie

TO THE *ST. LOUIS REPUBLIC*, 1890
To the Editor of The Republic.

St. Louis, Oct. 18—Will you kindly permit me through the columns of your paper to set <u>The Republic</u> book reviewer right in a matter which touches me closely concerning the use and misuse of words? I cannot recall an instance, in or out of fiction, in which an American "country store" has been alluded to as a "shop," unless by some unregenerate Englishman. The use of the word depot or station is optional. Wm. Dean Howells employs the former to indicate a "railway station," so I am hardly ready to believe the value of "At Fault" marred by following so safe a precedent. Very respectfully yours,
KATE CHOPIN.

TO THE *NATCHITOCHES ENTERPRISE*
Saint Louis, Dec. 9, 1890

To the Editor of the ENTERPRISE:

While thanking your reviewer for the many agreeable and clever things said of my story, "At Fault," kindly permit me to correct a misconception. Fanny is not the heroine. It is charitable to regard her whole existence as a misfortune. Therese Lafirme, the heroine of the book is the one who was at fault—remotely, and immediately. Remotely—in her blind acceptance of an undistinguishing, therefore unintelligent code of righteousness by which to deal out judgments. Immediately—in this, that unknowing of the individual needs of <u>this</u> man and <u>this</u> woman, she should yet constitute herself not only a mentor, but an instrument in reuniting them.

Their first marriage was an unhappy mistake; their re-union was a crime against the unwritten moral law. Emerson says: "Morals is the science of substances, not of shows. It is the <u>what</u> and not the <u>how</u>. * * * It were an unspeakable calamity if anyone should think he has the right to impose a private will on others. That is a part of a striker, an assassin."

Towards the close of the story, Therese acknowledges her error, and Hosmer reads her a brief lecture upon the "living spirit," the "dead letter," etc.

I ask to straighten this misconception—of Fanny having been "at fault," because it is one, which if accepted by the reader is liable to throw the story out of prospective.

Yours very truly,
KATE CHOPIN

TO THE *CENTURY*, 1891
3317 Morgan St.

St. Louis May 28

Editor Century—
Dear Sir: The accompanying story of some 10,000 words, entitled "A No-Account Creole" is submitted for publication in Century. If unavailable, will you kindly return it to me as soon as you can conveniently.

Very truly
Kate Chopin

TO R. W. GILDER

Sulphur Springs Mo
July 12 1891

R. W. Gilder
Editor the Century
Dear Sir,

The weakness which you found in "A No-Account Creole" is the one which I felt.

I thank you more than I can say, for your letter. My first and strongest feeling upon reading it, was a desire to clasp your hand. I hope I have succeeded in making the girl's character clearer. I have tried to convey the impression of sweetness and strength, keen sense of right, and physical charm beside.

I have further changed and eliminated passages that seemed to me crude; but I made no attempt to condense the story. I knew that I could not without evolving something totally different in the effort. The thing drags lazily I know—I hope not awkwardly, and I believe contains nothing irrelevant. I trust a good deal to the close for rousing the interest of the reader if it may have flagged by the way.

I shall confess that your letter has given me strong hope that you may find the story worthy of publication.

Believe me
very truly yours
Kate Chopin

TO MARION A. BAKER

Marion A. Baker esq N. O.
My dear Mr. Baker

Your letter of 28 has quite consoled me for the return of "Miss McEnders." The sketch has already been to the <u>Arena</u>. When I sent it to you it had just come back from the New England Mag. without a word of apology for having been held precisely one year. The liberal views expressed by Mr. Walter Blackburn Harte in his "Corner at Dodsbys" had been my excuse for submitting it to them.

I leave tonight for a two weeks absence in New York and Boston, and shall combine the business of seeking a publisher with the pleasure of—well, not seeking a publisher. I want to say, that any suggestion, recommendation, helpful hint, you might be kind enough to offer in the matter would be gratefully accepted and appreciated.

I have the pleasure of meeting your charming daughter, Mrs. Chouteau quite often. Perhaps she has told you.

> Faithfully yours
> Kate Chopin

My address in N.Y. "The Gerlach"
In Boston The Thorndike

TO R. W. GILDER

> The Gerlach
> May 10 93

My dear Mr Gilder

I have left the MS of a novel—which I forgot to mention the other day—with the Messrs. Appleton. In using your kind note of introduction, however, I explained that it had no connection with the novel, of which you knew nothing, but had been written in reference to a collection of short tales that you had subsequently consented to have read by the Century company.

I hope my action will not seem objectionable to you, or that you will not consider it, in any sense, a misuse of your cordial assistance.

Thanking you heartily for the same,

> I am very faithfully yours
> Kate Chopin

TO STONE & KIMBALL, CHICAGO PUBLISHERS

> 3317 Morgan Street,
> St. Louis,
> Sep 10 '94

Messrs Stone and Kimball

> Chicago

Dear Sirs

I have today forwarded to you by express the M.S. of a novel entitled "Young Doctor Gosse and Theo" containing about 45000 words. The prologue introduces the reader to a Parisian scene: the story proper opens ten years later and is acted in America.

I beg that you will kindly consider the story with a view to publication, and would greatly appreciate an early reply.

If unavailable, please return M.S. to my address by express.

> Yours truly
>
> Kate Chopin.

TO WAITMAN BARBE
3317 Morgan Street, St. Louis, Oct. 2 '94

Mr. Waitman Barbe Parkersburg W Va

Mr. dear Mr. Barbe

I thank you for having selected me as one of the representative Southern Writers to appear in your series of sketches for Southern Magazine. You will find in the accompanying clippings more than the necessary data for a biographical notice.

In reply to some of your questions I shall say that I have no fixed literary plans, except that I shall go on writing stories as they come to me. It is either very easy for me to write a story, or utterly impossible; that is, the story must "write itself" without any perceptible effort on my part, or it remains unwritten. There is not a tale in "Bayou Folk," excepting the first, which required a longer time than two, or at most three sittings of a few hours each. A story of more than 3000 words which will appear in Dec. Century was written in a few hours, and will be printed practically without an alteration or correction of the first draught. I do not need to be secluded in order to write. I work in the family living room often in the midst of much clatter. I never discuss a story or sketch with any one before writing it.

I have ready another collection of Creole tales which I hope to have published in book form after they have made their slow way through the magazines.

My first efforts in literature took the form of two novels of fifty and sixty thousand words. They were written in 1890. The novel does not seem to me now be my natural form of expression. However should the theme of a novel present itself I should of course try to use it. I do not consider one form of more value than the other.

I send these two photographs not knowing which would better suit the purposes of the Mag. Would you kindly return the one not used?

I am greatly interested in the Southern Magazine and read it with pleasure. I hope it will keep up the high standard which it has adopted.

Let me say, My dear Mr Barbe, that the press notices of your poems have given me a great desire to read them. Were I anything of a reader the poems would no doubt by this time have been familiar to me.

Very sincerely yours
Kate Chopin

TO A. A. HILL
3317 Morgan Street,
St. Louis.
Dec 26 '94

Mr A. A. Hill
Managing Editor
American Press Ass.
Dear Sir

In reply to your letter of Dec 11th, I beg to state that my publishers, Messrs Houghton, Mifflin & Co have kindly consented to my submitting to you two stories from "Bayou Folk." They desire to be consulted about the selection of the stories and wish the copyright to be fully protected. I shall write to you when I hear further from them.

If you think you would like to use "Azelie" which appeared in Dec Century, kindly let me know and I shall ask Mr. Gilders permission to offer it to you.
Sincerely yours
Kate Chopin

3317 Morgan St
St Louis
Jan 1st '95

Mr A. A. Hill,
Managing Ed.
Am. Press Association
Dear Sir

In answer to your request, I beg leave to submit the accompanying two stories of 5000 and 3400 words "In and Out of Old Natchitoches" and "In Sabine." These stories appeared in "Bayou Folk" a collection of Creole and Acadian tales published last March by Messrs Houghton, Mifflin & Co.

Kindly let me know as soon as you can if the stories meet your desires. One of the stories appeared originally in Two-Tales, the other, In Sabine, was written expressly for the collection.

Very truly yours
Kate Chopin

3317 Morgan St
St. Louis
Jan 11 '95

Mr A. A. Hill
Managing Ed. American Press Ass.
My dear Sir

As stated in a former letter, I have already obtained Messrs
Houghton, Mifflin & Co's consent to submit to you two stories
from "Bayou Folk." The enclosed letter will testify to their
approval of my selection. Will you kindly return the letter to
me; and would you also state what amount you propose to pay for
the stories.

Very sincerely yours
Kate Chopin

3317 Morgan St
St Louis
Jan 16 '95

Mr A. A. Hill
American Press Association
N.Y.
Dear Sir,

Five dollars per 1.000 words seems to me fair enough
compensation for use of the two stories.

Yours sincerely
Kate Chopin

TO J. M. STODDART
3317 Morgan Street, St. Louis
March 31 '95

Mr J. M. Stoddart
63 Fifth Ave N. York
My dear Mr. Stoddart

Since receiving your letter of March 21 in reference to
"Young Doctor Gosse" I have undergone two or three changes of
mind regarding the book. It was written in '91—before I had
found my way to the short story. I have been told, and believe,
that it is interesting. As a piece of literature it does not
satisfy me, and certain of its features I would treat differently
to day. The MS was first offered to McClurg of Chicago (!) then
to Lippincotts—Belfords, who kept it a year and returned it at

my request. Berry R. Tucker held it also a long time. Cassell, Schulte, Appletons, Stone & Kimball have considered it, and the Arena wanted to publish it at my expense. That is all—quite enough, I have often thought.

I should like to know your charges for offering the novel, also for disposing of short stories. "Vogue," since its beginning, has been taking all my stories and sketches of the character that might suit "Variety." I would ask $20.00 a thousand words for stories offered to the latter publication, which is the price paid me heretofore by the Century & Youth's Companion. Vogue pays something less.

The American Press Association has already bought a couple of my "Bayou Folk" stories for reprinting. I did not know that they desired first hand matter.

I would like to ask if you have any market for disposing of translations of de Maupassant?—

I have a one act comedy and a story of 4800 words which I would like to dispose of. The story is, I think, one of my best and the editor of the Century complemented me upon it. The theme, alone, barred it from the columns of that magazine—a note which he feared to sound too often, he wrote me. I thought of offering it to the Yellow Book but did not know how to reach them.

     Awaiting an answer regarding terms & c—

     I am   Yours truly

          Kate Chopin

TO CORNELIA F. MAURY, DECEMBER 3, 1895

          3317 Morgan Street

             St. Louis.

Dear Miss Maury

I have received your kind invitation to attend the exhibition of Water Colors, and shall take much pleasure in doing so.

I hope to look into your Studio some afternoon before long, if you will let me.

     Faithfully yours

     Kate Chopin

TO STONE & KIMBALL

3317 Morgan St.   St Louis

Messrs Stone and Kimball
Chicago
Gentlemen

Your note of the 18 Dec accompanying a returned MS. is responsible for my further effort to have you accept some of my work for the Chap-Book.

In the collection of stories and sketches which you have under consideration, are two which I should like to submit to you: "Lilacs" and "Three Portraits" &c and the verses "Then Wouldst Thou Know" and "Under My Lattice." These things have not been printed. I would greatly like to see one of them—some of them—something—anything over my name in the Chap-Book.

Yours very sincerely
Kate Chopin

Jan. 2 1896

TO THE *CENTURY*

3317 Morgan St
St. Louis

Ed. The Century
My dear Sir:

I am going to ask you to kindly read the accompanying M.S which has already been submitted to you under the title of "In the Vicinity of Marksville." I have made certain alterations which you thought the story required to give it artistic or ethical value; and fully appreciating the regret which you expressed at returning it, I take the liberty of offering it again to your consideration.

The change in the story will be found to begin on page 53. The marriage is omitted, and the girl's character softened and tempered by her rude experience.

Wishing you a very happy New Year

I am most sincerely yours
Kate Chopin

January Fifth '97.

TO LYDIA ARMS AVERY COONLEY WARD

3317 Morgan St.
St. Louis

Dear Mrs. Ward

I feel as though I could not delay in expressing to you my
thanks for your kind attention during my brief visit in Chicago,
and also my regret at being unable to see you again and bid you
good-by. I shall cherish the hope of meeting you again. Wishing
to be affectionately remembered to your mother and the dear son,

I am ever sincerely yours
Kate Chopin

March twentyfirst '98

TO THE *YOUTH'S COMPANION*

3317 Morgan St
St Louis

Editor The Youth's Companion
Boston
Dear Sir:

I hope you will like the accompanying story well enough to
use it. If unavailable, kindly let me have it at your earliest
convenience.

Faithfully yours
Kate Chopin

Feb eleventh '99
Story 2640 words—title "A Little Country Girl."

TO HERBERT S. STONE

3317 Morgan St
St Louis

Dear Mr. Stone—

I shall have another photograph taken for the Critic and
send it to you as soon as possible.

Very sincerely yours
Kate Chopin

May Twenty first
'99

Letter to Herbert S. Stone, 1899
3317 Morgan St
St Louis

Dear Mr Stone

I mailed a photograph this morning before receiving your letter. Will follow it with another today and others as soon as possible.

What are the prospects for the book? I enclose a notice which you may not have seen—from the Post Dispatch. It seems so able and intelligent—by contrast with some of the drivel I have run across that I thought I should like to have you read it when you have the time.

Very Sincerely
Kate Chopin

June 7th

TO RICHARD B. SHEPARD
3317 Morgan St
St. Louis

Hon. Richard B. Shepard
Salt Lake City
Dear Sir

Following is a list of books I have published:

At Fault—a novel published in St. Louis in 1891
Bayou Folk—Houghton, Mifflin & Co Boston 1894
A Night in Acadie—H S Stone & Co Chicago 1897
The Awakening—H S Stone & Co Chicago 1899

Any of these books, with the exception of the first named, which I will be pleased to send you, may be obtained of the publishers or any bookseller handling such literature.

Thanking you for your kind interest—

sincerely yours
Kate Chopin

August twenty fourth 1899

Hon. Richard B. Shepard
House of Representatives
Salt Lake City, Utah

3317 Morgan St.
St. Louis

Richard B. Shepard Esq.
Salt Lake City—
My dear Mr. Shepard

    Since receiving and answering your letters last July I have had a severe spell of illness and am only now looking about and gathering up the scattered threads of a rather monotonous existence. Kindly let me know if you have procured my books or if it is still your desire that I send them to you.

    Hoping you will pardon my unavoidable neglect in responding to your wishes

Yours very sincerely
Kate Chopin

November Eighth '99

TO THE *CENTURY*

3317 Morgan St
St. Louis

Editor The Century Magazine
Dear Sir:

    I beg to offer the enclosed story for publication in Century Magazine. The title—"Ti Demon" is one which I have offered before to the Century, but the story is entirely new. Hoping for an early reply

Yours very sincerely
Kate Chopin

December First '99

TO *YOUTH'S COMPANION*
3317 Morgan St
St Louis

Editor the Companion
Dear Sir:

I can't imagine that you will care for this little sketch, or impression of one snowy day last winter when I arrived in Natchitoches, but I send it anyway, hoping that you might. The impression of that snowy day in the old Southern town and the snow in the forest and upon the cotton fields was fantastic and beautiful and I cannot forget it.

Most sincerely yours,
Kate Chopin

February 15th 1900

TO R. E. LEE GIBSON
St. Louis, Mo.
3317 Morgan St

Dear Mr Gibson

I wish I could convey to you some idea of the pleasure which your poems have given me in their handsome new garb. They show a fine, fine spirit and I am proud to know you. What a speaking likeness! Do come when you can and let us talk them over. Mr. Deyo and I have enjoyed reading some of the sonnets together.

Believe me my dear Mr Gibson, with congratulations and sincere esteem

cordially yours
Kate Chopin

Oct 13th 1901

TO MARIE BREAZEALE, FEBRUARY 4, 1902
3317 Morgan St
St. Louis

My dear Marie

I certainly appreciate your letter very much because I know that letter-writing is not one of the things that you enjoy most in life. Indeed it was mighty nice of you to write and I hope you will keep that New Year resolution of letting us hear from you often. I suppose you will be going to join Phanor pretty soon. I don't see how you manage to exist apart from each other unless your affections have somewhat cooled since I was with you. How I should love to see Phanor in Washington. I know he is just the same old Phanor that he is in Natchitoches. I can't think of anything changing him or moving him from his good humored whimsical self.

You must have that Womens Federation send you up to our Worlds Fair. It isn't going to be next year, notwithstanding the assurances of the officers, not unless they can get some spooks and fairy godmothers to do the work for them.

How are the little ladies? Marie must be nearly a young lady now. Are they all as pretty as ever and is July still in the lead?

Nini writes me that Eugenie continues to improve. But I know she must still be far, far from her old self. I can't bear to think of her condition. What do the doctors say of her prospects of getting entirely well. Let me know what progress she makes. I should love to write to her if I thought there was any use. I hope you have told her of our solicitude.

We are all well but the weather is so nasty and cold that I am actually unable to get about or accomplish anything. Aunt Amanda has been very ill off and on and I feel quite uneasy about her. She went through so much sorrow and uneasiness in poor Nina's sickness that she has never gotten over it.

Lelia and the boys send their love to all—always including Mrs. Walmsley's family.

Affectionately your sister

Katie

Can't you pass by St. Louis when you go to Washington?

Undated Letters

TO MRS. TIFFANY

3317 Morgan Street.

St. Louis.

Dear Mrs. Tiffany

It will give me great pleasure to see you tomorrow and also to be able to meet Mrs Francis again before her departure.

You are too amiable; I must thank you in person for your kindness in overlooking my lapse

Very faithfully yours

Kate Chopin

Sunday.

TO OTTO HELLER
3317 Morgan Street
St. Louis

Professor Otto Heller—
Dear Sir:

I cordially appreciate your invitation to hear Dr. Pearses paper. I am sure it will be of great interest to me; but let me hope that I may be excused from taking any part in the discussion of it.

Very sincerely yours
Kate Chopin

December twenty-sixth

TO MRS. DOUGLAS
3317 Morgan St.

Dear Mrs. Douglas
I have to express a double regret in writing to you. First that I missed your visit and Judge Douglas's the other evening, and second that I cannot accept your kind invitation for Friday. I am leaving for the country early tomorrow morning and shall be absent about a week. But my first pleasant duty when I come back will be to go out and see you. I hope I may have another opportunity to meet Mr and Mrs Stevens.

Let me congratulate you, my dear Mrs Douglas. I leave you to imagine why.

Sincerely yours
Kate Chopin

July 10th

Inscriptions

FOR RUTH MCENERY STUART

To Ruth McEnery Stuart
The snow lay everywhere, thick and soft; the tree-branches were bent like bows beneath its weight. A white silence muffled the earth and its chill reached my very soul.

But I heard the voice of a woman: it was like warm music; and her presence was like the sun's glow through a red pane.

The snow lay everywhere; but its silence and its chill no

longer touched me. For the voice of the woman lingered in my ears like a melting song, and her presence, like the warm red glow of the sun still infolded me.

Kate Chopin
February Third 1897

FOR MADISON CAWEIN

I shall never lose the delight which Madison Cawein has given me in his poems and his voice

Kate Chopin

Aug 17 '99

Kate Chopin's social circle, the habitués of her salon, was full of newspaper people. William Marion ("Billy") Reedy, brash editor and guiding spirit of *Reedy's Mirror*, was a constant Chopin booster—as was *St. Louis Life*'s warm and generous editor, Sue V. Moore. John A. Dillon and Dr. Frederick Kolbenheyer were among the founders of the *St. Louis Post-Dispatch*; Dillon later became editor of Joseph Pulitzer's *New York World*. Charles Deyo and George S. Johns continued writing for the *Post-Dispatch*, while Florence Hayward wrote for its rivals, the *Globe-Democrat* and the *Republic*, and was also a correspondent for London newspapers. St. Louis's working literary colony was small, inbred, and always gossipy.

Kate Chopin was often reviewed in newspapers, and several of her stories appeared first in daily papers. Her very first short story acceptance, in fact, came from the *Post-Dispatch*, for "A Point at Issue!" (published October 27, 1899). "Mrs. Mobry's Reason"—a story hinting at venereal disease—was rejected by more than a dozen magazines before the *New Orleans Times-Democrat* accepted it in April 1893. "Odalie Misses Mass," the unusual story of an interracial friendship between an old black woman and a young white girl, first appeared in the *Shreveport Times* (July 1, 1895).

Chopin herself occasionally wrote newspaper prose. Early in her career, she sold four translations to the *Post-Dispatch* (reprinted in this volume), and later wrote a series of essays for the St. Louis *Criterion*. In November 1899, the *Post-Dispatch* published a jaunty essay by Kate Chopin about her writing. (Per Seyersted later entitled the piece "On Certain Brisk, Bright Days.")

In St. Louis, though, Chopin was also a literary personality—which made her an appropriate subject for the two interviews reprinted here. In the discussion of "Is Love Divine?" the novel Chopin alludes to is *The Awakening*, and the passage is somewhat different from the final published description of Robert. Although Chopin claimed to be a breezy, spontaneous artist, this text shows that she did indeed revise.

Her last prose piece, "Development of the Literary West," is quite sober and suitable for the more conservative *St. Louis Republic*. Instead of the ethereal, evening-gowned portraits usually accompanying Chopin pieces, "Development" has a brisk drawing of Kate Chopin by her son Oscar, then a twenty-seven-year-old newspaper cartoonist. Oscar shows his mother wearing a suit and sporting glasses: she has large, capable hands and looks very businesslike. That was an image Chopin sought to foster after reviews of *The Awakening* condemned the book, if not its author, as morbid, immoral, and decadent.

"Development of the Literary West," Chopin's last essay, is neither decadent nor dramatic. She had lost her touch.

"Is Love Divine?" The Question Answered by Three Ladies Well Known in St. Louis Society.

"Love is not divine. It is a thing to be controlled by circumstances and environment."

By Gen. Louis Auer, whose fad for getting his friends married has made him famous as "The Matchmaker of Milwaukee."

MRS. TUDOR F. BROOKS,
Who is prominent in the Humane Society of St. Louis:

Is love an emotion that one can give birth to, or dispose of, at will? Are we, who call ourselves human beings, merely a set of machines who think and feel by rule? Is there nothing in us, nothing inborn, inexplicable, which finds satisfaction nowhere save in sympathy and love? Certainly it would be difficult and distressing to believe that love, the motive power of the universe, existed as a material something to be idly picked up or wantonly destroyed by creatures incapable of knowing or appreciating so great a blessing.

I think that love is certainly a divine emotion—a God-sent gift. "Amor esto perpetua"—and a thousand years from this time the world will still find itself irresistibly swayed and ruled by the "grande passion."

One could hardly say that the emotion is never influenced by circumstances. One's surroundings may have a very marked effect on one's spontaneous affections. But to me, it seems that the

St. Louis Post-Dispatch, January 16, 1898, p. 17.

magnetic spark frequently ignites in spite of adverse circumstances—and independent of all environment.

MRS. SHREVE CARTER.

A charming Virginia woman, who has been a distinguished St. Louis society leader for some years past:

Does one ever really know what one's thoughts about "love" mean? Is it quite possible or logical to judge broadly in regard to the many, when one's convictions are formed only by a single, personal experience? I have heard men and women of more than ordinary intelligence declare that love was no more than a delusion—a temporary fleeting fascination—a transitory magnetic attraction existing between two persons of unusual congeniality or similarity of tastes. I cannot help but feel some small degree of pity and a greater amount of contempt for just this class of persons. There is a crack in the vase somewhere. They have either "loved and lost" or their souls have become too puny, too cramped and marred by constant introspection and analysis, to recognize and appreciate the blessing of love when it comes to them.

For myself—well, all women think alike on this subject, do they not? It seems to me that all true women must cherish this belief, deep down in their hearts, that there exists, or will exist, some time and somewhere, their kindred soul—their dual spirit.

MRS. KATE CHOPIN,

Who has written stories of Southern life and as a novelist should know what love is:

It is as difficult to distinguish between the divine love and the natural, animal life, as it is to explain just why we love at all. In a discussion of this character between two women in my new novel I have made my heroine say: "Why is it I love this man? Is it because his hair is brown, growing high on his temples; because his eyes droop a bit at the corners, or because his nose is just so much out of drawing?"

One really never knows the exact, definite thing which excites love for any one person, and one can never truly know whether this love is the result of circumstances or whether it is predestination. I am inclined to think that love springs from animal instinct, and therefore is, in a measure, divine. One can never resolve to love this man, this woman or child, and then carry out the resolution unless one feels irresistibly drawn by an indefinable current of magnetism. This subject allows an immense field for discussion and profound thought, and one could scarcely voice a definite opinion in a ten minutes talk. But I am sure we all feel that love—true, pure love, is an uncontrollable emotion that allows of no analyzation and no vivisection.

"Has High Society Struck the Pace that Kills?"

"Within a month four young women of high social position have committed suicide under circumstances which seemed to indicate sympathetic motives. All of these young women were petted daughters of society. The condition of mind and body which would lead them to seek self-destruction was not caused by the pinch of poverty, the strain of work or the worries of women who must toil. Aside from the possibility of morbid emotional excitement there was no strain upon them, except the strain of social activity and rivalry. Does the conjunction of suicidal attempts indicate a tendency in that direction among the women of society? "Has high society struck the pace that kills?"

—Post-Dispatch Editorial, Jan. 23

"Society is an elixir of bon-bons. It represents the joy of being alive; the presence of beauty, usually of birth, occasionally of brains, but always wealth, and with it every opportunity for fastidious delight. The atmosphere seems a trifle heady. That it should lead to suicide is pathetic. It is worse. There is nothing as dismal as a young girl's death. She has lived so little. In her heart is the longing and the dream of beautiful to-morrows. 'Wait for me,' she cries. 'I am coming.' When the dream of the morrow retreats and the longing subsides; when the future narrows into a blind alley; when some formless thing, she knows not what, comes to her, plucks at her sleeve, sits by her, whispers to her and incites her to hide herself from life, then it is not death alone with has passed that way; it is tragedy!"

—EDGAR SALTUS.

St. Louis Post-Dispatch, February 6, 1898, p. 12.

MRS. MARIA I. JOHNSTON.
Lecturer for the Chart and Current Topic Clubs, which are composed of ladies of fashion.

Knowledge of society as it now exists convinces me that its conditions have nothing whatever to do with the tendency of society women to suicide, if it be true that they are so inclined.

If we may trust the pages of history, the disposition of society women to self-destruction has decreased of late years.

Both men and women now feel the weight of responsibility in regard to suicide which formerly sat lightly on their minds.

The causes of suicide count for nothing in the great population of this country.

For ages women have taken their lives to escape dishonor. In the present state of society, when women are so carefully guarded, this cause is infrequent.

The condition of mind that would bring about a desire for self-destruction in a child of fortune would be the result of disease or heredity, rather than of her social environment.

Society is a comprehensive term which means the association of human beings of all conditions.

Fashionable society is only a thin strata. I do not consider its present atmosphere unhealthful. It is an atmosphere in which like seeks like. The strain it occasions is even less than that of the lower grades.

MRS. JOHN GREEN
Litterateur, expert whist player and prominent society woman.

It is a benefit to women who have no definite occupation to employ themselves in attending to their social duties. It keeps their minds active and saves them from ennui. It has been the salvation of many a woman.

I believe that society is in a healthy condition. There is no especial tendency to suicide among society women. There have always been suicides and always will be, but the ratio has not increased. In fact, I believe that statistics will show a falling off in the number of society women who have taken their own lives in recent years.

The desire of young women to destroy themselves usually has its origin in family troubles or a love affair. Being sensitive and highly refined, they hesitate to confide their troubles to another, and brood over them until, to their morbid fancy, death seems the only relief.

There is certainly nothing about the prevailing conditions or duties of society that would tend to a nervous strain severe enough to produce a desire for self-destruction.

MRS. KATE CHOPIN.

Leader of a literary set in St. Louis society and author of many stories of Creole life.

Leadership in society is a business. It is a good thing for women who have no other occupation to engage in it and endeavor to keep up with the social whirl. There is nothing about it that I can see that would tend to produce an unhealthy condition of mind.

On the contrary, it prevents women from becoming morbid, as they might, had they nothing to occupy their attention when at leisure.

Business men commit suicide every day, yet we do not say that suicide is epidemic in the business world. Why should we say the feeling is rife among society women, because half a dozen unfortunates, widely separated, take their own lives?

The tendency to self-destruction is no more pronounced among society women than it ever was, according to my observation.

The desire seems to come in waves, without warning, and soon passes away. The mere reading of a peculiar case of suicide may cause a highly nervous woman to take her own life in a similar manner, through morbid sympathy.

But do not men do the same thing every day? Why all this talk about women?

MRS. MARTHA DAVIS GRIFFITH.

Lecturer, authoress and leader of the Literary Symposium, an organization of society women.

Languor is banished by the activity of modern society, but the consequent strain is too great for a person of nervous and excitable disposition. I can easily see how such physical and mental tension, seldom relaxed, would induce a frame of mind that would terminate in suicide.

At the very least it would produce a hysterical tendency in women, and hysteria is often a cause of suicide.

I do not believe the conditions of society as now organized are healthy. To persons who are weak, either in body or character, it is ruinous. Women, it must be admitted, are particularly susceptible to the effects of excitement. Many of them need a balance wheel. Strong will-power can overcome a woman's inclination to be flighty, whatever her station in life, but women who are so inclined would do well to keep out of society, as nearly as they can consistently with their station in life.

But in spite of these facts, I do not believe that the percentage of suicide among society women is increasing. There will always be isolated cases but the average, I think, will never be greater than now.

Development of the Literary West: A Review.

By Kate Chopin

What would Father De Smet with his Indian sketches have thought of Bret Harte and his "Luck of Roaring Camp?"

That was the beginning—that "Luck of Roaring Camp"—so we have all come to acknowledge. It was the first resounding note. It reached across the continent and startled the Academists on the Atlantic Coast, that is to say, in Boston. They opened their eyes and ears at the sound and awoke to the fact that there might some day be a literary West. Something different from the East, of course, and alien, but to be taken seriously, to be observed and considered.

Personally, I like to give precedence to our own well-beloved Father De Smet and his Indian sketches. The little volume with its quaint complimentary offering on the fly-leaf, no doubt, reposes, musty, on many a library shelf in St. Louis, libraries that perhaps ceased to grow when St. Louis began to spread.

The dear old man spoke the English language indifferently well, but he wrote with simplicity and directness. Pinning his faith in God and General Harney, he invaded the great unknown West and conquered it with the abundance of his love. The red man was his most noble friend. Savage tribes became his "dear spiritual children." Hell's Gate Fork and Bitter Root Valley held no terrors for him. The mountains and the great plains were his inheritance. Of all this he tells, and when one has read there is left upon the mind a well-traced picture of the early West, by no means devoid of atmosphere and color.

St. Louis Republic, December 9, 1900, Special Book Number, p. 1.

But the West of to-day is by no longer the West of Father De Smet and Bret Harte. The red man is vanishing. The buffalo has become a zoological specimen. Trails of the prairie schooner are obliterated. Mining camps are not so very far from the police station, and the bucking broncho is colliding with the automobile.

There is an intensely interesting story developing in the West. Hundreds of men and women, keen with artistic perception, are telling it and telling it well. There is sometimes a two obvious lack of reserve in their work, often tawdriness, but there is always vigor. Bret Harte has naturally had his followers, but it is pleasing to note that the great majority of Western writers have observed with their own eyes and have chronicled their individual impressions.

What pleasure have we not felt, for instance, in reading the stories—so genuine—of Mary Hallock Foote? Hers is excellent work, with a fine literary quality, damaged somewhat by a too conventional romanticism. But she knows her territory and leaves in the mind of the reader no inclination to question.

Then there is Ambrose Bierce away off in California. He, too, is a product of the West, but he has that peculiar faculty or privilege of genius which ignores subservience. He acknowledges no debt and pays no tribute. His "Soldiers and Civilians" might be called an eccentricity of genius. It is certainly a marvelous flash of the horrors of the possible. Depicting not so much what we are familiar with as what might be, hence, the shudder. His originality defies imitation.

Another Western writer of note is Owen Wister, in whose work there is a suggestion of the spectacular. This effect may be partly due to the profuse illustrations, which usually accompany it. But he gives the impression of a stagy fellow with an eye on his audience in the East. Yet his stories are greatly liked, and this may be a squeamish opinion, not wholly just.

Sincerity, on the other hand, strongly marks the work of Octave Thanet. One almost feels that she and A. B. Frost were created for each other, so graphically does he catch the spirit of her inspirations.

Her heart is essentially with the plain, everyday people. We meet her characters everywhere—crowding the department stores on bargain days, hurrying with bundles through the streets; thronging the lodge meetings and church sociables. She must walk about our Middle Western towns with her mental notebook open, chuckling to herself. But how she gets A. B. Frost to see exactly what she sees is a mystery.

Along with Bret Harte, the man, it seems to me, who most subtly reflects the western spirit, is Hamlin Garland. At his worst, Hamlin Garland has been guilty of inexcusable crudities in handling men and women. At his best, he has not been surpassed in his field. His best, to my mind, is represented by the long short-story entitled "In The Land of the Straddle-Bug," published several years ago in the Chap Book. Nowhere, except in Tolstoi's "Master and Man," and perhaps Mary Wilkins's "A Solitary," has any recent writer so vividly portrayed an atmospheric condition. The march, the sweep of the season on the Northern prairies, as he depicts it, is like a noble epic. The dreariness, the sinister, gray gatherings of clouds; the bleak rainfall; the still and killing cold and great winding sheets of snow; the flaming splendors of the sun, could only have been told by one whose soul is close to nature. He believes in himself and follows his own light. May he never be tempted to follow false gods.

Chicago has recently developed, among many writers of talent, a group of young men whose mental vision seems to be impaired by the city's skyscrapers, and who are apparently fascinated by the hideous complexities of life which so phenomenal and abnormal a growth has produced. Their work has its place in the great mosaic word-picture of the West, but it makes unpleasant reading.

Here, at home, Winston Churchill has had marvelous success with his historical romance. He is said to be engaged upon a novel depicting life in St. Louis during the days of Lincoln and Grant. This is good news. It is not well to let the age slip by unchronicled, and Winston Churchill, of all young writers, seems best fitted to tell the story of so important an epoch in the West.

After all, where are we to draw the line? May we not claim Mrs. Catherwood of the Northwest? James Whitcomb Riley and the whole State of Indiana that abounds in novelists and minor poets? Will the South cede to us Madison Cawein, John Fox or the incomparable James Lane Allen? Perhaps we are claiming too much, but draw the line ever so taut and we still have enough to be proud of if it were only Mark Twain. The West will surely continue to develop along the lines of a natural and wholesome growth, as yet unimpaired by intellectual complications.

 TRANSLATIONS

Kate Chopin seems to have been genuinely bilingual. At home with her great-grandmother, Madame Victoire Verdon Charleville, she presumably spoke only French. Kate's mother, Eliza Faris O'Flaherty, spoke English with a French lilt, and her French-speaking relatives never could manage to pronounce "O'Flaherty."

Young Kate grew up among Francophiles in St. Louis, where her formal education at the Sacred Heart Academy was based on the French educational principles of the Society's founder, Phillippine Duchesne. Sacred Heart events had French names: a refreshment break was *goûter*; hide-and-seek was *cache-cache*; and a play day was a *congé* (see Kate O'Flaherty's poem "The Congé" in her Commonplace Book, pp. 35–36). Their use of French marked Sacred Heart girls as an intellectual and social elite, for most were also daughters of the old French ("Creole") families of St. Louis.

On her honeymoon, Kate O'Flaherty Chopin spoke French in France, apparently with ease. As her honeymoon diary shows (earlier in this volume), she wrote French spontaneously, omitting accent marks—just as, in English, she frequently omitted or even misplaced apostrophes.

As a new bride in New Orleans, Kate Chopin probably spoke a French *patois* to the servants, and both English and French to friends and Oscar's colleagues. (If she met the painter Degas, presumably they spoke French.) The vernacular New Orleans Creole *patois* appears in such Chopin stories as "La Belle Zoraïde" and "A Lady of Bayou St. John," and the term "Creole" was already shifting meaning in her day. In *The Awakening*, it means a white person of French or Spanish ancestry—but in Chopin's short stories, it sometimes has today's most common meaning: a light-skinned person of color.

New Orleans, then as now, was a multilingual city—but Cloutierville, Louisiana, where the Chopins moved in late 1879, was purely French. There Madame Chopin would have had to speak the small village's common language. Even legal papers were often, though not always, written in French, and the baby Lélia Chopin's baptism appears in the church ledgers in French. Except for a few outsiders, such as Dr. Samuel Scruggs, the Chopins' friend and family physician, English speakers were rare in the Cloutierville area until after World War I.

But in St. Louis, where Kate Chopin returned to live in 1894, German-Americans predominated, and there were half a dozen daily German-language newspapers. The newly widowed Kate Chopin would have used English almost exclusively for daily life—but as a member of the city's literary and artistic circles, she regularly read French literature. Along with her friend and occasional publisher, *Mirror* editor William Marion Reedy, Chopin believed that the best and most avant-garde literature was coming from France. Yet she was not uncritical: Emile Zola's *Lourdes*, which she read in French, was ponderous and dull, she wrote in a review. The author seemed unable to rid himself of the notion that he must instruct his audience, whether they wished to be lectured to or not.

She had been "groping around," she wrote in 1896, looking for something else in her reading, when she discovered Guy de Maupassant. The daring French author was "a man who had escaped from tradition and authority . . . who, in a direct and simple way, told us what he saw. . . . I even like to think that he appeals to me alone." She evidently devoured his work: the Maupassant stories she chose to translate come from six different collections.

Kate Chopin hoped to make extra money through translations, and in 1891 she sold three translated articles to the *Post-Dispatch*: "The Shape of the Head," "The Revival of Wrestling," and "How to Make Manikins." The first drew on her interest in psychic phenomena, scientific discoveries, and paradoxes. She loved ghost stories, but gently mocked believers in extrasensory perception in her story "A Mental Suggestion" (1896). The other two are more for young people. "The Revival of Wrestling" would have had special appeal to her youngest son, Felix, a Central High School athlete. "How to Make Manikins," instructions for making paper dolls, may have had some interest for eleven-year-old Lélia Chopin. The *Post-Dispatch* evidently retitled the translations: in the Wondra Account Book, they are called "A Study in Heads," "Wrestling," and "Cut Paper Figures."

A year later, Chopin sold a more adult translation to the *Post-Dispatch*: the passionate marital drama of Adrien Vely's "Monsieur Pierre." She also translated at least three other pieces, now lost, for which we have only the tantalizing titles in the Wondra book: "A Trip to Portugese Guinea," "A Visit to the Planet Mars," and "Transfusion of Goat's Blood."

Her major translation interest was, however, Maupassant's stories of suicide, madness, solitude, disillusionment, and illicit love. Between 1894 and 1898 she translated eight of his tales but managed to publish only three: "It?" and "Solitude" in *St. Louis Life*, edited by her friend Sue V. Moore, and "Suicide" in the conservative *St. Louis Republic*. Chopin offered an edition of six of Maupassant's "Mad Stories" to Houghton, Mifflin, her *Bayou Folk* publishers. They declined, saying they did not publish translations from contemporary literature.

In fact, for most American readers, Guy de Maupassant was considered too racy. American public libraries generally shunned his works, along with those of Zola and Gustave Flaubert, as immoral.

Kate Chopin, however, disapproved of censorship. She kept Thomas Hardy's much-reviled *Jude the Obscure* on display in her house and wrote that she hoped young people would read it; she also wrote that Zola's melodramatic writings might actually be valuable for Catholics to read. Because her own friends were cosmopolitan readers, she may not have known how restricted Americans generally were in their reading and writing. Adultery, a routine subject in Maupassant's fiction, had been virtually banned from American literature in her time. "Guilty love" was not permitted in magazines and books edited for "The Young Person," the assumed general reader.

While she was making her last (unpublished) Maupassant translation, Kate Chopin was also writing *The Awakening*—a novel which would have been considered exquisite and perfectly acceptable in France. In the United States, however, the portrayal of a woman who commits "guilty love" without feeling guilty was considered "too strong drink for moral babes." Chopin's critics found her book downright wicked, sensual, even French in its outlook.

Kate Chopin and Guy de Maupassant were exactly the same age, but by the time her career was truly launched, his had ended prematurely: he died of syphilis in 1893. Chopin's career also ended abruptly—from discouragement, ill health, and too many other cares. But in one of her last reported public appearances, on May 2, 1902, she was one of the patronesses for a lecture sponsored by the French Benevolent Society of St. Louis. The speaker, M. Hugues Le Roux, was a distinguished literary figure who had known Gustave Flaubert, served as Alphonse Daudet's secretary, and was "an intimate friend of Renan, Maupassant, and President Faure." Still, the admiration and translation of French authors was never Kate Chopin's forte. Her own fiction was her true calling.

Until Thomas Bonner's *Kate Chopin Companion* (1988), Chopin's unpublished translations of Guy de Maupassant stories existed only in manuscript. For her last one, "Father Amable," she did not make a clean copy, and Bonner's transcription from her virtually illegible pencil draft is an extraordinary achievement. Interested readers are directed to Bonner's work for all of Kate Chopin's translations of Guy de Maupassant.

Her other translations are reproduced here.

The Shape of the Head.
Remarkable and Peculiar Variations That Have Been Observed

THE RESULTS OF A STUDY MADE BY A PARISIAN—HOW THE SIZE AND SHAPE
VARY—THE HEADS OF SOME PROMINENT FRENCHMEN—HINTS FOR SCULPTORS.

Mr. Henry Havard, a Parisian, has lately, for his own
satisfaction and the edification and instruction of his versatile
fellow-townsmen, made a study of heads. Apart from scientific
reasons, he has been moved in this practical study, to furnish
thereby a hint to sculptors in their methods of work. For it must
be known that there is scarcely a man of any note in France
whether he be artist, literateur, inventor or successful
merchant, who may not be certain that his bust will descend to
posterity. Here are a few results of Mr. Havard's researches in
anthropology, through the medium of famous hatters of Paris!
While it is gratifying to note for instance that the head of the
lamented Paul Bert is singularly like in form to that of
Voltaire, is it not deplorable that the cranium of the esteemed
and talented M. Milne-Edwards offers nearly the same conformation
as that of Ribot the assassin?

On the other hand we find the heads of certain remarkable
men, who in the exercise of a common profession have acquired
almost an equal notoriety, presenting projections absolutely
different. There are few lawyers of higher repute than Messrs.
Caraby, Demarge and Clery. Observe the diagrams of their heads,
and decide if it be possible to make a useful deduction from
them.

Messrs. Atthalin and Goron have won a merited renown in the
arts of cross-examining criminals. Well, follow with the eye the
vertical line which divides their respective diagrams and which
marks the mesial plane of each. You will observe that with
Atthalin the left side is more largely developed, while with
Goron it is the right. An astonishing contradiction.

Similar surprises await us in passing from the bar to the
army. Gens. Gallifet and Lebrun present extremely elongated
heads, while those of Ferron and Brugin are decidedly round.
Among the politicians who have governed the destinies of France
for twenty years, the differences of cranium are not less
considerable or strange.

It will be noticed that the diagrams of Giambetta and Bardoux

St. Louis Post-Dispatch, January 25, 1891, p. 12.

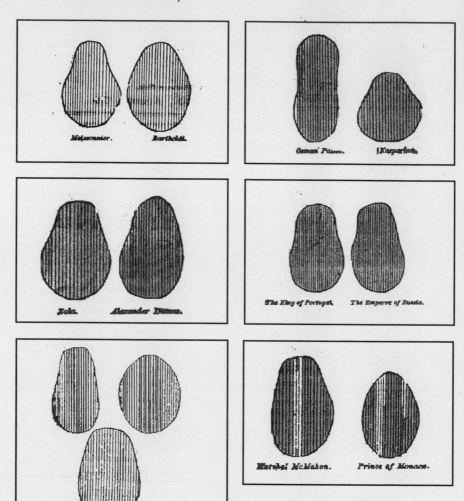

are admirably proportioned. Again, considering persons of high
social rank and those who exercise or have exercised a supreme
authority, these assertions will not seem less varied nor
astonishment. Certainly the head of the Duc [about two lines lost—paper
damaged]
could be desired, and that of the Duc de Montpensieur one of the
largest known. On the contrary, those of Mareschal MacMahon and
the Prince of Monaco are startlingly diminutive.

We may gather from these strange and confusing examples that

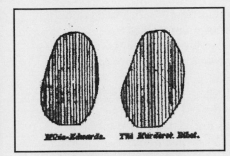

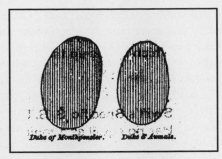

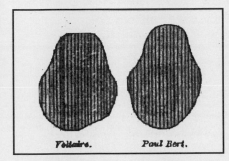

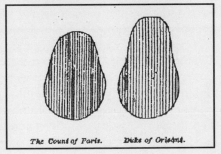

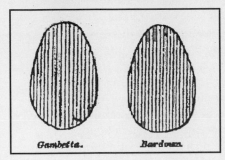

it is impossible to determine a priori the exact formation of
man's head even in strictly acquainting ourselves with his
special qualifications, whether moral or intellectual, or with
his work or actions.

Notwithstanding the surprising diversity of shape which we
have noted as existing in the skulls of certain of our great
contemporaries, we know that the general form of the head depends
upon race, and varies with it.

So we may conclude that there are poets, painters,

mathematicians, sculptors and merchants whose heads are decidedly oval; that there are mathematicians, poets, painters and sculptors whose heads are round. Because there are races which present these differences. It is a question of origin and not of aptitude. Yet miscalculations are frequent.

Within the confines of Europe, for instance, all peoples of Cimbric origin, those inhabiting the borders of the Mediterranean, North-Germans, Swedes and Norwegians are dolicocephalous (having elongated skulls), whilst peoples of Celtic origin, Southern Germans, Austrians, Hungarians, Swiss, Irish and Gaelic are on the contrary, brachy-cephalous (round-skulled). Compare the head of Osman Pacha with that of Dr Kasparian of Pesth, for example.

But the theoretically certain becomes practically uncertain, because of the incessant migration and resultant crossing of races. Such migration began with the quarternary epoch. So we may judge of the alliances, the mixtures of blood and consequent curious modifications which have come about since that remote period. If we needed proof that all a priori reasoning must be advanced with caution, it would only require that we contemplate the diagrams of the accompanying heads of Breal and that of Henri Rochefort. The former being of Semitic origin, should display an oval type; the other being of Franco-Celtic race should be slightly round, but it is exactly the contrary.

We see by these few examples how much it is to be wished that all illustrious men of our day would submit to an exact measurement of their skulls. Sculptors would not be so liable then to commit awful blunders; and posterity would be able to handle with more certainty those problems which are at present agitating the anthropological world.

Revival of Wrestling.

THE FAVORITE SPORT OF ANCIENT TIMES THE FASHION NOW IN PARIS.

HISTORY OF WRESTLING THROUGH THE AGES—THE ROMAN WRESTLERS—THE
GREAT PIETRO—HIS CHARACTERISTICS—THE FRENCH WRESTLERS—SWELL
AMATEURS IN PARIS.

Written for the Sunday Post-Dispatch.

So early as the sixth century, B. C., we hear Xenophon complaining that the wrestler's strength was preferred to the wisdom of the philosophers. Plutarch seems to have been more in sympathy with the manly exercise, for he calls it "the most artistic and cunning of athletic games." If we needed further evidence of the remote and very respectable lineage of this neglected science—or art—we have but to turn to the paintings in the Egyptian grottoes at Beni Hassan. Here are wrestlers presented in all attitudes—certainly faulty from a modern art standpoint, but no doubt highly satisfactory to the ancient Egyptians. As for the real origin of gymnastics we have no record. It lies in pre-historic times. We have seen that the old Egyptians practiced it. Homer, in his second and twenty-third books of the "Iliad" chants of athletic sports. That it formed a necessary part of the education of the Greek youth we know, and that the Spartans began the bodily training of their boys at the age of 7. Their boys, mind you, for as a quaint old Roman chronicler tells us: "Gymnastics were considered unbecoming and indecent for women (!)"

With the Greeks athletic sports were universally indulged in and thought to be ennobling. In such high repute were running and wrestling held that the victors in the Nemear games were rewarded simply with a wreath, that they might not stoop to the cultivation of their bodily faculties for gain.

The Romans, with whom wrestling was the sport par excellence, practiced it on a very magnificent scale in their famous Circus Maximus; but it was considered by them an occupation unbecoming the patricians, and they employed well paid hirelings for purposes of exhibition. The exercise seems to have been practiced there very much as it is now, except that the third throw decided the victory. Besides, it was the custom for the combatants to anoint their bodies with oil to insure suppleness to the limbs,

St. Louis Post-Dispatch, March 8, 1891, p. 12.

and to sprinkle themselves afterward with sand to enable the
adversary to secure a firmer hold in the contest. So the bath,
which invariably followed, was rather a driving necessity than
the luxurious indulgence which we like to imagine it.

DECLINE OF GYMNASTICS.

Gymnastics went out of repute and were abandoned entirely
during the Middle Ages, the days of chivalry. Feats of
horsemanship, skill with the broadsword and crossbow, and later
the invention of gunpower, made the cultivation of bodily
strength and agility a secondary consideration.

It was only in the beginning of the present century that a
rival of the long forgotten exercise set in again. It began in
Prussia, when Jahn with his gymnasium, rendered the science so
popular, that to its universal practice is largely attributed the
success of the Germans in driving out the army of the first
empire.

The system was introduced into the French army in 1844 by
Louis Philippe, since which time gymnasts have formed a feature
of all continental armies except those of England.

But Plutarch was right when he called wrestling the most
artistic and cunning of athletic games. He might have lauded it
more highly and still not said enough in praise of it. There is
no exercise so healthful, bringing into play as it does all the
physical faculties; developing as none other can the wonderful
mechanism of the human body.

Nearly all other exercises fail in some one thing. The legs
work too much or too little; certain muscles, remaining
unemployed, lose in strength; the equilibrium is destroyed. But
wrestling calls for strength, agility, suppleness, shrewdness,
tact and resistance. The weakness or absence of any one of these
six qualities gives the different sorts of games remarked among
athletes. The wrestler who feels himself infirm in one, endeavors
to turn his other qualities into the balance in larger
proportion. The perfect wrestler is the one who unites in himself
these physical and intellectual points.

THE FAMOUS PIETRO

Such a union is rare, but it is to be found in one man whose
fame comes to us through French channels. He is a South
American—one Pietro; apostrophised as the great, the only, the
incomparable Pietro, superior to all known wrestlers. His feats
have been the admiration of Paris, but he has partly retired now

from the arena, and lives upon his gains, most of the time at his
superb home in Buenos Ayres. His distinguished qualities might be
given as natural strength, remarkable muscular development,
dexterity, agility and judgment. He attacks as readily with the
left as with the right hand, and possesses enormous tact, which
enables him to take advantage of the first mistake of his
adversary. No athlete possesses in the same degree so many
qualities mentioned. As agile as a cat, and as dexterous as a
monkey, he attacks with the rapidity of lightning: He is simply
irresistible.

In France wrestling is indulged in as a game rather than a
combat, and is conducted by rule, regulated by formal convention
and marked always by a character of courtesy. Unlike American
methods—which admit of every and any thing—with them the
contestants are required to seize each other by the upper
portions of the body and are permitted to resort to no tricks
such as tripping to overthrow an adversary, but must rely upon
their strength and dexterity to gain their point.

The very excellent and graphic illustrations accompanying
this sketch represent certain French wrestlers indulging in their
favorite pastime. The grapple, indicated in figure 1, naturally
marks the opening of the contest. The athletes have approached
and have clinched hands; each endeavoring by some skillful move
to get the start on his opponent. Often the success of an
engagement depends upon this first encounter.

In figure 2 the wrestlers stand face to face, looking into
each other's eyes, ready for an emergency. The one who has
grasped his antagonist around the waist counted upon taking him
by surprise, but the other evidently has quickly folded his
arms—a simple movement which deprives his opponent of a support
in attacking and spoils his game.

THE BRIDGE

Figure 3 represents a combination known in the parlance of
wrestling as "the bridge." To avoid touching the ground with both
shoulders, which would close the contest, one of the wrestlers
has thrown his head violently back and endeavors to turn while
his opponent bears with full weight upon him.

The end of a conflict is portrayed in figure 4, in which the
exultant conqueror is seen pinning his man firmly to the ground
by the two shoulders. The elation depicted in his face is
especially such a good-natured one that it is difficult to
believe that even his vanquished foe could bear him ill will.

THE CONQUEROR.

THE GRAPPLE.

Pietro

THE BRIDGE.

THE BACK CLINCH AND FORE-ARM GUARD.

But it is through the amateur rather than the professional that wrestling is in a fair way to regain the high favor to which it has an incontestable right. So it is in France at all events, where gentlemen have made the sport fashionable to-day. It is quite the thing for the jeunesse dore of Paris to appear at the Hippodrome or the Cirque Moliere and meet professionals in the arena. The only mark to distinguish them from their plebeian antagonists, being a difference of costume, if such scanty attire as a pair of black tights covering the lower portions of the body can be called a costume. M. San-Marine appears to hold among amateurs the position which Pietro holds with professionals. He has often wrestled in the Cirque Moliere, has performed feats of strength that are astounding to think of and has even measured his strength with the famous South American. But Pietro is Pietro, the invincible!

Though we can hardly hope soon to see our American youth doing such unconventional things as that, it is very much to be wished that wrestling would grow more in favor with us than it is at present. When we come fully to realize the intimate relation existing between body and brain, the healthful influence which a sound physical condition exerts upon the intellectual faculties, we will perhaps be more ready to admit the importance of careful bodily training for men and women.

The old Greeks taught many lessons that we would do well to go back and learn. And in the studying we might find that true civilization may not mean gunpowder and electricity after all.

C.

How to Make Manikins
Ingenious ways to Cut Amusing Figures Out of Paper.

A PLEASANT AND AMUSING PASTIME FOR THE LITTLE PEOPLE—A SISTER OF CHARITY AND A LITTLE GIRL AND SEVERAL OTHER FIGURES EASILY MADE.

Written for the Sunday *Post-Dispatch*.

The only working materials necessary to shape the amusing little figures shown in the accompanying illustrations are a few visiting cards, a piece of strong white paper, black and colored pencils and a pair of scissors.

St. Louis Post-Dispatch, April 5, 1891, p. 12.

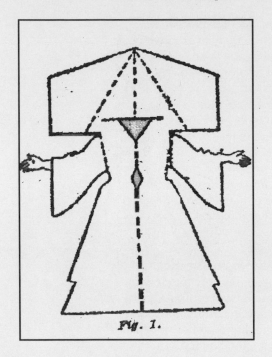

Fig. 1.

Fig. 2.

Fig. 5.

Fig. 6.

Fig. 7.

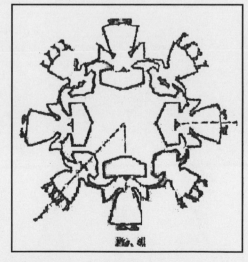

Fig. 8.

Double a visiting card lengthwise. Then upon a piece of transparent paper trace and cut out the half of fig. 1; having done that transfer the design to one side of the folded card, the central dotted line corresponding with the fold in the card. Having outlined this demi-figure it only remains to cut the card accordingly. Upon opening it, a figure resembling that of No. 1 will be disclosed.

What remains to be done now is to shape it into the Sister of Charity shown in fig. 3. In order to do this refold the card in central line, bring the arms forward, creasing them in dotted lines indicated in the model; then form the bonnet by means of two oblique folds, also in designated dotted lines. The shape of this bonnet may be slightly varied at pleasure, but it should always be fashioned with the idea of concealing the face, which is not there. The pencils now do their work. Color the skirt and sleeves a dark blue, leaving the large apron white, against which may be designed a rosary, a bunch of hanging keys, etc. A candle or a folded card representing a prayer-book might be placed in the hands. Such accessories may be varied according to taste.

Following the outline of fig. 3, another order of sister may be found without difficulty, differing chiefly in the matter of bonnet from her predecessor. Slightly spreading the two sides of the card will enable these small personages to stand solidly upon a table or other smooth surface.

ANOTHER LITTLE GIRL.

Passing to fig. 5 we see the plan of a little girl having four legs! In so representing the child, the designer has no intention of wounding the popular prejudice which favors little girls with the usual number of legs. What we want to do—having created and cut fig. 5 as we did the preceding ones—is to lop off the supplementary legs, on one side the right leg, and on the other side the left one, so that viewing the little one in profile, we find that she has two very nice legs, as correctly balanced as a little girl's legs need to be. The pencils will enable us to give her a red bonnet, red stockings and a blue-dotted gown. The little girl may be made to stand very securely by placing her feet in two slits made in a mustard bottle cork.

To represent a very pleasant scene, in which four sisters are shown dancing around in a ring with four of their little pupils, secure a sheet of stiff white paper. Double this. Then by a second crease, perpendicular to the first one, fold it in four.

Finally an intermediate fold will give you the paper doubled eight times. On the upper surface trace (as shown in fig. 7) the half outlines of a sister and a little girl. Having cut those out and unfolded the sheet we have a duplicate of fig. 8.

In coloring and shaping these frail manikins, care must be taken not to tear them, especially at the joining of the hands which are very fragile. Handle each figure as though it were separate and distinct from the others, cut away the superfluous legs and the work is finished. The little people will be found to stand upright without any trouble. Further embellishment of these figures and groups are left to the skill and fancy of the young people who may like to fashion them.

Monsieur Pierre.

HOW FRANCOIS LOST HIS LIFE AND HIS WIFE BY THE SAME SHOT.
FROM THE FRENCH OF ADRIEN VELY, BY KATE CHOPIN.

It was night, and intensely cold. Anne Marie, all wrapped about in her shawl, was hurrying with rapid strides toward the village. She had been engaged in sewing at a neighboring chateau, and was now hastening to reach home before the hour of dinner, knowing as she did, that her husband would not willingly wait.

Suddenly she was met by a young soldier, who, having recognized her, stopped at once.

"Good evening, Anne Marie?"

"Good evening, Monsieur Pierre."

"How pale you are," he said, "and you must be frozen! Have you been working again at the Chateau?"

"Yes, and I had forgotten the hour. I fear that it is late."

"And fear, above all, to be scolded, maltreated! Poor Anne Marie."

"You are mistaken, I assure you, Monsieur Pierre. I shall be neither scolded nor maltreated."

"I am not mistaken, Anne Marie. I know that your husband repays your care and devotion with hard words. I know that you toil like a slave to support your child, forgetful of self, whilst he muddles himself with drink."

"Oh, Monsieur Pierre! Believe me, you are wrong."

"Come, now! He beats you—the wretch! Do not deny it. I know that he has beaten you."

"Monsieur Pierre, you are cruel. Well, yes; all that you say

St. Louis Post-Dispatch, August 8, 1892, p. 2.

is true. But is it right for you to thus accuse my husband to me?"

"How can I help it, Anne Marie? I suffer so in knowing your unhappiness. You are so gentle, so worthy, so courageous. I suffer so in being powerless to help you; you whom I love so well. For I do love you, Anne Marie. I love you to distraction."

"M. Pierre!" cried the young woman, affrighted, "hush—I must not listen to you. I implore you to say no more." She retreated to a neighboring tree, against which she leaned, shivering from head to foot.

"Yes, I know," said Pierre, "everything separates us, and I should not have spoken—but that was more than I could do. I have kept this secret closed so long in my heart, suffering in silence. Oh, I repeat it. I adore you. But you are troubled—and how you tremble. Are you angry with me? Have I offended you? Why do you not answer? You are weeping. Ah no! There is a smile through your tears! Oh, Anne Marie, that would be too much happiness—I cannot believe that you love me."

"M. Pierre, I beg of you!" murmured the young woman faintly.

"Ah! you do love me, I feel it—I see it. Why try to hide it? You may yet be happy since we love each other."

"Monsieur Pierre," replied Anne Marie gravely, "you force me to speak the word that must separate us forever. Well, yes, I love you and with all my heart. I love you because you are kind and noble, because you have always shown an interest and affection for me. But I am married and I am honest. After what I have told you, we must never see each other again."

"You are right, Anne Marie. It is better so—that we should never meet again."

"Monsieur Pierre, did you not hear the sound of a footstep?"

"No, it is only the wind blowing the fallen leaves."

"I must make haste; it is late. From to-day we are strangers. Good-by."

"Good-by, Anne Marie."

It was the night following. A freezing night. Pierre, enveloped in his large, hooded cloak, had mounted guard at the powder mill just beyond the town. Suddenly a man advanced toward him.

"Qui vive!" called Pierre.

"How? You do not know François, the husband of your good friend?"

"Halt or I fire!"

"Fire on me? Come now! But if you killed me you could never marry Anne Marie."

"Wretch!"

"Oh, abuse me if you want. I have you in my power and I defy you to fire on me. I heard you both last night. It was charming—it was touching! Truly, I was moved to tears, and I pitied you both from my soul. What an immense favor to you two if I should disappear now—if I should die. No more obstacles, my good friends. A bullet in the head and that would end it."

"My duty is to fire on you!"

"Your duty! Now if you fired on me, my fine fellow, do you think Anne Marie would believe you did it from duty? Would she not rather suppose your object was to be rid of me? And would she be willing to marry you under such conditions? With a single motion you could, you ought to put an end to me. But that motion you will not make. And I have come expressly to tell you this. Kill me, and Anne Marie is lost to you forever. Spare me and you forfeit your honor—your honor of a soldier, to which you hold more than life. What do you say to this little revenge? Is it not well thought out? But this is only the beginning. I have some pleasant surprises of the same nature in reserve. I shall see you again."

And while Pierre stood immovable, dumb with rage, and powerless, the scoundrel retreated whistling.

He then hastened, as was his custom, to the ale house and in an hour's time was stupefied with drink.

Then there came to him a drunken, ferocious whim.

He started in the direction of his house, and once there, entered the room where Anne-Marie was sleeping, and brutally laying hold of her, dragged her from her bed.

"What is the matter!" cried the trembling woman still half asleep.

"Dress yourself."

"But why?" she asked timidly. "It is not yet morning."

"Will you dress yourself?" and he advanced upon her, enraged, with uplifted arm.

Poor Anne Marie, seeing that it was useless to resist and knowing that he would beat her rather than abandon his purpose, dressed herself hurriedly.

Then he seized her violently by the wrist, dragging her after him into the street.

"Oh, where are you taking me?" she moaned.

"Where am I taking you? You wish to know? I am taking you to a tender rendez-vous, my sweet one. I thought you might find the time long away from your lover, Pierre; that you dreamed of him, perhaps. So I concluded it would be a charity to unite you both."

"François, have pity! What do you mean to do? Oh, this is

terrible! Let me return."

"No, no," cried the wretch, hurrying her violently over the road. "He is sad out there all alone. You must go and keep him company—go and distract him. Come on."

When they reached the powder mill it was midnight and the silhouette of the sentinel stood out sombre and immovable.

"Qui vive!"

"Come, do not get excited. See how kind I am; I bring you your good friend. I am amiable."

"Halt, or I fire!"

"Oh, no, my brave fellow; you would not kill me in face of your sweetheart—you"—

A shout resounded through the plain and François fell in a senseless heap, muttering a last imprecation. Anne-Marie had fainted away.

The report brought the Sergeant of the Post at once to the spot.

"What has happened?" he cried.

"Why?" replied the sentinel. "I had just relieved my comrade, Pierre, and had taken his watch, when a man approached me with threats. I cried, 'Qui vive, halt!' He continued to advance; then I obeyed orders and fired. I believe that he has his deserts."

"The novel does not seem to me now [to] be my natural form of expression," Kate Chopin wrote to the West Virginia editor Waitman Barbe in 1894 (see Letters and Inscriptions, this volume).

Indeed, Kate Chopin wrote more short stories than any other form: it was more congenial to her imagination. Although both she and her friends claimed that she wrote spontaneously, often producing a story in just one sitting, her best stories do not appear to be dashed off. She certainly planned stories carefully in her mind before she grabbed the pencil and cheap newsprint paper she traditionally used to write early drafts. In Chopin's most famous short story, "The Story of an Hour," for instance, every detail contributes to the emotional impact. Mrs. Mallard's heart condition, mentioned only in passing in the first paragraph, leads to the story's deadly, shocking finale.

Most of the stories reprinted here show that Kate Chopin did revise, rework, and polish. The drafts or fragments come from various sources (see Notes), but the four shortest ones—"The Boy," "Doralise," "Misty," and "Melancholy"—are in the undated manuscripts Daniel Rankin borrowed from the Chopins in 1932 and never returned. The handwritten, newsprint scraps languished in a Massachusetts warehouse for sixty years, until Linda W. Marhefka found them in 1992. (See "Kate Chopin, 1885–1904," this volume).

The stories in the Rankin-Marhefka Fragments will be discussed separately, below.

"A Lady of Shifting Intentions," "A Horse Story," "Ti Frère," and "Alexandre's Wonderful Experience" are reproduced as they first appeared in *A Kate Chopin Miscellany* (1979). The Rankin-Marhefka Fragments transcribed are from the cache discovered in the Worcester warehouse. The transcriptions were produced over five months of meetings by a group of patient, diligent, and keen-eyed graduate students at Louisiana State University: Brian

Arundel; Phyllis Catsikis; Kevin Dwyer; Chris La Jaunie; Cynthia Maxwell; Anna Priddy; Leonard Vraniak; and Steve Weddle.

After laboring mightily, the transcribers brought forth the discovery that the Rankin-Marhefka manuscripts of "A Little Country Girl," "Alexandre's Wonderful Experience," "The Gentleman from New Orleans," and "Charlie" (also known as "Jacques") are substantially the same as earlier published versions. We encourage those interested in minute textual variations to compare the versions (all are housed at the Missouri Historical Society), but we have chosen not to reprint the almost-identical texts. Not all transcribers agree on all readings, and Emily Toth sometimes served as final arbitrary arbiter.

The Fragments, scrawled in pencil on crumbly newsprint, are often virtually unreadable. Crossed-out words are reproduced as strikeovers, and empty brackets indicate thoroughly illegible words.

Fragment of
A Lady of Shifting Intentions

and lit the gas in there: there was an old looking brussels carpet on the floor—the white marble mantle looked like a sepulchre—the wood and coal in the grate were all fixed ready to be started—Nora fell upon her knees before the sepulchre and held a match to the sooty paper stuffed between the bars—"Where's sister Bess?" asked Stetson—

"It isn't back from the club meetin' that she's come yet, sir—" "An' father won't be back from the office for an hour—I'll run up and see mother—you know she doesn't get downstairs—I guess she'll have you come up presently"—and he left the room, all excitement. To Stetson, this was the most beautiful spot on earth—He knew every brick along the pavement of the narrow dingy street—the arm-railings were interwoven in his life—the sepulchre and parlor grate fire were connected with all his youthful dreams and ambitions—It would never have entered his mind to suspect that they were producing other than a genial impression upon his friend—

Beverly seated himself in a little brown rep rocker—that worked in a jerky way on springs—and gave himself up to contemplating the blaze that was catching the kindling—he assisted matters a little with the poker—and with the spirit of an eighteen-year old boy, was prepared for anything—presently there was the sound of a latch key in the lock—the front door was flung open & shut with a determined swing—a charge was made upon the parlor door—it yielded—and a young woman stalked into the room—She had left the umbrella in the rack and was wearing her mackintosh as she entered—She was robust, fully as tall as Beverly—a thick-waisted young woman of thirty—her light hair combed back under a felt walking—her eyes round and questioning—her cheeks round and wet with rain. "She looked a blank question—" Beverly arose and bowed as he had been taught to bow at dancing school. "My name's Beverly—I came with Will—he's up stairs," he said with a flush of embarrassment—"Oh Beverly—why, I'm delighted—and she gave him a vigorous handshake. I guess you know who 'sister Bess' is. Will up stairs. I'll run up and give him a hug." Beverly fell back in his chair. He felt as if he were being buried beneath crumbling illusions. He had formed in his mind a composite picture . . .

Ti Frère

If Ti Frère had had any sense,—well, he was tired of working in the cotton patch: of being poor; of hearing himself called Ti Frère when his name was Joe. He was skilful enough with the hoe. Yet he brought the sharp blade down upon his foot, cutting an ugly gash through the worn shoe, deep into the flesh. He had been chopping weeds along the outside row of cotton; he was in a bad, careless humor, and had slashed himself severely. With a sharp cry he flung the hoe away and sitting upon the ground bared his wounded foot.

Azémia, who had witnessed the accident, came running toward him as fast as her feet could carry her. She was lithe and supple; sure of herself; yet she grew faint at sight of the blood that trickled down upon the ground. With quivering fingers she unknotted the soft handkerchief from her neck.

"Oh, Ti Frère! Yere, wrap my han'k'chief 'roun' it." But he reached back and gathered a fistful of cotton from the low-hanging bolls; with this he staunched the blood as he refused her offer of the handkerchief.

"This'll do," he said sullenly without looking up, adding with rude impatience: "an' besides that I a'nt yo' brother; my name's Joe."

Azémia stood speechless with amazement. She had never heard him called otherwise than by the endearing nickname. No one remembered, save by an effort, that he had any other.

It was only a day or so ago, however, that a Texan whom he met down at Nat Bower's cabin had laughed at his name and waxed humorous on the subject; and Ti Frère had then and there resolved to "call people down"—an expression also acquired from the Texan—who "called him out of his name."

Azémia's young face, which a moment before had glowed with solicitude, became rigid and cold—oh, so cold; as if an icy blast had swept across it.

Ti Frère, looking up quickly after he had spoken, caught a breath and a flash of the cold as she turned from him.

She walked away with her chin in the air. She did not know that holding her chin in the air gave her head with its smooth black hair a very fine poise. Ti Frère did not know it either.

If he had had any sense,—but he went on daubing the blood with the raw lint; finally drawing on his stocking over a thick wad of it. He managed to get on his shoe by tearing away the flap from the old brogan. Then he went and picked up his hoe; drew his old felt down over his troubled brown eyes and started limping toward his home—away over on the other side of the big field where he lived with a widower brother-in-law and a disagreeable cousin.

He looked back as he went limping; but Azémia was not noticing him. She was sweeping the gallery with useless flourishes of the broom, and talking in a loud and cheerful tone to her old grandmother within doors.

The following morning Ti Frère presented himself at Azémia's house with a dozen very magnificent peaches tied up in a bandana. He held his foot slightly from the ground as he stood handing the peaches up to Azémia on the gallery.

"Yere are some peaches I brought you, Azémia," he said, "You can't get any peaches like Leonce's anyw'ere 'roun' 'yere. I picked 'em early so's they'd be cool an' fresh."

"Thank you," she replied, looking through him as though she were contemplating some object of interest seen through his substantial frame. "Gra'ma is very fon' of peaches," and she called out:

"Tiens, Grand'mère! des pêches de chez M'sieur Léonce."

Grand'mère, at the mention of peaches, came out on the gallery, fat and waddling, fanning herself. Grand'mère was always fanning herself.

The peaches were luscious things. Grand'mère carried them inside telling Ti Frère to wait for his bandana. He seated himself on the upper step and stretched out the wounded foot before him. When Grand'mère came balancing back, he told her all about his mishap.

He began at the very beginning: how things had aggravated him all day; and how he was thinking of those things and not of the weeds, when he brought the sharp blade down upon his foot.

"And then," he went on, "I lost my temper completely. I could not have spoken a decent word to anyone. If you—why, even if my poor mother had come back at that moment, I'm afraid I would have said something rude to her."

He was talking to Grand'mère, but he was looking at Azémia throwing corn to the chickens. She paid not so much heed to his words as she did to the clucking of the hens; yet he continued his depressing story, describing the sleepless night he had endured, tormented by pain and by remorse.

Grand'mère's sympathy failed to make amends for Azémia's lack of attention. When the old lady kindly brought him out a vial of some soothing ointment and gave him minute directions for applying it, he put the thing gratefully enough into his pocket and went away.

He spoke to Azémia again that day and the next. She answered him but did not address him, and never once called his name. He had never before realized how formal, how altogether desolate a thing it was to be spoken to in that way by some one he cared for.

It seemed now that the mere mention of his name was what had heretofore given a certain tenderness to everything she said to him. He fancied if he could hear it again, all the warmth that had suddenly gone out of his existence would be restored to him.

He did not a second time take anyone to task for calling him Ti Frère; even not the little darkies who called him "Mr. Ti Frère."

He wondered if that Texan, Bud Aiken, were still in the Parish. He treasured seriously a scheme of waylaying the fellow and doing him some bodily injury. He longed to lay his hands upon Bud Aiken and pound and punch and pummel him in fact as he was doing to his heart's bent in fancy.

When Saturday came Ti Frère hoped for a recurrence of a naive little performance that Azémia had gone through for many consecutive Saturdays. He had grown accustomed to it and had come to look for it.

"Ti Frère," she would say, calling him from the field or addressing him as he passed trailing his hoe or leading his mule along the path. "Ti Frère, w'at are you goin' to do tonight?" And Ti Frère would stop and abandon himself to reflection, searching his memory for a possible engagement.

"Because," she would go on, "we are goin' to have veillée at the house an' I want you to come," or "we are goin' to pass veillée down at Cousine's." It was always veillée somewhere and she would not listen to the excuses which Ti Frère sometimes manufactured for the sole purpose of inciting her to insistence.

He knew as well as she did why she inveigled him into the harmless veillée of a Saturday night: it was to lead him away from the allurements of Nat Bower's cabin down the bayou. The solicitude which Azémia had always evinced to entice Ti Frère from the dangerous allurements of the cabin had seemed to indicate on her part an interest in his welfare which not alone flattered him, but gave a motive and a meaning to his existence.

He was sure she would not fail him this time; and all day Saturday he waited for her to speak to him, but she evidently had no intention of doing so on that particular Saturday. She even seemed mildly astonished when he took the initiative and stopped to ask her if there were no veillée in prospect for the night.

Veillée, indeed! as if she had no other things to think of!

He asked if she would like to have his pony to ride to church next morning, and offered to bring it around to her. No, she did not want the pony; she was going to Mass with the Chotards in their cart. Ti Frère turned away filled with unutterable discouragement.

Azémia watched him furtively as he went along stumbling over the rough ground. This time he did not look back. His wounded foot seemed to have grown worse: it was evidently painful for him to touch it to the ground. He had not taken the rest which Grand'mère had advised. Grand'mère believed greatly in rest; in repose of body and mind; in "des petits soins."

Ti Frère was in that state of mind which is usually described as "looking for trouble." He mounted his pony a good bit after dusk and started down the bayou road. His foot pained him cruelly; but he took a morbid satisfaction in letting it bump and dangle against the pony's fat flank, while the throbbing and twinges served him as pretext for an ugly mood.

It was a warm night and so still that the rhythmic pound of his pony's hoofs and creaking of his saddle seemed to fill the night immeasurably. Occasionally there was the sound of other hoofbeats coming out of the silence, meeting and mingling with his own and passing on. There was the faintest pale glow in the east across the fields where the moon would be up before long.

Ti Frère, still following the bayou's course, had soon left the great sweep of open fields behind him. The road had gradually narrowed to the faintest trail, indiscernible at times and almost impassible by reason of intersecting branches and a stubborn tangle of sprawling undergrowth. Voices and other sounds began to reach him. The bullfrog and the hooting owl mingled their uncanny night-calls with rasping, monotonous insistence. Some black thing slid from a nearby shiny log and dipped into the water with a dull splash. A pirogue glided lazily by; a voice from the pirogue called out: "C'est toi, Frézime?"

Ti Frère did not answer. He was near the lake at the head of the bayou and he could distinctly hear the flapping of great wings as an army of buzzards circled down upon the moss-draped branches of the cedars that reared their grim heads in mid-water.

Nat Bower's cabin was on the very rim of the lake. It was a species of boat-house, and in the gloom of the night it was hardly distinguishable from the distorted growth that crowded, overlapping to the water's edge. The light from the open door reached out along the water, and bats were darting in swift, aimless flights across its faint beam.

Ti Frère entered the cabin without attracting special attention; one man looked up from a game of craps and nodded absently to him. The cabin room was dismal, the light of two oil lamps serving rather to emphasize the gloom than to lighten it. A profusion of fishing tackle, guns, hung along the logs and the walls and the rafters. Men were playing cards at two tables, others were playing craps while a group stood about the improvised bar from which Nat Bowers—a half-breed—was dispensing whiskey by the glass. A Negro sat in the open window playing a low monotonous tune on an accordeon.

Ti Frère stood for a while watching the dice players. He had no desire to join them: he was gathering and reserving his energy for some other purpose. One man who was pleased to believe that Ti Frère had brought him luck standing at his elbow insisted upon his taking something at the bar. Ti Frère did not want anything to drink, and the generous crap player wanted to know what then, in the infernal regions, had brought him there.

Ti Frère strayed to one of the card tables and stood rather aimlessly by, till a man who was losing heavily turned upon him calling him a hoodoo, besides other uncomplimentary names, and the youth, having no desire to quarrel with the fellow, strolled across to the other table. "Hello, Ti Frère," greeted him amiably one individual who was drawing together in a pile a number of white, blue and red bone "chips."

"Hello, Ti Frère!" called the big Texan looking up from the other side of the table. "Hello, Ti Bébé."

"You want to look out," retorted Ti Frère sullenly, whereupon he was laughed at and his sullenness deepened. He pushed his broad felt back on his head and mopped his thin pale face with a red bandana; his hand shook nervously.

"Does your mammy know you are out, Ti Bébé," continued the facetious Texan, winking indiscriminately at his companions, while he shuffled the cards with marvelous dexterity.

"Did baby get its face washed and say its little prayers before it started out, hey?"

A quick blow struck Aiken. Another and again others rained down in swift succession. At the very first blow the man had lost his balance, tilting sideward from his chair, grasping at the table as he went over. The occupants of the cabin gathered about in noisy confusion; but none lifted a hand to interfere.

Then a strange feeling overtook Ti Frère. He did not know what had caused it; as if all energy had been stunned within him. There was a spontaneous cry of indignation.

Some one caught hold of him.

"Take him out to the do'!" cried another. Ti Frère was led from the room.

He steadied himself, once in the open air, and drew away from his supporters.

"Let me be," he protested.

"Put him on his hoss an' turn 'im loose, the fool!" suggested some one.

He reached his pony without assistance, and after a struggle or two succeeded in mounting; seeing which, the men who had accompanied him re-entered the cabin.

All sense of reality had deserted him as he threaded his way through the tangle that skirted the bayou. The path was unfamiliar. The moon, of which he caught glimpses through the trees, was like a lamp in the sky, and its light played fantastic tricks.

A swinging vine struck Ti Frère on the head. It was very unkind, he thought, striking a man thus on his defenceless, hatless head. He swayed and his head fell forward on the pony's neck, and his fingers got tangled in the animal's thick mane.

How comfortable it was to rest thus against the pony's neck! How pleasant was the rocking lope when they struck the bayou road! But a pony has no sense to go galloping on when a man is swerving, clutching, reeling—.

Ti Frère lay upon the road with his face bare to the moonlight. He could hear the pony pounding away and he tried to lift his voice to arrest the animal's flight. Then he felt that it made no difference. Nothing made any difference. He laid his

hand upon his side and held it there while the blood oozed
through his fingers.

Ti Frère had given a beating to Bud Aiken.
[Probably a few paragraphs missing.]
His people found him unconscious in the lane
at daylight, twenty paces from his home—his pony galloping away
as fast as his firm feet could carry him toward the Sabine hills
where he had been born and raised.

Ti Frère's case presented a most serious and vicious
complication. The wound in the side was bad enough, but the foot
was worse, inflamed and threatening, and the disagreeable cousin
vowed that he had tramped needlessly about and come and gone with
a raging fever on him the whole week. The wisest of the doctors
who saw him said it would be a miracle if Ti Frère recovered. And
then every one felt very sorry, for they suddenly remembered his
kind heart and forgot his quick temper. Grand'mère lamented
openly and drew a moral to embellish her theory of
rest—repose—des petits soins.

When someone told Azémia that Ti Frère was going to die she
shook all over and set down her milk pail and left it there
without rinsing. She walked straight out of the house to escape
further chatter of the visitor and her grandmother's monotonous
reiterations. She went out and leaned over the gate and looked
across the path, across the cotton field, toward Ti Frère's home.
She could not see the house—the cotton was so full and tall—but
her eyes strayed in that direction and they were full of tears
that glistened and fell upon her cheeks and she made no effort to
wipe them away. Through a sudden overwhelming flood of emotion
there came a subtle knowledge of other things that she had not
thought of—the conviction that there are natures which seem born
to lean upon and be guided by other stronger and tender ones. How
often she had heard people say: "If Ti Frère had had any sense:
he would have done thus or so or this and that," when in reality
he was like one in the dark feeling for a friendly hand to lead
him.

Azémia did not think in any logical, practical way of
this—it was rather like an illumination that came to her with
the pain of loss. And there came an impulse that she obeyed. She
opened the gate and went out—went over across the field along
the narrow footpath that cut its way through the cotton. It was
stifling with this world of green closing in about her, reaching
above her head. The dry bolls scraped her dress; her skirts
gathered wisps of lint as she passed that clung to her. She was

crossing Ti Frère's patch, where he would have been picking cotton if—. She could not bear to think the rest, but hurried forward with a quicker, keener impulse than before.

Azémia did not present herself in the character of a nurse, and surely not in the one of a physician; therefore the disagreeable cousin was disinclined to permit her to see Ti Frère. But Azémia with a new and big resolve in her heart was not to be stayed; all the way through the cotton she had been uttering a holy intention: If Ti Frère could be spared, never again would she turn from him so long as she lived; never, never! And it was at the feet of Mary the Virgin that she unfolded this promise, and it was her patron saint she called upon to witness the sincerity of her resolve.

She had intended to sit beside his bed and speak to him; but she stood staring down at his pallor and the stupor in which he lay. The speech which she had intended to utter shrank from her lips and in its stead came a sob. She sank upon her knees beside the bed and clasped his hand.

"Ti Frère," she whispered. "Ti Frère; oh, Ti Frère." She could say nothing else. She wanted to say nothing else. He turned his gaze upon her, and as he looked long, his eyes began to gather intelligence from the promise in hers.

A Horse Story

Herminia, mounted upon a dejected looking sorrel pony, was climbing the gradual slope of a pine hill one morning in summer. She was a 'Cadian girl of the old Bayou Derbanne settlement. The pony was of the variety known indifferently as Indian, Mustang or Texan. Nothing remained of the spirited qualities of his youth. His coat in places was worn away to the hide. In other spots it grew in long tufts and clumps. To the pommel of the saddle was attached an Indian basket containing eggs packed in cotton seed; and beside, the girl carried some garden truck in a coarse bag.

From the moment of leaving her home on the bayou, Herminia had noticed a slight limp in Ti Démon's left fore foot. But to pay special attention to his peculiarities would have been to encourage him in what she considered an objectionable line of conduct.

"Allons donc! You! Ti Démon! W'at's the matter with you?" she exclaimed from time to time. They had long left the bayou road and had penetrated far into the pine forest. The ascent at times was steep and the pony's feet slipped over the pine needles.

"I b'lieve you doin' on purpose!" she exclaimed vexatiously. "If I done right I would walked myse'f f'om the firs' an' lef' you behine." Ti Démon held his leg doubled at a sharp angle and seemed unable to touch it to the ground. At this, Herminia sprang from the saddle, and going forward, lifted the animal's foot to examine it.

The leg was shaggy and might have been swollen; she could not tell. But there was no sign of his having picked up a nail, a stone, or any foreign substance.

"Come 'long, Ti Démon. Courage!" and she tried to lead him by the bridle. But he could not be persuaded to move.

The girl stayed wondering what she should do. The horse could go no further; that was a self evident fact. Her own two legs were as sturdy as steel and could carry her many miles. But the question which confronted her was whether she should turn and go back home or whether she should continue on her way to Monsieur Labatier's. The planter had his summer home in the hills where there were neither flies, mosquitoes, fevers, fleas nor any of the trials which often afflict the bayou dwellers in summer.

It was nearer to go to the planter's—not more than three miles. And Hermania cherished the certainty of being well received up there. Madame Labatier would pay her handsomely for the eggs and vegetables. They would invite her to dine and give her a sip of wine. She would have an opportunity of observing the toilets and manners of the young ladies—two nieces who were spending a month in the hills. But above all there would be young Mr. Prospere Labatier who perhaps would say:

"Ah! Herminia, it is too bad! Allow me to len' you my ho'se to return home," or else:

"Will you permit me the pleasure of escorting you home in my buggy?" These last considerations determined Herminia beyond further hesitancy.

With the piece of rope which she carried on such occasions she tied Ti Démon to a pine tree near the sandy road in a pleasant, shady spot.

"Now, stay there, till I come back. It's yo' own fault if you got to go hungry. You can't expec' me to tote you on my back, grosse bête!" She patted him kindly and turning her back upon him, proceeded to ascend the hill with a little springy step. She wore a calico dress of vivid red and a white sun bonnet from whose depths twinkled two black eyes, quick as a squirrel's.

Ti Démon observed her with his dull eyes and continued to hold his foot from the ground like a veritable martyr. It was still and restful in the forest and if Ti Démon had not been suffering acutely, he would have enjoyed the peaceful moment. Patches of sunlight played upon his back; a couple of red ants crawled up his hind leg; he slowly swished his long, scant tail. The mocking birds began to sing a duet in the top of a pine tree. They were young; they could sing and rejoice; they knew nothing of the tribulations attending upon old age. Ti Démon thought to himself:

"If this thing keeps up, there's no telling where it will land me."

While he understood Herminia's broken English and her mother's 'Cadian French, Ti Démon always thought in his native language, that he had imbibed in his youth in the Indian Nation.

He stood for some hours very still listening to the drowsy noises of the forest. Then a blessed relaxation began to invade the afflicted foreleg. The pain perceptibly died away, and he straightened the limb without difficulty. Ti Démon uttered a deep sigh of relief. But with the consciousness of returning comfort came the realization of his unpleasant situation. He could fancy nothing more uninteresting than to be fastened thus to a tree in the heart of the pine forest. He already began to grow hungry in anticipation of the hunger which would assail him later. He had no means of knowing what hour Herminia would return and release him from his sad predicament. It was then that Ti Démon put into practice one of his chief accomplishments. He began deliberately to unknot the rope with his old, yellow teeth. He had observed Herminia give it an extra knot and had even heard her say:

"There! if you undo that, Ti Démon, they'll have to allow you got mo' sense than Raymond's mule." The remark had offended him. He hated the constant association with Raymond's mule to which he was subjected.

He managed after persistent effort to untie the knot, and Ti Démon soon found himself free to roam whithersoever he chose. If he had been a dog he would have turned his nose uphill and followed in the footsteps of his mistress. But he was only a pony of rather low breeding and almost wholly devoid of sentiment.

Ti Démon walked leisurely down the slope, following the path by which he had come. It was a pleasing diversion to be thus permitted to roam at will. He did not linger, however, to nibble here and there after the manner of stray horses, for he knew well that the pine hill afforded little sustenance to man or beast; and he preferred to wait and whet his appetite with the luscious bits that grew below along the bayou. He appeared like a wise old philosopher plunged in thought.

By frequent stepping upon the rope dangling from his neck, it at length gave way, much to Ti Démon's satisfaction.

"Now! if I could get rid of the saddle as easily!" thought he.

It was impossible to reach the girth with his teeth; he tried that. Then Ti Démon shook himself till his coat bristled; he rubbed himself against the tree; he rolled over on his side, on his back, but the only result which he reached was to turn the saddle so that it dangled beneath him as he walked. At this he swore lustily to himself, as his master, Blanco Bill, used to swear so many years back in the Nation. He did not feel now like nibbling grass or amusing himself in any way. His one thought was to get home to his dinner of soft food and be rid of the hateful encumbrance beating against his legs.

When Ti Démon found himself standing before his home, he viewed the situation with sullen disapproval. The little house was closed and silent. The only living thing to be seen was the cat sleeping in the shade of the gallery. A line of yellow pumpkins gleamed along the boards in the sun. There was a hoe leaning up against the fence where Herminia's mother who had been hoeing the tobacco plants had left it.

"Just as I thought," grumbled Ti Démon. "I could 'a sworn to it. That woman's off galavanting down the river again; dropped her hoe the minute Herminia's back was turned. An' them kids ought to be back from school; drat 'em! A thousand dollars to a doughnut they gone crawfishing. If I don't shake this whole shootin' match first chance I get, my name ain't Spitfire." It was the name Blanco Bill had given him at birth and the only one he acknowledged officially.

"There's no opening gates or lifting latches or anything since they got them newfangled padlocks on," he further reflected, "if there was, I'd get inside there an' them cabbages an' cowpeas 'ld be nuts for me. Reckon I'll stroll down an' see if I c'n ketch Solistan at home." Ti Démon turned again to the road and with a deliberate stride which sent the saddle bumping and thumping, he headed for the neighboring farm up the bayou.

There was nothing startling to Solistan in seeing Ti Démon staring over his fence. He simply thought Herminia had returned from the pine hall, that the animal had got loose from the "lot" and he went forward to drive him into his own enclosure, intending to take him home later, when he should be at leisure.

But Solistan's astonishment was acute when he discovered Ti Démon's condition; covered with clay and bits of sticks and bark,

Herminia's saddle hanging beneath him, and the blanket gone. It was but the work of a moment to drive the pony back in the lot; to throw a measure of corn into the trough; to saddle his own horse and start off at a mad gallop.

"Wonder what all the commotion's about," thought Ti Démon as he attempted to munch the corn from the cob. "He didn't take much trouble to pick an' choose when he gave me this mess. This here corn mus'be a hundred years old; or my teeth ain't what they used to be."

Solistan knew Ti Démon too well to believe that he had cut any capers which could have resulted in harm to Herminia. But the saddle must have turned with her; he might have stumbled and thrown her. A hundred misgivings assailed him, especially after he had been to her house and discovered the place deserted by all save the cat asleep in the shade of the gallery.

Solistan had started away just as he was, in his blue checked shirt and his boots heavy with the damp earth of the fields. He never dreamt of stopping to make a bit of toilet. He could not remember when he had in his life been a prey to such uneasiness. He had known and liked Herminia all her life; but she was always there at hand, seeming to be a natural part of the surroundings to which he was accustomed. It was only at that moment, when the menace of some dreadful and unknown fate hung over her, that he fully realized the depth and nature of his attachment for the girl.

Solistan rode far into the forest, his anxiety growing at every moment, and sick with dread of what any turn or bend in the road might reveal to him. He could not contain himself. He shouted for joy when he saw Herminia standing unharmed and motionless beneath a tall pine tree, as though she were holding a conversation and even some argument with his rugged majesty.

Her sunbonnet hung on her arm and her whole attitude was one of deep dejection. Herminia was in truth helplessly surveying the spot where she had so insecurely fastened Ti Démon, who had disappeared, leaving not so much as a hair of his hide or tail to say that he had ever been there. This seeming treachery on the part of Ti Démon marked the culmination of Herminia's mortification, and the tears were suffocating her.

Oh! it had been very fine up at the planter's! Too fine indeed. There was a large house-party congregated for the day, and little Herminia standing on the back gallery with her eggs and garden truck had been scarcely noticed.

She had been permitted to dine with them, wedged in between two stout old people; but she felt like an intruder and even perceived that the servants gave themselves the air of forgetting her. The young ladies' volubility and ease of manner made her feel small and insignificant; and their fluffy summer toilets conveyed to her only the bitter conviction of never being able to reproduce in calico such intricacy of ruffles and puffs. As for Mr. Prospere, he had only exclaimed: "Hello! Herminia!" in passing hastily along the gallery when she sat with her garden truck and eggs.

She could scarcely eat, for mortification and disappointment. She had not had an opportunity of relating the misadventure to her pony, and when, at leaving, the planter solicitously asked how she was going to get home, Herminia replied with forced dignity that she had left her horse tied a little below in the woods.

There was the wood all right, and there was Herminia, but where was the pony? That was the question which Herminia seemed to be asking of the big pine tree when Solistan rode up in such hot haste and flung himself from the saddle as if to reach out for some prize that he had pursued and captured.

"Oh! Solistan! I lef' Ti Démon fasten' yere this mornin'; he couldn' walk; an' now he's gone! Oh! Solistan! Someone mus' 'ave stole' 'im!"

"Ti Démon is in my lot eatin' co'n fo' all he's worth. The saddle was turned under 'im. I thought you'd got hurt." Solistan wiped his steaming, beaming face with his bandanna; and Herminia felt at beholding him that she had never been so glad or thankful to see any one in her life. And she could not think of any one whom she would rather have seen at that moment; not even Mr. Prospere. Not even if he had come along and said:

"Allow me the pleasure of escorting you home in my buggy, Herminia!"

Solistan's was a big, broadbacked horse, and Herminia sat very comfortably behind the young man on her way back to the bayou; holding on to his suspenders when the occasion required it.

After they had reached Solistan's home and he had brought forth Ti Démon resaddled and refreshed, the following bit of conversation took place between them. Herminia was mounted, ready to start, and Solistan was still holding the animal's bridle.

"That Ti Démon of yo's is played out, Herminia. He isn't safe, I tell you. He'll play you a mean trick some these days. I been thinkin' you better use that li'l mare I traded with Raul fo' las' spring."

"Oh! Solistan! it would take too much corn to feed 'im. We

got Raymond's mule to feed; an' Ti Démon eats fo' three, him—"

"Oh! shoot Ti Démon; his time's over."

"Shoot Ti Démon!" cried the girl, flushing with indignation. "You talkin' like crazy, Solistan. I would soon think o' takin' a gun an' shootin' someone passin' 'long the road."

"I'm jus' talkin'," laughed Solistan, perceiving the impression which his heartless remark had produced. "Ole Démon's good fo' a long time yet. He's plenty good to haul water or tote the children up an' down the bayou road. But don't you ever trus' yo'se'f in the woods with 'im again."

"You c'n be sho' of that, Solistan."

"An' 'bout feedin'," he went on, greatly occupied with the buckle of Ti Démon's bridle, "I could keep on feedin' the ho'se, an' if that plan don't suit you, w'at you think 'bout takin' me 'long with the ho'se Herminia?"

"Takin' you, Solistan!"

"W'y not? We plenty ole 'nough; you mus' be mos' eighteen, an' I'm goin' on twenty-three, me."

"I better be goin'. We c'n talk 'bout that 'nother time."

"W'en, Herminia! W'en?" implored Solistan holding on to the bridle of her pony, "tonight if I come down yonder? Say, tonight?"

"Oh Solistan, le' me go!"

"An' w'at will you tell me, Herminia?"

"We'll see 'bout that," she laughed over her shoulder as Ti Démon started away with a stiff trot.

But all the joy of life had forever left the breast of Ti Démon. Solistan's sinister remarks had made a deep and painful impression which he could not rid himself of.

When, in the autumn following, the young farmer took Herminia home to be his wife, and also took Ti Démon with the benevolent intention of feeding him all the rest of his life, it was then that Ti Démon's days were given over to brooding upon the possible fate which awaited him.

Once in an unguarded moment, Ti Démon walked himself off, across Bayou Derbanne, along the Sabine and away from the haunts which had known him so long.

"If there's goin' to be any shootin'," reflected Ti Démon as he limped along, swishing his tail, "it's time fo' me to be pullin' my freight."

It was during the winter following that Solistan one evening said to his wife as she bent over the fire, getting their evening meal.

"W'at you think, Herminia? Raul tole me w'en he was drivin'
his drove of cattle into Texas las' month, they came 'cross Ti
Démon layin' dead in the Bonham road. The li'le rascal mus'
a'been on his way to the Indian Nation."

"Oh! Po' Ti Démon!" exclaimed Herminia holding aloft the huge
spoon with which she had been stirring the couche-couche. "He was
a good an' faithful ho'se! yes!"

"That's true, Herminia," replied Solistan with philosophic
resignation, "but who knows! maybe it is all fo' the best!"

Alexandre's Wonderful Experience

As Alexandre was vigorously polishing one of G. Catalan's
"Antiques" he was greatly startled by the sudden appearance of a
tall, slender lady standing beside him. She had entered the store
as noiselessly as a ghost. She was dressed in black, however, and
Alexandre, remembering the well known predilection of ghostly
visitants for white, was at once reassured and politely asked the
lady what he might do for her. Never in his life of fourteen
years had he beheld such a smile as softly illumined her eyes and
whole visage as she spoke to him.

"I have not come to buy anything," she said, "I was passing
by and thought I would stop and ask Mr. Catalan if he would like
to purchase a very old chest of drawers that I have at home that
I can say truthfully is in my way." She passed her gloved hand
in a lingering fashion over the rosewood chiffonniere that
Alexandre was polishing and praised his skill and energy in
producing so fine a luster on its delicate surface.

"I'll call Mr. Catalan," said the boy making a bow and
feeling as if he were plunged in an atmosphere of kindness and
gentleness as in a bath.

G. Catalan brought his short bulk slowly from some mysterious
depths. He was in shirt sleeves with vest unbuttoned, and seemed
indifferent and somewhat bored at being interrupted, a manner
rather effective in a business wherein there is little
competition.

A chest of drawers! of all things! No one wanted them any
longer, old or new. He had not had a call for a chest of drawers
in two years! Alexandre groaned inwardly and thought of the
doctor out on St. Charles Avenue who was turning heaven and
earth.

"I am sorry to have troubled you, sir," and the lady bowed

loftily, seeming to Alexandre's eyes to have changed from a Madonna most amiable to the personification of pride and condescension. G. Catalan took a card and the stub of a pencil from his pocket. He was not unwilling to jot down her address. He might stop and look at the chest of drawers some time when in her neighborhood. She gave the number of her residence, but not her name.

Alexandre detected that she was not rich and he felt sorry for her. How much more deserving of wealth she seemed than some he could name not a thousand miles away! For that matter he was not rich himself, but he meant to be some day. His present employment was infinitely better than selling clothes-poles on the street—he thought of that time with a shudder—but it was nothing more than a stepping stone, the very beginning of those steps that were to lead him to Canal Street. His secret and consuming passion was an ambition to rise in the world, and if a lively imagination was to count for anything he would reach the heights in no time.

While Alexandre rubbed and polished in G. Catalan's shop day after day, his fancy ran riot. One of his favorite dreams was that of a rich gentleman driving up in a handsome equipage—a rich gentleman, at once struck by Alexandre's air of refinement and intelligence, engaging him in conversation. Upon this foundation of moonbeams and cobweb, how many dreams had Alexandre not woven! He was assisting at his own magnificent wedding to the rich gentleman's beautiful daughter before the altar at the Cathedral when the lady in black appearing at his side shattered that pleasing vision. Now, the lady was gone, and yet she was not gone so far as Alexandre was concerned.

He could not get her kindly manner, her smile, her beauty, out of his mind. And the thought that she was not rich continued to distress him. While poverty rendered her ineligible as an actress in any of his dramas it drew all of his sympathy. He knew perfectly well what would happen, what G. Catalan would do. He could see him gazing upon that article of furniture with pity, and regret that he had wasted his time. He could hear his offer—the paltriest sum! Alexandre wondered how poor she really was, if she were poor enough to accept the paltry sum? Without any ultimate intention of being disloyal to G. Catalan he had a keen desire to be loyal to the lady.

It was nearly dusk when Alexandre quitted the shop. The electric lights shone like a row of stars down the long, narrow street. It was warm and murky and the banquettes were slimy with a thick ooze. The air was not refreshing nor invigorating, but

Alexandre walked nimbly and sometimes skipped along. He was thin and undeveloped. His hair was black and a little too long and his eyes were almost round, they stared and glowed so.

Often after hours he did errands for G. Catalan, but tonight there was nothing for him to do but stop for his roll and cup of coffee at the lunch-stand and get back to his bed of rags at the clothes-pole-man's. But he had an intention which took him quite in an opposite direction. He had not forgotten the address which the lady had reluctantly mentioned in the shop.

It was fully half a mile away and in an unfashionable though respectable neighborhood. The tall brick house stood directly on the banquette, and was placarded with a large for rent sign. Nevertheless there was a light glimmering between the half closed shutters of the lower room and Alexandre heard the tinkle of an old piano. Some one was playing a slow tune like a minuet.

He was filled with inward reluctance but his action was decided enough when he went and gave three raps with the knocker. The piano ceased and presently there was a turning of keys and drawing of bolts within, and when the door opened, there stood the amiable lady holding up a candle in a quaint old brass candle-stick and peering out at Alexandre.

"I'm the boy from G. Catalan's," he said with surprising presence of mind.

"Oh!" uttered the lady motioning him to enter. The hall was large, gloomy and bare and it rang with the sinister echo of her relocking and rebolting. When she opened the door at hand and Alexandre stood on the threshold he was amazed at the aspect of the room.

The first object that caught his attention was a delicate little child half reclining in a long chair. There was no covering on the white boards of the floor. The only light in the room was from a cheap coal oil lamp that stood on the high mantel. But never did coal oil lamp shine upon anything more rich, more rare than the almost priceless antique furnishings that crowded the apartment.

The piano—it was a spinet with yellow keys—must have been a hundred years old. There stood the chest of drawers in almost perfect condition, its glass knobs would have made G. Catalan's mouth water. There were chairs, sofas, tables, screens, chiffonnieres, heaven only knows what, crowding each other for place: and not a stick of it all but bore the imprint of distinguished old age. Alexandre was offered a chair in which Napoleon might have sat unless looks were deceiving.

"Did Mr. Catalan send you to look at the chest of drawers?"

asked the lady who, but for her simple and poor cotton gown could have reminded one of a lady of the First Empire, seated in her sofa corner. "This is the boy I told you about, Chérie," she said in French, turning to the little invalid on the chair.

Alexandre's heart thumped in his bosom to think she had remembered and spoken of him.

"Did Mr. Catalan send you?" she asked again.

"Yes," he answered; and then "no: that is, I didn't know how soon he might get around and I thought so long as I was passing by I'd tell you about a doctor out on St. Charles Avenue that wants an old chest of drawers the worst kind."

She was looking at him intently with her hands pressed down in her lap; and comprehending his action and being extremely sensitive the tears came into her eyes.

"I thought I'd give you the doctor's address," he went on, feeling in his pocket. But with a sudden caution worthy of G. Catalan himself he changed his mind. "No—I reckon I better not. He might think you were too anxious. I'll give him your address and you can sell it to him or not, like you want. Are these things for sale? everything in here?"

"No, no! jamais de la vie! heaven forbid!" she cried with a look of distress. Arising she walked over to the chest of drawers and leaned her cheek against the sombre wood as though it were alive with human sympathy.

Alexandre felt greatly embarrassed and stood up to say good night. He was permitted to shake hands with the little girl and the lady accompanied him out in the hall, out upon the steps beyond hearing of the little one. He told her his name was Alexandre when she asked him.

"You are a kind boy, Alexandre; you have a good heart, I knew that when I first looked at you this morning." He must have seemed to the lady much older and wiser than he was, or it may be she had had no one to talk to for a long time.

He could not understand that almost passionate idolatry for inanimate things which the lady revealed—just because they were heirlooms! She was making this heartbreaking sacrifice for her sick child and yet she dreaded that it was only the beginning—she could see no brighter future. As for herself she would have washed, scrubbed, worked her fingers to the bone if she had been alone in the world rather than part with a stick of it.

Dear! dear! what a puzzling proposition to Alexandre, who could look upon old furniture only as a marketable commodity. But since it was going to be so hard for her to part with the chest

of drawers he was more than anxious for her to get all she could
for it.

He started straight for the doctor's regardless of the hour
and the miles ahead of him. He forgot, as he walked, his own
personal romance which had been interrupted at so engaging a
chapter that morning. But he made quite a pretty story for the
lady. It had to do with a secret drawer in the old escritoire;
the accidental discovery of a long lost will; a title to
millions! She was descending the marble steps of her Chateau in
France, in a trailing purple velvet gown, when Alexandre rang the
doctor's bell.

It was late by that time. It was later still on his return,
when he seated himself exhausted on the stone step at the base of
an imposing statue that commanded the avenue. The street cars
rattled by; an occasional cab swung around the circle, its lights
reflected on the glistening asphalt. There were few people
abroad. Overhead the stars were dim through the mist. It was a
long way off to the clothes-pole-man's. Too far. Alexandre heaved
a sigh and stretched himself in the shadow along the step. No one
molested him. A careless negro shuffled by singing: "Jordan am a
hard road to trabble." He kept it up until his voice died away
in the distance. That was the last thing Alexandre remembered.

That seemed to be the only thing Alexandre remembered for
many a day. "Jordan am a hard road to travel." It was the reply
he made to the policeman who attempted to arouse him in the chill
dawn. It was the theme upon which he wove a variety of fancies
when he lay upon his clean cot in the hospital. How far was
Jordan? was it as far as the doctor's? The path was filled with
stones and there was a procession of spindle-legged furniture
traveling the road with him; getting in his way, tripping him up,
mincing ahead, toppling along like drunken things. But when a
good-humored white-capped young woman asked him one morning,
leaning over his bed: "Well, what about Jordan and the hard
road?" Alexandre looked at her vaguely and shook his head. He
was so comfortable, so hungry, so sleepy.

Before very long he was up again on his feet, all dressed
from head to toe and they told him he was well, that he might go
home and good luck to him. He went around and thanked everybody,
which made some of them snicker. But the good-humored young woman
said any one could see he had had good bringing up! Well, there
might have been good bringing up at some remote period of
Alexandre's family history.

They told him he might go home: but he went out and sat on

the warm stone coping in the sun. The flush of rushing spring
tide was in the air and the people all seemed light-headed and
glad. Alexandre, too, rejoiced to be alive and to feel himself
again one of the multitude.

By slow and broken stages he took his way to G. Catalan's,
where he found another boy there polishing the furniture, a stout
German lad. G. Catalan came forward and turned Alexandre away,
calling him hard names. He had never been called thief before,
and Alexandre was too feeble to do more than protest with a
shrill, uplifted quaver, that made the passers-by linger,
scenting trouble. But there was no further trouble. Alexandre
could do nothing but walk away muttering and wiping his eyes on
his coat sleeve. A small band of curious urchins followed him a
bit, hoping for enlightenment.

The doctor had bought the chest of drawers, of course. He had
turned it over to G. Catalan for touching up, and had thanked the
dealer for sending his boy out with the information through which
he had procured it. All of which had aroused G. Catalan's ire
towards Alexandre, whose guilt seemed further established by his
failure to re-appear at the shop.

As the days went by and Alexandre was unable to obtain work
it became more and more apparent that he would have to take to
the clothes-poles. His ambitious spirit rebelled at the descent.
But however ambitious spirits may rebel, they are oftentimes
broken. And a morning came after a night of weeping on his bed of
rags when Alexandre started out with the clothes poles slung on
his little skinny shoulder.

They did not seem so very heavy at first; but the load was
not lightened; nobody bought any though it was Monday morning.
Soon they began to accumulate weight as though the delicious
spring atmosphere were charging them with lead. When he reached
the French Market, Alexandre was well nigh staggering, and he
stopped there on the sidewalk and leaned his bundle against an
awning post.

They are very light-hearted people who sell wares at the
French Market. They like to laugh and to talk to each other: all
except the Choctaw women who sit before their pepper and
sassafras bottles as solemnly as though guarding the tombs of
their ancestors.

Alexandre's appearance seemed to be mirth-provoking.

"C-l-o-t-h-e-s p-o-l-e-s," drawled a young banana vendor in a
high nasal twang. It must have been excruciatingly funny, for
every one laughed. Even the thread and needle man laughed
silently in his beard.

"Dat boy look like he b'en dug up," spoke up a big mulatto woman with a large market basket.

"Look lak he b'en washed and hung up to bleach on his own clothes poles," simpered a little mulatto woman with a small market basket.

"Yo! ho!" screamed the greasy banana boy, and Alexandre looked around for something to throw at him. But the boy's sister—swarthy, with gold hoops in her ears—came forward and offered him an orange. Her brother dashed to the rescue and snatched it away from her, whence ensued a spirited battle that for the moment distracted attention from Alexandre.

"Whar yo' eyes? you, boy! you plumb deaf?" blustered the big mulatto woman in his face. "You don' heah dat lady yonda callin you?"

In fact Alexandre heard his name called and turning, bewildered, perceived the fair lady of his dreams leaning from a carriage door at no great distance. His first thought was: "She has sold all the furniture and bought herself a carriage!"

"Where have you been, Alexandre?" she exclaimed at his approach. "Oh! how pale! how thin! Where have you been? We looked and looked for you. Mr. Catalan directed us to a place—there was a clothes-pole-man; he said you had run away."

"I was in the hospital," he replied. Although not arrayed in the splendor in which Alexandre had once pictured her, there was no trace of that old poverty in the lady's appearance which had once so distressed him. The little girl sat snugly beside her, smiling contentedly out of her innocent blue eyes. There were packages and market stuff piled up before them.

"We are going to the train," she said; and after a waver of reflection—"Get into the carriage, Alexandre. Move those packages aside; we have no time to lose."

"I—I have some poles—some clothes-poles. They are not mine; I can't leave them."

"We will send the money to the owner. Come, hurry get in."

Alexandre trembled with excitement as he sank on the comfortable seat of the carriage. His brain whirled and it was with a great effort he kept himself from fainting away.

"Lean back," said the lady, and he obeyed her.

"Do you know what happened, Alexandre?" she asked him with smiling eyes.

"You sold it all—everything—and brought a carriage." She laughed.

"This is not my carriage, it is hired. I have sold nothing, nothing but the chest of drawers. You will see all the dear old

furniture in a big beautiful house that is worthy of it, down on
the Mississippi."

"You found a will in a secret drawer," he whispered in all
seriousness. Even the little girl laughed at that.

"No, no. I will tell you. Here, take this orange—it will
refresh you. The doctor, you know, came the very next day and
bought the chest of drawers. Ah! how I wept when it went away.
He looked at Chérie and said he would cure her with God's help.
He came every day, every day to see her. Oh! he was so good, so
noble, so beautiful! One day he said that Chérie would have to go
to the country. Imagine! the country—impossible! Not at all. He
had an old plantation. He was—why, Alexandre, can't you guess?"

Alexandre shook his head, hopelessly.

"Why, we were married. I am his wife. Oh! you are a
blessed boy. The doctor said only this morning he would find you
if he had to turn heaven and earth."

There was a spasm of disappointment. The doctor! after all.
So the beautiful lady would never marry a marquis and live in a
French Chateau! But the pang did not last. When he had left the
grime and noise of the city behind him; when the scent of fields
was wafted in to him and long vistas unrolled beneath the blue
sky, he was overcome with happiness.

To have a strange, delicious, beautiful dream come true! That
was Alexandre's wonderful experience.

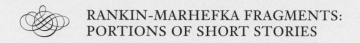

RANKIN-MARHEFKA FRAGMENTS: PORTIONS OF SHORT STORIES

"The Boy" Fragment

This fragment anticipates Kate Chopin's "A Vocation and a Voice," one of her longest short stories, evidently inspired by her editor-friend William Marion Reedy's struggles with the spirit and the flesh. A former altar boy, Reedy was a heavy drinker noted for boorish and lecherous conduct. He married a madam and later defied the Catholic Church with his demand for a divorce. He even chortled rudely about young writer Fannie Hurst's first name. Yet, singlehandedly, Reedy opened up St. Louis for modern literature and continental tastes through his weekly newspaper, the *Mirror* (later known as *Reedy's Mirror*).

Kate Chopin originally wrote "A Vocation and a Voice" in 1896, according to her manuscript account book; it was not published until 1902, in *Reedy's Mirror*. She may have been tinkering with it for much of that time, and "The Boy" seems to be a direction she tried and then rejected. It does not appear in the published version of "A Vocation and a Voice." The fragment is untitled.

2

men, & the boys looked at him as they passed but did not question him. He proceed on his way overtaking a small group of the black frocked figures who were walking seemingly for recreation along the brick paved walk that encircled the building—A brisk wind was blowing there on the summit and it fluttering their black gowns.—Some of them held their hats down & they seemed cheerful and even enjoyed lively and jovial conversation

✳ 1/3

when the boy appeared. He removed his hat as he drew near. "What
will you have?" asked one of the men whose ~~healthy face~~ ruddy,
sunburned face still [   ] reflected the laughter ~~with which~~
~~he had received~~ Which their pleasantries had inspired. He could
see ~~that~~ this boy bore no appearance of a tramp, yet his [   ] anxiety
~~alone~~ uninspired mannered, made him doubt he might
be one.

    "Will you have something to eat?" the man asked kindly.
    He had just dined himself and

4

as the odor of ~~stewed onions~~ soup & repast came up from a
basement window near at hand.

    "Thank you I'm not hungry," said the boy. "I want to see the
Superior."

    "It's Brother John he'll be wanting to see" chimmed in a
smaller man in spectacles. as if to say he it's the high muck
muck and no other will suit him.

    "And its brother John that'll not be troubled at this hour to
see him or the next one" proclaimed a ~~a second man~~ a second.

    "Come - come on with me." offered ~~the first speaker~~ the man
who had first addressed him, disengaging himself from the group
and motioning the boy to follow him. Something

5

in the youth's face & appearance had arrested his attention and
awakened his sympathy. They mounted a short flight of stone steps
and entered a long bare hall, a corridor—[   ]& unfurnished
save for a few chairs standing at wide intervals against the wall
and—upon which hung ~~some~~ a half dozen religious prints
~~hanging against the wall~~. When they had proceeded some little
way the man stopped and seating himself—instructed the boy to do
like wise—"Brother John does not like to be disturbed

6

at this hour" he said "unless on important business. If you tell
me what you wish perhaps I can attend to you—assist you" he
corrected himself—the man was a little bald—with a sprinkle of
gray in his temples—his countenance was open & merited
confidence. "I want to go to confession," avowed the boy frankly
- and then [   ] hesitatingly—"I would like to stay here."

The man smiled. ~~Confessions are hours~~ you could go to
confession in the morning" ~~assured~~ the man smiling, "when the
priest

7

is here who comes to say mass. It is then he hears confessions.
We are not an ordained priesthood you see. This is a church
house of "The Brothers of Christ". It is here that we prepare
young men for the brotherhood—and we also receive a traditional
number—of boys whom we educate free of charge and who are taught
some useful trade or employment ~~which will~~ whereby to earn a
decent livelihood in the world. Whom do you know here have you
any friends? any references?" The boy thought of the priest who
had befriended in the South

8

and also of Father Dorian. Brother Philip wrote both nains &
addresses on a card which he took from a table nearby and slipped
the card in ~~the~~ the ample pockets of his gown.
   "I'll speak to brother John & he'll see what he can do for
you." he said reassuringly. He left the boy sitting there. There
was the sudden loud clatter of ~~loud sounding bell~~ of a
bell—followed [   ] by the sound of many feet going & coming
hither and thither—the group that had met ~~him~~ walking
outside—entered and [   ] they

9

all looked at him as they passed silently & soberly along the
corridor—

XI

Brother Ludovic was so strong so stalwart that the boys of
the Institution often whished he might be permitted to give an
exhibition of his prowess or to enter upon a contest—a match
which they might shine in the reflected hour of his achievements.
Some said it all came of sleeping with open windows—winter and
summer—because he could not abide the

"Doralise" Fragment

The fragment we are calling "Doralise" does not correspond to any of Kate Chopin's published works. It bears a slight tonal resemblance to her early short stories "A Harbinger" and "Caline," and she did use the name Doralise for a mixed-blood servant in the story "The Return of Alcibiade."

The tale of a poor, beautiful, artistic young woman was one that attracted Kate Chopin, and she played some variations on that theme in other stories, including "Wiser Than a God" (her first published story) and "Cavanelle." The finest artist in *The Awakening* is the pianist Mademoiselle Reisz—who first appears in chapter IX wearing "a batch of rusty black lace" in her hair, like Doralise's here.

One trial was sufficient to convince Doralize that she

Doralise with her dozen ~~twelve~~ water color sketches under her arm made her way into the very heart of French N. Orleans—she had hoped to place the sketches before the Xmas holidays. But Xmas had come & now so far past that the city was getting ready her cap & bells for Mardi Gras. Doralize stood looking into a little shop window on Conti street. She was a ~~golden-haired~~ Creole girl with a bit of black net ~~lace~~ resting Spanish fashion in [   ] her gold color hair—~~Any non conventional head covering she removed for her visits to Canal street~~. She had worn a hat the day she went to Canal street with these sketches, alas! it had taken her but a short after noon to discover that the Canal st merchants would have none of them.

"Misty" Fragment

Kate Chopin worked for several years on an essay called "In the Confidence of a Story-Writer," published in the *Atlantic Monthly* in January 1899 with no byline. Three years earlier, *Atlantic* editor Walter Hines Page had invited her to contribute to his "Men and Letters" series, but he found her piece too indirect, and urged her to revise.

The "Misty" fragment (untitled by Chopin) may be a more fanciful precursor to the draft Chopin submitted in 1896 (it and the Atlantic final version appear in *The Complete Works of Kate Chopin*). In the 1896 draft, Chopin discusses her debt to Guy de Maupassant and also addresses an imaginary

Madame Précieuse: "I have discovered my limitations and I have saved myself much worry and torment by recognizing and accepting them as final" (CW 702). The final published version also includes lines similar to those in this fragment, including "But the story failed to arouse enthusiasm among the editors. It is at present lying in my desk" (CW 704).

9

they were misty and I looked around. What a great big story book the world is! It turns over Stories whose beginnings we need not seek and whose endings we must not follow. Suggestions, that are poignant with reality. Impressions, that come & go with the charm of illusions that are never shattered: but we hold for a time unuttered; like ~~the~~ a dim exquisite dreams that can never be told. ~~But sometimes we do strive to tell what we see~~

Madame Precieuse - a dear little woman who makes up beautiful stories as she goes, tells me that she sees them with her soul. It is a pretty idea, and I dropped

9 ~~8~~

~~illustrious and successful example~~ as I have offered you—" He [   ] nothing of the sort; his touching speech is far more subtle. ~~He said "they [   ] Madame—please do not commit the folly of trying to imitate. You [   ] my stories as well you [   ] find they are grand things. Be yourself," he said~~ ~~"use~~ "Let me down," he said "use your own faculties. You have only two eyes, it is true, while I have a hundred—but it is already still a blessing to have discovered that you have eyes at all—use them." whereupon I rubbed my eyes—for

19

But someway the story failed to arouse enthusiasm among the editors. It is at present lying there in my desk. Even Madame Precieuse has declined to listened to it when I offered to read it to her during one of her "avid enjoyment" hours. In this, ~~Do~~ I feel the mistake was mine. ~~I should~~ in not having stretched the hour which she has set apart for ministering to her afflicted fellow beings.

"Melancholy" Fragment

The fragments we are calling "Melancholy" and "Doralise" are the only Rankin-Marhefka Fragments which do not correspond to any published Chopin stories. They are the only abandoned efforts we have from her pencil.

Kate Chopin wrote frequently about maladjusted, melancholy, and misanthropic men, as in such stories as "After the Winter," "The Blind Man," and "An Easter Day Conversion." She rarely wrote about melancholy women, however. Her unhappy women characters usually have specific woes or grievances leading to their discontent—as in, for instance, "A Matter of Prejudice," "Regret," and "The Godmother."

Most likely, the melancholy tone and Parisian setting of "Melancholy" were inspired by Kate Chopin's reading and translating stories by Guy de Maupassant. Maupassant's story "Night" includes descriptions of the luminous Parisian sky; his story "Suicide" features a protagonist who remembers his childhood love for his mother.

Although both stories end in death and grief, Chopin was able to publish the "Suicide" translation in the daily *St. Louis Republic* in 1898. That story's mention of a "solitary existence left without illusions" clearly anticipates *The Awakening*, published a year later.

Edouward de Savignole stepped from his room out upon the
narrow stone balcony that hung high above the shadowy garden
~~beneath~~ Myriad stars powdered the heavens and the lights of
Paris shone out from the darkness below like a resplendant
firmament. There was a gentle ~~rain~~ wind shaping over the city.
As its cool breath met him, he pushed the damp ~~matted~~ hair up
from his forehead and lifted his face to its soft & soothing
caress.

2

His whole being was in revolt; ~~and Tonight~~ his sensitive
and outraged soul had reached the limit of its endurance. He
wanted to lean his head down upon the stone railing and weep—as
he had ~~not~~ never wept—~~Since he was a boy sobbing out his
troubles upon his mothers sympathetic bosom~~, in his life before.
He was a man who all his life had been misunderstood and who all
his life had hopelessly, helplessly, resented it. He could have
been sympathetic, yet no one had ever sought him with their
confidence—he was capable

3

of deep & lasting affection; yet no man had ever called him friend—and of womens love, he only knew such as his gold had ~~paid for~~ bought. What trick could so have damned him in his cradle? Was it a droop of the eye - a turn of the lip - a manner of quiet speech or glance - something [   ] he might have labored to overcome or was it some thing more bitter - a trick of the soul - that eluded his research

"A Little Country Girl"

Kate Chopin wrote "A Little Country Girl" in February 1899, two months before the publication of *The Awakening*. In March, according to her manuscript account notebooks, "A Little Country Girl" was accepted for publication by *Youth's Companion*, which paid her $50. It was advertised as forthcoming in 1900 ("The Best of Reading for Girls"), but it never appeared. Sometimes *Companion*—as Chopin called it in her notebooks—bought stories and did not run them, perhaps because of editorial staff changes.

It is also possible, though unlikely, that *Youth's Companion* cancelled the Chopin story because of her notoriety after publication of her scandalous novel, *The Awakening*. Early in 1900, *Youth's Companion* also accepted Chopin's "Alexandre's Wonderful Experience," "The Gentleman from New Orleans," and "A December Day in Dixie"—and never published any of them. But the author did receive a total of $150, a good price, for the four stories.

The transcription published here, from the Rankin-Marhefka Fragments, is similar to Per Seyersted's in CW. We include it to illustrate Kate Chopin's methods of composition, her sometimes faulty proofreading and spelling, and her vacillation about the names of characters.

1

Ninette was ~~polishing~~ scouring the tin milk pail with sand and lye soap, and bringing it to a high polish. She used for that purpose the native scrub brush, the fibrous root of the palmetto, which she called <u>latanier</u>. The long table on which the tins were ranged stood out in the yard under a mulberry tree. It was there that the pots and kettles were washed, the chickens, the meats and vegetables cut up and prepared for cooking. Occasionally a drop of water fell with a faint splash ~~and~~ on the polished surface of the tin, whereupon Ninette would wipe it away, and the carrying

2

the corner of her checked apron up to her eyes, she would wipe them, & proceed with her task. For the drops were falling from Ninette's eyes. Trickling down her cheeks & sometimes dropping from the end of her nose. It was all because two disagreeable old people who had long outlived their youth, no longer believed in the spring circus as a means of cheering the ~~fretful~~ human heart, nor could they see the use of it. Ninette had not even mentioned the subject to them. Why should she? She might as well have said: Grandfather & Grandfather, with your permission

3

and a small advance of fifty cents, I should like, after my work is done, to make a visit to one of the distant planets this afternoon."—It was very warm & Ninette's face was red with heat and ill humor. Her hair was black & straight & kept falling over her face—it was an untidy length—her grandmother having decided to let it grow about six months before. She was barefooted and her calico skirt reached a little above her thick brown ankles.—Even the negroes were all going to the circus—Suzan's black girl had lin-

4

gered beside the table a moment before on her way through the yard. "You aint gwine to the suckus?" No" "bang" went the bread ~~pail~~ pan on [down] on the table." "We alls goin', pap & Mammy an' all us is goin'"—with a complacent air and a restful pose against the table." "Where you all goin to get the money, I like to know." "oh, Mr Ben advance Mammy a dollar on de crap—an Joe he got six bits lef' from las pickin' and pap sole ~~is~~ a ole no-count plow to Dennis." We all's goin. Joe say he seed em pass yonder back Mr Ben's lane. Dey a elephant mos as big as dat corn crib, walkin along

5

des like he somebody—an' a whole pa'cel wild critters shet up in a cage sot up yonder in a wagon. An' all kine o' hosses & little

ponies [dis' like/little] dogs; an' ole ladies [~~dey~~] ridin'
& prancing in red skirts all fill up wid gole & diamonds. We
all's goin. Did you axe yo' gra'ma? W'at she say? W'y you dont
ax yo' gran'pap?"—'That's my business, taint ~~none~~ o' yo's
Black Gal. You better be getting yonder home, tendin' to yo'
work, I think." "I aint got no work cep iron out my

6

pink flower dress fo' de suckus." But she took herself off with
an air of lofty content—swinging her tattered skirts. Ninette
polished the pans, more [vigorously] than ever ~~after [Black~~
~~Gal left]~~,but it was then that the tears began to ~~splash~~ drop
& splatter. ~~And~~ resentment rose & rose within her like a
leaven—causing her to ferment with wickedness and to make all
manner of diabolical wishes in regard to the circus. The worst
of these was that she wished it would rain. "I hope to goodness
it'll rain; po' down rain'; po' down rain!" She ~~pro~~ uttered

7

the wish with the air of a young Medusa pronouncing a blighting
curse—"I like to see 'em all drippin' wet; Black Gal with her
pink flowers all drippin' wet." She spoke these wishes in the
very presence of her grandfather & grandmother, for they
understood not a word of English, and she used that language as a
medium to express her individual opinion on [~~all~~] many
occassions—

"What do you say Ninette?" asked her grandmother. She had
brought in the last of the tin pails & was rinsing them on a
shelf in the kitchen—"I said I hoped

8

it would rain" she answered wiping her face & fanning herself
with a pie pan as though the oppressive heat had suggested the
desire for a change in the weather."

"You are a wicked girl said her grandmother turning on
her—when you know your grandfather has acres and acres of cotton
ready to fall to the ground—that the rain would ruin. He's angry
enough too, with every man woman & child leaving the fields to
day to take themselves off to the village. There ought to be a
law to compel them to pick their cotton—those trifling
creatures! Ah it was different in the good old days."

9

 Ninette possessed a sensitive soul & she believed in
miracles. For instance, if she were to go to the circus that
afternoon; she would consider it a miracle. Hope follows on the
heels of fFaith. And the white-winged goddess—which is
Hope—did not leave her, but prompted to many little
surreptitious acts of preparation in the event of the miracle
coming to pass. She peeped into the clothes press to see that her
gingham dress was where she had folded & left it the Sunday
before, after mass. She inspected her shoes and got out a clean
pair of stockings

10

which she had beneath the pillow—In the little tin basin behind
the house she washed & rubbed her face & neck till they were red
as boiled crawfish—and her hair which was too short to plait,
she tied smothered & plastered and tied back with a black
green ribbon—till it stood out & in a little bristly in
like a little stiff tail.
    The noon hour had scarcely hardly passed than an unusual
agitation began to be visible throughout the surrounding country.
The fields were deserted. People, black and white, began passing
along the

11

road in little squads & detachments.
    Ponies could be seen galloping ahead on both sides the river,
carring two and as many as three on their backs. Blue and green
carts with rampant mules—Top buggies & no-top buggies—old,
[rattling] family carriages that groned with age & decrepitude;
heavy cotton farm wagons filled with picaninnies made a
procession along the road that nothing short of a circus in town
[,] could have accounted for—Grandfather ÐBezeau was too
angry to look at it. He retired indoors to

12

the hall where he sat, gloomily reading a two weeks old paper—He
looked about ninety years old—He was in reality not more than
seventy. Grandmother Bezeau stayed out on the gallery—apparently
to cast ridicule & contempt upon the heedless and extravagant

multitude; in reality, to satisfy a womanly curiosity and a
natural interest in the affairs of her neighbors. As for Ninette
she found it extremely difficult to keep her attention fixed upon
the task of shelling peas and her inward supplications that
something might happen. But something

13

<u>did</u> happen. Jules Perrote with ~~his big farm wagon packed with~~ a
family load in his big farm wagon stopped before their gate. He
handed the reins to one of the children and he himself got down
and came up to the ~~the house~~ gallery where she & her
grandmother were sitting. "What's this! What's this! he cried
out in French—"Ninette not going to the circus—not even ready
to go. "Par exemple!" exclaimed the old lady, looking daggers
over her spectacles. She was binding the leg of a wounded
chicken, that squawked & fluttered with excitement—"Par exemple
or no par exemple she's going, and she's going with me—and her
grandfather [is —] going to ~~pay~~ give her the money—Run in
little one—get ready, make

14

haste we'll be late. She looked appealingly at her grandmother
who said nothing—she was ashamed to say anything in face of her
neighbor Perrote of whom she stood a little in awe. Ninette
~~looked~~ taking silence for consent, darted into the house to get
herself ready—And when she came out, wonder of wonders! there
was her grandfather ~~drawing~~ taking his purse from his pocket.
He was drawing it out slowly & painfully, with a hideous grimace
as though it were some vital organ that he was parting with. What
arguments could Mons Perrote have used. They were certainly
convincing. She had heard them in wordy discussion as she
nervously laced her shoes; dabbed her face

15

with flour, hooked the gingham dress, and balanced upon her head
a straw hat which looked like an inverted pie plate decorated
with roses that had stayed out over night in a frost. But no
triumphant queen on her throne could have presented a more
beaming and joyful countenance than did Ninette when she ascended
and seated herself in the big wagon in the midst of the Perrote
family + She took the baby from Madame Perrolte & held it and

felt supremely happy. The more the wagon jolted and bounced the
more did it convey to her a sense of reality, and less did

16

it seem like a dream. They passed Black Gal and her family in
the road, trudging ankle deep in dust. Fortunately, she was
barefooted, though the pink flowers were all there and she
carried a green parasol. Her mother was semi-decolleté; ~~which~~
and her father wore a heavy winter coat while Joe had secured
piece meal, a species of cake-walk costume for the occasion. It
was with a feeling of lofty disdain that Ninette passed & left
the Black-Gal family in a cloud of dust.
X   Even after they reached the circus grounds which were just
outside the village, Ninette

17

continued to carry the baby. She would willingly have carried
three babies had such a thing been possible. The ~~youngster~~
infant took a wild and noisy interest in the Merry go round with
its hurdy gurdy accompaniment. Oh! that she had had more money!
that she might have mounted one of those flying horses & gone
spinning round in a whirl of ecstasy! There were side shows, too.
She would have liked to see the lady who weighed 600 pounds or
the gentleman who tipped the scales at [   ], and she would
have wanted to peep in at the curious animal captured after a
dangerous & desperate

18

struggle in the wilds of Africa. Its picture painted in red &
green on the flopping canvas was certainly not like any thing she
had seen in her life or ever heard of. The lemonade was tempting;
the pop corn, the pea nuts the oranges were delights that she
could only gaze upon and sigh for. For Jules Perrot was not
extravagant. He took his people straight to the big tent, bought
the tickets and entered. Ninettes pulses were thumping with
excitement. She sniffed the air ~~with~~, heavy with the

19

smell of sawdust and animals—and it lingered in her nostrils
like some delicious odor. Sure enough, there was the elephant

that Black Gal had described; a chain was about his leg and he
kept reaching out his trunk for tempting morsels. The wild
creatures were all there in cages—and the people walked solemnly
around looking at them,—awed by the ~~unnovelty~~familiarity of
the scene. But Ninette never forgot that she had the baby in her
arms. She talked to it and it listened & looked with round
staring eyes. She felt as if she were a person of

20

distinction assisting at some royal pageant when the bespangled
Knights and Ladies in plumes flowing robes went prancing round on
their beautiful white & black horses. The people all sat on the
circus benches—& Ninette's feet hung down, because an irritable
old lady objected to having them thrust into the small of her
back. Madame Perotte offered to take the baby, but Ninette clung
to it. It seemed to be a pleasing object to visit her excitement
upon. She would whisper into its ear—and squeeze it spasmodically when
her emotions be-

21

came uncontrolable.
    "Oh! bébé! I believe I'm goin' to split my sides! Oh, la la!
if grandma could see that—I know she laugh hersef sick! It was
none other than the clown who was producing this agreeable
impression upon Ninette. She had only to look at his chalky face
to go into contortions of mirth. No one had noticed a gathering
obscurity—and the ominous growl of thunder made every one start
with apprehension & disappointment. A flash and a second clap
that was like a crash followed—it came just

22

as the ring master was cracking his whip with a "hip la—hip la!"
at the bare back rider and the clown was standing on his head.
There was a sinister roar, ~~the~~ a terrific stroke of the wind;
the center pole [swooned] and snapped. The great canvas swelled
and beat the air with bellowing resistance. Pandemonium reigned.
Ninette found herself down beneath the ~~benches~~ piled up
benches—and, still clutching the baby, proceeded to crawl out
~~from beneath~~ of an opening in

23

the canvas. She staid huddled up against the fallen tent clasping
the baby that shriekinged lustily & thinking her end had come.
The rain poured in sheets. The cries of the frightened animals
were like unearthly sounds. Men called and shoted, children
screamed; women went into hysterics and the negroes were having
fits. Ninette got on her knees & prayed God to keep her and the
baby and everybody from [injury] and to take them safely home.

24

It was thus that Mons. Perringault discovered her, half covered
by the fallen tent.

——— ——— ——— ——— ——— ———

    Days afterward Ninette was going about in a most unhappy
frame of mind with a wretched look upon her face. ~~and~~ She was
often discovered to be in tears ~~by her grandmother~~. When her
condition began to grow monotonous & depressing, her grandmother
insisted upon finding the cause of it. Then it was that she
confessed her wickedness and claimed

25

the guilt of having caused the terrible catastrophe at the
circus. It was her fault that a horse had been killed, it was her
fault if an old gentleman had had a collar bone broken and a lady
an arm dislocated and several persons thrown into fits and
hysterics—all her fault. She it was who had called the rain down
upon their heads, and thus had God punished her!
    It was a very delicate matter for Grandmother Bezeau to
pronounce upon—far too delicate;

26

so the next day she went over ~~and got the priest to come and~~
and explained it all to the priest and got him to come over and
talk to Ninette. The girl was at the table under the mulberry
tree peeling potatoes when the priest arrived—He was a jolly
little man who did not like to take things too seriously. So he
approached Ninette bowing low to the ground & making deep
salutations with his hat. "I am overwhelmed he said at finding
myself in the presence of the celebrated

[p. 27 missing]

28

shamed. But Mons. Perrault came over; he understood best of all.
He took grandfather & grandmother aside and told them the girl
was morbid from staying as much with old people and never
associating with those of her own age. He was very impressive &
convincing. He frightened them, for he hinted vaguely at terrible
consequences to the child's intellect. He must have touched their
hearts, for they both consented to let her go to birthday part
over at his house the following day. Grandfather Bizeau even
declared that if it was necessary—if it was necessary, mind
you—he was willing to contribute one dollar towards providing
her a suitable toilet for the ocassion.

Kate Chopin
Feb 10th
99

"Alexandre's Wonderful Experience"

As noted above, Kate Chopin wrote "Alexandre's Wonderful Experience" in early 1900. It was accepted, but never published, by *Youth's Companion*. The untitled draft of this story in the Rankin-Marhefka Fragments is essentially the same as Per Seyersted's transcription, elsewhere in this volume (pp. 261–268), of another version held by the Missouri Historical Society.

Slight differences may be illustrated by the final page of the Rankin-Marhefka version:

~~Alexandre resigned himself to a fate that seemed to him marvelous +~~ To have a strange, delicious, beautiful dream come true! that was his wonderful experience.

When ~~they~~ he had left the grime + noise of the city behind ~~them~~ him, when the scent of the fields + dew wafted in to him and long vistas unrolled beneath the blue sky—Alexandre for the first time knew ~~his first~~ happiness which was, not a dream. To have a +c—

K. C.— Jan 22—19—

"The Gentleman from New Orleans"

As noted above, Kate Chopin wrote "The Gentleman from New Orleans" in early 1900: the draft in the Rankin-Marhefka Fragments is dated February 5. The story was rejected by the *Century* magazine and then accepted by *Youth's Companion*, but it was never published. An earlier version, transcribed by Per Seyersted in CW, is essentially the same as the Rankin-Marhefka version. CW has five extra lines; Rankin-Marhefka is missing one page; the extra lines do not seem to correspond with the missing page. "Aunt Crissy" in CW is called "Aunt Suzan" in the Rankin-Marhefka draft; "Parkins" in CW is "Carrington" in Rankin-Marhefka.

Because the texts vary very little, we have chosen not to reproduce the Rankin-Marhefka version of "The Gentleman from New Orleans." Interested textual scholars may compare the drafts held by the Missouri Historical Society (which will also provide photocopies).

"Charlie"

We have more manuscript pages for "Charlie" than for any other Kate Chopin story, and they present a rat's nest of possibilities.

In the Bonnell Manuscript Account Book, Chopin recorded "Charlie" as a 15,000-word story written in April 1900. She sent it to *Youth's Companion* and *The Century*, both of whom rejected it. Her tale of a tomboy tamed was not published until Per Seyersted's edition in CW. Seyersted transcribed "Charlie" from a manuscript owned by Robert Hattersley, Kate Chopin's grandson, but an earlier draft called "Jacques" is owned by the Missouri Historical Society. "Jacques," in which the tomboy heroine is called Jack, is also in a different handwriting, one much more legible than Kate Chopin's.

The Rankin-Marhefka manuscripts include 55 pages entitled "Jacques"; 25 pages of a draft of part IV of "Charlie"; and 33 pages of a draft of part V. Some of the pages have game scores on the backs, or household lists: one says, "630 to 7–30 write—write(3)—house work(2)—sew 2—go out and read (1)." The handwriting is often close to illegible, and the pages are in no particular order. Working with the manuscripts is an intricate, mind-numbing experience.

We have tried gamely to decipher and transcribe the Rankin-Marhefka drafts, but it would require textual and technological techniques not available to us to make a readable text that would also indicate variants in punctuation, spelling, and the like. We have chosen not to do so.

The essential story is the same throughout the drafts of "Jacques" and "Charlie." Some drafts, as with Chopin's other manuscripts, are written using dashes instead of periods to end sentences. Characters' names sometimes vary: "Gus" is "Stevens" in one draft.

Among the drafts there are some changes in wording. In the published version, for instance (CW 641), Charlie writes "Relentless Fate, and thou, relentless Friend!" and the story continues: "Its composition had cost Charlie much laborious breathing and some hard wrung drops from her perspiring brow." For the same sentence, the Rankin-Marhefka version reads: "Its composition had cost Jack much laborious breathing many drops of perspiration that had profusely besprinkled the sheet."

Sometimes the changes involve telling (narration) versus showing (quotation). At the end of part IV, for instance, Charlie receives a telegram summoning her home. In the published version (CW 663):

> Terror seized her like some tangible thing. She feared some one was dead.
> Her father had been injured, they told her. Not fatally, but he wanted her.

In the Rankin-Marhefka draft, Chopin wrote:

> She grew faint with terror—She feared someone was dead—"Your father has been injured—Charlotte, dear—not fatally—and he wants you—

Many of the drafts are, however, almost indecipherable. Except for textual study, we find the canonical text, the CW version of "Charlie," to be the most useful version.

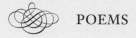 POEMS

      As a child, in the years when future writers are unconsciously absorbing the words and figures of speech and twists of language that they will use later, Kate O'Flaherty did not read much poetry.

      She and Kitty Garesché were avid and precocious readers. Before the summer of 1863, when the thirteen-year-old best friends were separated by war, they had read together, according to Kitty, "the metrical romances of Scott" and "some of the chosen poems of Pope, Collins, and Gray." But mostly they read popular novels by women writers, among them Susan Warner, Jane Porter, Grace Aguilar, Margaret Oliphant, and Dinah Mulock. With *Blinde Agnese*, a novel by Cecelia Mary Caddell, the two girls tried to learn Italian— and failed, comically and miserably.

      Clearly, the young Kate O'Flaherty preferred prose to poetry, and so did her adolescent self: her Commonplace Book includes passages from Byron and Longfellow (revised by K. O'Flaherty), but most of the writings she chose to copy were from novels, memoirs, and essays. Likewise, the mature Kate Chopin seems to have read little or no poetry, although would-be poets were often thrusting their verses upon her.

      Yet there were times when Kate O'Flaherty Chopin chose to express herself through poetry. Her schoolgirl poem "The Congé" is one of the gems of her Commonplace Book, and as an adult she sometimes wrote short verses to accompany Christmas or other gifts. She also wrote poems about nature, going a-Maying, love, sensual temptations, and the night—but whether they were intended to express her own emotions cannot be determined. On the back of one poem, "An Hour," which asks for more time to live and love, Chopin wrote, "This is not dedicated to you or to anybody."

      Per Seyersted reprinted twenty Kate Chopin poems in *The Complete Works of Kate Chopin* (1969). Reprinted here are others discovered since his edition, besides those in the 1894 diary. His notes are reprinted in this volume. "I Opened All the Portals Wide" was published in the prestigious *Century* magazine in July 1899, three months after *The Awakening*. The others were unpublished during Chopin's lifetime.

Per Seyersted believed that Kate Chopin's love poems were about her longing for her late husband, Oscar; Emily Toth has suggested that they express bittersweet memories of her romance with Albert Sampite. But Kate Chopin was, as always, very private about her personal life—and so her poems, while they do not refer to you or me, may be about "anybody."

A FANCY

Happily naught came of it.
'Twas but a fancy born of fate and wishing.
But I thought all the same of it.
Now that the wishing's dead,
I find that naught remains of it.
Fancy and fate are fled.

IF THE WOODS COULD TALK

O! if the woods could talk
Of all they know
Would they tell of a summer's walk
Long years ago?

But the woods they never will talk
Nor the birdlings tell
What happ'd in the summer's walk.
And indeed it is just as well.

A SENTIMENTAL SERENADE

If I were a star, thy star I'd be.
I'd fill the sky with splendor and the night,
Until thine eyes perchance in soft delight
Would beam glad thanks to me.
Then might those dear lips tell:
"Ah, star that shines for me, I love thee well!"

If I were the South-breeze onward blown,
Laden with rose-scents and entrancing sighs,
Soft would I come and touch those sleeping eyes
With kisses, sweet my own.
Then might those dear lips tell:
"Ah zephyr mine that breathes for me, I love thee well!"

But neither zephyr soft nor star nor ought
Am I, save only one that loves thee and would give
All that the world holds best to live
Enfolden in thy thought,
To hear those dear lips tell:
"Ah, heart that beats for me, I love thee well!"

A MESSAGE

A thought has gone from me, swifter than bird on the wing.
How my soul trembles yet from its rapturous swing
As it left me! Fly, O thought to my loved one, and say
To her heart what thou knowest. Away! Fly away!

THE ROSES

I'll gather the roses tomorrow, dear,
That are blooming over the way.
For the dread of an unknown sorrow near
Is holding my heart today.

But gone were the roses white and red!
So the scattered crumbs I swept
In a little mound all dry and dead
And sat me down and wept.

LINES TO LINN

A little boy should have a toy
Or something else to play with.
Perhaps his joy without alloy
A "Tiger"'d be to play with.

A mug of beer may soothe or cheer
I often have been told so.
The cards entice, but they're not nice
For all the preachers hold so.

The pleasing glance that lights perchance
The fair face of a maiden
May drive to folly or melancholy
For 'tis with danger laden.

But one thats good when understood
That neer plays scurvy tricks O'

Fast friend of mine—true friend of thine—
Is Gracious Lady Nick O'.

WHITE OAKS

Of all the places on earth I know
I'd rather stay where the white oaks grow.
From dawn till night, the whole day long
They sing their musical, mystical song
Of "rest, rest, for the time is flying,
Dream, dream, for the day is dying."
O! that tomorrow were far away
And all "forever" a long "today"
When the world stands still and the soft winds blow
In the beautiful land where the white oaks grow.

LINES SUGGESTED BY OMAR

I

Wake! for the night is past, the dawn is nigh,
The little stars have faded one by one.
See where the melting rose-tint lights the sky
And tells the radiant coming of the sun.

II

Bright morning pours from out its crystal bowl
The limpid honey-dew of life supreme—
That nourisheth the new-awakened soul
Born yesterday of Darkness and a Dream.

III

This is God's wine-shop;—linger a while and sip
The ruby sparkle with the drunken Noon
God's self doth tilt the rim upon your lip,
The cup of rapture, emptied all too soon

IV

The purple clusters, drowsing in the sun
That swoons and sinks into the arms of Night,
Are sweet and warm to gather, one by one
Before the waning of the evening light—

V

Ah! drink, my soul, the splendor of the day;
Quaff from the golden goblet oft and deep.
Darkness will come again; too long 'twill stay—
The everlasting night of dreamless sleep.

THE LULL OF SUMMER TIME

The lull of summer-time, a day in June;
The gold wine of a golden, drowsy noon;
The mystic whisper of the leaves—and thou,
Reading the page that ended all too soon.

TO HENRY ONE EVENING LAST SUMMER

The trials of today and the tasks of tomorrow—
The troubles we have and the many we borrow—
That are sometimes enough to make saint into sinner
God lets us forget with a friend and a dinner.

OLD NATCHITOCHES

It wasn't so very long ago,
Tho' I can't remember and neither can you—
A couple of hundred years or more
When the moon was old and the town was new.
O! the people and places that neer stand still!
They've none of the wisdom that gathers riches,
In the dreaming old town at the foot of the hill
That is old as the moon and world and as wise.

BY THE MEADOW GATE

Over the hill and across the ford and down by the meadow gate
A girl is asleep in the long, cool grass.
The soft winds blow and the soft winds pass;
The birds call: "awake!" but they do not stay
While the maid is dreaming the time away
    By the meadow gate.

Over the hill and across the ford and down by the meadow gate
A youth with the light of the boundless skies
A glow in his soul and a flame in his eyes,
Follows a voice that is never still,
Treading the path to the distant hill
    By the meadow gate.

Over the hill and across the ford and down by the meadow gate
The voice and the dream are near—so near,
That if he but listened his heart might hear.

Now he may follow the years and afar,
He may walk from the world to the evening star
   Past the meadow gate.

Over the hill and across the ford and down by the meadow gate
May her days be many, her days be few,
The dream of the maiden will never come true.
For the soft wind carried the moment away,
And the birds they sang, but they would not stay
   By the meadow gate.

AN HOUR

If yesterday were but to-day
   And I could gather all tomorrow
Into an hour that would stay,
   No further time I'd seek to borrow.
For life is long enough to live it;
   And love is deep enough to give it;
Since you are love and life is sorrow.

If yesterday were but to-day
   And I could gather all tomorrow!

O FAIR, SWEET SPRING!

I opened all the portals wide
   To swallows on the wing.
It matters not what e'er betide,
   I've had the taste, the touch, the breath,
     The scent and song of spring!

Oh, fair, sweet spring! abide with me
   In joy the whole time long!
Bring all thy life, thy light with thee.
   I fain would keep thy taste, thy touch,
     Thy breath, oh spring! thy song!

MY LADY ROSE POUTS

Oh dear! in the garden is all dismay!
My lady rose pouts and will not speak
To the violet meek
Nor the pansies over the way.

Thrice has the blue bell nodded her head
With graceful pleading; whilst star-eyed pink
And daisy, shrink,
Hiding, a tear to shed.

Perchance has a rival blossomed more red;
Or south breeze lingered too long on the way;
Or sun beams ray
More light on the lily shed.

However it be, there is all dismay
My lady rose pouts and will not speak
To the violet meek,
Nor the pansies over the way.

COME TO ME

Bathe your face in the dew and come to me with clean, cool lips.
Bring the scent of the grass upon your cheeks
And the light of the morning in your eyes.

O! BLESSED TAVERN

O blessed tavern wherefore art thou hidden
I've journeyed far with fears and cares beridden,
Longing to find a shelter and a rest.
Wilt thou not open thy door if kindly bidden?

AS CARELESS AS THE SUMMER BREEZE

As careless as the summer breeze that blows,
    She knows! She knows!
She claps her hands: red wine! red blood! red rose!
    She knows! She knows!

ONE DAY

Wait for me friend, until the day be past;
This one most perfect summer day,
That hold me with an hundred varying spells
Of warmth, of rose scents and entrancing lights.
I'll stop to place this flower on my breast;
'Tis called anemone, and spake to me but just a moment gone
The softest, faintest speech that heart could listen to.
Now will I lie upon the sward
Plunging my hands deep in the rippling brook.

Now turn and gaze into the blue white sky
And laugh, and only laugh to hear the hills laugh back at me.
Let me but call the day my own,
And when the sun's last kiss hath touched the earth
Then will I join thee on thy sober way
Whither thou wilst—nor linger—nor regret
Nor even keep the little flower at my breast.
Only but wait until the day be past.

AH! MAGIC BIRD

In summertime a bird sang on the bough.
His fluty throat throbbed rapture all day long.
I stopped to listen to his wondrous song
And catch the glinting shadows of the bough.

Ah! magic bird whose voice I loved so well!
No longer in the noontide will he sing.
I heard the last faint flutter of his wing,
The last note of the song I loved so well.

But yonder where the flaming poppies grow,
More soft than sleep upon the breast of night
Is song of birds that never take their flight
Yonder in fields where flaming poppies grow.

WITH A VIOLET-WOOD PAPER KNIFE

When you tire of the violet whose perfume lasts
With its charms but a space of a day, and is past:
When you long for the fragrance that time hath withstood—
Then seek you the violet that's hid in the wood!

A LITTLE DAY

A little day is mine 'twixt night and night
So short 'tis nearly done—
There might have been more joy more light
Yet do the shades come without the sun—

I'll be no grumbler—take it all in all—
'Tis better than t'have had no day at all

ALONE

I see the sights that I saw in the Sight
  Of Love's dawn-light in its morning's glow:

I dream the dreams that I dreamt in The Dream
When hopes ran high over fears lain low:
I live the life that I lived in The Life
    Of our living Love in the Long Ago.

Golden lights are the lights that yet Light
    That Love Day Morn of the Time Gone By:
Bright are the blushes that blush in The Blush
    In the zenith of high of the Love-Lit Sky:
Sweet are the kisses that kissed in The Kiss
    That welcomed a Love not born to die.

Fearful the fears that fear in the Fear
    That fills the space to my distant Star:
Black the darkness that darkens The Dark
    From high o'erhead to the horizon's bar:
Sad are the sighs that sigh in The Sigh
    That thrills my world while you are afar.

Sweet are the hopes that hope in The Hope
    That shows through the Future's Door ajar:
Bright is the light that lightens The Light
    That shines from my heart to you afar:
Lovely the Life that shall live in The Life
    When the Distance no longer my Kisses bar.

When Kate Chopin decided to answer the critics of *The Awakening*, she chose *Book News* as her venue—and with good reason. In March 1899, the periodical had published the first notice of *The Awakening*, calling it "a remarkable novel," one

> so keen in its analysis of character, so subtle in its presentation of emotional effects that it seems to reveal life as well as to represent it. In reading it you have the impression of being in the very heart of things, you feel the throb of the machinery, you see and understand the slight transitions of thought, the momentary impulses, the quick sensations of the hardness of life, which govern so much of our action. It is an intimate thing, which in studying the nature of one woman reveals something which brings her in touch with all women—something larger than herself. This it is which justifies the audacity of "The Awakening" and makes it big enough to be true. . . .

Kate Chopin, wrote the reviewer, was "an artist in the manipulation of a complex character, and faulty as the woman is, she has the magnetism which is essential to the charm of a novel." Overall, the reviewer wrote, "the thing shows a very subtle and a brilliant kind of art."

The review was in no sense impartial. Its author, Lucy Monroe, was the chief reader and literary editor for Herbert S. Stone, *The Awakening*'s publisher, and almost certainly was responsible for Stone's buying the book. An art critic, a member of Chicago literary and artistic circles, and a "New Woman" who cared passionately about opportunities for women, Lucy Monroe was the ideal reviewer and promoter for *The Awakening*.

Others were not so in tune with Kate Chopin's sensibilities. Her first St. Louis review, in the April 22 *Republic*, called *The Awakening* "the story of a lady most foolish." A few days later, the reviewer for the St. Louis *Mirror* said the novel "leaves one sick of human nature," while the *Globe-Democrat* called it "a morbid book." The *Post-Dispatch* review, by Chopin's friend Charles Deyo, was more intelligent, but ironic enough so that it could be understood as condemning Edna's extramarital desires: "A fact, no matter how essential, which we have all agreed shall not be acknowledged, is as good as no fact at all." And then, in an extraordinary move, the *Post-Dispatch* published a second review by "G. B." (otherwise unidentified), who damned *The Awakening* as "too strong drink for moral babes, and should be labeled 'poison.'"

By the end of May 1899, only *Book News* and the St. Louis newspapers had reviewed *The Awakening*. Still, Chopin—perhaps egged on by Lucy Monroe in Chicago—felt moved to write the *Book News* statement on *The Awakening*.

She wrote in on May 28, but it did not appear in print until July—by which time she had achieved some national notoriety. Her novel had received negative reviews from newspapers in Chicago, New York, Providence, New Orleans, and Los Angeles, as well as in *Public Opinion* and *Literature*. Although the New York *Times* and Boston *Beacon* praised it, most other papers called the story unpleasant and immoral. Several directed particularly vicious attacks upon the main character Edna Pontellier, as a discontented "fool woman" who went outside marriage to seek sexual fulfillment.

By July 1899, then, Kate Chopin might already have realized that she would not be able to write about life as she saw it. She was receiving warm letters of praise from friends, but the powerful reviewers would determine what she could publish in the future.

Perhaps she already knew that her writing career was almost over.

The following was published in *Book News*, July 1899, p. 612, under the heading "Aims and autographs of authors."

THE AWAKENING. By KATE CHOPIN.

Having a group of people at my disposal, I thought it might be entertaining (to myself) to throw them together and see what would happen. I never dreamed of Mrs. Pontellier making such a mess of things and working out her own damnation as she did. If I had had the slightest intimation of such a thing I would have excluded her from the company. But when I found out what she was up to, the play was half over and it was then too late.

ST. LOUIS, MO., May 28, 1899. Kate Chopin

This fragment, now in the Missouri Historical Society, also includes a photograph labeled "Kitty Garesché 1870"—the year that Kate O'Flaherty married and Kitty Garesché became a Sacred Heart nun.

From the time they began school until age thirteen, Kate and Kitty were neighbors who climbed trees, shared candy, and took their first Communions together. Reading was their great shared passion, and among their favorite popular novels were those by the English authors Grace Aguilar (*Days of Bruce*) and Sir Walter Scott (*Ivanhoe*). Years later, Kate Chopin drew on her memories of Aguilar's and Scott's fair heroines for Adèle Ratignolle in *The Awakening*: "There are no words to describe her save the old ones that have served so often to picture the bygone heroine of romance and the fair lady of our dreams" (IV).

The character of Kitty herself may also be reflected in *The Awakening*, when Edna remembers her "most intimate friend at school," a girl of "rather exceptional intellectual gifts, who wrote fine-sounding essays, which Edna admired and strove to imitate; and with her she talked and glowed over the English classics, and sometimes held religious and political controversies" (VII).

But Kate Chopin's later reminiscence does not mention that the two girls were separated in 1863 when Kitty and her family, punished for their Confederate sympathies, were banished from St. Louis. Kitty went to school in New York, and did not return until 1868. Two years after that, on her honeymoon with Oscar Chopin, Kate noted Kitty's August 24 birthday in her Commonplace Book (in this volume): "I had not forgotten her."

The two women probably corresponded, and occasionally met, throughout the rest of Kate's life (Kitty lived until 1940). Kate may have been thinking of Kitty when she wrote "Two Portraits" (1895—also called "The Nun and the Wanton"), two contrasting stories about a beautiful young woman named Alberta. In one section, molested as a child by a young male student,

Alberta grows up to be a sensual demimondaine, and carries a knife. In the other, Alberta, taught at an early age by a very holy woman, falls in love with spiritual things and becomes a nun. The story represents, in extremes, the paths Kate O'Flaherty and Kitty Garesché took in 1870: one sexual, one spiritual.

In 1900, on Kitty's fiftieth birthday, Kate wrote a poem:

To the Friend of My Youth: To Kitty

It is not all of life
To cling together while the years glide past.
It is not all of love
To walk with clasped hands from first to last.
That mystic garland which the spring did twine
Of scented lilac and the new-blown rose,
Faster than chains will hold my soul to thine
Thro' joy, and grief, thro' life—unto its close.

As a child, Kitty had been an excellent seamstress and pianist; as an adult, she was a superb administrator and intellectual leader. She had a reputation as "a brilliant teacher" and "a true friend of the young, preferring to stress the good side of each one, and to provide plenty of fun for them all, with an acceptable joke often taking the place of an expected scolding."

Recognizing her talents, the Sacred Heart nuns often sent Kitty to initiate new projects. While her friend Kate was in Louisiana giving birth to and raising six children (1870–1884), Kitty was moving around. In 1877–1880, for instance, she was teaching in Chicago; in 1880 she was sent back to Maryville, in the country outside St. Louis, as "surveillante of novices." Three years later, Kitty was in Omaha, where she had become Mistress of Studies for the whole academy. By 1885, the year her mother and Kate's mother died, Kitty was in Chicago. She moved on to San Francisco and then was back at Maryville in 1891, for the next ten years. (Whether she read Kate Chopin's writings, virtually all of which appeared during that period, cannot be known.)

At Maryville Kitty was devoted to teacher training, helping younger nuns, playing the organ, and teaching the highest class in religious instruction. According to Sacred Heart historian Marie Louise Martinez, Kitty "seems to have been one of the most lovable and approachable persons on campus—popular, in fact—and a great help to young teachers making their first efforts and first blunders."

Kitty was at Maryville for her fiftieth birthday in August, and presumably received Kate's poem there. A year later the Sacred Heart Vicar, Henrietta Sarens, moved to the New City House in the city of St. Louis and took Kitty Garesché as her secretary—which put Kitty very close to the home of her old friend Kate. From her new home on McPherson, Kate could easily walk to see Kitty at the Sacred Heart convent, on Maryland and Taylor. The front door, known as the parlor entrance, opened onto Taylor, and convent parlors were very discreet places for old friends to meet. Possibly one such visit inspired Kate to write down a few memories of Kitty. But the rest of this fragment, which cannot be dated, was lost long ago.

[. . .] mental and physical relaxation: under the special supervision and instruction of one of the "ladies." It was at this time that I formed a friendship with Kitty Garesché: a friendship which last all through our childhood and youth & which, I will not say ended—but was interrupted by her entering the Sacred Heart Convent as a religious in 1870—the year that I married. We divided our "picayune's" worth of candy—climbed together the highest cherry trees: wept in company over the "Days of Bruce," and later, exchanged our heart secrets. The step which

As the sole support of a large family, Kate Chopin almost certainly had written wills before 1902, but this is the only one that has survived. By that December, Chopin had good reasons for writing a will. Her grandmother had died of bronchitis in early 1897; her mother had already been dead for seventeen years (and her father for forty-seven). Oscar's sister, Eugenie Chopin Henry, who had died in March 1902, was just two years older than Kate. John A. Dillon, *Post-Dispatch* editor when Chopin was beginning her literary career, died in October 1902 after a fall from a horse led to pneumonia and pleurisy.

There would also be future changes: Chopin's son Jean, the first of her children to wed, had married Emelie Hughes in June 1902. By December they were expecting their first child. (Emelie Hughes Chopin would die in childbirth in July of 1903).

Kate Chopin was ailing herself, perhaps from a combination of diabetes (which could have caused her eye trouble) and emphysema (which could have come from her cigarette smoking, as well as St. Louis's foul air). Many of Chopin's stories from 1900 on are about disabilities, especially blindness, and her letter to Richard Shepard (in this volume) hints at illness, depression, or both.

Chopin's December 1902 will was witnessed by Isabel Willcox and Linn R. Brokaw, to whom Chopin probably addressed her poem "Lines to Linn" (in this volume). Kate Chopin enjoyed the company of younger people, and Brokaw was a twenty-three-year-old law student at the time he witnessed the will. Two years later, he would be one of Kate Chopin's pallbearers.

The 1902 will is simple, directing that all of her property be divided equally among her five sons—except for her jewelry and clothes ("my personalty"), which went to her sole daughter, Lélia. Most intriguing, though, is Chopin's providing for Lélia to be an independent woman: Lélia alone received the most valuable property, the city land which Thomas O'Flaherty had wisely purchased half a century earlier. Lélia would not have to marry for financial support, and the will gave the property to her exclusively, for "her sole and separate use, free from any debts or claims against her husband."

As a child, Kate O'Flaherty had grown up in a household of widows who managed their money wisely. She obviously wanted no less for her daughter. Her will gave Lélia what Virginia Woolf would say a woman writer needs: an independent income and a room of her own.

Like her mother, grandmother, great-grandmother, and great-great-grandmother, Lélia eventually was widowed at a young age—and she did have a successful writing career. The author of six books on bridge and backgammon, she made her living as a professional bridge player and teacher in New York and Palm Beach. Her articles on New York drama were also praised for their "literary attainments" and "engaging style." Perhaps her mother's independence also encouraged Lélia's eccentricities, for "Aunt Lil" delighted in embarrassing her young nieces and nephews. She loathed poor service and canned orange juice, and liked to say so in dramatic, hysterical scenes in restaurants. As she was six feet tall, dark, intense, and flamboyant, no one could ignore her. She reminded her blushing younger relatives of Margaret Dumont, the dowager in Marx Brothers films.

Lélia, like the widows for generations before her, did not remarry, but she did have an eye for the gentlemen. She would sometimes ride up and down New York's Park Avenue in a chauffeured open car—from which, in a loud voice, she would comment on the faces and bodies of any men who passed by. She was a true character, perhaps a fit daughter for Kate Chopin, who, half a century earlier, had scandalized Cloutierville, Louisiana, by smoking cigarettes, showing her ankles, and flirting with other women's husbands.

Lélia had simply moved onto a larger stage.

I, Kate Chopin, of the City of St. Louis, State of Missouri, being of sound mind and disposing memory, do make, publish and declare this my last will and testament.

I. I direct all my just debts, my funeral expenses, and the expenses of my last illness be first paid, as soon as possible, and if possible out of my personal estate.

II. I direct that my daughter Lelia, have the lot and stable located thereon and situated on west side of Seventh Street between Franklin Avenue and Wash Street in the City of St. Louis, and at present leased by one Berger; to have and to hold the same to her sole and separate use, free from any debts or claims against her husband.

III. I direct that my daughter Lelia have all my personalty of the nature of jewelry and wearing apparel, to hold to her separate use.

IV. All the rest of my property, both real and personal which I may own at the time of my death I direct be divided equally, share and share alike, between my sons, or the descendants of such as may be living at the time of my death.

V. I do hereby appoint my sons Jean and Felix executors of this, my last will and testament, to serve without bond, and should neither be living, or in any manner incapacitated from serving, I desire that my oldest living son capable of serving, do execute my will without bond.

In witness whereof I have hereunto set my hand this _____ day of December, 1902.

<u>Kate Chopin</u>

Signed, published and declared by the above named Kate Chopin to be her last will and testament in the presence of us who at her request and in her presence and in the presence of each other have hereunto subscribed our names as witnesses thereof.

Witnesses: <u>Isabel Willcox</u>.   <u>Linn R. Brokaw</u>

Appendix: Complete Works of Kate Chopin

This list includes all of Kate Chopin's known writings, both published and unpublished. Also listed here are writings recorded in her manuscript account notebooks, but now destroyed or lost. The items are arranged in order of composition, with final title, date of composition, first appearance in print, and inclusion in collections. Where titles vary, we have listed variations. CW includes information about changes from manuscript to print versions.

ABBREVIATIONS

BF = Kate Chopin, *Bayou Folk*. Boston: Houghton, Mifflin, 1894.

CW = Per Seyersted, ed., *The Complete Works of Kate Chopin*. Baton Rouge: Louisiana State University, 1969.

DIR = writings appearing in "Impressions," Kate Chopin's 1894 diary, reprinted in this volume (KCPP)

DSR = Daniel S. Rankin, *Kate Chopin and Her Creole Stories*. Philadelphia: University of Pennsylvania, 1932.

KCM = Per Seyersted and Emily Toth, eds., *A Kate Chopin Miscellany*. Natchitoches and Oslo: Northwestern State University Press and Universitetsforlaget, 1979.

KCPP = Emily Toth, Per Seyersted, and Cheyenne Bonnell, eds., *Kate Chopin's Private Papers* (this volume).

NA = Kate Chopin, *A Night in Acadie*. Chicago: Way & Williams, 1897.

PS1 = Per Seyersted, "Kate Chopin: an Important St. Louis Writer Reconsidered," *Missouri Historical Society Bulletin* 19 (January 1963), 89–114.

PS2 = Per Seyersted, "Kate Chopin's Wound: Two New Letters," *American Literary Realism* 20:1 (Fall 1987), 71–75.

RMF = Rankin-Marhefka Fragments, found in a Massachusetts locker in 1992 (see notes in this volume).

SCB = Per Seyersted, *Kate Chopin: a Critical Biography*. Oslo and Baton Rouge: Universitetsforlaget and Louisiana State University, 1969.

TB = Thomas Bonner, Jr., *The Kate Chopin Companion*. Westport: Greenwood, 1988.

TKC = Emily Toth, *Kate Chopin: A Life of the Author of "The Awakening."* New York: Morrow, 1990. Austin: University of Texas, 1993.

VV = Kate Chopin, *A Vocation and a Voice: Stories*. Ed. Emily Toth. New York: Penguin, 1991.

WORKS OF KATE CHOPIN

"Leaves of Affection." Autograph book (with pictures, poems, brief comments by Kate O'Flaherty). 1860—. KCPP.

"Katie O'Flaherty, St. Louis. 1867" (diary and commonplace book). 1867–1870. DSR (in part). KCM (in part). KCPP (in full).

"Emancipation. A Life Fable." Undated: late 1869 or early 1870. PS1. CW.

New Orleans diary. 1870—. Seen by Rankin; later lost.

Letter to Marie Breazeale. June 21, 1887. KCM. KCPP.

"Lilia. Polka for Piano." Undated. Published for the author by H. Rollman & Sons, St. Louis, 1888. KCM. KCPP.

"If It Might Be" (poem). Undated. *America* (Chicago) 1 (January 10, 1889), 9. CW.

"Euphrasie" (story). 1888. See "A No-Account Creole."

Manuscript Account Books (2—now called Bonnell and Wondra). 1888—. KCPP.

"Unfinished Story—Grand Isle." 1888–89. Destroyed.

"A Poor Girl" (story). May 1889. Destroyed.

"Wiser Than a God" (story). June 1889. *Philadelphia Musical Journal* 4 (December 1889), 38–40. CW.

"A Point at Issue!" (story). August 1889. *St. Louis Post-Dispatch*, October 27, 1889. CW.

"Miss Witherwell's Mistake" (story). November 18, 1889. *Fashion and Fancy* (St. Louis) 5 (February 1891), 115–117. CW.

"With the Violin" (story). December 11, 1889. *Spectator* (St. Louis) 11 (December 6, 1890), 196. CW.

At Fault (novel). July 5, 1889–April 20, 1890. Published for the author by Nixon-Jones Printing Co., St. Louis, September 1890. CW.

"Monsieur Pierre" (story; translation from Adrien Vely). April 1890. *St. Louis Post-Dispatch*, August 8, 1892. TB. KCPP.

"Psyche's Lament" (poem). Undated; probably 1890. DSR. CW.

Letter to the *St. Louis Republic*. October 18, 1890. *St. Louis Republic*, October 25, 1890. KCM. KCPP.

"Young Dr. Gosse" (novel, also called "Young Dr. Gosse and Théo"). May 4–November 27, 1890. Destroyed.

"A Red Velvet Coat" (story). December 1–8, 1890. Destroyed or lost.

"*At Fault*. A Correction" (letter). December 11, 1890. *Natchitoches Enterprise*, December 18, 1890. TKC. KCPP.

"Mrs. Mobry's Reason" (story). January 10, 1891. *New Orleans Times-Democrat*, April 23, 1893. CW.

"The Shape of the Head" (translation of an article listed in Chopin's account book as "A Study in Heads"). Undated. *St. Louis Post-Dispatch*. January 25, 1891. KCPP.

"A No-Account Creole" (story). 1888 as "Euphrasie"; rewritten January 24, 1891– February 24, 1891. *Century* 47 (January 1894), 382–393. BF. CW.

"Octave Feuillet" (translation?) February 1891. Destroyed or lost.

"Roger and His Majesty" (story). March 1, 1891. Destroyed.

"Revival of Wrestling" (translation). Undated. *St. Louis Post-Dispatch*, March 8, 1891. KCPP.

"For Marse Chouchoute" (story). March 14, 1891. *Youth's Companion* 64 (August 20, 1891), 450–451. BF. CW.

"The Christ Light" (story). April 4, 1891, as "The Going and Coming of Liza Jane."

Syndicated, American Press Association. December 1892. In CW as "The Going Away of Liza."

"Cut Paper Figures" (also entitled "Manikins" and "How to Make Manikins"; translation?) Undated. *St. Louis Post-Dispatch*, April 5, 1891. KCPP.

"The Maid of Saint Phillippe" (story). April 19, 1891. *Short Stories* (New York), 11 (November 1891), 257–264. CW.

"A Wizard from Gettysburg" (story). May 25, 1891. *Youth's Companion* 65 (July 7, 1892), 346–347. BF. CW.

Letter to the *Century*. May 28, 1891. KCM. KCPP.

"A Shameful Affair" (story). June 5, 7, 1891. *New Orleans Times-Democrat*. April 9, 1893. CW.

Letter to R. W. Gilder. July 12, 1891. KCM. KCPP.

"A Rude Awakening" (story). July 13, 1891. *Youth's Companion* 66 (February 2, 1893), 54–55. BF. CW.

"A Harbinger" (story). September 11, 1891. *St. Louis Magazine* 12 (apparently November 1, 1891: no copies can be found). CW.

"Dr. Chevalier's Lie" (story). September 12, 1891. *Vogue* 2 (October 5, 1893), 174, 178. CW.

"A Very Fine Fiddle" (story). September 13, 1891. *Harper's Young People* 13 (November 24, 1891), 79. BF. CW.

"Boulôt and Boulotte" (story). September 20, 1891. *Harper's Young People* 13 (December 8, 1891), 112. BF. CW.

"Love on the Bon-Dieu" (story). October 3, 1891, as "Love and Easter." *Two Tales* (Boston) 2 (July 23, 1892), 148–156. BF. CW.

"An Embarrassing Position. Comedy in One Act." October 15–22, 1891. *Mirror* (St. Louis) 5 (December 19, 1895), 9–11. CW.

"Beyond the Bayou" (story). November 7, 1891. *Youth's Companion* 66 (June 15, 1893), 302–303. BF. CW.

"Typical Forms of German Music." Paper read at the Wednesday Club, St. Louis, December 9, 1891. Possibly the same as "Typical German Composers," essay offered in 1899 to the *Atlantic*. Destroyed or lost.

"After the Winter" (story). December 31, 1891. *New Orleans Times-Democrat*. April 5, 1896. NA. CW.

"The Bênitous' Slave" (story). January 7, 1892. *Harper's Young People* 13 (February 16, 1892), 280. BF. CW.

"A Turkey Hunt" (story). January 8, 1892. *Harper's Young People* 13 (February 16, 1892), 287. BF. CW.

"Old Aunt Peggy" (story). January 8, 1892. BF. CW.

"The Lilies" (story). January 27–28, 1892. *Wide Awake* 36 (April 1893), 415–418. NA. CW.

"Mittens" (story). February 25, 1892. Destroyed.

"Ripe Figs" (story). February 26, 1892. *Vogue* 2 (August 19, 1893), 90. NA. CW.

"Croque-Mitaine" (story). February 27, 1892. PS1. CW.

"A Trip to Portugese Guinea" (translation?) February 27, 1892. Destroyed or lost.

"A Visit to the Planet Mars" (translation?) March 1892. Destroyed or lost.

"Transfusion of Goat's Blood" (translation?) March 1892. Destroyed or lost.

"Miss McEnders" (story). March 7, 1892. *Criterion* (St. Louis), 13 (March 6, 1897), 16–18, signed La Tour. CW.

"Loka" (story). April 9–10, 1892. *Youth's Companion* 65 (December 22, 1892), 670–671. BF. CW.

"Bambo Pellier" (story). May 1892. Destroyed or lost.

"At the 'Cadian Ball" (story). July 15–17, 1892. *Two Tales* (Boston) 3 (October 22, 1892), 145–152. BF. CW.

"A Visit to Avoyelles" (story). August 1, 1892. *Vogue* 1 (January 14, 1893), 74–75. BF. CW.

"Ma'ame Pélagie" (story). August 27–28, 1892. *New Orleans Times-Democrat*, December 24, 1893. BF. CW.

"A Fancy" (poem). Probably 1892. DSR. KCM. KCPP.

"Désirée's Baby" (story). November 24, 1892. *Vogue* 1 (January 14, 1893), 70–71, 74. BF. CW.

"Caline" (story). December 2, 1892. *Vogue* 1 (May 20, 1893), 324–325. NA. CW.

"The Return of Alcibiade" (story). December 5–6, 1892. *St. Louis Life* 7 (December 17, 1892), 6–8. BF. CW.

"In and Out of Old Natchitoches." (story). February 1–3, 1892. *Two Tales* 5 (April 8, 1893), 103–114. BF. CW.

"Mamouche" (story). February 24–25, 1893. *Youth's Companion* 67 (April 19, 1894), 178–179. NA. CW.

Letter to Marion A. Baker. May 4, 1893. KCM. KCPP.

Letter to R. W. Gilder. May 10, 1893. KCM. KCPP.

"Madame Célestin's Divorce" (story). May 24–25, 1893. BF. CW.

"The Song Everlasting" (poem). Before June 1893. Published in program for St. Louis Wednesday Club's "Reciprocity Day: An Afternoon with St. Louis Authors." November 29, 1899. CW.

"You and I" (poem). Before June 1893. Published in the program for the St. Louis Wednesday Club's "Reciprocity Day: An Afternoon with St. Louis Authors." November 29, 1899. CW.

"It Matters All" (poem). Before June 1893. DSR. CW.

"If the Woods Could Talk" (poem). Before June 1893. KCM. KCPP.

"A Sentimental Serenade" (poem). Before June 1893. KCM. KCPP.

"A Message" (poem). Before June 1893. KCM. KCPP.

"An Idle Fellow" (story). June 9, 1893. CW. VV.

"A Matter of Prejudice" (story). June 17–18, 1893. *Youth's Companion* 68 (September 25, 1895), 450. NA. CW.

"Azélie" (story). July 22–23, 1893. *Century* 49 (December 1894), 282–287. NA. CW.

"A Lady of Bayou St. John" (story). August 24–25, 1893. *Vogue* 2 (September 21, 1893), 154, 156–158. BF. CW.

"La Belle Zoraïde" (story). September 21, 1893. *Vogue* 3 (January 4, 1894), 2, 4, 8–10. BF. CW.

"At Chênière Caminada" (story). October 21–23, 1893. *New Orleans Times-Democrat*, December 23, 1894. NA. CW.

"A Gentleman of Bayou Têche" (story). November 5–7, 1893. BF. CW.

"In Sabine" (story). November 20–22, 1893. BF. CW.

"A Respectable Woman" (story). January 20, 1894. *Vogue* 3 (February 15, 1894), 68–69, 72. NA. CW.

"Tante Cat'rinette" (story). February 23, 1894. *Atlantic Monthly* 74 (September 1894), 368–373. NA. CW.

"A Dresden Lady in Dixie" (story). March 6, 1894. *Catholic Home Journal* (March 3, 1895). NA. CW.

Bayou Folk (collected stories). March 1894, Houghton, Mifflin & Co., Boston.

"The Dream of an Hour" (story). April 19, 1894. *Vogue* 4 (December 6, 1894), 360. In CW as "The Story of an Hour"; modern editors use that title. VV.

"Impressions. 1894" (diary). May 4, 1894-October 26, 1896. Published in part in SCB. KCM. KCPP.

"Lilacs" (story). May 14–16, 1894. *New Orleans Times-Democrat*, December 20, 1896. CW. VV.

"Good Night" (poem). Undated. *New Orleans Times-Democrat*, July 22, 1894. CW.

"The Western Association of Writers" (essay). June 30, 1894. *Critic* 22 (July 7, 1894), 15. CW. DIR.

"A Divorce Case" (story; translation of "Un cas de divorce," by Guy de Maupassant). July 11, 1894. TB. DIR.

"A Scrap and a Sketch": "The Night Came Slowly" (story), July 24, 1894; "Juanita" (story), July 26, 1894. *Moods* (Philadelphia) 2 (July 1895), n. p. CW prints the two separately as "The Night Came Slowly" and "Juanita." DIR. VV.

"Dorothea" (untitled story, possibly a real-life observation—not listed separately in manuscript account notebook, and not sent out separately for publication). July 25, 1894, in 1894 diary. KCM. KCPP. DIR.

"Cavanelle" (story) July 31–August 6, 1894. *American Jewess* 1 (April 1895), 22–25. NA. CW. DIR.

"Mad?" (story; translation of "Fou?" by Guy de Maupassant). September 4, 1894. TB. DIR.

Letter to Stone & Kimball. September 10, 1894. KCM. KCPP.

"Regret" (story). September 17, 1894. *Century* 50 (May 1895), 147–149. NA. CW. DIR.

"The Kiss" (story). September 19, 1894. *Vogue* 5 (January 17, 1895), 37. CW. DIR. VV.

"Ozème's Holiday" (story). September 23–24, 1894. *Century* 52 (August 1896), 629–631. NA. CW. DIR.

"'Crumbling Idols' By Hamlin Garland" (essay). Undated. *St. Louis Life* 10 (October 6, 1894), 13. CW.

Letter to Waitman Barbe. October 2, 1894. KCM. KCPP.

"The Real Edwin Booth" (essay). Undated. *St. Louis Life* 10 (October 13, 1894), 11. CW.

"Emile Zola's 'Lourdes'" (essay). Undated. *St. Louis Life* 10 (November 17, 1894), 5. CW.

"A Sentimental Soul" (story). November 18–22, 1894. *New Orleans Times-Democrat*, December 22, 1895. NA. CW.

"Her Letters" (story). November 29, 1894. *Vogue* 5 (April 11, 18, 1895), 228–230, 248. CW. VV.

Letters to A. A. Hill. December 26, 1894; January 1, 11, 16, 1895. KCM. KCPP.

"Odalie Misses Mass" (story). January 28, 1895. *Shreveport Times*. July 1, 1895. NA. CW.

"It?" (story; translation of "Lui?" by Guy de Maupassant). February 4, 1895. *St. Louis Life* 11 (February 23, 1895), 12–13. TB.

"Polydore" (story). February 17, 1895. *Youth's Companion* 70 (April 23, 1896), 214–215. NA. CW.

"Dead Men's Shoes" (story). February 21–22, 1895. *Independent* (New York) 49 (February 11, 1897), 194–195. NA. CW.

"Solitude" (story; translation of "Solitude," by Guy de Maupassant). March 5, 1895. *St. Louis Life* 13 (December 28, 1895), 30. TB.

"Night" (story; translation of "La Nuit," by Guy de Maupassant). March 8, 1895. TB.

Letter to J. M. Stoddart. March 31, 1895. KCM. KCPP.

"Athénaïse" (story). April 10–28, 1895. *Atlantic Monthly* 78 (August and September 1896), 232–241, 404–413. NA. CW.

"A Lady of Shifting Intentions" (story). May 4, 1895. Destroyed or lost; extant fragment in KCM, KCPP.

"Two Summers and Two Souls" (story). July 14, 1895. *Vogue* 6 (August 7, 1895), 84. CW. VV.

"The Unexpected" (story). July 18, 1895. *Vogue* 6 (September 18, 1895), 180–181. CW. VV.

"Two Portraits (The Nun and the Wanton)" (story). August 4, 1895. DSR. CW. VV.

"If Some Day" (poem). August 16, 1895. CW. DIR.

"Under My Lattice" (poem). August 18, 1895. KCM. KCPP. DIR.

"The Falling in Love of Fedora." November 19, 1895, as "Fedora." *Criterion* (St. Louis) 13 (February 20, 1897), 9, signed La Tour. In CW as "Fedora." VV.

Letter to Cornelia F. Maury. December 3, 1895. KCM. KCPP.

"For Mrs. Ferriss" (poem). December 1895. KCM. KCPP. DIR.

"To Hidee Schuyler—" (poem). Christmas 1895. CW. DIR.

"To 'Billy' with a Box of Cigars" (poem). Christmas 1895. CW. DIR.

"To Mrs. B———n" (poem). Christmas 1895. CW as "For Carrie B." DIR.

"To a Lady at the Piano—Mrs. R——n." (poem). Christmas 1895. DIR.

"To Blanche" (poem). December 1895. KCM. KCPP. DIR.

"Vagabonds" (story). December 1895. DSR. CW.

"Suicide" (story; translation of "Suicide," by Guy de Maupassant). December 18, 1895. *St. Louis Republic*, June 5, 1898. TB.

Letter to Stone & Kimball. January 2, 1896. KCM. KCPP.

"Madame Martel's Christmas Eve" (story). January 16–18, 1896. CW.

"The Recovery" (story). February 1896. *Vogue* 7 (May 21, 1896), 354–355. CW. VV.

"A Night in Acadie" (story). March 1896. NA. CW.

"A Pair of Silk Stockings" (story). April 1896. *Vogue* 10 (September 16, 1897), 191–192. CW.

"Nég Créol" (story). April 1896. *Atlantic Monthly* 80 (July 1897), 135–138. NA. CW.

"Aunt Lympy's Interference" (story). June 1896. *Youth's Companion* 71 (August 12, 1897), 373–374. CW.

"The Blind Man" (story). July 1896. *Vogue* 9 (May 13, 1897), 303. CW. VV.

"In the Confidence of a Story-Writer" (essay). October 1896. *Atlantic Monthly* 83 (January 1899), 137–139, published without byline. CW. (An earlier version, written September 1896 and entitled "Confidences," is also published in CW.)

"Ti Frère" (story). September 1896. KCM. KCPP.

"For Sale" (story; translation of "A Vendre," by Guy de Maupassant). October 26, 1896. TB. DIR.

"A Vocation and a Voice" (story). November 1896. *Mirror* (St. Louis) 12 (March 27, 1902), 18–24. CW. VV.

"A Mental Suggestion" (story). December 1896. CW. VV.

"To Mrs. R" (poem). Christmas 1896. CW. DIR.

"Let the Night Go" (poem). January 1, 1897. CW.

Letter to the *Century*. January 5, 1897. KCM. KCPP.

Inscription for Ruth McEnery Stuart. February 3, 1897. KCM. KCPP.

"Suzette" (story). February 1897. *Vogue* 10 (October 21, 1897), 262–263. CW. VV.

"As You Like It" (a series of six essays). Undated, individual essay titles supplied by Per Seyersted. *Criterion* (St. Louis) 13:

    I. "I have a young friend . . . " (February 13, 1897), 11. CW.

    II. "It has lately been . . . " (February 20, 1897), 17. CW.

    III. "Several years ago . . . " (February 26, 1897), 11. CW.

    IV. "A while ago . . . " (March 13, 1897), 15–16. CW.

    V. "A good many of us . . . " (March 20, 1897), 10. CW.

    VI. "We are told . . . " (March 27, 1897), 10. CW.

"The Locket" (story). March 1897. CW.

"An Easter Day Conversion" (story). April 1897, as "A Morning Walk." *Criterion* (St. Louis) 15 [*sic*] (April 17, 1897), 13–14. In CW as "A Morning Walk." VV.

"An Egyptian Cigarette" (story). April 1897. *Vogue* 15 (April 19, 1900), 252–254. CW. VV.

A Night in Acadie (collected stories). November 1897, Way & Williams, Chicago.

The Awakening (novel). April 1897–January 21, 1898, listed in Chopin's notebook as "A Solitary Soul." Published April 22, 1899, by Herbert S. Stone & Company, Chicago & New York. CW.

"A Family Affair" (story). December 1897. Syndicated—American Press Association, January 1898. *Saturday Evening Post* 172 (September 9, 1899), 168–169. CW.

"'Is Love Divine?' The Question Answered by Three Ladies Well Known in St. Louis Society" (interview). *St. Louis Post-Dispatch*, January 16, 1898, 17. TKC. KCPP.

"Has High Society Struck the Pace That Kills?" (interview) *St. Louis Post-Dispatch*, February 6, 1898, 12. TKC. KCPP.

Letter to Lydia Arms Avery Coonley Ward. March 21, 1898. PS2. KCPP.

"Elizabeth Stock's One Story" (story). March 1898. PS1. CW. VV.

"A Horse Story" (story). March 1898. KCM. KCPP. VV.

"Father Amable" (story; translation of "Le père Amable," by Guy de Maupassant). April 21, 1898. TB.

"There's Music Enough" (poem). May 1, 1898. DSR. CW.

"An Ecstasy of Madness" (poem). July 10, 1898. DSR. CW.

"The Roses" (poem). July 11, 1898. KCM. KCPP.

"The Storm" (story). July 19, 1898. CW.

"Lines to Linn" (poem). July 31, 1898. KCM. KCPP.

"White Oaks" (poem). August 24, 1898. KCM. KCPP.

"Lines Suggested By Omar" (poem). August 1898. KCM. KCPP.

"The Lull of Summer Time" (poem). Undated, but probably August 1898. KCM. KCPP.

"To Henry One Evening Last Summer" (poem). October 21, 1898. KCM. KCPP.

"By The Meadow Gate" (poem). October 24, 1898. KCM. KCPP.

"Old Natchitoches" (poem). December 1898. KCM. KCPP.

"An Hour" (poem). Undated, but before January 1899. DSR. KCM. KCPP.

"In Spring" (poem). Undated, but before January 1899. *Century* 58 (July 1899), 361. KCM. KCPP.

"I Wanted God" (poem). Undated, but before February 1899. CW.

"My Lady Rose Pouts" (poem). Undated, but before February 1899. KCM. KCPP.

"Come to Me" (poem). Undated, but before February 1899. KCM. KCPP.

"O! Blessed Tavern" (poem). Undated, but before February 1899. KCM. KCPP.

"As Careless As the Summer Breeze" (poem). Undated, but before February 1899. KCM. KCPP.

"One Day" (poem). Undated, but before February 1899. KCM. KCPP.

"Ah! Magic Bird!" (poem). Undated, but before February 1899. KCM. KCPP.

"With a Violet-Wood Paper Knife" (poem). Undated, but before February 1899. KCM. KCPP.

"Because—" (poem). Undated, but probably 1899. CW.

"The Godmother" (story). January—February 6, 1899. *Mirror* (St. Louis) 11 (December 12, 1901), 9–13. CW. VV.

"The Haunted Chamber" (poem). February 1899. CW.

Letter to the *Youth's Companion*. February 11, 1899. KCM. KCPP.

"A Little Country Girl" (story). February 11, 1899. CW. RMF.

"Life" (poem). May 10, 1899. DSR. CW.

Letter to Herbert S. Stone. May 21, 1899. KCM. KCPP.

Statement on *The Awakening*. May 28, 1899. *Book News* 17 (July 1899), 612. KCM. KCPP.

Letter to Herbert S. Stone. June 7, 1899. KCM. KCPP.

"A Little Day" (poem). Undated, but probably 1899. KCM. KCPP.

Inscription for Madison Cawein. August 17, 1899. KCM. KCPP.

Letter to Richard B. Shepard. August 24, 1899. KCM. KCPP.

Letter to Richard B. Shepard. November 8, 1899. PS2. KCPP.

"A Reflection" (story). November 1899. DSR. CW.

"On certain brisk, bright days" (untitled essay, title supplied by Per Seyersted). Undated, but undoubtedly November 1899. *St. Louis Post-Dispatch*, November 26, 1899. CW.

"Ti Démon" (story). November 1899. CW. VV.

Letter to the *Century*. December 1, 1899. KCM. KCPP.

"A December Day in Dixie" (story). January 1900. DSR (in part), CW (in full).

"Alexandre's Wonderful Experience" (story). January 23, 1900. KCM. KCPP. RMF.

"The Gentleman from New Orleans" (story). February 6, 1900. CW. RMF.

Letter to the *Youth's Companion*, February 15, 1900. DSR. KCM. KCPP.

"Charlie" (story). April 1900. CW. RMF. Also in RMF as "Jacques."

"The White Eagle" (story). May 9, 1900. *Vogue* 16 (July 12, 1900), 20, 22. CW. VV.

"Alone" (poem). July 6, 1900. KCM. KCPP.

"To the Friend of My Youth: To Kitty" (poem). DSR (dated as August 24, 1900). CW. KCPP.

"Development of the Literary West: a Review" (essay). Undated. *St. Louis Republic*, December 9, 1900, 1. TKC. KCPP.

Letter to R. E. Lee Gibson. October 13, 1901. KCM. KCPP.

"Millie's First Party" (story). Also called "Millie's First Ball." October 16, 1901. Destroyed or lost.

"The Wood-Choppers" (story). October 17, 1901. *Youth's Companion* 76 (May 29, 1902), 270–271. CW.

"Toots' Nurses" (story). October 18, 1901. Destroyed or lost.

"Polly" (story). January 14, 1902 as "Polly's Opportunity." *Youth's Companion* 76 (July 3, 1902), 334–335. CW.

Letter to Marie Breazeale. February 4, 1902. KCM. KCPP.

Kate Chopin's Last Will and Testament. December 1902. KCPP.

UNDATABLE MATERIALS

Reminiscences about Kitty Garesché. 1900? DSR. KCM. KCPP.

Letter to Mrs. Tiffany. KCM. KCPP.

Letter to Professor Otto Heller (Washington University). December 26, no year. KCPP.

Letter to Mrs. Douglas. July 10, no year. KCM. KCPP.

"The Impossible Miss Meadows" (story). CW. Possibly a sketch for "The Falling in Love of Fedora."

"The Boy." RMF. KCPP.

"Melancholy." RMF. KCPP.

"Doralise." RMF. KCPP.

"Misty." RMF. KCPP.

Notes

ABBREVIATIONS

ACQ = Acquisitions Folder. Chopin family. Private file, MHS.

CW = Per Seyersted, ed., *The Complete Works of Kate Chopin*. Baton Rouge: Louisiana State University, 1969.

DSR = Daniel S. Rankin, *Kate Chopin and Her Creole Stories*. Philadelphia: University of Pennsylvania, 1932.

HKT = Heather Kirk Thomas, *"A Vocation and a Voice": A Documentary Life of Kate Chopin*. Diss. University of Missouri–Columbia, 1988.

KCM = Per Seyersted and Emily Toth, eds., *A Kate Chopin Miscellany*. Oslo: Universitetsforlaget and Natchitoches: Northwestern State University of Louisiana, 1979.

KCPP = Emily Toth, Per Seyersted, and Cheyenne Bonnell, eds., *Kate Chopin's Private Papers*. Bloomington: Indiana University Press, 1998.

MHS = Missouri Historical Society, St. Louis.

SC = Seyersted Collection. Collection of Per Seyersted's Chopin research notes and materials, at Missouri Historical Society.

SCB = Per Seyersted, *Kate Chopin: A Critical Biography*. Baton Rouge: Louisiana State University. Oslo: Universitetsforlaget, 1969.

SH-VD = National Archives of the Society of the Sacred Heart, Villa Duchesne, St. Louis.

TB = Thomas Bonner, Jr., ed., *The Kate Chopin Companion, with Chopin's Translations from French Fiction*. Westport: Greenwood, 1988.

TKC = Emily Toth, *Kate Chopin: A Life of the Author of "The Awakening."* New York: Morrow, 1990. Austin: University of Texas, 1993.

GENERAL INTRODUCTION

xix: rumored book banning: "The Alleged Banning of *The Awakening*," TKC, 422–425.

xx: "rogue in porcelain": TKC, 303.

xx: Kate Chopin's business papers: TKC, esp. chap. 11. Lost diary: DSR, 92–95.

xxii: Seyersted's correspondence about publishing "The Storm": ACQ, April 25 and May 27, 1962.

1850–1870: KATE O'FLAHERTY

Material on Kate O'Flaherty's childhood can be found in TKC, chaps. 1–5. Chaps. 6–7 treat her years as a debutante and as a new bride on her honeymoon.

LEAVES OF AFFECTION

4: Kitty's contributions: Kitty Garesché's letter, dated October 29, 1930, is quoted from DSR, 41. "We have been friends together" is published in Caroline Elizabeth Sarah Norton, *The Undying One, and Other Poems* (London: Henry Colburn and Richard Bently, 1830), 215–216.

COMMONPLACE BOOK

Janet Wondra deserves particular thanks for tracking down the most obscure quotations in this section.

TKC, chaps. 5–7 provide additional background on the Commonplace Book (which was given that name by Per Seyersted).

10: Oscar Chopin's flirtatious past is described in a letter to his cousin Louis Chopin in France (TKC, 93). The translation in TKC, by Jean Bardot, may be more vague or discreet than Oscar Chopin actually meant. Oscar wrote about a place of entertainment called the Boum Magenta, "où ces demoiselles ont bien voulu nous faire un punch et nous donner quelques renfoncements à nos pauvres boisseaux," which Bardot translated as "where the girls were kind enough to make us punch and give our pipes a bashing." According to Katherine Jensen, the passage is actually more racy and phallic, and should be rendered something like this: "where the girls were happy to make us punch and give us some reinforcements to our poor little rods." Bardot and Jensen agree on the next line ("Le mien n'est plus favorable, pauvre tuyau"): "Mine is no longer in good condition, poor thing." For Oscar's years in France, see Jean Bardot, "*L'influence française dans la vie et l'oeuvre de Kate Chopin*," *Thèse de doctorat*, Université de Paris-IV, 1985–1986, esp. 43–45, 286–287, 292–293, 298. Katherine Jensen translation: personal communication.

14: "policy (?)": The question mark is Kate O'Flaherty's.

17: Madame Swetchine: Reading *The Life of Madame Swetchine* was sometimes assigned to rebellious Sacred Heart students as a punishment. See TKC, 77 and 441, n. 77. Kate O'Flaherty's quotations are all from early in the text: possibly she had no intention of finishing it. She was evidently copying from the H. W. Preston translation of *The Life and Letters of Madame Swetchine by Count De Falloux* (Boston: Roberts Brothers, 1867), but she changed the wording at the end of the passage that she copied. Preston's translation of the last sentence reads: "A remarkable king in this respect, that he is sovereign in small matters as well as in great" (37).

18: Minnie Ervinger: or Enninger, was probably a classmate. She may have died in the cholera epidemic which swept St. Louis in 1866. Nothing is known about her.

30: Charles Lamb quotation: Where Kate O'Flaherty wrote, "Between the affirmative and negative there is no broader band with him," Charles Lamb actually wrote "border-land" rather than "broader band." Young Kate's mistranscription suggests that she may have read passages aloud while she wrote them, since "broader band" and "border-land" are so similar. Sometimes Sacred Heart students were read to while they did needlework. See *The Complete Works and Letters of Charles Lamb* (New York: Modern Library, 1953), 52.

31: "beauties celestial and terrestrial": This phrase was previously transcribed incorrectly in both KCM, 52 and TKC, 79. We are never too old to confess our mistakes and remedy them.

33: "a Venus a Hebe or an Achilles": What looks like "Hebe" in Kate O'Flaherty's convoluted handwriting could be intended as "Nike."

35: Congé and Mother Galwey's feast: Kate O'Flaherty means Reverend Mother Margaret Gallwey, who was later present when Kitty Garesché made her vows on February 2, 1872. Mother Gallwey was Superior during Kate and Kitty's childhood at the Old City House (Sacred Heart Academy), and also served as Vicar, Superior, and Mistress of Novices. Source: Marie Louise Martinez, R. S. C. J. Materials from SH-VD. Nina is Kate O'Flaherty's little cousin Nina McAllister: see notes below, 315.

38: Grissberg: Kate O'Flaherty copied Longfellow's "Geissberg" incorrectly. See Henry Wadsworth Longfellow, *Hyperion and Kavanagh* (Boston: Houghton, Mifflin, 1886), 42.

40: "Martin Luther (?)": The question mark is Kate O'Flaherty's, not Longfellow's (52). As a Catholic, Kate O'Flaherty would have been taught to disapprove of Martin Luther's rebellion against her church.

45–46: "Le Montagnard Emigré": This is a song from François-René de Chateaubriand, *Les aventures du dernier abencérage* (Paris: Garniers Frères, 1958), 316–318, originally published in 1806. Kate O'Flaherty miscopied (or edited) Chateaubriand in several places. His "son coeur joyeux" became "son sein joyeux"; "blancs cheveux" became "blonds cheveux"; "Tendre compagne" became "Douce compagne"; and "ceuillant" became "cenillant."

48–49: Sicilian Vespers: Although Kate O'Flaherty writes that the massacre took place on March 20, 1232, it was actually on March 30, 1282. The events are described in W. Carew Hazlitt, *The Venetian Republic: Its Rise, Its Growth, and Its Fall, vol. I (421–1422)* (London: Adam and Charles Black, 1900), 431–437, originally published in 1858. According to Hazlitt (436), the massacre was precipitated by a rough Frenchman's grabbing the breast of a young Sicilian woman on her way to church. Her fiancé and hundreds of armed Sicilians rose up to defend her honor and massacre the French. We do not know whether Kate O'Flaherty knew this story—nor why she copied the text about the Vespers massacre.

51–55: "Mrs. Jamison": Kate O'Flaherty is copying from *Sketches of Art* by Anna Brownell Jameson, an Irish-born author of books on travel, art, and literature and a strong supporter of women's rights and writings. Jameson promoted the *Englishwoman's Journal*, a periodical that helped create the women's movement in England. See "Anna Jameson (1794–1860)" in Dale Spender, *Women of Ideas and What Men Have Done to Them* (London: Routledge & Kegan Paul, 1982), 155–157. Jameson also wrote on authors quoted by Kate O'Flaherty in her Commonplace Book, among them Byron, Schiller, and Rückert. See Anna Jameson, *Studies, Stories, and Memoirs* (Boston: Ticknor & Fields, MDCCCLXV).

55: "grösse Wäsche": Written in German script.

55–56: "Mignon's Song": This is the translation by Thomas Carlyle, originally published in 1824 and reprinted in 1839 with slight changes. Kate O'Flaherty changed (or miscopied) one word in the last line of Carlyle's first stanza: for his "O my belov'd one," she wrote "O my true loved one." Either is an accurate rendering of Goethe's "O mein Geliebter." See Johann Wolfgang von Goethe, *Wilhelm Meister's Apprenticeship*, trans. Thomas Carlyle, with a new Introduction by Franz Schoenberner (New York: Heritage Press, 1959), 137. Kate O'Flaherty copied the German text later in the Commonplace Book, on her page 155.

64–65: "Bilderbuch ohne Bilder von Hans Christian Andersen: Erster Abend": Kate O'Flaherty originally copied this story into her notebook in German script. The tale is reprinted in *Bilderbuch ohne Bilder von Hans Christian Andersen*, ed. Wilhelm Bernhardt (Boston: D. C. Heath, 1891), 2–3. Kate O'Flaherty's difficult handwriting makes it impossible to claim that this transcription is absolutely correct, and researchers working on this text should consult the original.

65–66: "Gefunden. Von Göthe" and "Schlaf ein mein Herz": Copied in German script. Friedrich Rückert (1788–1866) was a patriotic lyric poet and a professor of Oriental languages at the University at Erlangen. He is discussed in Anna Brownell Jameson's *Studies, Stories and Memoirs*, 105, which may be where Kate O'Flaherty encountered him.

69: "Au moins le souvenir": Probably inadvertently, Kate O'Flaherty omitted the next stanza of Lamartine's poem:

Qu'il soit dans ton repos, qu'il soit dans tes orages,
Beau lac, et dans l'aspect de tes riants coteaux,
Et dans ces noirs sapins, et dans ces rocs sauvages
Qui pendent sur tes eaux.

See Alphonse Marie Louis de Lamartine, *Méditations poétiques*, Vol. I, ed. Gustave Lanson (Paris: Librairie Hachette, 1922), 140.

70–71: La Petite Mendiante: Jacques Boucher de Perthes (1788–1868) was a tax collector and amateur paleontologist living near Abbéville in northern France. He collected fossils showing that humans, as well as elephants and rhinoceroses, had existed in the Somme area before recorded history. Abbéville has a museum displaying the stone tools and other relics he discovered. See Charles Tanford and Jacqueline Reynolds, *The Scientific Traveler: A Guide to People, Places & Institutions in Europe* (New York: John Wiley, 1992), 183, 196–197.

73: "Kennst du das Land": See note to 55–56, above. Copied in German script.

73–75: "Erlkönig": Copied in German script.

76–77: Gottfried August Bürger: Best known to English speakers for *Baron Münchhausen's Narrative of His Marvellous Travels and Campaigns in Russia*. See William A. Little, *Gottfried August Bürger* (New York: Twayne, 1974), esp. 192–193.

77–78: "Das Schloss am Meere": Copied in German script. Uhland's poem appears in *Gedichte von Ludwig Uhland*, eds. Erich Schmidt and Julius Hartmann (Stuttgart: Verlag der J. G. Cotta'schen Buchhandling, 1898), 150–151.

78–81: "Healing of the Daughter of Jairus": The poem appears in *The Poems, Sacred, Passionate, and Humorous, of Nathaniel Parker Willis* (New York: Clark & Maynard, 1868), 17–21. Willis (1806–1867) was an American magazine editor and friend of Lady Blessington and Bulwer-Lytton, two English authors quoted elsewhere in the Commonplace Book. Kate O'Flaherty miscopied (or edited) several of Willis's lines. On her p. 121 she changed his "pilgrim's scallop-shell / And staff—" to "pilgrim's staff" alone, and added the word "meek" in the line beginning "Alone," on the same page. On her p. 123 she omitted the line after Willis's "The silken curtains slumbered in their folds": "Not even a tassel stirring in the air—"

81–82: "What is it makes a house bright?": When she copied "it is idle for them to chatter about their rights," Kate O'Flaherty underlined the entire phrase, and underlined "rights" twice. *The Woman's Kingdom*, a British novel by Dinah Mulock Craik, includes characters who embrace and who rebel against women's traditional domestic role. One, the fond mother, is named Edna. Kate Chopin's links with popular fiction are discussed in Emily Toth, "That Outward Existence Which Conforms: Kate Chopin and Literary Convention," diss. Johns Hopkins University, 1976, esp. chapter 2: "The Cult of Domesticity and Sentimental Fiction," 28–57.

84: "Harry Lorrequer": A comical character created by the Irish novelist

Charles Lever (1806–1872). First introduced in *The Confessions of Harry Lorrequer* (1839–1840), Lever's first novel, the Irish-born hero starred in numerous humorous stories and exciting military adventures. See Robert L. Meredith and Philip B. Dematteis, "Charles Lever," in *Victorian Novelists Before 1885* (Dictionary of Literary Biography, vol. 21), eds. Ira B. Nadel and William E. Fredeman (Detroit: Gale, 1983), 217–222.

84: "The Man Who Laughs": This story of a man and a wolf seems to have inspired Kate O'Flaherty's earliest surviving short story, "Emancipation: a Life Fable." See TKC, 97.

84–85: New Orleans trip: At the time of this trip in 1869, Kate was 19, her mother, Eliza, was 40, and Mamie Sloan was Kate's age. (Mamie Sloan later married Sylvestre Pratte, from an old St. Louis family Kate knew well.) Kate's cousin Nina McAllister, also mentioned in the poem "The Congé," was the daughter of Eliza's sister Amanda. The McAllisters lived in the same household with the O'Flahertys. Rosie, possibly a servant, cannot be identified. At the time of this trip Kate had probably already met Oscar Chopin, a Louisianian working in St. Louis. His parents lived in New Orleans, but whether Kate visited them is unknown: this diary entry is the only record of her trip.

Kate O'Flaherty may also have begun smoking on this trip: young society women from St. Louis traditionally learned to smoke on trips to New Orleans. The men smoked cigars, but carried cigarettes for the young women. According to Norton Schuyler, son of Kate Chopin's friend William Schuyler, Kate Chopin smoked cigars in the privacy of her own home. (Norton Schuyler letter to Per Seyersted, September 30, 1969, in SC.)

"Schauspielerin": One of Kate Chopin's earliest short stories, "Wiser Than a God," describes a woman musician who performs on stage to support indigent parents—but the woman in the story declines to marry her rich suitor. Three decades after this first New Orleans trip, Chopin used Esplanade Street in the French Quarter for the Pontelliers' home in *The Awakening* (1899).

85–90: "Graziella": As this text shows, Kate O'Flaherty frequently omitted French accent marks. She also made slight changes which may be miscopyings. Her handwriting is difficult, and I have sometimes made educated guesses by using the French text for comparison: A. de Lamartine, *Graziella* (Paris: Albin Michel, 1979). Her last paragraph does not appear after "embaumer de moi" at the end of *Graziella*, and it may be her own invention.

90: "Fisher Maiden": She left the rest of this page blank, evidently intending to copy from Björnson's novel but never doing so.

90–91: "The Siege of Corinth": The poem is by George Gordon, Lord Byron (1788–1824). Possibly Kate O'Flaherty did not list an author's name because the handsome, wicked poet was so well-known, especially to young women. As the next section shows, she was very familiar with his writings.

91: Colton: Kate O'Flaherty's quotations are from the Rev. Charles Caleb Colton (1780–1832), an English essayist and poet. Colton was an eccentric character who wrote treatises promoting Manichean philosophy and the existence of ghosts. His parishioners called him both a fine scholar and a hopelessly impulsive hypocrite who used to hide his cigars in his church and was "a man of low, groveling, and vicious propensities." After he was dismissed as a parson because of his gambling and wine dealing, Colton escaped to the United States and then to Paris, where he shot himself to death in 1832. His best-known work, originally published in 1820, is *Lacon; or Many Things in Few Words: Addressed to Those Who Think* (New York: William Gowans, 1855), with an introduction to the life of the author, 1–23. Kate O'Flaherty's first quotation ("A man who knows the world") is from p. 92 of *Lacon*, and Colton's essay continues with an obscure series of Latin-related puns. Colton's best-known aphorism from *Lacon* is "Imitation is the sincerest of flattery" (127).

92: Lavater: Johann Kaspar Lavater (1741–1801) wrote *Aphorisms on Man* (1788), a widely quoted work, privately annotated by William Blake.

92: Hare: The aphorism about atheism comes from Julius Charles Hare and Augustus Hare, *Guesses at Truth* (London: Macmillan, 1867), 492.

92–93: Byron: The quotations are largely from Byron's *Don Juan*: "Her glossy hair . . ." is from Canto 1, v. 61.

94: "That is not the most perfect beauty . . .": From Charles Caleb Colton's *Lacon* (noted above), 137.

94: Fuller: The quotation attributed to "Fuller" is actually the work of Jeremy Collier: "A man may well expect to grow stronger by always eating as wiser by always reading. . . . 'Tis thought and digestion which makes books serviceable, and gives health and vigour to the mind." Quoted in Burton Stevenson, ed., *The Home Book of Quotations: Classical and Modern* (New York: Dodd Mead, 1967), 1676, citing Collier's *Essays: Of the Entertainment of Books*.

94: "Books like friends": The indecipherable author's name after this quotation looks like "Joineriana," but it could be something else.

95: "They love their land": This is by Fitz-Greene Halleck (1790–1867) from his poem *Connecticut*, as quoted in *Bartlett's Familiar Quotations* (Boston: Little, Brown, 1955), 462–463.

> They love their land because it is their own,
> And scorn to give aught other reason why:
> Would shake hands with a king upon his throne,
> And think it kindness to his Majesty.

96: "God made the country": This very famous quotation is from Book I, "The Sofa," ll. 749ff. in William Cowper, *The Task* (Yorkshire and London: The Scholar Press Limited, 1973), 40. *The Task*, first published in 1785, was widely praised for its originality, blank verse, and poignant satire, and it made Cowper into a major literary figure in England.

97, 98: Young: See Edward Young, *Night Thoughts*, ed. Stephen Cornford (Cambridge: Cambridge University Press, 1989), III, ll. 526–529 and IV, ll. 97–100. Originally written in the early 1740s, Young's book was widely read and emulated, and in 1795 William Blake was commissioned to do a series of illustrations for it.

102: Miss Clafflin: Either Tennessee Claflin or her sister Victoria Woodhull. Both were women's rights activists, suffragists, and mediums. Their patron, Commodore Cornelius Vanderbilt, set them up as stockbrokers on Wall Street. The sisters published their own women's rights newspaper, *Woodhull & Claflin's Weekly*, and in 1872 Victoria Woodhull ran for President of the United States, the first woman to do so.

102: the Park: Central Park, the famous urban oasis of greenery designed by Frederick Law Olmsted.

105: Bunnie Knapp: presumably Vernon Knapp, whose family had been Eighth Street neighbors of the O'Flahertys. The Knapps edited the conservative *Missouri Republican* (later the *St. Louis Republic*), and Bunnie, twenty-three years old, was evidently on a Grand Tour. Half a century later, after a long law career in St. Louis, Knapp would write an article calling Kate Chopin "the most brilliant, distinguished and interesting woman that has ever graced St. Louis." KCM 151–153; TKC 206.

112: My grenadine: Grenadine is a open weave fabric, something like gauze, usually striped or checked, although the term is also used for a kind of black silk lace worn in France in the eighteenth century. Janet Wondra's costume research (unpublished) also refutes the possibility that Kate Chopin meant "gabardine." Gabardine is a tightly woven, hard-twisted fabric especially appropriate for rain gear—so it would not have been ruined.

112: "die schöne Dame": Written in German script.

113: Lil Chouteau: Lélia Clemence Chouteau (1850–1932), Kate O'Flaherty's friend and friendly academic rival at the Academy of the Visitation. The youngest of ten children, "Lil" also lost her father when she was just five. Lil married John Still Winthrop of North Carolina in 1874 and gave birth to five children. See Paul Beckwith, *Creoles of St. Louis* (St. Louis: Nixon-Jones, 1893), 24. The MHS copy has excellent handwritten emendations by one Nettie Harney Beauregard. See also William E. Foley and C. David Rice, *The First Chouteaus: River Barons of Early St. Louis* (Chicago: University of Illinois, 1983), 213, and TKC 112, 144.

No letters between Lil Chouteau and Kate Chopin survive, but Chopin's naming her only daughter Lélia, and calling her own first publication "Lilia. A Polka," suggests a continuing connection. (Lil Chouteau Winthrop's only daughter was named Evaline Susan.) Both Lélia Chouteau and Lélia Chopin's names were continually miswritten as "Lilia" or "Lillian" and both used "Lil" as a nickname. Lil Chouteau was part of St. Louis's intertwined kinship networks: her distant cousins included Blanche Valle (who married Kate Chopin's newspaper friend John A. Dillon), and Sylvestre Pratte (who married Kate O'Flaherty's New Orleans traveling companion Mamie Sloan). See Beckwith 19, 110, and his genealogical charts.

116: Letter from Nina: Nina McAllister; see references to 84–85, above.

121–122: List of Books: After six blank pages, Kate O'Flaherty Chopin's "List of Books" is on two facing pages just inside the last page of her notebook. It is noteworthy that she lists the author of *Shirley*, Charlotte Brontë, as "A. Bell." Brontë's pseudonym was "Currer Bell"; her sister Anne wrote as "Acton Bell."

1 8 7 1 – 1 8 8 4 :   K A T E
O ' F L A H E R T Y   C H O P I N

The fullest biographical treatment of Kate O'Flaherty Chopin's Louisiana years is TKC, chaps. 8–11. Most materials in this essay are from those chapters.

123: Lines quoted by Rankin: DSR 94–95. His chaps. VI and VII cover Chopin's Louisiana years. Lost diary: Per Seyersted letter to Charles van Ravenswaay, March 11, 1962, ACQ.

123–124: Births and baptisms of children: Jean Baptiste, Oscar, and George were baptized in St. Louis and Lélia in Cloutierville. No baptismal records exist for Frederick and Felix in St. Louis or in the New Orleans churches named to me by the Archdiocese of New Orleans: St. Patrick's, St. Stephen's, St. Alphonsus. But Sister Marie Louise Martinez, R. S. C. J., suggests that the Chopins may have attended church at St. Theresa of Avila or St. Michael's. Those church records have not been checked.

124: Oscar's mutual aid society membership: Jean Bardot, "Kate Chopin's French Culture," diss., Sorbonne–University of Paris–IV, 1985–1986, 75. This is the English translation of the dissertation in the note to p. 52, above.

124: Degas connection: I am indebted to Michelle Bergeron for noticing the name Edma Pontillon in her research on Berthe Morisot, and linking it with Kate Chopin's Edna Pontellier. In one Morisot book, Anne Higonnet mentions Chopin's *The Awakening* as a book about a woman who paints and whose physical and emotional desires are thwarted. But Higonnet mistakenly calls Chopin's character "Edna Montpellier" and therefore fails to see the striking similarity with "Edma Pontillon." See Higonnet's *Berthe Morisot's Images of Women* (Cambridge: Harvard University Press, 1992), 203 and *passim*. Higonnnet also writes about Edma Morisot Pontillon in *Berthe Morisot* (New York: Harper & Row, 1990), *passim*. For the restoration of the Degas house in New Orleans, see "Persistence Pays Off in Renovation of Historic Home," *Baton Rouge Advocate* (August 9, 1996), 4-B. The house may be opened to the public for special events.

124–125: Battle of Liberty Place: An obelisk honoring the White League militiamen at the Battle of Liberty Place was erected on Canal Street in 1891. In 1932 an inscription praising "white supremacy" was added; in 1974 a plaque was attached, calling white supremacy repugnant to modern New Orleanians. In 1989 the obelisk was removed from Canal Street as part of a street repair project, and in the early 1990s, attempts to return it to its old spot led to anti-racist protests and arrests. As of mid-1995, the Liberty Place monument was sitting in an obscure corner behind the Westin Hotel, a short block from Canal Street.

125: Ogden Guards: HKT 163.

125: In New Orleans: Re Mrs. Tyler, see DSR 89–90; see SCB 38 about Mrs. John Tritle. Mrs. Tritle, the former Nelly Hoblitzelle of St. Louis, would already had been known to Kate Chopin: see notes in SC. For the New Orleans years, also see Emily Toth, "Kate Chopin's New Orleans Years," *New Orleans Review* 15:1 (Spring 1988), 53–60.

125: About Chopins' long separations: HKT 240, 242–245, 257.

126: Chopins' Cloutierville home: The house is now the Bayou Folk Museum/Kate Chopin Home, with national historic landmark status.

1 8 8 5 – 1 9 0 4 :   K A T E   C H O P I N

For the fullest biographical treatment of Kate Chopin's last twenty years, see TKC chaps. 12–24.

129: "literally prostrate with grief": DSR 105; HKT 298 about cancer.

129: New house: Information about Chopin's house comes from Frederick Medler, St. Louis architectural historian: interview with Emily Toth, 1997.

129: Frederick Kolbenheyer: The doctor was the author of a somewhat sentimental and sensational novella called *Jewish Blood*, serialized in *The American Jewess* (1896), which was edited by Kate Chopin's friend Rosa Sonneschein.

129–130: Chopin's discovering Guy de Maupassant: "Confidences," CW 700–701.

130: Chopin's telephone number: *Telephone Exchange Directory No. 124* (St. Louis: Bell Telephone Company of Missouri, July1902), 103, at MHS. The number is actually listed under the name of Chopin's son: "Chopin, G. F. Physician," and his medical duties may be the reason she had a phone.

130–131: Felix Chopin's description: "Statement on Kate Chopin by Felix Chopin," KCM 166–168, also cited at several points in TKC. The original is at MHS. None of Chopin's grandchildren know what the "eccentric clothing" was like.

131: quiet manner: William Schuyler, "Kate Chopin," *The Writer* VII (August 1894), 115–117, reprinted in KCM 118 and discussed in TKC, 243–245. According to Schuyler's son Norton, his father used to pass Chopin's house on his walk home from teaching at Central High School, and would have an impromptu visit. Norton Schuyler's letters (September 30, 1969, and January 17, 1970) are in SC.

131: sewing or polishing a table leg: See Chopin's 1899 essay, "On Certain Brisk, Bright Days," CW 721–722.

132: not shutting herself off from family: See Lélia Chopin Hattersley's 1907 letter, quoted in DSR 116, repeated in SCB 60.

133: For a full discussion of "The Alleged Banning of *The Awakening*," see TKC 421–425.

133–135: Discovery of Rankin-Marhefka Fragments: Emily Toth interview with Linda W. Marhefka, November 3, 1995. Papers relating to the discovery and to the transfer of other manuscripts are at MHS, some in ACQ. I am indebted to Peter Michel for sharing them with me. Rankin's recollections, recorded in an interview with Per Seyersted, are in SC. George Chopin's recollections about Daniel Rankin:

interviews with Emily Toth in 1975, 1984. Further information about Rankin: TKC 402–403.

135: al fresco suppers, lone wolf: Felix Chopin, "Statement on Kate Chopin," KCM 166–168, quoted at various points in TKC, original at MHS.

"IMPRESSIONS": KATE CHOPIN'S 1894 DIARY

176: "Kolby had eyes for Mom": quoted in TKC 261.

177: Elise Miltenberger: Interview and materials from Marie Louise Martinez, March, 1994.

178: "woman of mysterious fascination": DSR 106. Rankin told Seyersted (SC) that in 1929 he met with several St. Louis men who had known and admired Kate Chopin. He claimed that they had spoken with him confidentially, and he declined to identify them. Some of her admirers whose names we know—such as Dr. Frederick Kolbenheyer and newspaper editor John Dillon—were dead by then, but *Post-Dispatch* editor George Johns was still alive. Still, Rankin's claims always have to be taken with some skepticism.

Much more detailed information about individuals mentioned in the 1894 diary appears in TKC, esp. chaps. 15–17.

179: Mrs. Moore: Sue V. Moore, editor of *St. Louis Life*, and apparently the only female editor-in-chief of a St. Louis publication. She was a close friend and booster of Kate Chopin and author of an important 1894 profile (KCM, quoted in TKC 242–243, original at MHS).

In 1888 Sue V. Moore's husband, Henry Moore, managing editor of the *Post-Dispatch*, had left her for another woman, the former Emma Stockman, an actress and wife of actor-manager John Norton. Moore and Mrs. Norton fled to Australia, then separated, and he died in the mid-1890s in New York City. With her son, Sue V. Moore transcended the scandal, and wrote warm notes to Kate Chopin, especially when *The Awakening* was published (KCM 133, TKC 338, original at MHS). Sue V. Moore's marital troubles no doubt contributed to the story in *The Awakening*.

180: Mrs. Hull: Lizzie Chambers Hull, mother of four, wife of a coal merchant, and member of the Wednesday Club.

180: Ferriss: Judge Franklin Ferriss. His wife is mentioned later in the diary.

180: The Doctor: Dr. Frederick Kolbenheyer.

180: Cable: George W. Cable, Louisiana-born author of *Old Creole Days*, *The Grandissimes*, and other works.

181: Miss Jewett, Mary E. Wilkins: Sarah Orne Jewett and Mary E. Wilkins (later Freeman) are two of the best short story writers New England ever produced. Both flourished in the 1890s.

181: Miss Breddon and E. P. Roe: British novelist Mary Elizabeth Braddon was best known for the sensational *Lady Audley's Secret*; Reverend Edward Payson Roe was the best-selling American author of such novels as *Barriers Burned Away* and *What Can She Do?* Both wrote about women's need for money and for creative outlets for their energies and talents.

181: Blanche: Kate Chopin's cousin Blanche Bordley, to whom she also wrote the verse "To Blanche," later in this diary.

181: James Lane Allen: A very popular American novelist whose sensual *Summer in Arcady* probably inspired the title of Kate Chopin's second short story collection, *A Night in Acadie*. TKC 297–298.

182: "Liza": Elise Miltenberger. See Editor's introduction to the diary.

182: Jean's birthday: Jean Baptiste Chopin, Kate Chopin's first child. Jean was also the first of her children to die (in 1911); the others all died in the same order they were born, ending with daughter Lélia in 1962.

183: Old Doctor Faget: Dr. Charles Jean Faget, a unique and progressive medical figure who supported the use of chloroform for women in childbirth when many medical men insisted that women should feel the pain. See TKC 127–128.

183: Mr. and Mrs. Schuyler: William and Hidee Schuyler, to whom Kate Chopin wrote a verse, "To Hidee Schuyler," in this diary. William Schuyler was a musician, poet, and schoolteacher whose later star pupil was the novelist Fannie Hurst. In 1894 he wrote an excellent Chopin profile for *The Writer*: see note to 131, above.

184: Mr. Dillon: John Alvarez Dillon, former editor of the *Post-Dispatch*, by 1894 editor of the *New York World*. Dillon may have been a romantic admirer of Kate Chopin. He and his wife, the former Blanche Valle of St. Louis, had seven children. See TKC, *passim*.

184: Hamlin Garland: American novelist of a somewhat naturalistic bent. Chopin generally disliked his work, and wrote about him unfavorably in "'Crumbling Idols' by Hamlin Garland,"CW 693–694, and more favorably in "Development of the Literary West," reprinted in this volume.

185: Mrs. Walsh: Mrs. Julius Walsh, the former Josephine Dickson, mother of seven and an inveterate card player and club woman.

185: Mrs. Stone: Mrs. Margaret M. B. Stone, novelist, social reformer, and author of an 1892 pamphlet, "The Problem of Domestic Service." She also founded St. Louis's Modern Novel Club.

185: Deyo's: Charles Deyo, *Post-Dispatch* editorial writer, who held his own visiting days, complained a great deal (see references later in this diary), but wrote a very intelligent review of *The Awakening*.

185: Mrs. Ferriss: wife of Judge Franklin Ferriss (see p. 180 above and poem later in this volume).

185: Mrs. Blackman: Carrie Blackman, a painter who, with her husband George, organized soirées and the St. Louis Artist's Guild. Also see p. 193, this volume.

185: Mrs. Sawyer and Miss Sawyer: Harriet Adams Sawyer, a would-be poet and her daughter Bertha.

185: *Heavenly Twins*: British novel by Sarah Grand, an impassioned attack on the double standard that allowed men to visit prostitutes, contract deadly venereal diseases, and pass them on to their wives. The success of *The Heavenly Twins* probably enabled Kate Chopin to publish, finally, "Mrs. Mobry's Reason," her most-rejected story, which hints at venereal disease.

186: "I am younger today at 43": When she wrote this entry, Kate Chopin was actually 44—but there seems to have been much confusion about her birthdate. Her tombstone says 1851, but her baptismal record and the 1850 census say 1850.

186: "My friend whose birthday I remembered": Dr. Frederick Kolbenheyer.

186: Felix Morriss: British actor, greatly admired. According to the Wondra Manuscript Account Book (in this volume), Kate Chopin tried to send him her play, *An Embarrassing Position*, via the St. Louis actor-manager John Norton (see note about Sue V. Moore, above).

187: Mary Wilkins Pembroke: Mary E. Wilkins' novel *Pembroke*, a striking and dramatic portrayal of a man's "New England will" and its terrible consequences for women.

188: Streets of Anderson: Kate Chopin was attending the Western Association of Writers meeting in Anderson, Indiana. See TKC 229–231.

188: "Critic accepted my paragraph": When her essay "The Western Association of Writers" was published in *The Critic*, Kate Chopin was attacked for elitism in newspapers all over the Midwest. See TKC 230–231.

189: The Cedars: According to Per Seyersted's interview with Mrs. John Tritle (SC), Kate Chopin and her children spent most summers at the Cedars, a former plantation and resort village in Sulphur Springs, Missouri. There the boys lived in a cabin, while their mother liked to sit around talking and smoking, between bouts of writing. She wrote "The Night Came Slowly" there in 1894 (TKC 231).

190: "Cavanelle": This story appeared in the first issue of *The American Jewess*, edited by Kate Chopin's friend and fellow smoker Rosa Sonneschein. Chopin was the only gentile contributor in that issue.

192: "For Mrs. Ferriss": See notes above.

192: "To Hidee Schuyler": See notes to William Schuyler, above. For Hidee Schuyler, as with so many of the wives of men Kate Chopin knew, it is impossible to get much information. She died in 1897: Norton Schuyler letter of January 17, 1970, SC.

193: "To 'Billy' with a box of cigars": William Marion Reedy, raffish editor of the *St. Louis Mirror*, later called *Reedy's Mirror*. Reedy was a progressive thinker and writer with an intense sense of humor, who helped inspire Chopin's short story "A Vocation and a Voice." See introduction and notes to "The Boy," elsewhere in this volume.

193: "To Mrs. B——n": Undoubtedly Carrie Blackman. See note above to p. 185.

193–194: "To Blanche": Chopin's cousin Blanche Bordley. See note above. Some readers think the text says "muffins" rather than "puffins." The original is at MHS.

THE "LILIA POLKA"

195: TKC discusses Chopin's love of music.

LETTERS AND INSCRIPTIONS

Further information about recipients of these letters is in TKC.

200: Edwin Booth: See "The Real Edwin Booth," CW 695.

201: Marie Breazeale: Oscar Chopin's sister, some seventeen years younger, was married in 1884 to the Natchitoches attorney and politician Phanor Breazeale. They had four daughters, and Phanor—besides being an agnostic and a great storyteller—was elected to the U. S. Congress. He may have given Kate Chopin an idea that led to *The Awakening*. Cora is Cora Henry Chopin, the wife of Oscar's younger brother Lamy; she died in 1892, leaving a daughter Eugenie ("Nini").

201–202: Responses to reviews: The original reviews to which Chopin is responding are quoted, in full or in part, in TKC.

203: R. W. Gilder: Richard Watson Gilder, editor of the *Century*, the most prestigious and best-paying magazine for short stories.

203–204: Marion A. Baker: editor of the *New Orleans Times-Democrat*, which published many of Chopin's short stories. His wife, Julia Wetherell Baker, was also a writer.

205: Waitman Barbe: A West Virginia-based teacher, author and editor. Despite this correspondence, he does not seem to have written a sketch about Kate Chopin. See "In Memory of Dr. Waitman Barbe," *The School Journal* (Charleston, W. Va.) 58:7 (March 1930), 215–216. Copy is in SC.

207–208: J. M. Stoddart: New York magazine editor who served with *Lippincott's Monthly Magazine*, and then with *Collier's Weekly*, *New Science Review*, and *Information*.

208: Cornelia F. Maury: St. Louis painter who specialized in children.

210: Lydia Arms Avery Coonley Ward: Member of Chicago literary and intellectual circles.

211: Notice from the *Post-Dispatch*: Almost certainly the review by Charles Deyo, published on May 20.

211: Richard B. Shepard: Salt Lake City attorney and legislator.

213: R. E. Lee Gibson: St. Louis poet who often seemed to be currying favor with Kate Chopin. His day job was as head clerk at the St. Louis Insane Asylum. He later wrote a sonnet "To the Author of 'Bayou Folk,'" and his autographed copy is in the Bayou Folk Museum/Kate Chopin Home in Cloutierville, Louisiana. His sonnet is published in TKC 385.

214: The little ladies: Marie and July (Julia) were two of the Breazeale daughters; Gladys and Katherine were the others. All became deeply involved in Louisiana politics, esp. July Breazeale Waters. Her contributions to civil rights and women's rights in Louisiana are discussed in Pamela Tyler, *Silk Stockings and Ballot Boxes: Women and Politics in New Orleans, 1920–1965* (Athens: University of Georgia, 1996), a book for which July Waters was a major source.

214: Eugenie: Eugenie Chopin Henry, Oscar Chopin's sister, who died that year.

214: Aunt Amanda and Nina: Chopin's aunt, Eliza O'Flaherty's sister, and Chopin's former Sacred Heart schoolmate, Nina McAllister, who also died that year.

214: Mrs. Tiffany: Mrs. Dexter Tiffany, active in St. Louis charity balls.

214: Mrs. Francis: Probably Mrs. David Francis, whose husband was best known as the administrator in charge of the St. Louis World's Fair of 1904.

215: Otto Heller: St. Louis autograph collector and a Washington University professor. His autograph collection is now in the special collections at the Washington University library.

215: Mrs. Douglas: Mrs. Walter Douglas, wife of a St. Louis judge.

215–216: Ruth McEnery Stuart: Louisiana author of "Carlotta's Intended" and other stories. Chopin admired her work very much, and said so in an essay (CW 711–713).

216: Madison Cawein: Kentucky-born poet. With his friend R. E. Lee Gibson, he seems to have fawned on Kate Chopin. See TKC, esp. chap. 23.

NEWSPAPER PIECES

217: Interviews: For further information about Chopin's interviews, see Emily Toth, "Kate Chopin on Divine Love and Suicide: Two Rediscovered Articles," *American Literature* 63:1 (March 1991), 115–121.

TRANSLATIONS

226: Kate O'Flaherty's bilingualism is discussed in fascinating detail in Bernard Koloski, *Kate Chopin: A Study of the Short Fiction* (New York: Twayne, 1996), *passim*.

227: Kate Chopin's review of Emile Zola's *Lourdes* is in *CW* 697–698.

228: Chopin's appearance at French Benevolent Society: Joan Mayerson Clatworthy, "Kate Chopin: The Inward Life Which Questions," diss. State University of New York at Buffalo, 1979, 108. Clatworthy was also the first to question the story that *The Awakening* had been banned. See TKC 424.

REDISCOVERED SHORT STORIES

245: Dating: "A Lady of Shifting Intentions" was a story of 1600 words, written on May 4, 1895; only this fragment survives. Four extant manuscript versions of "Ti Frère" show that it was written September 27 and 19, 1896. Kate Chopin was revising "Ti Démon" in March 1898.

272: Walter Hines Page: Chopin's correspondence with Page is discussed in TKC 294–295.

POEMS

286: Kitty about their reading: TKC 51–52.

286: "You, me, anybody": TKC 326.

286: Poems' probable dates of composition (from Seyersted, KCM 191–192): "A Fancy"—1892.

"If the Woods Could Talk," "A Sentimental Serenade," "A Message"—earlier than June 1893.

"The Roses"—July 11, 1898.

"Lines to Linn" (previously read as "Lines to Him")—July 31, 1898, probably written for Linn R. Brokaw (see Kate Chopin's will, later in this volume).

"White Oaks"—August 24, 1898, White Oaks, Wisconsin. Barbara Sims has an autographed book from Kate Chopin using the words "live oaks" instead of "white oaks." In 1995 book collector George Koppelman found another *Bayou Folk* copy autographed with this poem, using the words "live oaks," but the handwriting does not look like Kate Chopin's.

"Lines Suggested by Omar," "The Lull of Summer Time"—August 1898.

"To Henry One Evening Last Summer"—October 21, 1898.

"Old Natchitoches"—December 1898.

"By the Meadow Gate"—October 24, 1898.

"An Hour"—earlier than January, 1899

"O Fair, Sweet Spring"—submitted to *Century* as "Abide With Me" on January 6, 1899; published as "I Opened All the Portals Wide" in July 1899; also part of the program honoring Kate Chopin and others on "Reciprocity Day: an Afternoon with St. Louis Authors," held by the Wednesday Club November 29, 1899. This event was important for honoring Kate Chopin and showing she was not ostracized after publishing *The Awakening* the previous April.

"My Lady Rose Pouts, "Come to Me," "O! Blessed Tavern," "As Careless as the Summer Breeze," "One Day," "Ah! Magic Bird," "With a Violet-Wood Paper Knife"—all undated, but before February, 1899.

"A Little Day"—undated, but probably 1899.

"Alone"—July 6, 1900. See SCB 226 n. 50.

286: "I Opened All the Portals Wide" was also set to music by C. B. Hawley, under the title "The Joy of Spring." A copy of the sheet music, either donated or published in 1931, is at MHS.

STATEMENT ON *THE AWAKENING*

295: Lucy Monroe: See TKC 328–329 for Lucy Monroe; chap. 22 for reviews.

296: Letters from Kate Chopin's friends praising *The Awakening* appear in KCM and TKC. Originals are at MHS.

REMINISCENCES ABOUT KITTY GARESCHÉ

298: "To the Friend of My Youth": CW 735.

298–299: Kitty's positions, visiting Kate: This information is from Marie Louise Martinez, R. S. C. J.

LAST WILL AND TESATMENT OF KATE CHOPIN

300, 302: "Isabel Willcox": The signature is probably the same Miss I. Willcox who taught English and history at Central High School in 1904. It is noteworthy that Kate Chopin had her will witnessed by a woman, at a time when women lacked many legal rights, including the right to vote.

300–301: Lélia Hattersley: Her eccentricities are described in TKC, Epilogue; other information comes from 1984 interviews with Lélia's nephews David and George Chopin and niece Marjorie McCormick.

Core Bibliography for Kate Chopin Scholars

Bonner, Thomas, Jr. *The Kate Chopin Companion, with Chopin's Translations From French Fiction*. Westport, CT; Greenwood Press, 1988.

Boren, Lynda S., and Sara de Saussure Davis, eds. *Kate Chopin Reconsidered: Beyond the Bayou*. Baton Rouge: Louisiana State University Press, 1992.

Chopin, Kate. *A Vocation and a Voice: Stories by Kate Chopin*. Ed. Emily Toth. New York: Penguin, 1991.

Ewell, Barbara C. *Kate Chopin*. New York: Ungar, 1986.

Koloski, Bernard, ed. *Approaches to Teaching Kate Chopin's "The Awakening."* New York: Modern Language Association, 1988.

Koloski, Bernard. *Kate Chopin: A Study of the Short Fiction*. New York: Twayne, 1996.

Rankin, Daniel. *Kate Chopin and Her Creole Stories*. Philadelphia: University of Pennsylvania, 1932.

Seyersted, Per, ed. *The Complete Works of Kate Chopin*. Baton Rouge: Louisiana State University, 1969.

Seyersted, Per. *Kate Chopin: A Critical Biography*. Baton Rouge: Louisiana State University Press and Oslo: Universitetsforlaget. 1969.

Seyersted, Per, and Emily Toth, eds., *A Kate Chopin Miscellany*. Oslo and Natchitoches: Universitetsforlaget and Northwestern State University Press of Louisiana, 1979.

Toth, Emily. *Kate Chopin: A Life of the Author of "The Awakening."* New York: Morrow, 1990.

Toth, Emily. *Unveiling Kate Chopin*. Jackson: University Press of Mississippi, 1999.

Toth, Emily, Per Seyersted, and Cheyenne Bonnell, eds. *Kate Chopin's Private Papers*. Bloomington: Indiana University Press, 1998.

Index

Emily Toth, Professor of English and Women's Studies at Louisiana State University, is the author of *Kate Chopin: A Life of the Author of "The Awakening"* and the forthcoming *Unveiling Kate Chopin*; editor of Kate Chopin's *A Vocation and a Voice*; co-editor of *A Kate Chopin Miscellany*; and author/editor of five other books, including a novel and an academic advice book.

Per Seyersted, Professor Emeritus of English and American Studies at the University of Oslo, is the author of *Kate Chopin: A Critical Biography*; editor of *The Complete Works of Kate Chopin*; co-editor of *A Kate Chopin Miscellany*; and author/editor of seven other books in comparative literary studies.

Cheyenne (formerly Marilyn) Bonnell, who teaches English at Northwest College in Powell, Wyoming, has written on women's studies, pedagogy, and the novelist Sarah Grand.